Mysterium and Mystery
The Clerical Crime Novel

Studies in Religion, No. 6

Margaret R. Miles, Series Editor

Professor of Historical Theology
The Divinity School
Harvard University

Other Titles in This Series

Mysterium and Mystery
The Clerical Crime Novel

by
William David Spencer

 U·M·I Research Press

Ann Arbor / London

Produced and distributed by
UMI Research Press
an imprint of
University Microfilms Inc.
Ann Arbor, Michigan 48106

Library of Congress Cataloging in Publication Data

Spencer, William David, 1947-
   Mysterium and mystery : the clerical crime novel / by William
David Spencer.
      p. cm—(Studies in religion ; no. 6)
      Bibliography: p.
      Includes index.
      ISBN 0-8357-1936-7 (alk. paper)
      1. Detective and mystery stories—History and criticism.
2. Clergy in literature.   I. Title.   II. Series: Studies in
religion (Ann Arbor, Mich.) ; no. 6.
PN3448.D4S64   1989
809.3'872—dc19   88-39773
                                                           CIP

British Library CIP data is available.

To my wife, Aída Besançon Spencer,
whose perspicacity unlocks the great mysteries

In the Company of Killers

I. Evil Enters Eden

What strange beast is this
     that slithers through the grove,
down among the sacred trees
     in the sheltered cove?
Mark its progress by our fear,
     flocks flung into flight,
waking to a nightmare
     in the garden of delight.

II. Evil Exits Earth

Mocking, jeering as they strung 'em up,
The monster fed us all the good lines,
"Come down! Heal yourself! Show us Elijah!"
We spat ourselves as the monster drooled and danced in glee.

And then as the warrior bellowed, "It is finished!"
One foot kicked free,
Swift, sure, it crushed the monster dead.
And stunned, we lie a lifetime,
Caught where heel meets head.

III. Picking up at Palestine

Like a child at the end of day,
God picks up at Palestine,
The tomb empty, the saviour back in place,
Both on the best shelf and in God's mind,

The beast dying but snapping yet,
As the child's breath whips by,
And we—precious little people,
handcrafted and greatly prized—
scattered across the world and the ages.

> \- William David Spencer
> 1987

Contents

Preface

The adventures of Joe Pooh, Teddy Bear Detective, were the most exciting mysteries I have ever heard. I would sit spellbound as my sister spun them out, plot heaped on plot like an investigator's Arabian Nights. No doubt she borrowed liberally from A. A. Milne's Winnie the Pooh and perhaps Walter Brooks' Freddy the Pig, noted senior detective of the firm Frederick and Wiggins the cow, but the bulk of the excitement came from her vast creativity. When Joe Pooh took on a case, I was in for high adventure. I lost my sister when I was just six and she eleven. Perhaps, my search through the mystery is in part a quest for stories as exciting as hers. That longing to go back to our past, back to find those we have lost, back to walk again with God through Eden is the quest for the mysterium that lies behind the mystery. I still have the mystery genre my sister gave to me to enjoy and the mysterium that gave her to me. In my own quest through the mystery for its source I have also many fellow investigators of the great mysterium to appreciate and acknowledge.

If my sister first opened my eyes to the delights of detection, my parents first taught me to read adventure tales. From the moment my mom, exasperated at hearing her fifth grade son gripe about nothing to do, ordered, "Why don't you go down to the P. M. Bookstore and buy a Tarzan book?" I was off into the wonderful world of popular fiction. My dad whisked me off to New York City, where on many Saturdays for the next several years we would haunt the book shops up and down the Bowery. Then we headed for the Olde Book Shoppe in Morristown, New Jersey, the Salvation Armies, Good Will Missions, Mount Carmel Guilds of Newark and Plainfield, and eventually one summer for a several-state and four-province ramble book collecting. By tenth grade I had a four-room attic filled with stock, a thriving mail order book business and an outstanding Burroughs collection. I had also read hundreds and hundreds of westerns, mysteries, adventures, sea sagas, science fiction and fantasy tales, horror novels, true classics and children's classics and that genre of the teens and twenties called the boys' adventures, even romances, gothics, and "modern novels" as well, and, of course, a never-ending kaleidoscope of nonfiction books. Was ever a child blessed with such a family?

Today I have a companion who is herself a superlative scholar, my wife Aída. I owe much of the refinement of my thought and any accomplishment I achieve to her inexhaustible well of support and encouragement. She was the Livingstone who through the thick morass of my 800-plus-page draft blazed a thematic trail to follow in reducing this manuscript to a manageable size. My own son, Stephen, follows in his mother's footprints with a mind that penetrates to the core of issues and a spirit loving and strong for high adventure.

I also owe an inexpressible debt to Elizabeth Bettenhausen and Carter Lindberg, the first and second professors I met in the graduate program at Boston University's School of Theology and two of the finest scholars I have ever had the privilege to meet. They took what was a struggling study and helped channel it into something from which I gained continual insight. Socrates could take lessons from their maieutic method of helping scholars become what they, themselves, want to be. Hulane Ross also offered an excellent course on the hard-boiled novel at Boston University, and Linda Clark team-taught a superb one on theology and the arts.

No one can do a study of this magnitude, of course, without access to a multitude of books, and, despite my remaining shelves and boxes of classic mysteries, I had no Clerical Crime novels but the Father Brown collections. As a child I was more interested in the Saint's swagger and Reggie Fortune's flippancies than in Buell's or the Archdeacons' eccentricities. But, of course, in the years I was collecting, only a sixth of the books had even been written. The present study would not have been possible without several key people and their institutions. Roger Nicole, evangelical statesperson and as expert in the mystery novel as he is in Christian theology, kindly put at my disposal his collection of 3,000 mysteries. It was through his reading that we learned about Allen Hubin's authoritative work (though too late to save my weeks in the various cumulative book indices of Great Britain and the United States). Through his collection I gained access to the rare Sister Ursula and Mary Finney books. I owe a great debt of gratitude, too, to his continual encouragement. How the Library of Congress ever let Cynthia McCue escape to the Wenham Public Library I shall never know. A magician of a librarian, she can use the inter-library loan system to find books that no one else can. The bulk of the books I used were found by her and Frances Moscovitch of her staff. Shirley Kerr, Eric Stancliff, and Beth Rutledge, too, of the Gordon-Conwell Theological Seminary library, kindly supplied me with a steady stream of theological books. The Hamilton area is blessed with a number of superb libraries. Annette Janes, Diana Ward, who also reviewed my Eco study, Nancy Day, Jean Buckley, and the rest of the Hamilton library staff were also a continual source of encouragement, assistance, and information. Beverly Library's reference librarians and staff were also always extremely helpful when I had all the local libraries backed up with the hundreds of books I reviewed to select the small percentage discussed here. They supplied answers to dozens of esoteric questions that cropped up. Finally, I wish to thank the main library of Louisville, Kentucky, as well as its St. Matthews and Chestnut Hill branches, Newark's public library and the staff and collections at the Beverly Farms branch, the Southern Baptist Theological Seminary Library, Harvard University's Widener Library, and Boston University's staff at both the seminary and university libraries, where over the years I discovered many of these series. Thank you all.

While I am thanking magicians, I want to acknowledge warmly Judith A. Richmond, who took on the typing of the huge draft of this manuscript like a general conducting a campaign. Military field marshalls could well applaud the army of typists she organized, marshalling supplies, regularizing typefaces, and pacing us all through a timetable that produced the copy in record time. And before Ms. Richmond, Pamela McDonald, faculty secretary, typed the earliest chapters, which were developed from lectures for the classes TC 261 *Sin, Justice, and Mercy in Contemporary Literature* and PR 261 *Theology and the Arts,* which I taught in the summer program of Gordon-Conwell Theological Seminary. I also warmly thank my students, who have added their own astute reflections; Wesley Roberts, who helped these classes become a reality; Robert Cooley, Garth Rosell, Father Dean Borgman, and my friends on the faculty; Anne Marie and Sean Cullen, whose warm home welcomed Stephen on the Wednesdays Dad was at Boston University; R. K. Harrison, who suggested to me that if one is going to the effort to write in a field one might as well attempt to produce the master work; and everyone who assisted me at the Boston University School of Theology, the Reverend Earl Beane, Jean Osborn, and the Reverend William Zimpfer. Thank you every one.

As I stand now on this side of the study, I find my final emotion is humility. One cannot look through the mystery without being ultimately humbled by the shocking realization that the great God of the universe has afforded us—animated dust—a glimpse into the great mysterium.

Modus Operandi

Mysterium into Mystery

In one very real sense the story of Jesus is a murder mystery. "Why did Jesus have to die?" an avid and expert mystery reader once asked me. The murder story of Jesus is the enactment in history of his parable of the vineyard owner who, seeing his messengers rebuffed, sent his own son thinking his unruly employees would surely respect and obey him. The murder of the vineyard owner's son is the bad news that sets the scene for the discovery of good news: Jesus as victim, humanity as murderer, God as judge. The quest of the theologian for the truth about Christ begins like the search of the detective for the mystery of evil. And what the honest detective finds is an Agatha Christie-like violation of Father Ronald Knox's decalogue of rules. At the end of the quest each honest detective finds the murderer's bloody hands are his or her own. The blood of the slain innocent still cries out against humanity as Abel's did from the violated edenic earth. Before the bar of God's justice people stand convicted and condemned. If an eleventh hour pardon comes, it is not by means of any atoning act of restitution humanity has done. No amount of good work can ever raise Abel again from the ground, can ever knit back dead limbs, breathe back in the breath of life. The mysterium of Christ is that suddenly the victim takes the murderers' places on death row and himself receives the death sentence. Then that victim becomes counsel for the defense! The mysterium of God's revealed grace is that Christ's death at human hands on humans' behalf fulfills the just decrees of God. Its enigma is that this substituted, executed convict comes back to life. Unruly humanity, having seized God's earth and killed God's messengers, need no longer be condemned for its crimes but has been provided a means of full pardon through Christ's payment of its debts to the laws of divine and secular society.

If some Christians question whether a mystery story can be a Christian story, they do not know their own faith thoroughly enough. And every detective of the full implication of any mystery ends in the mysterium that comes from this great source, which is the well-spring of morality as well. The following study is my quest for the primal mysterium in the mystery.

Mystery

Μυστήριον: *musterion* or *mysterion* in Greek; the very word is enigmatic. To trace the progress of the Greek word *mysterion* from its origin to its present form in the English language is like trying to trace the undercover passage of a spy. As it boarded ships and slipped across the linguistic boundaries of multinational sailors, it changed its case endings and accent, adapting itself to Latin *mysterium* for worship, blending with *ministerium* for occupation or office, into Old French *mestier* and Middle English *misterie, mysterie* (standing for the trades or crafts which were later to produce the plays). Thus it invaded England in the tongues that eventually fused with others to form the English word *mystery*.

In the Greek, *mysterion* is as much an enigma as that which it represents. The New Testament scholar Gunther Bornkamm notes, "The etymology of the word is itself a mystery." Its derivation is uncertain. From early on, the term, predominantly in the plural, was applied to the ancient cults from the seventh century B.C./B.C.E. to the fourth century A.D./C.E., for "mysteries are cultic rites in which the destinies of a god are portrayed by sacred actions before a circle of devotees in such a way as to give them a part in the fate of the god" (Kittel, 803). Bornkamm observes the rites' holy mystery is the "sanctifying union between the suffering deity and the devotees, who in the mysteries acquire a share in the destiny of the god and hence in the divine power of life" (Kittel, 805). This mystery usually includes a vow of silence placed on the devotees, hence one reason for our connotation of "the secret" or "the hidden" for the word *mystery*. Such an appealing word would be easily appropriated, as did Plato for the mysteries of philosophy or as did the magic texts that divorced magic from worship (Kittel, 808, 810).

The Septuagint, the Greek translation of the Hebrew Scriptures and apocryphal additions, employs the term in a number of extracanonical books. In the joyful ending of *Tobit* the incognito angel Raphael uses it in a proverb, "A king's mystery is good to conceal, but the works of God honorable to reveal" (12:7, 11). In 2 Maccabees 13:21 we find out what happens to one who does reveal the king's secret plan. When the unfortunate Rhodocus passes the mysteries to the enemy, he is sought out and clamped into prison. In *Judith* 2:2 Nebuchadnezzar calls together his cabinet of officers and nobles and lays before them "the mystery of his decision." He reveals what he has decided to do. *The Wisdom of Solomon* moves this earthly use of *mysterion* to a heavenly and religious sphere, identifying God's *mysterion* as recompensing a holy life, giving innocence a reward (2:22). The writer promises to hide no "secret" about the nature and origin of wisdom from the reader (6:22). The writer proceeds to examine pagan religious "mysteries" that counterfeit true religion, ones that may have begun with innocent grieving for a dead child and then have institutionalized the grieving into religious rites (14:15), frenzied orgies, secret ceremonies, and ritual murder (14:23). These are "mysteries" with a diabolical cast, like the deep evil that often surfaces when a detective searching for a motive tracks down the past of a victim in the hard-boiled subgenre.

The book of *Sirach* deals with more benign secrets, those of a friend. According to 22:22 and 27:16, 17, and 21, if we betray a friend's secrets, we will drive that friend away. Alternate readings of *Sirach* 3:18 add what is often listed as verse 19. The variant claims inclusion for a thought that will figure significantly in Paul's understanding of the *mysterion* of Christ, that while many are exalted and mighty, God reveals "secrets" to the modest. Strangely, however, despite its prevalence in the translation into Greek of the Old Testament text, such a potent word as *mysterion* is not used regularly in the canonical Scriptures. Rather it is only employed in the Septuagint for a particular word used only in Daniel.

Hatch and Redpath in their authoritative concordance note that *mysterion* translates the word *raz*. Some, like Benjamin Davidson, see *raz* as a Chaldean word, others as a Persian word (James Montgomery in the International Critical Commentary), still others as an Aramaic word based on a Persian original (Gunther Bornkamm). Still, though the concept of mystery may occur earlier in the Old Testament text, such as in the account of Joseph interpreting dreams, the word translated *mysterion* in both the Septuagint and Theodotion's version occurs principally in Daniel and in the Apocrypha.*

Outside of the book of Daniel, Theodotion also uses *mysterion* beyond the Apocrypha's limits to translate Job 15:8 (as does Symmachus), substituting it for the word *sod,* secret counsel, a word that depicts God as a Nebuchadnezzar or a king of Israel holding a secret council, outlining the ruler's plan, the king's wisdom. This same *sod* is later employed for the fourth level of Jewish exegesis, the inner, spiritual meaning incorporated in the concept of *raz,* the hidden or secret mystery. As an exegete progressed from "Peshat" (the first simple sight meaning, the literal interpretation), through "Remuz" (that meaning which the passage implies, to which it alludes, the typical or allegorical meaning), through "Derush" (the meaning induced from research or investigation), one finally arrived at "Sod," the hidden or deep meaning. To enter through these four meanings and at last to achieve the "Sod" interpretation was to enter the Holy of Holies of the text. This was "Pesher," the solution/interpretation of a divine secret mystery. As Nebuchadnezzar receives that mystery vision (the gigantic tree and its fall), Daniel pierces to the secret interpretation. As F. F. Bruce points out in *Biblical Exegesis in the Qumran Texts,* "Not until the mystery and the interpretation are brought together can the divine communication be understood" (Bruce, 8). This is what young Joseph does in Genesis 40–41, first for

---

*Hatch and Redpath in their concordance to the Septuagint, the ancient Greek translation of the Hebrew scriptures, list nine occurrences in Daniel.

the butcher and the baker and then for the great Pharoah himself. *Sod* is also used again in both Theodotion's and Quintilianus' translation of Psalm 25:14 for those purposes of God revealed to the ones who fear God. Theodotion further adds Proverbs 20:19, which has to do with a gossip betraying secrets, and both Theodotion and Symmachus add Isaiah 24:16, which has to do with treachery. Symmachus finally appends Proverbs 11:13, which also has to do with gossip, the revealing of secrets.

But the use of *mysterion* in Daniel means something far greater than gossip, something deeper than revealing the king's secret, something more akin to the mysteries pierced by Joseph. Concentrated primarily in Daniel chapter 2, this instance of spiritual detecting becomes a life and death matter when the *mysterion* has to do with the fate of a whole nation, and the lives of the king's individual counselors are at stake in its discovery. Troubled by a dream, the despot of Babylon throws the lives of his wise men on the block. Daniel, in verses 2:18, 19, 27, 28, 29, 30, and twice in 47, seeks God's indulgence to reveal the *raz,* the *mysterion* to pierce through to God's intention communicated in the parable of the king's nocturnal vision. Later in 4:6 Daniel is terrified by his own nocturnal *mysterion.*

These visual parables in Daniel are like the later audible parables of Jesus that will blind those who see, deafen those who hear, confusing the understanding of those who witness them in the New Testament. God unlocks the *mysterion* to God's servant Daniel, who unlocks it to the king. In the same manner Jesus comes telling parables in the parallel accounts of Luke 8:10, Matthew 13:11, and Mark 4:11, the famous parable of the sower. Understanding is given to the disciples. God's sovereignty is displayed. No one pierces to the meaning alone. But free will is here, too. One has to have cultivated within one's active life such an environment that the word of God implanted can grow through the rich soil of one's own faithfulness and obedience. Ironically, the disciples to whom understanding is given do not understand. But then Jesus becomes the giver. He explains that the mystery herein is that the kingdom is ripped from those in the exclusive kingdom class—the scribes, the Pharisees—and is given to the humble obedient. Jesus ends his ministry giving the great commission, commanding his disciples to go to the Gentiles.

Paul sees as a mystery that Gentiles are included in the inheritance of Israel. To the lifelong Pharisee Paul, such an action is baffling. It is a great *mysterion.* It stands against strict Pharisaical interpretation of Old Testament teaching. It takes the exceptions, the Rahabs and Ruths, and makes them part of the rule, seeing them as synecdoche of a great principle: that all the nations in the world will be blessed through Abraham, as Genesis 12:3 promised the great patriarch, he whom all rabbis, all scribes, all Pharisees claimed as progenitor. Paul's writings are a continued grappling with this enigma, this great mystery.

In Romans 11:25, Paul wants "the family" to understand that a part of Israel will remain hardened until the full measure of Gentiles enters in. Israel then will be saved by the deliverer coming out of Zion. According to 16:25 the gospel and preaching of Jesus now manifested through the prophets was also concealed for ages since those hearing and seeing did not understand. Now it is made known to the Gentiles to bring about the obedience of faith. So verse 27 claims Christian unity mirrors the one wise God, who conceals and reveals through Jesus Christ. Thus, in the unity Christians are one while in the plurality they are Jews and Gentiles. In 1 Corinthians 2:7 (and possibly 2:1) the wisdom of God which is in mystery contrasts with the wisdom of this age. God's mystery had been concealed so that with their lack of knowledge of this wisdom earthly rulers crucified the Lord of Glory. Christian leaders, however, are supposed to be stewards of the mysteries of God (4:1). Still, Paul warns, even if one knows all wisdom and all mysteries, one is nothing without love (13:2). Though the spirit of one speaking in a tongue speaks mysteries, the speaking is not done with the mind. These mysteries are only communicated to God (14:2). Though this speaking may not be apprehendable, some mysteries, such as that in 15:51 of the transforming of people in the resurrection of the dead, are. At least they are apprehendable by analogy. Ephesians 1:9 states the mystery of God's will is for unity.* The mystery of God's will, God's set plan, is to summarize all things on heaven and earth in Christ. A specific example of this summarizing is found in the case of the Gentiles' adoption to the faith (Ephesians 3:3,4). This mystery made known to Paul by revelation was a mystery of Christ now revealed that Gentiles are fellow heirs who share God's promise. Ephesians 3:9 states that this mystery that had been hidden for ages in God is God's many-sided wisdom and is able to be known (3:10). Another example of unity is the two partners of a marriage becoming one flesh—a great mystery that Paul identifies as imaging Christ and the Church in 5:32. Paul ends his letter to the Ephesians asking that he be granted the opening and courage to speak the mystery of the good news that the Gentiles are co-heirs. To the Colossians in 1:26–27 he notes that the

---

*Readers will note that in this study I accept the traditional attributing by such witnesses as Irenaeus, Tertullian, Clement of Alexandria, the Muratorian Canon, Polycarp, and Clement of Rome of such presently disputed epistles as what since Paul Anton of Halle (1726) have been called the Pastoral Epistles, Ephesians, and Colossians to Paul. Linguists Mosteller and Wallace, computer studies, and studies in the new field of stylistics, like Aída Besançon Spencer's *Paul's Literary Style* (1984: Eisenbrauns Publishing Company), suggest that a 100,000 word sample is needed to establish authorship. The entire New Testament only contains about 180,000 words (A. B. Spencer, *Style*, 218). No serious ruling on authorship can therefore be made or could ever have been made on the sole basis of characteristics or peculiarities of style. However, for traditional arguments for the authenticity of the Pastorals, Ephesians and Colossians, readers may consult Donald Guthrie's *New Testament Introduction*, Inter-Varsity Press, 3rd ed., 1970, and for arguments particularly against Paul's authorship of the Pastorals and Ephesians, Werner Kummel's *Introduction to the New Testament*, which encapsulates clearly the histories of the authorship questions.

mystery is Christ among you (plural), the hope of glory, Christ in whom all the treasures of wisdom and knowledge are hidden (2:2–3). He explains this mystery of Christ is the object of his preaching (Colossians 4:3,4). He writes to Timothy that deacons should possess this mystery with a good conscience (1 Timothy 3:9). In verse 16 he explains the mystery of godliness has appeared in flesh, been justified in spirit, seen by angels, preached among Gentiles, believed in the world, taken up in glory—obviously Jesus the Christ. There is also an evil mystery of lawlessness Paul identifies that is already at work but is being restrained (2 Thessalonians 2:7). Paul, then, speaks of a number of mysteries, such as the mystery of God's will, which is that Gentiles have a share in God's promise, a mystery of lawlessness, a mystery of godliness which is Christ.

John, who would appear to be overwhelmed by mystery in that great vision of the Apocalypse, strangely enough uses the term less than Paul, a mere four times in twenty-two chapters, compared to Paul's potential six times each in the sixteen chapters of 1 Corinthians and the six of Ephesians and a potential twenty-one times throughout his writing. In Revelation, John, staggered by the first burst of his vision (1:20), is told by the theophany of the one who died and is alive of the mystery of the seven stars and gold lampstands which image the seven angels and the seven churches of Asia Minor. In 10:7, a seventh angel eventually reveals the mystery of God as announced through the prophets, a remarkable echo of the doxological ending of Romans 16:25 and 26, which talks about the mystery kept secret from long ages but now announced to all Gentiles: that the reign of the world has become the reign of the Lord and of God's Christ and that the Lord will rule forever (Revelation 11:15). Again in the Apocalypse an evil mystery is contrasted. It is one written on the forehead of the terrifying monster who rides glutted with the blood of the saintly martyrs. On it is "a name written, a mystery, Babylon the great" (17:5), a counterfeit religious statement. The mystery of this monster and the beast that carries her is revealed by the angel who guides John (17:7), in essence the angelic sleuth who interprets the hidden secrets of these great eschatological mysteries (the beast is not yet but is to come) of the war of good with evil, a war in heaven fought on earth.

But how did this religious word for God's secrets in Christianity and in the mystical religions of the East come to be used for fictional literature dealing with human crimes? According to *The Oxford English Dictionary,* which lists "A mystery story" as one of the meanings for mystery in its 1976 supplement, the term *mysterion,* from which is derived "mystery," classically denotes certain secret religious ceremonies whose initiates were sworn not to reveal them. This idea of secret counsel or purpose was retained in the Septuagint. By the time of the New Testament, it had come to mean a religious truth long kept secret but now revealed through Christ to the Church. In later Greek writings, when the Christian religious sense became stabilized as a reference to the sacraments, the term was still used, according to the *Oxford English Dictionary,* "even when it means only 'secret.'" In the medieval mystery plays the term meant incidents or events in the life of Christ and the saints having mystical significance. Thus, Christian usage of the term up to the threshold of the modern period retained a connotation of secrecy.

Interestingly, the development of the mystery play may have contributed to preserving and resuscitating theater itself. Because of the gross immorality and pagan blasphemies associated with the Roman theater and the bloodshed and persecution of Christians associated with the Colosseum and the other Roman theaters of games, creative popular and particularly dramatic entertainment had come to be shunned by the Church. Of course, the creative literature we now call generally the Pseudepigrapha or New Testament Apocrypha continued to pour out, amplifying—sometimes fantastically—the canonical New Testament gospels, Acts, epistles, and Apocalypse from early in the second century on, but the Church did not energetically pursue creative literature.

As Alfred W. Pollard in *English Miracle Plays, Moralities, and Interludes* has noted:

> Under the later Roman Empire the drama died a natural death, not because the Church condemned it, but by a lust for sheer obscenity and bloodshed which made true dramatic writing impossible. Until the theatres in which men were made to die and women to prostitute themselves, not in show but in reality, had long been closed and forgotten, the stage was something too vile and horrible for any attempt to Christianize it; nor could the innate dramatic instincts of mankind again find free play amid the unhealthy surroundings of a dying civilization. (Pollard, xi)

The few exceptions to this embargo include a disputed drama on the passion of Christ in the Greek tragic mode *Christos Paschon* ("Christ Suffering," or perhaps, "The Suffering Christ"), often attributed to St. Gregory Nazianzene of the fourth century (but perhaps, some speculate, really belonging to a period six hundred years later) and the six plays of Hroswitha, the nun who was "Germany's first poet and playwright" (Tucker, Liefield, 145) and of other scattered monastics in other monasteries.

When finally the memory of pagan theatrical atrocities had faded far enough into the past to allow a return to creativity, the apocryphal tales, along with the stories of Scripture and the lives of the saints, provided the cloth to be embroidered into the new medieval popular arts. New Testament scholar Bruce M. Metzger notes of the primal detective tale *Susannah:*

> During the Middle Ages the story attained great popularity in various literary forms among the nations of Europe. About the beginning of the twelfth century Hildebert, Archbishop of Tours, paraphrased the story in a lengthy Latin poem. During the fourteenth and fifteenth centuries at least five versions in alliterative and riming stanzas circulated in Scotland. In these versions the original story is much adorned with imaginative details. In the sixteenth century

a translation from German into Ladino, the dialect used in the Upper Engadine Valley in
Switzerland, was adapted for presentation as a drama. (Metzger, 113)

Among the Scottish poems were the popular fourteenth- to fifteenth-century
"The Pistill of Susan" (a corruption of "The Epistle of Susannah"), usually
attributed to one Huchown (Hugh) of Ayrshire in West Scotland. Also balladeer
William Elderton turned out a medieval hit, "The Constancy of Susanna," which
reportedly turned in a healthy number of the Renaissance equivalent of mechani-
cals for Thomas Colwell, who licensed it in 1562–63. According to Metzger,
"The tune to which the words were set was catchy, and the ballad had a wide
sale" (Metzger, 208). Sir Toby Belch belts it out in Shakespeare's *Twelfth
Night* (II,iii,84). Shylock alludes to the tale in *The Merchant of Venice,* and
Metzger adds provocatively that Shakespeare's daughters were, after all, named
Judith and Susanna—a not unthinkable coincidence since Richmond Noble has
recognized at least eighty passages in his plays that allude to eleven Apocryphal
books (Metzger, 207–9). *Susannah* also lives in early Christian art in the Roman
catacombs, on sarcophagi in Italy and Southern Gaul, in a painting in the
cemetery of Praetextatus with a Latin inscription. Even the somewhat misogy-
nistic St. John Chrysostom preached a sermon praising Susannah (Metzger,
112).

But besides all these, chief among her popular artistic appearances are in
the now famous dramas called the mystery plays. Perhaps more than any other
popular artistic expression the mystery play cycles wedded religion, enjoyment,
and creativity together. We have already seen how in the Apocrypha the term
mysterion was appropriated and how later in the New Testament it was Chris-
tianized to depict the deep secrets of God made manifest to the faithful. Following New Testament times the term was adopted by Ignatius and then by the
Didache, passing into the literature of the early Church. As it wended its way
across Christendom, it stood in for the sacraments (Kittel, 826), the deep participation in the signs and experiences of God's grace. Thus, when the era of the
early Church closed, the term came infused with profound religious significance
when the populace added dramas of faith to the entertainment of tournaments,
holiday festivals, folk plays, sword dances, civil pageants, juggling, mimes and
dance. For the people and the sponsoring guilds "mystery" retained the significance of the deep mystery, the mysterium of God, and the term was restricted
to plays drawn from what was recognized to be Scripture.

However, the term was probably not as widely employed in English as it
was in French (from the fourteenth century on), nor did it apply to all popular
plays with religious themes (Thomas, 6–7). Eleanor Prosser, in her reevaluation
of the phenomenon, notes there were two other large classifications of religious
plays: "The religious drama was flourishing: the mysteries (based on biblical
stories), the miracles (based on the lives of the saints), and the allegorical

moralities (treating man's struggle against death and sin)" (Prosser, 4). Thus, the term mystery was reserved for the enigma revealed in the Scriptures. The mystery play did not preempt the Latin liturgical drama. As critic Rosemary Woolf notes, "Firstly, liturgical drama never left the church but co-existed with the mystery plays almost throughout their lifetime" (Woolf, 3). Thus, the Latin liturgical drama held solemn mass in the church, while the mystery play danced and reveled out into the market place. In the latter the somber secrets of the faith became lively events of massive pageantry, glittering costumes, triumphing saints, and prancing and plummeting devils. The delights of the *mysterion* spread out among the revelers of the market place, finding their way over the centuries into the other folk arts: religious dance, story telling, art.

Thus, the English word mystery not only stood for the crafts or trades that produced the Scripturally-based plays that came to bear its name, but also retained its profound theological referent to the themes of the two primal apocryphal mysteries. Perhaps the prior claim of God's law on human law, God's justice on human enforcement, God's enigma on human secrets, God's revelation on detection and exposure informs the secularized modern mystery genre as well. Because these tales are mysteries by designation, they point back to the great mysterium of existence. They are images of the hidden enigma of God. They stand in the way of affirmation, they image a truth in the nature of God about the eternal order, the primal goodness, justice, love, and mercy which human existence in the image of God reflects.

The clerical detectives, then, stand at the core, the heart of the origin and main intention of the mystery genre. The newly arrived police inspectors, private eyes, detecting citizens, in spite of their multiplicity, finally congregate around them. Anyone who penetrates the secular deeply enough will reach the borders of the sacred.

Nontheological uses of the term mysterium, or mysterie, began appearing as early as 1194, denoting a riddle, an enigma, a secret or hidden matter or event. Early nontheological uses were for political secrets, which, of course, bred intrigue; secrets of nature such as the hatreds and affections of animals; and a whole corpus of literature from 1382 to 1884 which turned the biblical phrase "mystery of iniquity" into a seamy category of secret events that bode evil. A nineteenth-century example is, "The great city (of London) is full of many mysteries—not a few of them . . . mysteries of iniquity" (OED, 815). Thus, the term mystery, which originally referred to divine events and incidents in the enigmatic life of Christ, had acquired a sinister cast. In the early gothic novels of terror that were so popular in the 1700s, such as Horace Walpole's *The Castle of Otranto* (1764) or Ann Radcliffe's *The Mysteries of Udolpho* (1794), supernatural events secreted in gloomy castles were used to create tales of evil and horror. When those events began to contain murders of humans by other humans, such as in Matthew Gregory Lewis' religious horror tale *The Monk*, a rudimentary form of detection began. In *The Monk,* a sibling, a lover, and a nun all contribute to gathering evidence and bringing an indictment that eventually topples a clerical criminal. By 1794, the year of *The Mysteries of Udolpho,* William Godwin had created a murder mystery featuring two detectives, one amateur, one professional, and had written one of the first attempts at a psychological study of the criminal mind. In the United States the first thoroughly modern mystery of detection was to be recognized in Edgar Allen Poe's 1841 "Murders in the Rue Morgue." But Charles Brockden Brown's *Ormond; or The Secret Witness* and *Edgar Huntley* (1799) had earlier presented tales of pursuit, and eventually in James Fenimore Cooper's *The Pathfinder* (1840) and *The Deerslayer* (1841), among others of his tales, the redoubtable Hawkeye reconstructs the character of a criminal from his footprints, a feat worthy of the later Holmes. In Great Britain Edward Bulwer-Lytton (Lord Lytton) had already written two novels containing systematic detection by an amateur in *Pelham* (1828) and *Eugene Aram* (1832). The rise of Vidocq and the Sûreté, the first truly professional detective police force, and the publication of Vidocq's memoirs in 1828 captured the imagination of a host of writers, including such luminaries as Honoré de Balzac, Victor Hugo in *Les Misérables* and Dumas (Stevenson, *Collier's,* 146). By 1842–1843 this trend peaked in Eugène Sue's most popular novel, *Les Mystères de Paris,* mysteries that exposed the defects in the Parisian social system. By the time Poe's detective, C. Auguste Dupin, arrived upon the scene, eccentric, analytic, magnificently contemptuous of the police, the term "mystery" was regularly employed for hidden incidents of a horrifying nature shrouded in secrecy. These secret horrific incidents were now synonymous with such crimes as murder, and the detecting of these mysteries, no longer supernaturally good but now humanly evil, gave birth to a whole corpus of literature, the detective or mystery novel. But corrupt though the term had now become, it still bore in its name the vestiges of something supernaturally good.

As the literature of the mystery genre became a secularization of the concealing/revealing quality of the great mysterium, God as orderer and focal point of unity was displaced by secular society, priest displaced by police, and the sacred act of repentance and reconciliation displaced by indictment and punishment. The detective as secular priest now identified the person out of unity, the antisocial criminal, and exacted society's punishment. Criminals were called to pay their debt to society. Social unity was in that way restored.*

But, as the present study will reveal, the detecting cleric, when functioning in the proper atavistic sense, the radical sense that recalls the primal function

---

*This priestly function is echoed in Walter Hill's Nick Nolte/Eddie Murphy hard-boiled movie, *48 Hours,* when Jack Cate's girlfriend complains that the detective has placed his job over their relationship, over his own health and sanity as some kind of "sacred" trust, and he snarls back in all seriousness, "That's right."

of the mysterium, reaches back to the root meaning and claims by discovery, by manifestation, to bring God's perspective on the criminal. Repentance is called for by the clearing of the mystery, and mercy is discovered by the disclosing of God's wonderful mysterium. In the case of Father Brown, the criminal is brought solely before God's bar of justice for judgment, in the case of Father Dowling, before both God's and society's. The clerical sleuth understands that the great mysterium demands that the lawbreaker be reunified with God through repentance and grace through penitence. Often penance *and* restitution are the result, as in Brother Cadfael's ministry.

All of life is to be lived under God's expressed intentions. Laws are societal attempts to form these into decrees, into secularized commandments. Breaking laws violates God's intentions and directives. So the clerical detective reaches back to the great Μυστήριον and attempts the unity of all transgressors back under God's reign. When the detective feels this reign is better served directly, however, societal laws are bypassed.

A Note on the Literature and Its Classification

This book will engage in theological analysis of the subgenre of popular mystery literature I call the clerical crime novel. These fictional, secularized mystery novels present an ordained cleric who steps in when the police and their consultants are thoroughly baffled by a crime or series of crimes and who then with a perspicacity illumined by God's wisdom solves the crime(s). I use the term "ordained" in a nontechnical sense for any religious professional who has taken vows, who has received a church's public affirmation of God's calling, who serves in a professional capacity for which others in other churches are ordained or (in the case of women) for which their churches now ordain. My theory is that the modern mystery novel is a secularized form structured on the ancient mysterium or revelation of God's judgment and grace. Fictional mystery literature began in the Apocrypha's primal tales of *Bel and the Dragon* and *Susannah,* two stories in which the young Daniel, filled with God's sagacity, solved crimes, wedding detection and solution with revelation from the sacred. Today's proliferation of clerical sleuths testifies to continuing interest in seeing the sacred mysterium behind the secular mystery. The mystery story itself, in its quest for the criminal and the interdiction of evil and restoration of the good, images the quest through a fallen world for the great good God. The deeper one delves in the secular mystery, the closer one travels to the borders of the great sacred mystery. This latter point is addressed throughout the study. The clerical sleuths from the beginning to the present, because of the nature of their function and their quest, stand in the center of the mystery novel's quest for solution, justice, punishment, penance, forgiveness, redemption. In so doing, the clerical sleuth graphically illustrates the popular thirst for a cosmos put right by God.

The clerical crime novel may be subdivided into three classifications. First, the most general category would be any tale that involves the clergy and crime. Practically every tale about active ministers could be a part of this category. However, clergy serving in chaplaincy positions with the police or regularly accompanying detectives (as in Jack Webb's or Thurmin Warriner's tales or in a lesser sense in Christopher Leach's *Blood Games* or Dorothy Salisbury Davis' *Where the Dark Streets Go*) I would call "saintly sidekicks" rather than clerical sleuths. To a lesser or greater degree in detecting activity, they comprise a vast bulk of the fiction about clerics, for the line between dealing with sin and crime is a slim one. Sin normally subsumes crime, yet at times, as with civil disobedience or, more arguably, some of the machinations of the clerical sleuths in the name of God's justice, all sin is not crime and all crime may not be sin. In the gap stands the clerical sleuth. But in that gap stand these many other active clerics of category one as well. In distinguishing between category one and category three, the saintly sidekick and the clerical sleuth, I draw the demarcation of the subgenre tightly at those present clerics or religious professionals, who, themselves, name the criminal and solve the crime.

A second great division of the clerical crime novel might well be tales that feature crime by a cleric. This would be a clerical crime novel in the most literal sense of the words. It certainly began with the deceitful priests of *Bel and the Dragon* and could have embraced those despicable elders of *Susannah* if they were drawn from the priestly class. From Matthew Gregory Lewis' 1795 *The Monk* through A. E. W. Mason's sinister Reverend Mr. Bernard Simmons, whose syncretism argues "Buddhism makes murder worthwhile" (*Dilemmas*, 107), to C. E. Vuillamy's ordained lunatic, the Rev. Gregory Virgil Pardicott of *The Vicar's Experiments* (a.k.a. *Clerical Error* in the U.S.A.), the list seems endless. In mainline fiction, clergy sin at an appalling rate in the seemingly endless variations of *Night of the Iguana, The Tight White Collar, The Thorn Birds, The Runner Stumbles,* in movies like *True Confessions,* as well as on television in regular series. Even that great American novel, *The Scarlet Letter,* features a nefarious Reverend Arthur Dimmesdale. The "bigger than both of us" sexual sin, which can lead to heinous crime, is the theme of most of the stories already listed as well as, for example, such television episodes as "Premium for Murder" in the Jack Warden detective series, *Crazy like a Fox,* among numerous others. True life scandals involving clergy are fictionalized and explored in such novels as ex-Jesuit priest Robert Casey's *The Jesus Man.* Clerical crime is a fully developed form of literature (a counterpart of life) in itself. Since the only qualification for becoming a Christian is being a repentant sinner, this is certainly understandable. I allude to representative tales from this category throughout the text whenever appropriate. Some novels, like *Reverend Randollph and the Unholy Bible* or *Through the Valley of Death,* fit all three categories: a crime tale with a cleric committing the crime and a cleric solving the crime.

The third category, as I have noted, however, is my focus—mysteries solved primarily by the cleric. When I use the term clerical crime novel, such is my primary reference. Just as the "police procedural" focuses on police solving the crime through police procedure, not on police losing culprits through the procedure or manipulating the procedure to pick up graft, so, too, the clerical crime novel focuses on clerics solving mysteries—not creating them.

What separates mystery from thriller or crime adventure (with which I do not primarily deal) is that mystery involves detecting, a secret that has to be discovered, a secret that has to be revealed. Its fictional form, too, invokes the stories that Jesus and the prophets told. As storytelling came to duplicate in fictional form the confessional literature exemplified by Augustine in his confessions and later developed fully by eighteenth-century pietistic writers, it produced the psychological novel, a precursor of the mystery. The romance derives from the great comedy, that primal epic of peril and rescue, the great human adventure of fall and redemption, sin and salvation, mirrored now in crime and restoration. The literature literally spans the ages.

Part One

Rabbis and Robbers

1

Rabbis and Robbers in the Past:
Bel and the Dragon and *Susannah*

Two of the first mystery novels that initiated the tale of detection are clerical detective thrillers in the Judeo-Christian tradition and can be found among the books of the Apocrypha. Consequently, the clerical crime novel can hardly be considered a subdivision or a development of the genre of mystery fiction.

In 1929 crime writer Dorothy Sayers, creator of that detecting dilettante Lord Peter Wimsey, compiled what has now come to be regarded as a classic collection of modern crime fiction, *The Omnibus of Crime*. In her introduction she observed, "The detective-story has had a spasmodic history, appearing here and there in faint, tentative sketches and episodes, until it suddenly burst into magnificent flower in the middle of the last century" (Sayers, 9). Among the spasmodic appearances she noted are occurrences in Aesop's beast fable of the lion and the fox, in the tale of Hercules and Cacus in Virgil's *Aeneid,* book 8, in the story of Rhampsinitus' Treasure-House in Herodotus, book 2, in German and Indian folk tales, and in the Apocryphal tales of *Susannah* and *Bel and the Dragon*. Of these last two she writes, "The Jews, with their strongly moral preoccupation, were, as our two Apocryphal stories show, peculiarly fitted to produce the roman policier" (Sayers, 10). In a footnote she writes, "In *Bel and the Dragon* the science of deduction from material clues, in the popular Scotland Yard manner, is reduced to its simplest expression. *Susanna,* on the other hand, may be taken as foreshadowing the Gallic method of eliciting the truth by the confrontation of witnesses" (Sayers, 11). Diana L. H. Butler in her unpublished study "Lord Peter Wimsey and the Theological Art of Detective Fiction" (July 24, 1985) has dubbed *Susannah* and *Bel and the Dragon* respectively a "frame up" and a "set up" (Butler, 7). Thus, one who seeks the *habeas corpus* of the first appearance of the mystery genre itself will trace back the clues to two clerical detective novels which themselves were hidden in a collection of books intentionally shrouded in mystery.

The term Apocrypha, first traced to Jerome and Cyril of Jerusalem (died 420 and 386, respectively), was applied to a collection of some fifteen books, whose origins remain obscure. The term *apokruphos* means literally "from secret," "hidden, concealed, secret, obscure, hard to understand." The word was applied variously to hieroglyphics; krúphios was the title given to one grade of initiates in the mysteries of Mithras, that Persian Sun-worshipping military cult so popular with the pre-Christian Roman emperors, and was even applied to a fabulous gem, "The Secret One" (Liddell, 1000). So in its popular and cultic use the word carries the connotation of the mysterious, the hidden secret, the mystery to be revealed.

All the books we now call the Apocrypha were written in the last two centuries B.C./B.C.E. Its wide dispersion throughout the ancient world shows how popular this literature was in the intertestamental period.

This example of ancient popular literature appears to contain the distant ancestors of today's bestsellers. Genre literature in particular can trace its sources to the Apocrypha. Gothic romances can find their flame in the romantic tales of Tobit and Judith, complete with love interest, wild demons, a *femme fatale,* dastardly villains, and a handsome hero. Historical adventure epics from Tolkien to John Jakes thunder to us across the ages not only from the *Iliad* and the *Aeneid* but also from the adventures of the Maccabees, blood-thirsty tales of war and slaughter, intrigue and high adventure. Our "how-to" and personal enrichment books are foreshadowed by the first practical books of sage advice— the wisdom literature. Devotional and inspirational books find their inspiration in the Apocrypha's liturgical psalm, and "whodunits" trace back to age-old thrillers of primeval crime and ancient detecting, appended to the canonical book of Daniel.

As the spiritual parents, the mystical forerunners of the later writers of the hidden books of the Cabala, the writers of the Apocrypha undoubtedly nourished as a primary intention the secreting of these books from the general public. As Fritsch notes, "As a literary term it was first applied to books which were to be kept from the public because of the esoteric wisdom they contained. In this sense it was a title of honor, since it referred to books whose secret doctrines imparted to them special authority" (Fritsch, 162). He traces such a design to passages like 2 Esdras 14:4–6, which reads:

> I led him [Moses] up on Mount Sinai, where I kept him with me many days; and I told him many wondrous things, and showed him the secrets of the times and declared to him the end of the times. Then I commanded him, saying, "These words you shall publish openly, and these you shall keep secret." (Fritsch, 162)

Fritsch identifies the words open for publication as the Torah of Moses and those closed to the public as what have come to be called the outside books, those multitudinous books which include the writings of the Apocrypha. Julius Wellhausen, of the famous Graf-Wellhausen theory of pentateuchal construction, speculated the source of many of these esoteric secrets may well have been the Essenes, that mystical Qumran community with its enormous library of outside books and cryptic scripts.

In a kind of performatory utterance the first clerical mysteries were themselves intentionally shrouded in mystery. Yet, so popular did these books become as entertainment literature that they burst out of the restricting limitations of the outside books and dispersed throughout the Near East. This wide distribution is what saved them from extinction, for after the fall of Jerusalem the appalled rabbis seized on these outside books as the rabble-rousing source of the calamity and outlawed them, taking the Apocrypha down with all the apocalyptic works.

Those dangerous apocalyptic daydreams had brought disaster on Jerusalem, and now Christians, who were starting to produce a Christian Aramaic literature, threatened to provide Christian interpretations for the outside books. So a definitive Hebrew canon was needed and with it a corresponding ban against the outside books.

Josephus explained the procedure in his *Against Apion:*

> For we have not an innumerable multitude of books among us, disagreeing from and contradicting one another (as the Greeks have), but only twenty-two books, which contain the records of all the past times, which are justly believed to be divine. . . . It is true, our history hath been written since Artaxerxes very particularly, but hath not been esteemed of the like authority with the former by our forefathers, because there hath not been an exact succession of prophets since that time: and how firmly we have given credit to these books of our own nation, is evident by what we do: for during so many ages as have already passed, no one hath been so bold as either to add any thing to them, to take any thing from them, or to make any change in them; but it is become natural to all Jews, immediately and from their very birth, to esteem those books to contain divine doctrines, and to persist in them, and, if occasion be, willingly to die for them. (Josephus, *Against Apion,* book 1:8)

Therefore, the principle adopted was that after the time of Artaxerxes, that is the time of Ezra, the Lord ceased to speak. Hence anything written afterwards was automatically noncanonical; it ceased to exist for the Jews or was systematically destroyed. As the Midrash Qoheleth 12:12 taught, "Whoever brings together in his house more than twenty-four books (the canonical Scriptures) brings confusion," and Rabbi Akiba ruled that among those who have no part in the world to come is "he who reads in the outside books" (Fritsch, 163). The only reason, then, that the Apocryphal mysteries still survive today is that Christians found them fascinating and copied them copiously into their own languages.

Bel and the Dragon

The elder of the two mysteries is *Bel and the Dragon*. It was written about 100 B.C./B.C.E., presumably, according to W. O. E. Oesterley, in the diaspora (Oesterley, 396–97). One of the difficulties in Apocryphal research, due primarily to the rabbis' zealous program of destruction aided by the ravages of time, is the difficulty in ascertaining what language served for each book's original composition. At Qumran two fragments of Ecclesiasticus were located in Hebrew or Aramaic, corroborating the theory that the Apocrypha first appeared in Hebrew, and two fragmentary manuscripts of Tobit were unearthed, one in Aramaic. If *Bel and the Dragon* was composed in the diaspora, however, one might argue for a Greek original, as Oesterley does, though on language characteristics R. H. Charles maintains it enjoyed a Hebrew original. On admittedly slight evidence Charles further speculates the Septuagint (LXX) version was extant in 100 B.C./B.C.E., ultimately guessing its date of composition to be about 136 B.C./B.C.E. (Charles, 655–57). B.C./B.C.E. 136 was a stormy time for the Jews, when Simon the last of the original Maccabees died at the hands of his son-in-law. Simon's surviving son John, killing those sent to murder him, routed Ptolemy only to be beseiged by Antiochus. John's tension at being forced first, to capitulate Joppa and pay tribute and second, by 129, to battle the Parthians forms the background. As John the ruler chafed, *Bel and the Dragon* was written. Oesterley, however, places the tale later, in the time of the notorious Alexander Jannaeus. The good ruling widow Alexandra's decision to marry her late husband's eldest brother Alexander Jannaeus precipitated disaster. Jannaeus had the unique ability to bungle every campaign while still landing on his feet. Defeated by both Ptolemy and Cleopatra, he managed to retain his rule. He conquered Gaza and ignited a civil war at home, thereby setting himself up to be beaten by Demetrius II of Syria. Still he overcame every adversity but a decadent and debauched life, to which he succumbed in 88 B.C./B.C.E. Jannaeus' sole accomplishment appears to have been the curing of Alexandra's desire for another husband. The result, when she decided to rule herself, was one of the first decades of God-fearing rule in an otherwise bleak and troubled time.

If Oesterley is correct, *Bel and the Dragon* was written during the first years of Jannaeus' reign, with Aristobulus freshly dead and Egypt threatening. If the author was in the diaspora, (s)he would probably be aware of the situation at home while enduring the corresponding turmoil in Rome, Syria, Egypt or wherever. Perhaps Charles' honest summary, "Nothing whatever is known of the author of this work and nothing that is definite of the place or date of composition" (Charles, 656) is the best conclusion, though most speculation seems to fall into the 136–100 B.C./B.C.E. range.

Understanding its construction seems to be as difficult as pinning down the origins of the tale.* *Bel and the Dragon* appears to many scholars to be two separate tales linked episodically in either piecemeal or picaresque fashion, in effect a sort of clumsy melding of two similar tales together to make a book. But a careful reading will reveal that such is not actually the case. The two tales intrinsically interrelate as one.

As *Bel and the Dragon* opens after the mandatory establishing of the tale's credential in the Septuagint version and a locating of it in an historical setting in Theodotion's (ca. late 200s), we are introduced to the first of the Judeo-Christian clerical detectives. Daniel is presented as a priest who has risen, as did the canonical Daniel, despite the odd circumstances of the captivity, and who is in secular employ as companion of the King of Babylon. As we soon see, his specialized ministry, however, in no way mutes his vows.

The King of Babylon introduces him to the idol Bel, the Greek rendering of the usual Baal. The idol establishes its priority on the people by purportedly consuming an enormous amount of bread, mutton chops, and olive oil, as well apparently as a hearty ration of the local wines. For this feat of being a good trencherman, it is supposed to be worshipped. One would suppose they would have done better to have molded it in the form of a huge locust since this seems to have been its chief claim to fame—besides having a good priestly press. Daniel is, of course, hardly impressed and continues to pray to the Lord while the king goes each day to pray to Baal. Collision is inevitable in a two-faith household, and theirs comes when the king asks bluntly, "Why do you not worship Baal?"

Daniel fires back, "I worship no one except the Lord who created the heavens and is holding Lordship over all flesh." The seeds of both stories are germinating in this pregnant reply. As a maker is superior to that which is made, Daniel's God is the chief craftsperson (i.e., superior to the crafted Baal) and the Lord over all flesh (i.e., superior to the revered dragon, who is mere flesh).

The king is understandably annoyed and at Daniel's persistent skepticism flies into a rage. The upshot of their falling out is a dangerous wager in which Daniel and his household are stacked against the alimentary feats of Baal. "If I do not show that it is not Baal who eats these things," declares Daniel in the Septuagint version, "I will die and all those of mine."

---

*Most scholars consider it not one but two tales (e.g., Hoenig, 376; Metzger, 117; Oesterley, 395; Charles, 652; Dentan, 41). Dentan rules, "The other story, that of the dragon, is much inferior," labeling it "a second-rate version of the canonical story of Daniel in the lions' den" (Dentan, 42–43). Even in the Syriac translation the story of Bel is entitled "Bel the Idol," with the second part beginning "Then Follows the Dragon." The Vulgate, however, puts the tales together to comprise a single chapter 14, while neither Vaticanus (B) nor Alexandrinus (A) emphasizes their distinctness, leaving them as a single straight account with no title except "Vision . . . xii" (Charles, 652).

At this point the author slips a clue in, making the bland statement, "But they were to Baal seventy priests besides women and children." The author says no more, content as was Agatha Christie many years later to dangle the solution before the reader's eyes in a seemingly irrelevant bit of data.

Now comes the experimental test. The king lays out a sumptuous meal before Baal as Daniel makes suggestions. First, Daniel confirms the arrangements, then he commands that the temple be sealed. He remains to lay a trap out of the sight of everyone, anticipating the modern police procedural techniques of finger-printing and tire and foot plaster casting by spreading ashes on the floor to record the mark of tracks. Counting on the ashes to remain unobserved in the darkened temple, Daniel orders the door sealed. And now the author tips us off. As in television's celebrated Columbo series, we see the crime committed in Theodotion's version, and we are told of it in the other. The suspense lies in our watching the hero unravel the way it was done.

When the next day dawns, the Septuagint's Daniel makes a point of showing that the king's seal remains, then allows the triumphant king to exult for a while in the apparent performance of his idol and the vindication of his worship, ending in the eulogy, "Great is Baal, and there is not from him deceit." In reply, "Daniel laughed very much and he said to the king, 'Come behold the deceit of the priests,'" picking up the king's word and flinging it back at him in a change of context. "Whose footprints are these?" The stupefied king can only exclaim in stunned polysyndeton, "Of men and women and children."

Immediately Daniel shows the king the false door where the priests have been lugging the food off to eat and stockpile. Thus, the doom Daniel risked falls on the priests, and the king himself overturns the idol of metal, "and the money spent to him he gave to Daniel, but the Baal he overturned."

Thus, one would think that Daniel had won his point, but now the king offers Daniel an alternative. Now that Daniel has discredited an object of worship made of metal, the king offers him a deity not made of metal but of flesh and blood—the dragon. The second part of Daniel's declaration is coming under challenge. God is not only the master craftsperson, but also the Lord over all flesh and blood, hence the unity of the story and the complementary functions of its two parts as illustrations of the two halves of God's full sovereignty: over all that is made and all that is living.

The king, taking pains not to be misunderstood as falling back into his old error, observes, "You will not say that this also is copper? Behold it lives and eats and drinks. Worship him." The king's display of intelligence throughout both episodes certainly supports the argument that the chief factor establishing kings in those days was a predilection for violence. It also illuminates the worship of metal idols and snakes, which most scholars suppose the dragon-worship in the story represents.

Daniel tolerantly offers the king a second challenge: he will kill the dragon without iron and stick (or sword and staff). The appropriateness of his offer justifies our pejorative remarks about the king's mental prowess, since the feat, obviously going beyond the limits of the king's own vision of how such a task could be accomplished, wins Daniel the king's assent. There is some disagreement about whether Daniel's concoction of pitch, hair, and suet could even give the dragon a bellyache. Some argue the sheer harmlessness of it establishes the Living God as the one who slays. Whether the resulting motza (as the text actually calls it) is lethal or not in real life, it rips the dragon apart and leaves Babylon godless.

Now the mere apparentness of the king's blustering sovereignty is revealed. The enraged people form a mob screaming, "The king has become a Jew. The Baal he overturned and the dragon he killed," their reaction making a good case for slow religious reform. The frightened king hands Daniel over to them, preserving his reign for another day.

As producer of a conscious supplement to the Book of Daniel, the writer has Daniel once again thrown to the lions, seven of them, in fact, for six days. These lions are already acclimated to "long pig," having been accustomed to feed on two unfortunate rebels a day, according to the LXX version. Theodotion turns this into two carcasses and two sheep.

So the crowd solves the pestiferous problem of Daniel. Or so they suppose. But they have not taken his theological claims seriously enough. His God holds sovereignty over *all* flesh, including the lions, and six days later Daniel is discovered having lunch with the supposed author, if we credit the tale's claim that Ambakoum (rendered Habbakuk) of the tribe of Levi is its author—which is as credible as the tale itself.*

In a rather comic exchange an angel appears ordering lunch for Daniel from the stunned Levite. When Ambakoum babbles he has not even seen Babylon, not to mention the pit, the angel proceeds to give him a lift, literally, dangling him by the hair, to the land of Babylon. Sure enough he arrives about the noon hour. This may be the origin of take out/delivery service. After his no-frills flight, the no doubt shaken Ambakoum serves lunch. Of this happy comestible scene the mournful king gets an eyeful as "he stooped down and peered into the pit and saw him sitting."

Daniel's point is finally made as the overjoyed king cries out, "Great is the Lord God, and there is not like him another," proving that idols and dragons are alright, but when they cost such an entertaining companion as Daniel, they cost too much. To a God who can deliver even out of the lions' den this recently insurrection-threatened potentate gladly turns. And again the price in grief ex-

---

*This Ambakoum can hardly be the great Habakkuk whose prophecy is normally placed at the end of the seventh century, since Daniel's events occur in the sixth century, and the tale was written in the second or first.

acted on the guilty is excessive, as the lions make up for six days of breakfasts, lunches, suppers and snacks on "the ones causing his destruction."

The tale of *Bel and the Dragon* has everything: carnage, vindication, detection, humor, striking personalities, witty exchanges, lots of violence, and a memorable clergy sleuth fronting for a magnificent Deity. What a great thriller it is! In respect to the question of its unity, we can see at the end the essential interrelatedness of its two parts. The king must be shown that the Living God of Daniel is superior to both his alternatives, a deity made of metal and one made of flesh. When Daniel triumphs, his deity is authenticated.

The technique employed of solving a crime (as Daniel does by exposing the duplicity of the priests of Baal) but then going on to a fuller and usually unwanted exploration of the wellsprings and exigencies of that crime is a model plotting technique that has been repeated again and again throughout contemporary mysteries. In Dashiell Hammett's *Red Harvest,* often called the first of the hard-boiled novels, the Continental Operator is hired to work for a newspaper editor. When that editor is killed, the Op's job is terminated. He gets himself rehired to find the killer. When he does, again his services are no longer desired, but the Op decides to go on his own and clean up the town, causing distress to his employers and havoc everywhere. In Raymond Chandler's *The Big Sleep* Philip Marlowe is hired to eliminate a blackmail scam that threatens a well-moneyed California family. When the job is done and we would suppose the story is over, Marlowe on his own decides to nose deeper into the family's troubles expressly against their wishes and stirs up a sinkhole of problems. Ross Macdonald's Lew Archer does the same thing in *The Chill.* Refusing to be paid off or fired, he solicits a new employer to stay on a supposedly solved case. Sara Paretsky's V. I. Warshawski not only refuses to be paid off or fired when her investigation is completed, but also withstands a beating to delve deeper into her former employer's troubles until the whole root of the trouble is eradicated. One can even read a variation of this theme in John D. MacDonald's *The Deep Purple Lament.* And, of course, as we shall see in the next section, the Rabbi Small series is initiated with a complete vignette that sets the scene and the themes not only for the larger tale of *Friday the Rabbi Slept Late* but also for the entire series that follows.

In each example the real story commences after the opening story is supposedly complete, precisely as in *Bel and the Dragon.* The first and second parts of Daniel's declaration set the impetus for the first and second activities of his exposing Babylon's deities, and only after this full purgation can the king give complete allegiance to the Living God. While a rival deity exists, the king cannot worship in defiance of the custom of such a volatile, warlike people, able to mob up against him. Daniel, at great risk, or not so great considering the Living God supports him, eliminates these obstacles and frees the king to act on Daniel's proof.

As we can see, whoever the author is, (s)he has done an excellent job of creating a fictional archetype that has lasted over the years and has presaged this century's hard-boiled detective tradition.

Susannah

Seventy-five to one hundred years is a long time to wait to write a sequel, so we can suppose that the author of *Bel and the Dragon,* whose date of composition we have seen is estimated as about 100 B.C./B.C.E., is not the author of the sequel, the tale of *Susannah.* A number of stylistic differences between the two books further support this conclusion. One such distinction I noticed in the vocabulary of *Susannah* is the prevalence of words formed by compounding a preposition with a verb, such as *ekpheugo, ekbiazo, exomologeo.* Aída Besançon Spencer notes the same characteristic in her stylistic studies of the writings of the Apostle Paul. In addition Bauer's and Newman's lexicons for New Testament and patristic translation contain more vocabulary items from *Susannah* than from *Bel and the Dragon,* whose translation depends more heavily on the vocabulary gathered by Liddell and Scott in their classical lexicon. Of course, some of *Susannah's* vocabulary harkens back to an age before the composition of the New Testament. Still, these observations confirm that the style and vocabulary of *Susannah* is closer to the Koine Greek of the New Testament than is the Greek of *Bel and the Dragon.* Thus *Susannah* can be linguistically dated to a later period more approximating the time of the New Testament (or at least, if its original language is Hebrew or Aramaic, its translation into Greek can be dated later, perhaps, but not necessarily, supporting its later composition). Speculations like Oesterley's on other grounds have dated *Susannah* in the last quarter of the first century B.C./B.C.E. in Jerusalem or at least Palestine. Oesterley believes "the language was in all probability Hebrew" (Oesterley, 394). Charles, on the other hand, for stylistic and vocabulary reasons, also supposes a Hebrew original but places the tale's composition back in the time immediately following the death of the fortunate/unfortunate Jannaeus, whose dismal history we reviewed earlier (Charles, 641–42). Charles sees it as a pharisaical satire of the rival Sadducees, done in scathing fashion by a follower of the celebrated and legendary Simon ben Shetach. If we question whether the Pharisees could be so caustic against their opponents, we have only to recall that they made the day of Jannaeus' death an annual festival. Thus, in contemporary religious parlance, this would make *Susannah* a kind of ancient prototype of "The Wittenburg Door" and place it between the years 95 and 80 B.C./B.C.E. in his estimation—some fifty years after *Bel and the Dragon.*

If Oesterley's later dating is correct, however, the last quarter of the first century is that time which Emil Schuerer generally calls the period of Herod's "splendour and enjoyment" (Schuerer, 304). Though 25 B.C./B.C.E. itself saw an ordeal of famine and pestilence, Herod's political courtship of the Roman emperor Augustus was paying off as he gained territory, indulged his passion for building, restored the temple, and benefited in numerous ways from his friendship with the Romans, enjoying prosperity until his appalling family relations finally blighted his life.

Still, though my own study supports Oesterley's late dating, Charles persuasively notes that after Jannaeus' debacles a legal reform called for more careful questioning of witnesses, a event which would fit the theme of the story. Simon ben Shetach is considered the champion of the cross-examination of witnesses, a procedure that became intrinsic to Jewish law as we can see from this quotation from The Mishnah, Sanhedrin 5:2:

> The more a judge tests the evidence the more is he deserving of praise: Ben Zakkai [ca. A.D. 10–80 (Danby, 799)] once tested the evidence even to the inquiring about the stalks of figs. Wherein do the inquiries differ from the cross-examination? If to the inquiries one [of the two witnesses] answered, "I do not know," their evidence becomes invalid; but if to the cross-examination one answered, "I do not know," or if they both answered, "We do not know," their evidence remains valid. Yet if they contradict one another, whether during the inquiries or the cross-examination, their evidence becomes invalid. (Danby, 388)

We, of course, still benefit from this procedure today. Charles also underscores the tale's essential fictional quality when he notes with irony, "In the heat of controversy neither party could well call the young detective Daniel" (Charles, 644).

Thus, for all these reasons, its dating, its improbabilities, the tale is obviously fiction. Why was it written and why did it survive? Martin Braun in *History and Romance in Graeco-Oriental Literature* notes that popular literature like *Susannah* has two chief functions. He believes that oriental nations "reacted to the Persian overlordship by the creation of national heroic myths or 'romances'" (Braun, 2). He asserts oriental fiction provided edification, consolation, revival of self-esteem, pride, appeasement of hatred and contempt. It was a literature filled with an oppressed people's own demands and ideals. Further, he sees "two distinct strata" within "national" literature. One emerges from the "better educated and socially superior class of the subjected people," which wishes to "display to the foreign ruling class the great antiquity, virtues and achievements of their own nation." At the same time, these spokespersons fight for "truth" against current rumors and false reports. They are personalities of good repute and social dignity who defend their own people while also entering the service of the Greek or Roman rulers (Braun, 3). Theirs is a campaign for equality. The second use nourishes the common people, the masses of the conquered nations, with what he calls their "spiritual bread," wherein their "ideals, needs, wishes and hopes" achieve self-expression. These tales provide the means by which a "proud people can stand the pressure of alien domination" by sublimating hostility into the creation of heroes and heroines (Braun, 3).

Susannah, however, does neither of these things. R. H. Charles points out the domestic scandal would hardly win repute from Gentiles, noting for proof the fact that Josephus, for one, kept silent about the tale toward the Romans (Charles, 644). In fact, such a silence did the Jewish elders maintain about *Susannah* that Origen could only catch vague rumors about it and Africanus concluded it must have simply been written in Greek and not Hebrew at all.

Thus, in contrast to Josephus and Philo, whose work is apologetic, praising Gentiles and uplifting Jewish heroes for praise in turn, *Susannah* makes its case by poleaxing leading elders of the people, while on its side *Bel and the Dragon* lampoons other religions and the quixotic, emotionally mercurial king of the representative Gentile Babylonians, dumping dozens of priestly families into destruction and tossing an undisclosed number of Daniel's accusers to the lions. No wonder the Apocrypha were the hidden books, B.C./B.C.E.'s underground literature.

In the light of their style and content these two works can hardly be construed as apologies to the Gentiles. Yet *Bel and the Dragon,* at least, may more likely be seen as having been written to Diaspora Jews like those at Elephantine in Egypt who were polytheistic, neglecting observing the law or living together in protective community. The book clearly counsels that a wise sojourner should act like the hero Daniel, rejecting the false gods of the foreigners and worshipping the one true Living God of Israel.

For Braun's second use of popular literature, an undercutting of respected leaders, of the oppressed people's own elders, could hardly serve to uplift a people, even with the elevation of the hero Daniel. More likely, a subjected people would make their villains outsiders.

Thus, *Susannah*, at least, may represent a third way. Perhaps it is a functional literature with which a party that wishes to rule the people, say in this case the Pharisees, jockeys for position by suggesting a better kind of rule, a new legal reform. On the other hand, perhaps the tale is simply a vibrant eulogy of youth against age—morally upright springtime against the decadent old and their hypocritical ways. Youth certainly comes in for lavish praise in the end. Perhaps what we have here is simply first-century adolescent fiction—the mother of the comic book, the James Dean movie, rock and roll, and *Rolling Stone* magazine.

There is no doubt, however, that as far as genre is concerned, *Susannah* is a pure suspense thriller. The tale of Susannah is a tight courtroom drama that exhibits in archetype the exact factors that make this kind of fiction so tense and thrilling. Salvation or disaster hinges completely on the tough legal mind of Daniel, as aided here in counsel by the messenger of the Lord.

The tale begins by setting the scene—an idyllic upper-middle-class villa with attached garden. The cast includes an extremely beautiful woman, not just a beautiful one but *kale sophodra,* an extremely beautiful one; a rich old man whose happiness may be just a fool's paradise, a December/May dream; two lascivious dirty old hypocrites whose machinations place the heroine in peril of death; and at the courtroom climax—the hero Daniel! In its plot structure—the setting of the scene, the buildup, the accusation, the trial, the repartee, the turn-around tactics by counsel of the defense, the sudden recognition of the guilt of the previously unsuspected, the succoring of the innocent and the denunciation and execution of the guilty in a climax of justice, and the celebration of the deliverer—we have the mother work from which Erle Stanley Gardner spun his stacks of volumes. Every tale of his I have read tends to be a reworking of the primal *Susannah* account, which had he written it he would doubtlessly have called *The Case of the Bathing Beauty.* Daniel, as the father of Perry Mason, even uses the courtroom methods employed today, attacking and berating witnesses, trying to shake their stories, undermining their confidence, provoking them into emotional self-betrayal. The difference is that he topples the chief prosecutors. In *Susannah* this ancient Perry Mason finally gets Hamilton Burger. The figure of Daniel in *Susannah* is not identified as a clergy sleuth as it is in the earlier *Bel and the Dragon;* instead he is presented simply as a young man.

As we noted, the tale opens with the idealized domestic scene—the rich man with the beautiful wife. As indicated by the use of the term synagogue of the city, a post-exilic phenomenon, the tale could not have been written in the time in which it claims to take place. Placed in Babylon, which R. H. Charles notes did not have the trees, the legal system, or the village life so intrinsic to the tale (Charles, 642–43), for no other reason apparently than the opportunity to make the hero Daniel its protagonist, the story moves immediately to its hot sex motif. In this dimension Erle Stanley Gardner stays true to its form. Braun has noted in his study of ancient popular fiction, and particularly in his comments on the expansion of the spicy details of Joseph and Potipher's wife, that preoccupation with sex is a peculiarity of pseudepigraphical literature and, I imagine, explains its vast popularity. After a few paragraphs chronicling the voyeurism of the elders, the Septuagint version races on to the proposition, Susannah's indignant refusal, and the backlashing accusation of the elders, as it speeds on to the trial. Not so Theodotion's version, which firmly camps out in the garden, no doubt earning the ancient equivalent of an "R" rating with its interpolation of a bathing scene against the LXX's more delicate solicitation while Susannah takes a healthful morning jog. After Susannah's brave refusal, the scorned and nervous elders feed her to the wolves, enacting plan B, the accusation against her to cover their perfidy, actually within that legal system, their crime.

The trumped-up charges carry weight since they are supported by two respected elders, who in their dastardliness even brashly order her unveiled so they can feed on her beauty—the kind of sordid sensationalism that keeps some paperback houses solvent year after year. All appears lost when Susannah cries out to the Lord God. God hears the innocent and activates Daniel by a shower of discernment from an angel.

Now proceeds a technique that Perry Mason can emulate. Daniel has the witnesses separated, and showering them with vituperation, fires a cross-examination off at each of them in turn, tripping them up over a small but cogent detail, the type of tree under which Susannah's alleged infidelity occurred.

At the confused contradictory answers Daniel exults, all in puns, and the crowd, knowing what to do with false witnesses, shouts aloud praise to Daniel and hurls the elders into a chasm. The angel of the Lord steps in and fires off an ending. The two versions then split off, the LXX giving all the credit to Daniel, while Theodotion's shares the credit between Susannah and Daniel.

Daniel certainly emerges in both these tales as a prototype of the violent defender of truth. The style of the vitriolic Daniel in his ridicule of the idol Bel or his defense of an innocent woman against the charge of adultery has echoed down to us in Daniel's descendent Perry Mason:

> "Take it easy, Perry," Drake warned. "Some of these guys are vicious."
> "I'm vicious myself," Mason said, "when some s.o.b. starts shoving a woman around."
> (Gardner, 95)

For those who recognize in Daniel the ancestor of the modern suspense hero, the figure of Daniel in both these tales, *Bel and the Dragon* and *Susannah,* is an archetype of the hard-boiled mystery hero, be he detective, lawyer, or clerical sleuth. Small wonder, then, when we listed the occurrences of the structural technique of *Bel and the Dragon* today, most examples that sprang to mind were drawn from the hard-boiled detective genre and one, *Friday the Rabbi Slept Late,* from the clerical sleuths. This is hardly peculiar since the hard-boiled detective particularly flaunts conventional behavior to elicit truth, as Daniel does in these prototypical tales. He is tough, persistent, sarcastic. He has his own code, his own set of values that clash with that of his superior and that of those in recognized authority, be they kings or judging elders. As a result he is submitted to physical violence in the first tale, gamely bouncing back. He alone attacks the solutions everyone else has found satisfactory, wreaking havoc without a qualm. In the resultant turmoil he precipitates truth, ferreting out guilt, saving the innocent, bringing about justice. I can easily picture him in a soft fedora and double-breasted suit, a lone knight with few friends but a soundly intact ideal and a tough eye.

Susannah and *Bel and the Dragon:* two two-thousand-year-old hard-boiled thrillers of a clerical sleuth. No wonder, despite the attempt to wipe them out, these tales remained popular and foreshadowed not only the contemporary roster of clerical sleuths but also the entire secularized mystery genre of today. These tales remained popular for they were just as exciting to their public as mysteries are to ours today. As is still done with our mysteries, translations were made into many foreign languages. Copies of these are extant and are still available for us to curl up with on dark and stormy nights.

2

Rabbis and Robbers in the Present:
The Hectic Week of Rabbi Small

Two thousand years after the Apocryphal tales one of the most celebrated of contemporary Judeo-Christian clerical sleuths paced methodically on the scene muttering Pilpul, making his debut just as *Susannah*'s Daniel did in the context of a Din Torah, the trial by religious elders of a case of the people. The name Daniel, after all, means literally "God (El) is my judge," and young, wise, bold to seek the truth, the Rabbi David Small is, indeed, a modern incarnation of *Susannah*'s figure of Daniel. Like Daniel he is merely a youth at the opening of his delightful series. Old Jacob Wasserman, "older than most of the members of the congregation" (*Friday,* 10), has risked bringing "the young rabbi" David Small (*Friday,* 11) to his first call as the founding rabbi of the new synagogue at Barnard's Crossing, Massachusetts. By virtue of his sheer youth David Small is an unknown commodity to the older professionals of the synagogue until he settles a dispute between two senior members, explaining:

> One of the rabbi's main functions—to sit in judgment. In the old days, in the ghettos of Europe, the rabbi was hired not by the synagogue but by the town. And he was hired not to lead prayers or to supervise the synagogue, but to sit in judgment on cases that were brought to him, and to pass on questions of law. . . . Like any judge, he would hear the case, sometimes alone, sometimes in conjunction with a pair of learned men from the village. He would ask questions, examine witnesses if necessary, and then on the basis of the Talmud, he would give his verdict. (*Friday,* 12)

Yet, if Rabbi Small exemplifies the Apocryphal Daniel in certain ways in his youth and in his discernment, theologically he differs. A remarkable aspect of the two Apocryphal tales was the active intervention of the Lord God to save Daniel and Susannah, and the messenger of the Lord to bring Daniel sustenance and torch the lying elders. For the Apocryphal Daniel the Lord God is indeed a living God, whose personal involvement in the affairs of humans affects them dynamically, but for Rabbi Small such an active God is not a Jewish God at all but a Christian God, as we see in his reaction to "evangelical preachers you see on TV" who claim, "Let Jesus come into your heart and your troubles will disappear":

> "Another function of religion is to provide us with a Father who is stern but just, and yet loving and forgiving. But as a Father, he can also be called on for help in an emergency."
> "And you believe that?" demanded Aaron.
> "*I* don't," said the rabbi simply. "While that picture of God as the rewarding and punishing Father is seen again and again in the Bible, I think we have outgrown it in the same way we have outgrown Genesis as a factual account of the creation." (*Conversations,* 95)

According to Rabbi Small:

> "With us, however, faith in the Christian sense is almost meaningless, since God is by definition unknowable. What does it mean to say I believe in what I don't know and can't know? Theoretically, Christianity has the same view of God, which is why His Son was born on earth and lived as a man. Because being a man, He could be known. But we don't share this belief. Our religion is a code of ethical behavior." (*Wednesday,* 227)

Thus, the God of the Judaism articulated by Rabbi Small is a departure from the God of the Judaism depicted in the intertestamental Apocryphal tales as they form an addendum to the Old Testament canon.

How, then, does this new Judaism of Rabbi Small's help him solve mysteries, rescue the innocent, and indict the guilty?

Rabbi Small does not understand himself as a minister, as do Roman Catholic and Episcopal priests and Protestant ministers, but as a scholar and a judge. In his view, "Judaism as it is today is the Judaism of the Scribes and of the Pharisees" (*Friday,* 27). Therefore, his province is a legal one much more than any other ordained person's sphere of activity is. Though his emphasis is on religious law, that province branches out to include civil law as "a matter of religion" (*Friday,* 29) and eventually encompasses all aspects, legal/illegal and moral/immoral, in the human condition.

As the first novel, *Friday the Rabbi Slept Late,* opens, we are reminded immediately of the young, ordained companion of the king, the faithful Hebrew in the diaspora of the Babylonian captivity. Young, ordained Rabbi David Small is also a Hebrew in the diaspora, and he soon serves as companion to Police Chief Hugh Lanigan in the "American diaspora" at Barnard's Crossing, Massachusetts.

We noted already the Din Torah that opens the series. In the spirit of *Bel and the Dragon* the novel has two distinct parts that interrelate. In this case the first vignette, a tale within a tale, sets out the themes that are to be developed in the larger murder mystery that comprises the remainder of the novel.

The initial hostility that greeted Rabbi Small at the Din Torah we soon see is generalized within the congregation, for like Daniel in both Apocryphal tales,

Rabbi Small has to contend with a hostile crowd before he can earn praise and acceptance. As the novel unfolds, we see both mob themes developed. Like the Daniel of *Susannah,* Rabbi Small must contend with opposition in his own constituency and like the Daniel in *Bel and the Dragon,* he and his congregation must remain mindful of the image they are creating as the new Jewish synagogue in the eyes of the implicitly, and at times explicitly, anti-Semitic, tight, conservative New England goyim of Barnard's Crossing.

When a murder takes place on synagogue property and, the evidence reveals, may have been done in the rabbi's car, then those two concentric circles of hostility become overtly evident. The murdered woman Elspeth Bleech is a young governess/maid who has gotten in the family way without benefit of a husband. While she tries to resolve her difficult situation with eventually fatal results, the board of directors of "the temple" are obstinately stalling on the renewal of Rabbi Small's year-by-year contract. In his first year of ministry the rabbi has alienated a number of members by such antics as turning the introduction of a baseball hero at a children's banquet into "a long spiel about how our heroes are scholars instead of athletes," and lecturing the Sisterhood during a Chanukah fundraising luncheon where forbidden shrimp is served on how "keeping Judaism in their hearts and a kosher home was more important for Jewish women than campaigning for gifts for the temple" (*Friday,* 32). If Rabbi Small illustrates any virtue, and he illustrates many, his chief one is the enduring sincerity of his convictions. Like the lawyer Daniel in *Susannah* he insists on what he feels is the truth no matter how numerous his opposition is or how incontrovertible the arguments for the other side appear.

The two spheres of tension, Elspeth's predicament and the board's hostile hesitation, build throughout the week until on Thursday evening they converge. Rabbi Small, having received the discouraging news that the congregation may not rehire him, experiences a normal human reaction, deciding to "sleep in" Friday morning rather than face his opposition over morning prayers. Roman Catholic police chief Hugh Lanigan visits him later that morning with inquiries about his car, which, with proverbial scholarly absent-mindedness, the rabbi, keyless, has left in the synagogue lot. The rabbi then turns upon the chief the penetrating scrutiny of Pilpul, the close rabbinic legal reasoning. "This is not permitted?" the rabbi asks in religiously legal language about the leaving of his car in the lot (*Friday,* 78), and carefully proceeding, penetrates the chief's questions and cross-examines his intentions until he has ferreted out the news of Elspeth's murder on synagogue grounds. The rabbi is quick to apprehend his own position as a suspect, but when Chief Lanigan demurs, Rabbi Small with ruthless legal objectivity comments:

"Come, Mr. Lanigan, evidently something has happened, a police matter in which my car is concerned—no, I myself must be concerned or you wouldn't want to know why I didn't go to morning prayers. . . .

"I would not presume to suggest what a priest would or would not do, chief, but anything that a man might do a rabbi might do. We are no different from ordinary men. We are not even men of the cloth, as you call it. I have no duties or privileges that any member of my congregation does not have. I am only presumed to be learned in the Law by which we are enjoined to live." (*Friday*, 79)

Thus, suspicion falls on a number of people, including the rabbi, and as the investigation continues, both Jews and Gentiles are exposed as having connections to the deceased and possible reasons for helping her reach that permanent condition.

The prospect of having both their rabbi and other members of the Jewish community suspected of the heinous crime of murder sends a shudder through the Jews of Barnard's Crossing. Like the captives and sojourners of the ancient diaspora, they are well aware of the excessive reprisals that might be exacted should the culprit prove to be Hebrew. Their deliberations on the rabbi's contract are thrown into turmoil:

How's that for public relations, Al? What are your Gentile friends going to think when they find out that two days after the rabbi becomes a suspect in a murder case, his congregation fired him? . . . I'm not concerned with the reaction to the rabbi. I'm concerned with the reaction to the temple, to the congregation. Some are going to say that we dropped him because we suspected he was guilty. And they'll say we must have a fine bunch of men in the rabbinate if one of them could be so quickly suspected of murder. And there'll be others who'll think it absurd that the rabbi could be suspected. And all they'll think is that we Jews don't trust each other and are willing to fire our spiritual leader just on suspicion. In this country where a man is considered innocent until he's proved guilty, that won't sit so well. (*Friday*, 133–34).

Thus, like the Hebrews of the diaspora, the Jews of Barnard's Crossing carefully weigh the effects of the accusations and their response to them against the opinions of the larger Gentile class that rules their adopted country. The rabbi, too, like the Daniel of *Bel and the Dragon*, finds his own life and safety on the line in this 1964 novel when the death penalty was again an appropriate legal response to murder. Thus, like Daniel he is compelled not to leave the administration of justice to the limited vision of the constituted authorities but strikes out on his own, turning his incisively trained mind on the evidence. And, similar to the findings exposed by Daniel in *Bel and the Dragon*, guilt is finally brought home to a Gentile holder of constituted authority. One who is supposed to uphold true law and rule has abused that responsibility with deceit. So just as the priests are removed from authority in the earlier tale, the abuser of authority is exposed and suspended awaiting trial in this one.

Vindicated and the vindicator of the rest of the suspects, Jew and Gentile,

Rabbi Small now deserves the accolades showered upon Daniel in the Apocryphal tales. But as a modern hero he must make do with the wintry gratitude of contemporary Americans. Only in a parallel vignette in the last chapter, when he duplicates his achievement in the opening Din Torah by cutting to the core of an issue and saving money, does the rabbi finally find his congregation regarding "their young rabbi with respect and admiration" (*Friday*, 223). Solving murders is not enough, holding forth with sincerity and integrity for the Hebrew law is not enough; to impress jaded consumer-oriented Americans the rabbi must save them money and shortcut their work as well! The satire is apt. So Rabbi Small finally achieves the respect and the accolades he deserves. And as well, he has won the respect of at least one member of the Gentile community. When Hugh Lanigan runs into a payroll problem connected with the murder, he is back knocking on the rabbi's door for advice. And Rabbi Small is still there to help in the big matters and the small ones. His invitation, "Shall we see what the Talmud says?" (*Friday*, 224) concludes the book.

The novel seems to emerge as a powerful apologetic for contemporary American Judaism. Its careful exoneration of the Jewish characters, its portrayal of their similarities to and differences from Gentile Americans, its expositions on Talmudic law, the function of the rabbi as lawyer, and the viability of the Talmud not only to mediate on purely religious matters but also on civil and economic ones summon up the image of Martin Braun's first function of ancient oriental popular literature, to "display to the foreign ruling class the great antiquity, virtues and achievements of their own nation. At the same time, they fight for 'truth' against current rumors and lies" (Braun, *History*, 3). The characters depicted within the Jewish community in the book certainly have as a chief concern their image before their Gentile neighbors. As we have seen, so strong is their concern that even hostile board members are prepared to table the decision of the rabbi's contract for the higher goal of preserving the reputation of the Jewish community among the goyim. In a larger sense, with the vindication of the suspected Jews, the careful illumination of Jewish faith and rabbinic practice, as well as the deft portrayal of the essential humanity of both the rabbi and his congregation, *Friday the Rabbi Slept Late* itself serves as a potent defense of American Judaism. Jews follow a highly ethical religion, and though they are as human as Gentiles with their petty squabbles, ambitions, and prejudices, their high ethics safeguard and encourage their integrity, industry, and humanitarian contributions.

Thus, if what we have observed is true, the nearly two thousand one hundred years that have elapsed between *Bel and the Dragon* and *Friday the Rabbi Slept Late* have not altered the function of the Jewish clerical mystery novel as disseminated throughout the Gentile world. The sad fact is that diaspora Hebrews of the contemporary age as of ancient times still feel called upon to defend themselves and their faith against oppressive Gentile "overlordship."

Therefore, it is not surprising that the pattern for all of the rabbi books (though not the addendum, *Conversations with Rabbi Small*) presents a murder which casts the shadow of guilt on a member of the Jewish community. While Rabbi Small battles his congregation over renewal of his contract steadily through the series, he also must serve accused Jews as a sort of investigating legal defense counsel to rescue the innocent, preserve the good name of the Jewish community of Barnard's Crossing, and find the adult Gentile usually responsible.

The lone exception, *Conversations with Rabbi Small,* is not a mystery. As the capping book to the initial Rabbi Small series it interestingly harkened back to a predecessor of the entire series itself. In the preface to his collection of short stories entitled *The Nine Mile Walk,* Harry Kemelman notes that he originally wrote a manuscript of a novel about "the sociological situation of the Jew in suburbia" (*Walk,* 11). He titled it *The Building of a Temple* but could not find a publisher until an editor suggested he blend it with the successful mystery stories he had been publishing since 1947 in *Ellery Queen's Mystery Magazine.* "The murder would provide only one thread, albeit an important one, of a longer narrative" (*Walk,* 12). Thus, the establishing of a temple and the solving of mysteries that came to comprise the ensuing Rabbi Small series provided a background for Kemelman's primary interest, which was a study of Jews in suburbia. *Conversations,* then, provided a summary of the findings of that chief interest and as such became a compendium of all the Judaism expounded in the preceding seven books. For example, the argument that a righteous Gentile has the same standing before God as the high priest of Israel from page 277 of *Wednesday the Rabbi Got Wet* appears on page 23 of *Conversations. Wednesday*'s argument against Judaism as a mystical religion on 276–78 is summarized on page 51. *Thursday*'s image of God as the Algebraic X factor is reintroduced and refuted on page 58. *Friday*'s definition of a rabbi as a judge on page 12 is amplified on pages 27–31. Having earned his right to speak by seven books of entertainment, Harry Kemelman now summarizes his serious points. As a thinker who proceeded to interrupt his "entertainments," as Graham Greene calls his suspense novels, with the treatise *Common Sense in Education* (a sort of companion *Conversations* to the three novels about college students), Professor Kemelman, an educator himself, seems to be making sure his serious intent is not missed. One could view the preceding and following novels as an elongated series of opening and closing anecdotes, and yet his points were thoroughly fleshed out in these parables, as we see by the extensive repetition in *Conversations.* Thus, the book is by and large a true summary, not primarily a new addition, as well as a partial fulfillment of his original intention: a straight novel about suburban Jews. It is an explanation for the less observant as well as an exposition of Harry Kemelman's deep theological concerns. In this sense, he himself is much like Rabbi Small, speaking to the two audiences of the diaspora, the surrounding ignorant Gentiles and his fellow "exilic" Jews.

While defining for us all the new post-Apocryphal Judaism through the scientifically enlightened modern Rabbi Small, who brands such traditionally held supernaturalistic events as the parting of the Red Sea and the tumbling of the walls of Jericho as "myth, legend and fable" (*Conversations,* 87), Kemelman also makes some telling points about other religions. Although mainly concentrating, of course, on explaining how Judaism is a system of ethics rather than a religion, the rabbi draws some perspicacious distinctions between it and other faiths. Thus, toward adaptive Christianity he throws this intriguing challenge:

> "I suppose," Joan said, "you are referring to Jesus as the son of God and the Virgin Mary. Well, enlightened Christians nowadays don't believe that either, not literally. Not even some of my Catholic friends."
> "Are what you call enlightened Christians really Christians then?" he asked. (*Conversations,* 40)

The rabbi's point developed through so many books, *Monday, Wednesday, Thursday,* and *Conversations,* is a provocative one: Judaism can abandon its supernatural trappings because it is a tribal expression and a set of ethics primarily. But Christianity as a mystical religion cannot and remain Christianity. To the counter "Christian ideals" are the definitive characteristics, the rabbi points out all civilized and probably even primitive people hold these. "What is it that makes it Christian?" (*Conversations,* 41). The rabbi assures us it is Christ and the theology of Christ's efficacious act.

Toward the Buddhist doctrine of reincarnation, that the good rise to a higher incarnation, say a prince, and the evil to a lower, say a dog, he objects:

> "But I'm sure you see that there are other objections," the rabbi said.
> "Like what?"
> "That prince, for one. Since he was presumably the result of thousands of previous reincarnations which finally brought him to his present eminence, he ought to be a saint. So, too, all other men of authority, wealth, and power. And there is no indication of it. And how about those who were reborn as one of the lower animals. How does a dog or a mouse rise on its next rebirth? Is it by being a good mouse?" (*Conversations,* 81)

Still, the balance of the book is an exposition of Judaism and through the conversations of a potential convert, an indifferent Jew, and Rabbi Small all the Apocryphal apology Braun highlighted comes to the fore as the exchanges carefully define Judaism for the insider and outsider, while highlighting various Jewish contributions to society from education to concern for animals to care for the poor (*Conversations,* 250). And, at the end, wonder of wonders, the book does turn out to be a kind of genealogical mystery wherein the perspicacious pilpul of Rabbi Small again saves the day—in regards not to laying to rest a murder, an ending of life, but to stirring a beginning of life.

Still, one further contribution of interest to the series is the full-length movie made out of *Friday the Rabbi Slept Late*. Anyone wishing to view the Hollywood transfiguration of the clerical detective to the screen could do a full-length study of Robert C. Thompson's and Rodrick Paul's Stuart Margolin/ Art Carney television pilot film, *Friday the Rabbi Slept Late*. Gone is the stooped, scholarly, bookish Rabbi Small, and in his place steps an attractive, boyish, beaming rabbi, seen playing basketball with the neighborhood kids (an act unthinkable for the novel's rabbi, who, we recall, introduced an athlete at a children's banquet by noting scholars are the true heroes (*Friday*, 32)). The new rabbi is a young, all-American rabbi next door. The movie is still amusing and entertaining, but it is not *Friday the Rabbi Slept Late* on film; it is a new characterization using the same character name.

Instead, we must look to books like *Someday the Rabbi Will Leave* to peer into the rabbi's address, Maple Street off Glen Lane, a typical North Shore locale in a wooded area which may have skunks and raccoons and is infested with pot holes (*Someday*, 132). Aging as the years pass, Rabbi Small's family is touched with the world of the 1980s even to the extent of suffering a Massachusetts adaption of the early eighties "Valley Talk" in the teenagers (e.g., "awesome").

We find out the Rabbi has a "sweet tooth" (*Someday*, 226), discover he may be Republican (*Someday*, 219), even learn his blood type—AB (*Someday*, 246). We have heard about his writing scholarly articles for the *Quarterly* before and have seen the high reputation that is garnered for him among such rabbis as his erstwhile potential replacement Rabbi Hugo Deutsch in *Monday*. As another potential replacement now repeats, David Small is a "real scholar" (*Someday*, 220).

Harry Kemelman has fully wedded his published interests in mystery and education in his protagonist. But best of all for us in this work as in all of them is the down-to-earth portrayal of a ministry-hardened religious professional, stripped of all the false expectations and unworldly ephemeral supra-sanctity of many fictional portrayals. As police chief Lanigan grins at the rabbi's jaded views of humanity, "Maybe that's the difference between a policeman and a rabbi. I tend to think well of my fellow men" (*Someday*, 244). As the archetypal Father Brown once argued, no one who spends his days listening to a recitation of sins can be wholly unaware of human evil.

Slender, stoop-shouldered, not particularly winsome but extremely helpful to those unjustly accused of murder, Rabbi Small continues succoring Jews, calling Gentiles to responsibility, interpreting his vision of the Jewish faith. And in his clerical detecting he takes his place alongside the Apocryphal Daniel in the canon of Jewish popular detective fiction. His theology may differ, but his apologetic function within and without the Jewish faith remains the same. Like *Bel and the Dragon* his novels encourage Jews and lecture Gentiles. Like *Susannah* they show that ethics are truly integral to faith and that guilt and innocence are the province of religion and the concern of God.

Part Two

Priests and Psychopaths

3

Holmes in a Tonsure:
Umberto Eco's *The Name of the Rose*

Penetrate the secular deeply enough, we have noted earlier, and one will reach the borders of the sacred. Back across these borders Italian semiotics professor Umberto Eco has gone to reapproach the enigma of the universe in the signs and signals of the world through the medium of the theological mystery locked deep in the ancient heart of the medieval Church, the abbey, in the golden age of the English "mysterie"—the fourteenth century. His novel, *The Name of the Rose,* which concerns the investigation of the serial murder of monks on the eve of a crucial summit whose clues lead to a forbidden abbey library, returns the theological dimension to the nature of the mystery explored. Like the medieval mystery play, Eco's novel reaches back through the parabolic trappings of the biblical book of the Apocalypse, Revelation, to detect the deep theological mystery that all the signs and symbols of human language, human art, and created nature itself employ to point back to the Master Artist, the enigmatic Creator God.

The detecting monk Eco sends on that quest is himself constructed as a unique blend of the ancient and the modern, Sherlock Holmes in a tonsure.

Syracuse University comparative literature professor Stefano Tani has claimed in *The Doomed Detective: The Contribution of the Detective Novel to Postmodern American and Italian Fiction* that the classic crime novel is not the literary *cul de sac* that writers like Raymond Chandler have slandered over the years; rather, it is a major influence on what he calls the current "postmodern" "antidetective" novels of Italo Calvino, Vladimir Nabokov, John Gardner, and Eco. Umberto Eco agrees with him, seeing "old fashioned" storytelling as a reaction to the literary dead-end of the narrative abstraction of the postmodernist writers:

> It is similar to what happened in painting. . . . The avant-garde painters went on destroying the human image, and they arrived at abstract painting, then action painting, then the blank canvas. At one point it became impossible to go forward, and you had to rediscover the image.

> This is what the writers have done who are coming back to plot. They exploit popular narrative forms, but they do it with an ironic, tongue-in-cheek kind of attitude. (Kakutani, 36)

Thus, Eco's own "exploitation" of the classic mystery genre, what he considers "among the model plots" to be "the most metaphysical and philosophical" (*Postscript*, 53), goes consciously back to the source, even as he produces "a mystery in which very little is discovered and the detective is defeated" (*Postscript*, 54). His "ironic, tongue-in-cheek" appropriation of Conan Doyle's archetypal scientific detective has produced one Brother William of Baskerville (the family and hall name of the Devonshire family of "Hound" fame), an English Franciscan who, late of the inquisitors, is like Holmes—tall, thin, acquiline, with "beaky nose" and "sharp and penetrating" eyes (*Rose*, 5). This Sherlockian prequel is given to Holmesian periods of vanity about his "acumen" (*Rose*, 23) and the "speed and accuracy" of his deductions (*Rose*, 209), as well as to emotional storms of frenetic activity followed by droughts of inertia (e.g., *Rose*, 287), a lethargy his duller-witted scribing "Watson" Adso suspects is due to "some vegetal substance capable of producing visions" (Holmes' infamous cocaine dependence?). He has even replaced Holmes' famous pipe with chewing tobacco (*Rose*, 16). His attention to details duplicates Holmes' astounding armchair revelations from first impressions, the science of deduction (actually induction) spiraling back in time.

Brother William is a strong advocate of Roger Bacon and friend of William of Occam, whose references at times threaten to make the book an odd hybrid of fiction and nonfiction (like Nicholas Meyer's prior adaption of Holmes, *The Seven-per-cent Solution*, wherein the fictional Holmes and Watson interact with such real historical figures as Sigmund Freud, George Bernard Shaw, and Bram Stoker). The opinions William espouses make him seem as much a modern as an ancient. Brother William moves in a world whose base is classic scholastic Thomism, as evidenced in Adso's reflections: "For three things concur in creating beauty: first of all integrity or perfection, and for this reason we consider ugly all incomplete things; then proper proportion or consonance; and finally clarity and light, and in fact we call beautiful those things of definite color" (*Rose*, 72), displaying the Thomist principles of order in proportion and consonance, evil as a deprivation, an incompleteness, and beauty as possessing definite color, thereby an identity, a sense of place, an assigned location in the divine order. And these attributes of order produce, we are further told, "peace" (*Rose*, 72). This is a Thomism also evidenced in Adso's perception of the telos of architecture:

> For architecture, among all the arts, is the one that most boldly tries to reproduce in its rhythm the order of the universe, which the ancients called "kosmos," that is to say ornate, since it is like a great animal on whom there shine the perfection and the proportion of all its members.

And praised be our Creator, who has decreed all things, in their number, weight, and measure. (*Rose,* 26)

Phrases like "the order of the universe" convey an Aristotelian Thomism. William himself will appeal to this Thomism in his argument at the council, wherein he espouses the Thomist concept of the separate orderly places of rule for prince and pope (*Rose,* 354).

Yet William brings to this scholastic theology a proleptic perspicacity that welcomes the new science of Bacon and da Vinci: "But in various countries I have seen new works made of glass which suggest a future world where glass will serve not only for holy purposes but also as a help for man's weakness" (*Rose,* 86). Hence, he wears eyeglasses (his counterpart to Holmes' famous magnifying glass?), a rare innovation in the fourteenth century, and appropriates the Occamites' "developed theory of signs" (*Postscript,* 26) to incorporate modern concepts and the language of semiotics, "signs," "signals," "design," in his speech. For example:

The print does not always have the same shape as the body that impressed it, and it doesn't always derive from the pressure of a body. At times it reproduces the impression a body has left in our mind: it is the print of an idea. The idea is sign of things, and the image is sign of the idea, sign of a sign. But from the image I reconstruct, if not the body, the idea that others had of it. (*Rose,* 317)

In fact Eco, a fantasizing "medievalist in hibernation" (*Postscript,* 14, 77) who wrote a book on medieval aesthetics and who is also an authority on Joyce, Eliot, literature, reading, language, art, and philosophy, even considered casting William of Occam as his detective but was put off by Occam's personality (*Postscript,* 27). Instead Occam lent William of Baskerville his first name and Eco, the nonfantasizing contemporary, gave him his contemporary outlook. William even seems to live to a modern life expectancy beyond what we might expect for Italy in 1327:

He explained to me that, when a man had passed the middle point of his life, even if his sight had always been excellent, the eye hardened and the pupil became recalcitrant, so that many learned men had virtually died, as far as reading and writing were concerned, after their fiftieth summer. (*Rose,* 74)

And he dies in "the great plague" "toward the middle of this century," at the very least in his seventies, perhaps eighties or nineties (*Rose,* 499).

But greatest of all these differences is William's modern sense of doubt. True, Brother William can be a stern defender of Neoplatonist Christian scholastic philosophy against the doubts of William of Occam, believing that machines to fly and navigate ships and lift great weights are willed by God "and certainly they already are in His mind, even if my friend from Occam denies that ideas exist in such a way" (*Rose,* 17–18). Still William is not so assured of his perceptions or his hermeneutics, and so "On other occasions I had heard him speak with great skepticism about universal ideas and with great respect about individual things; and afterward, too" (*Rose,* 28). He also doubts: "We are already hard put to establish a relationship between such an obvious effect as a charred tree and the lightning bolt that set fire to it, so to trace sometimes endless chains of causes and effects seems to me as foolish as trying to build a tower that will touch the sky" (*Rose,* 30). This is not the certainty of a good orthodox Thomist inquisitor; it is the doubt of a Franciscan, which when finally divorced from piety, reflects the doubt of a modern. And thus, William prefers to speak not of the Devil's prompting presence but of crime and guilt and personal blame. He is not prescientific but scientific in perspective. He is not so much scholastically Thomist as he is more modernly Franciscan in philosophy. He is a semiotically, scientifically oriented medieval modern who, when confronting the massive Thomist system, feels locked in the closed universe of traditional medieval Catholic thought. He reasons from poison to a poisoner. He precludes the intervention of the supernatural, not as impossible but as unascertainable, the *via moderna.** In this he is scientifically modern as well as authentically late medieval. Like us, he must grope along, puzzling. And the seal of the confessional assures us that even those who know will maintain the silence that forces the seeker to discern the design (*Rose,* 34). Thus, he is at best a hesitant scholastic theologian, arguing that "reasoning about causes and effects is a very difficult thing, and I believe the only judge of that can be God" (*Rose,* 30). And this hesitancy can break out into denials: "as a philosopher I doubt the world has an order" (*Rose,* 394). As his hesitancy accumulates, he ends the tale completely given over to doubt, affirming the validity of signs but doubting the entire Thomist presupposition of order in the universe (*Rose,* 492). He may be able to unravel the maze of the library and even of the murders, but he cannot unravel the eternally open maze of his own conjectures (*Postscript,* 57–58). This doubt, too, is communicated at last to his scribe Adso, who like William becomes unhinged from the security of his time and place, like Vonnegut's Billy Pilgrim unmoored in time, or H. G. Wells' time traveler locked in the past. Thus, both the detective and his scribe end as agnostics with respect to discerning meaning in the universe: "The more I repeat to myself the story that has emerged from them, the less I manage to understand whether in it there

---

*See Heiko A. Oberman's thought-provoking essay "Fourteenth-Century Religious Thought: A Premature Profile," in which he argues that Franciscan aversion to and suspicion of the vast Thomist system questioned the close association of God and necessity, refocusing instead eventually on the will of God, which, we can infer, might finally lead those not discovering that will, after losing piety, to modern doubt.

is a design that goes beyond the natural sequence of the events and the times that connect them" (*Rose*, 501).

Adso's view of death, too, takes on a modern cast of enigma, as opposed to the supposed fourteenth-century theological certitude that death meant entry into the presence of God, shared by doubting Franciscans and Thomists alike. Instead, as Adso through his relationship with William encounters such unanswered puzzles as whether affirming God's omnipotence precludes affirming God's free will, death becomes for him the complete Sheol of silence where the mysterious divine all is divine oblivion:

> Soon I shall be joined with my beginning, and I no longer believe that it is the God of glory of whom the abbots of my order spoke to me, or of joy, as the Minorites believed in those days, perhaps not even of piety. (*Rose*, 501)

Adso chooses eternally to beg the question, taking "flight into the divine nothingness, which was not what his master had taught him" (*Postscript*, 34):

> I shall soon enter this broad desert, perfectly level and boundless, where the truly pious heart succumbs in bliss. . . . I shall fall into the silent and uninhabited divinity where there is no work and no image. (*Rose*, 501)

Thus, William and his scribe seem at times almost modern people wandering through an ancient setting. William is modern in his opinions, his frame of reference, and his doubt, which he shares with all the clerical detectives, "that the truth was not what was appearing to him at any given moment" (*Rose*, 14). As a result, "The other monks looked at William with great curiosity but did not dare ask him questions," while Adso exults, "I felt proud to be at the side of a man who had something with which to dumbfound other men famous in the world for their wisdom" (*Rose*, 74). Eco is well aware of this anomaly, admitting he has disguised quotations of modern authors such as Wittgenstein, "passing them off as quotations from the period," while defending his actions by suggesting "the moderns" "were thinking medievally." He does, however, "ask myself if at times I did not endow my fictitious characters with a capacity for putting together, from the *disiecta membra* of totally medieval thoughts, some conceptual hircocervuses that, in this form, the Middle Ages would not have recognized as their own" (*Postscript*, 76). But for Eco this is the task of the historical novel, to show us the cradle of modern culture. Heiko A. Oberman provides partial support for him when he points out that a "new conception of Christian thought" was coming about:

> It involved a quest for an *Aggiornamento* of intellectual and spiritual life, and in this sense deserves the epithet "moderna." When this is not clearly seen we are bound to be led to such

> erroneous assumptions as that quattrocento humanist thought forms an erratic "modern" bloc
> in a "medieval" century. (Oberman, 92)

When that doubt is divorced from the piety that even the doubting Franciscans shared, and particularly when it involves the medievalizing of modern quotations, it strays into injecting the modern in the medieval more than revealing the modern as one strong option already in the medieval.

However, this objection, too, may be historically naive, for as far back as the ancient Hebrew Scriptures skeptical doubters and deniers were claiming "there is no God" (Psalm 14:1). All that is modern or medieval perhaps are the combinations and the exact turns of the arguments, but the basis or telos, doubt, is painfully, suprahistorically, consistently, fundamentally human. Doubt is not a modern invention, but it does historically adopt different dress. While both might doubt that God exists, Maoist doubt is not synonymous with Epicurean doubt, nor is Mao's ethic Epicurus' ethic.

Into the ancient world, then, comes Brother William, accompanied by the young monk Adso, who has been released by his father for a season from his own monastery to explore new possibilities. Brother William seems to Adso to be on a secret mission, a vague quest for truth under the suspicion we have noted that what was appearing to him at a given moment was not the truth. That quest becomes particularized when he is entreated by an abbot to investigate the suspicious death of a young illuminator who has been dashed to death days before an important conference between representatives of the pope and the emperor.

How Brother William's protomodern mind seeks to read the clues of the smaller mystery as they become signs of the greater mystery becomes the point of the book. As we have noted, William's assessment of the clues incorporates the language of the modern philosophy of semiotics, for Umberto Eco, professor of semiotics at the University of Bologna, has fleshed out his philosophy in this test case. Whereas Notre Dame medievalist Ralph McInerny has tried to flesh out the medieval philosophy of Saint Thomas in a modern tale, Eco has attempted to flesh out his modern philosophy in an ancient tale.

What exactly is semiotics? In *A Theory of Semiotics* Umberto Eco explains:

> Semiotics is concerned with everything that can be *taken* as a sign. A sign is everything which
> can be taken as significantly substituting for something else. This something else does not
> necessarily have to exist or to actually be somewhere at the moment in which a sign stands in
> for it. Thus *semiotics is in principle the discipline studying everything which can be used in
> order to lie*. If something cannot be used to tell a lie, conversely it cannot be used to tell the
> truth: it cannot in fact be used "to tell" at all. I think that the definition of a "theory of the lie"
> should be taken as a pretty comprehensive program for a general semiotics. (*Theory*, 7)

An alternative description might be that in its largest sense semiotics takes as its purview the metaphorical or significantly representative. Interestingly, Eco has chosen to introduce moral categories into his discussion of semiotics, just as he does in his novel. Those (like the ethicists) whose field is the moral, the biblical scholars, already know of the movement as it is reflected in structural exegesis or structuralism, which attempts to apply the findings and theory of semiotics to exegesis. Authentic semioticians such as The Entrevernes Group resist the suggestion that semiotics can be used for exegesis; hence my reluctance to be so clever as to attempt a semiotics-directed analysis of Eco's own book. While the results may be interesting, they would not yield an interpretation of the novel. Rather, through the construction of linguistic models in the adaptation of a metalanguage, semiotics applied to literature attempts to discover *how* meaning is communicated in a text. For Eco the novel itself is "a machine for generating interpretations" (*Postscript,* 2). Thus, the goal is not what the author meant, the goal of traditional literary analysis and my goal, but *"how* the text meant and means" as they express it, how meaning is created by the language of a text (Entrevernes, xv-xvi).

What the semiotician seeks to do is locate and trigger an internal unobservable mechanism in text that produces meaning, meaning not so much being there to be extricated as being produced (Entrevernes, 5). Thus, a semiotic reading attempts to describe through the production of linguistic models not what the text means but how it produces meaning.

Umberto Eco himself goes even farther in his "Concluding Remarks" to the First Congress of the International Association for Semiotic Studies in Milan, questioning whether semiotics is even limited to literary studies. Like Brother William he sees the activity as applicable to the reading of all of life:

> Is semiotics a branch of linguistics? As a matter of fact, one and only one of the 32 section meetings of the Congress was devoted to purely linguistic matters. But it is also true that, when dealing with music, architecture, theater, movies and so on, the linguistic model has frequently proved its leading power. . . .
>
> Semiotics describes comic strips, popular songs, obscene gestures, the Empire State Building and the Little Red Riding Hood story, looking everywhere for phonemes, phrases, double articulation, Boolean calculus, propositional functions, Venn's diagrams, syllogisms and so on. (*Proceedings,* 247-50).

He goes on to trace the history of the "rise of a theory of signs" within "the history of formal logic" from Aristotle to Occam, both of whom are frequently mentioned in *The Name of the Rose,* to Locke to Boole and the rise of the modern movement (*Proceedings,* 250).

Thus, for Brother William as for Eco the subject matter is everything in his quest for truth. The seeker for God, then, finds his subject matter is ultimate truth, embedded in the error of the world such that the signals seem obscure and amalgamated with evil. So the task of the theological seeker for God becomes defined in terms of the quest of the linguist to find the revelation through the symbols of imperfection. The theologian as the writer "interrogates the material on which he is working—material that reveals natural laws of its own, but at the same time contains the recollection of the culture with which it is loaded (the echo of intertextuality)" (*Postscript*, 10–11). In this sense, the theologian is like G. K. Chesterton's ideal reader, sketched in his "A Defense of Detective Stories," who emerges from his quest through a book with an eye now trained to read every brick, every tile, every twist of the road, every slate, every chimney as a hieroglyph of its human author, who is in turn a hieroglyph of the divine author, the living letter sent from God.

Similarly, Brother William's analysis of the clues in the novel is based on the ancient romantic presupposition that actual physical things have a higher meaning, which he seeks to read. Consequently, within the sphere of his tale the creator Eco appears to be infusing meaning into nearly everything William and the reader encounter. The novel depicts our joint quest through the medium of the aged monk Adso's attempt to record verbatim his experiences in hopes that others trained in discernment (the readers) will be able to discover a design in his "signs of signs, so that the prayer of deciphering may be exercised on them" (*Rose*, 11).

Beginning in the unnamed opening pages that serve as a fictional preface, Eco himself becomes a participant in the book, thus drawing the modern reader in with him. Handed a purported reproduction of a fourteenth-century manuscript, according to his fictional pose, the unnamed narrator, whom we take for Eco, is intrigued to learn there is no record of its origin or existence outside of itself. Supposed queries to authentic sources (Etienne Gilson) and fictional ones (a technique used so potently by H. P. Lovecraft) leave the narrator baffled since the book has disappeared with his estranged traveling companion and, like all diffident scholars, "I didn't dare go and ask it back from the person who had taken it from me" (*Rose*, 3). The narrator goes on to explain his struggle with what style to adopt to present this fourteenth-century work, for example whether to follow Italian models of the period or not. He thus prepares us to accept the scholastic theology of the monks framed in the otherwise jarring terms of modern semiotic theory. So *The Name of the Rose* begins where fact and fiction intertwine with scholarship and personal emotion, tying the narrator's passionate scholarship and passionate quest for companionship into a lover's knot.

Consequently, as the initial departure from the model of medieval romances should warn us, the present work will also differ in intent and mode from the classic modern mystery. According to Lionel Basney, the murder mystery witnesses to two moral laws: "Thou shalt not kill" and "Be sure your sin will find you out." As he notes:

The murder mystery assures us that sin is, and always will be, vulnerable. The orderly world in which the detective works delivers up its clues intact and intelligible; it offers the murderer no sanctuary, for the truth will always win out. "Thou shalt not kill," for the victim's blood calls to us from the ground. . . . To the clarity of its moral intention, the detective story sacrifices the complexity of real life. It is a type of "romance," with moral issues crystallized into good and bad, white and black. Like fairy tales or myths, therefore, the detective story is escapist. But as Tolkien has reminded us, though escape from duty is infamous, escape from prison is only what every prisoner desires. The murder mystery allows us, for a moment, to dwell in the tents of reason and symmetry. (Basney, 17)

The resulting tale *The Name of the Rose,* however, does not allow us this respite. It breaks from the classic pattern in its rejection of presented order, its frustration of the detective, its ultimate agnosticism, which leaves the reader a jumble of pieces instead of a neatly fitted pattern. The result is a kind of linguistic jigsaw puzzle; if the pieces are to be made into a coherent picture, as the scribe Adso warns us, the reader must do it.

Piece number one, one might say the large border that frames the puzzle, is the monstrous abbey wherein the action takes place. A stylistic analysis of its opening description will yield a fascinating picture of what Eco is attempting to portray.

On the opening page of "First Day: Prime," echoing the opening of Genesis, night has dropped three fingers of snow, leaving the world white and formless, the Tohu and Bohu of primal creation. Then morning dawns, night and day, and the sun appears. The abbey that looms up before William and Adso at the top of a mountain is an artfully crafted image of the book's main point. From a distance its Aedificium (the library and scriptorium where texts are copied)—forbidden because it contains books of falsehoods, Jewish cabala, Moslem science, pagan fables, books by wizards, a limited, ordered, censored world that violent death has broken open (*Rose,* 37–38)—appears to be a tetragon, "a perfect form, which expresses the sturdiness and impregnability of the City of God" (*Rose,* 21). But things are not as they appear, and in reality it is an octagon whose walls stand between the sturdy abbey, symbolic of the bulwark of Christendom, and the abyss, a sheer drop down the mountain back into Tohu and Bohu—chaotic nothingness. The cliff itself seems to reach to heaven, but that impression is tempered by the fact that it seems the work of earth and sky, ancient familiar giants (Genesis 6:4?), not celestial workers. Three triune rows of windows proclaim the trinity and yet sit as a square on the earth (who is the fourth member?—evil, the tempter?), while toward heaven they become "spiritually triangular" (*Rose,* 21). At each corner is a heptagonal tower (seven being the number of perfection) but from the outside these appear pentagonal (the figure used in black magic spell casting and demon control). The grotesque irony of Adso's naive assessment, "And thus anyone can see the admirable concord of so many holy numbers, each revealing a subtle spiritual significance"

(*Rose*, 22) and his theological assignment of values to those shapes and numbers do not belie their darker earthly values or their deceptive construction. In such a place evil can masquerade as good. Adso finds it "awesome" and "capable of inspiring fear" and is glad "I did not first see the building as it appears on stormy days" (*Rose*, 22). He will, he will. And even at the outset he senses not "jollity" but "fear" and "subtle uneasiness" (*Rose*, 22). In those visceral reactions he has sensed the truth behind the signals he has misread. His feelings rightly interpret the signs. The appearances are not solely invested with the pure significance of good, but his uneasiness rightly interprets the indubitable omens inscribed in the stone the day that the giants began their work, before the "deluded" monks began to misread those sermons in stone to the hymnody and ritual in the service of evil. For as the last page of "Prime" assures us, of all the arts, architecture seeks to duplicate the rhythm and order of the universe, the "kosmos," and this microcosmic universe's main door opens "perfectly westward" (*Rose*, 26). Thus, the great animal, this living Tiamat, progresses toward traditionally symbolic death.

In the same manner that the larger framework, the abbey, is infused with meaning, signs to be read or misread, its heart, the library, reproduces in microcosm the world. Therefore its grammars are listed under "Hibernia," while the volumes on the Apocalypse are incarcerated in Spain, "Yspania," where the inquisition currently rages, and in "Leones" (Africa) rest Moslem texts and the Koran. All are united together by the tie of Scripture in which "the text was more or less always the same, but we found a rich, fantastic variation in the images" (*Rose*, 314).

Stefano Tani further posits in a larger sense that the library "reflects the three stages of detection: labyrinth = the mystery to unravel; mirror = the distortion, the false solution; map = the solution" (Tani, 70), and suggests the vehicle of the library is a parody of Borges' "La biblioteca de Babel," while the murderer himself is an image of "Jorge Luis Borges, blind creator of erudite mysteries" (Tani, 73). Nearly seventy years earlier, G. K. Chesterton's archetypal Father Brown detailed for us the strong spiritual impact of just such a setting in "The Head of Caesar," collected in his second volume of adventures, 1914's *The Wisdom of Father Brown*, "'What we all dread most,' said the priest, in a low voice, 'is a maze with *no* centre. That is why atheism is only a nightmare'" (Chesterton, *Omnibus*, 319).

Similar to the library, the church is stratified, like a microcosmic empire's tell, one civilization tiered on a more ancient one. And, viewing it, Adso sees a theophany in his imagination (*Rose*, 41). But the God he sees is stern and glaring. So that while like John he receives a command to write of the terrible heavenly and hellish creatures he sees, he realizes that the revelations of Revelation, celestial carnage and all, are occurring in the abbey. Thus his eyes drop from the communicating frescos to confront the dirty, disheveled, heretical monster-monk Salvatore (*Rose*, 45). So the abbey's frescos mirror the true nature of the abbey's inhabitants, and while these frescos contribute to the message of the whole, they carry their own messages, as the narration notes in its references to the "silent speech of the carved stone" (*Rose*, 41), "language of limbs" (*Rose*, 42), "that enigmatic polyphony of sainted limbs and infernal sinews" (*Rose*, 43). Distortion is a form of denying images, the mystical path that rejects the gifts to isolate and eventually attain the Giver, and here William attributes such views to Dionysius the Areopagite and Thomas Aquinas (*Rose*, 81). In parallel fashion, the abbot, too, perceives meaning in stones, not the carved blocks of the frescos valuable only for the images they have recreated, but in the intrinsically valuable precious gems with which he has filled the abbey. "I perceive in these stones such superior things, the soul weeps" (*Rose*, 144).

A further sign is that of the people themselves. Like the solid stone abbey around them the monks in community are the Church, the community chanting, reflecting the solid stone structures around them, "And as if released from every fear by the confidence that the prolonged syllable, allegory of the duration of eternity, gave to those praying, the other voices (and especially the novices') on that rock-solid base raised cusps, columns, pinnacles of liquescent and underscored neumae" (*Rose*, 412–13). And in the multiplicity of orders the abbey has come to house is reflected the whole Church gathered. Even when the people are victims, they impart significance, as when William speaks of the "sign" of the leprosy of the lepers (*Rose*, 203), or as in the instance of the "girl" (*Rose*, 406–7, 432); poor simple people become symbolic scapegoats in the intrigue of the rich and positioned. For Adso the girl who seduces him is viewed "as the vessel of every grace" (*Rose*, 278); as in the symbol of the abbey, each value can be read differently. Perhaps, William suggests, even the murderer may act for symbolically philosophical reasons: "How do we know that the murderer killed Venantius because he hated Venantius? He could have killed him, rather than another, to leave a sign, to signify something else" (*Rose*, 106) (which puts the murderer rather on the level of the "Son of Sam"). William, however, recognizes eventually he has misread this sign. The murderer has merely set in motion the internal evil that on the domino theory takes one victim down after another. Still the murderer seems to the interpreter of clues to be following the seven angels' curses in Revelation—that same Revelation which supplies the interlinking verses for the rooms in the library (*Rose*, 171)—and the murderer, as opportunist (capitalizing, perhaps?), falls in with his interpreter's design.

Even nature joins in the imparting of significance through the invocation of the pathetic fallacy, first providing unclear natural signs to match the confusing messages William is receiving from those who inhabit the abbey: "Snow, dear Adso, is an admirable parchment on which men's bodies leave very legible writing. But this palimpsest is badly scraped, and perhaps we will read nothing interesting on it" (*Rose*, 105). Secondly, nature mirrors the tale's moral obscurity when the fog begins gathering as the papal and Franciscan legations gather, then becomes engulfing, indicating that moral ambiguity now infuses all (*Rose*, 335). Thus, the communicating vehicle becomes totally identified with what it relates: ambiguity. So Adso sees

> the whole universe is surely like a book written by the finger of God, in which everything speaks to us of the immense goodness of its Creator, in which every creature is description and mirror of life and death, in which the humblest rose becomes a gloss of our terrestrial progress . . . the great theophanic design that sustains the universe, arranged like a lyre, miracle of consonance and harmony. (*Rose*, 279)

William concludes, "The abbey really is a microcosm, and when we have Pope John's envoys and Brother Michael here, we'll be complete" (*Rose*, 196).

In that microcosmic fallen post-Edenic world the lament of the smith is general: "'It's hopeless,' he went on. 'We no longer have the learning of the ancients, the age of giants is past!'" (*Rose*, 85). Thus, the abbey plays out its destiny from the slaughter of the pigs, reminiscent of the desecration of the Temple in the years of the Maccabees, or perhaps of the slaughter of the innocents, to its final conflagration in a great inferno, replica of the end of time.

What has this all been about? On the surface William's quest has centered at last on a forbidden book, a quest carried on as the monks prepare for, ironically, the ultimate religious event of the year, "the Christmas High Mass" (*Rose*, 412). William believes that

> the learned must devote themselves more and more, not only to discover new things but also to rediscover many secrets of nature that divine wisdom had revealed to the Hebrews, the Greeks, to other ancient peoples, and even, today, to the infidels. . . . And of all this learning Christian knowledge must regain possession, taking it from the pagans and the infidels. (*Rose*, 87)

Such a hermeneutic puts him in direct conflict with the murderer's intention to obscure that knowledge. The priceless forbidden book ironically functions—like Reverend Randollph's unholy Gutenberg Bible or the lure of Sebastian's phantasmagorical original manuscript of the Pentateuch—as a catalyst for evil. It precipitates a conflict between the murderer's condemnation and William's elevation of, of all things, humor, that gift of God which reminds us of our temporal earthiness, which defines our essential humanity. As Adso quotes, "men are animals but rational, and the property of man is the capacity for laughing" (*Rose*, 197). The premium put upon humor in the novel is evidenced in William's and Eco's many quips, for example, those that deflate sanctimonious pride, such as "I believe he [Christ] never laughed, because, omniscient as the son of God had to be, he knew how we Christians would behave" (*Rose*,

161); those that spoof provincialism, such as "These are not letters of the alphabet, and it is not Greek. I would recognize it. They look like worms, snakes, fly dung. . . . Ah, it's Arabic" (*Rose,* 173); and those that mock decorum, as in the comic free-for-all that terminates the legations' debate on the fifth day (the day, after all, that God created parrots—and sea monsters). Ultimately traveling full circle to our introduction, the motive of the murderer defines itself against the levity of the mystery play which occurs in those times when "even the church in her wisdom has granted the moment of feast, carnival, fair" by arguing, "Laughter frees the villein from fear of the Devil, because in the feast of fools the Devil also appears poor and foolish, and therefore controllable" (*Rose,* 474). What this objection denies is that humans may ultimately laugh because evil is controllable by God. Instead, the somber mania of the murderer is ascribed by the murderer to the deity, as he raves in his sermon, "He who has killed will bear before God the burden of his guilt, but only because he agreed to become the vehicle of the decrees of God" (*Rose,* 398). Thus, in his tainted service to God's interpreted revelation, the murderer has sacrificed his victims to the secreting of words, the safeguarding of the dangerous words that the ferocious library whispers to itself in its dark age-long conjurations (*Rose,* 286).

Interesting to note is that the passage Eco has presented for Aristotle's second book of the *Poetics* has as its subject matter the central theme of semiotics theory:

> We will then show how the ridiculousness of speech is born from the misunderstandings of similar words for different things and different words for similar things, from garrulity and repetition, from play on words, from diminutives, from errors of pronunciation, and from barbarisms. (*Rose,* 468)

Compare with this the words we quoted earlier from Eco on the "theory of the lie," the reading and misreading of signs. Further, the theme of misunderstanding stretches to the explanation of the murders which, rather than following a conscious pattern, were at random. The pattern imposed on them from Revelation was solely in the eyes of the interpreter, just as ultimately William imputes a lack of order to the universe except what the believer wishes to see. Yet ironically, despite the nonintention of the murderer and beyond his control, in the larger context of the novel the "Revelation pattern" does exist. Is God the real murderer? Grim humor indeed.

Thus, words become centrally significant to the book, a matter, as the murders proclaim, of life and death. A person's handling of words is, therefore, a dire responsibility, its implications crucial:

> "Don't build a castle of suspicions on one word."
> "I would never do that," William answered. "I gave up being an inquisitor precisely to avoid doing that. But I like also to listen to words, and then I think about them." (*Rose,* 64)

What frustrates William and thus us as we seek to discern order in the book is the fluidity of words in the messages they convey:

> There is a mysterious wisdom by which phenomena among themselves disparate can be called by analogous names, just as divine things can be designated by terrestrial terms, and through equivocal symbols God can be called lion or leopard; and death can be called sword; joy, flame; flame, death; death, abyss; abyss, perdition; perdition, raving; and raving, passion. (*Rose*, 248)

Further, "Such is the magic of human languages, that by human accord often the same sounds mean different things" (*Rose*, 288).

Even the apparently rock-solid basis of Saint Thomas is shown to be cracked and pulverizing with this foundational weakness:

> And this, it seems, is the teaching left us by Saint Thomas, the greatest of all doctors: the more openly it remains a figure of speech, the more it is a dissimilar similitude and not literal, the more a metaphor reveals its truth. But if love of the flame and of the abyss are the metaphor for the love of God, can they be the metaphor for love of death and love of sin? Yes, as the lion and the serpent stand both for Christ and the Devil. (*Rose*, 248)

The result of this fluctuation is to undermine reason and ultimately bring about its fall, as in the experience of Adso: "I was upset. I had always believed logic was a universal weapon, and now I realized how its validity depended on the way it was employed" (*Rose*, 262).

So those who would be wise in the book retreat to the modern skeptical limitations of the certitude that mere reason can provide. Severinus, an herbalist like Brother Cadfael, who serves as William's forensic expert, claims merely, "I know what a physician, an herbalist, a student of the services of human health must know" (*Rose*, 262). And William himself confesses he does not reason from first causes, an activity of the "divine intellect," but maintains a multifarious view, allowing many conflicting hypotheses until the facts seem to suggest one (*Rose*, 305).

Appropriately, this confusion is ultimately centered on the figure of a book, Aristotle's second book of the *Poetics*, since by William's definition, "A book is made up of signs that speak of other signs, which in their turn speak of things" (*Rose*, 396). And we might add playfully that that centering upon a book reflects the widest context that contains the action of this subworld, the nature of the great container, Eco's novel itself.

Shakespeare, we recall, had Juliet cry out to the night, "What's in a name? that which we call a rose / By any other name would smell as sweet" (*Romeo and Juliet* 2.2., 43–44), indicating that it was the content not the designation that was significant (hence, whether assigned "Capulet" or "Montague" the basic humanity of her lover remained universally pure and unblemished from within). Eco, however, has entitled his book *The Name of the Rose*. As a semiotics scholar his focus is upon the designation as he searches the signs and symbols, essentially "what's in a name," for the traces of humans' and God's naming technique. Mirrored by the naming creativity of humanity, God's creating Word has spoken what is not into existence. In our handicraft we see the image of the Maker. In the same way human speech mirrors that creating Word. So speech, sign, symbol, as they name, reflect the creating naming by God, the mystery that has expressed itself botanically, zoologically, celestially. The name is as important as the rose itself. In fact, so important has the name and imagery of the rose become that Eco points out the rose in its multiple meanings has become so thematically gorged as to be in effect meaningless, as when an enthusiastic child mixes all the greens, blues, yellows, reds, and purples into a dingy murky gray:

> The idea of calling my book *The Name of the Rose* came to me virtually by chance, and I liked it because the rose is a symbolic figure so rich in meanings that by now it hardly has any meaning left: Dante's mystic rose, and go lovely rose, the Wars of the Roses, rose thou art sick, too many rings around Rosie, a rose by any other name, a rose is a rose is a rose is a rose, the Rosicrucians. The title rightly disoriented the reader, who was unable to choose just one interpretation; and even if he were to catch the possible nominalist readings of the concluding verse, he would come to them only at the end, having previously made God only knows what other choices. A title must muddle the reader's ideas, not regiment them. (*Postscript*, 3)

We might summarize Eco's position by citing the progression from Shakespeare's focus on essence, "a rose / By any other name would smell as sweet," through Gertrude Stein's melding of essence and designation, "Rose is a rose is a rose is a rose" ("Sacred Emily," 1913), to Eco's emphasis on the designation *The Name of the Rose,* which he likens to the intent of both Bernard of Morlay, the twelfth-century Benedictine whose poem "De contemptu mundi" provided the title for the novel, and Abelard, whose *Nilla rosa est* sentence also illustrated that all "departed things leave (only, or at least) pure names behind them" (*Postscript,* 1). Hence, the frustration of Adso in the conclusion is inevitable as he pokes through the "traces" of the library seeking a coherent epitaph for the tale, for all he will find are traces, the "left eye of the enthroned Christ," for example, like the proverbial left hand of God, the mythical image of the dark side of God, evil (*Rose,* 499). So he searches as if "a message might reach me" (*Rose,* 500), yet when he pieces the remains together, he concludes, "The more I reread this list the more I am convinced it is the result of chance and contains no message" (*Rose,* 501).

Philosophically and theologically the book ends in agnostic doubt of William's nonsensual God (e.g. *Rose,* 58), whom he once assumed was his ally,

"Give me light, by the Devil, [perhaps, illumination by the sensual?] and never fear: God is with us!" (*Rose,* 459), and whom William appears to die unapprehending (*Rose,* 493). But there is another political message that Eco clearly communicates. Umberto Eco once helped compile a collection of Maoist cartoons, entitled *The People's Comic Book,* containing such revolutionary looney tunes as "Red Women's Detachment," "Bravery on the Deep Blue Seas," and "Hot on the Trail." A thread of Marxism runs through *The Name of the Rose* as well. William notes, for example, the political aspect of the Church's rulings on heresy, which claims "orthodoxy" for "any heresy it can bring back under its own control or must accept because the heresy has become too strong" (*Rose,* 203–4). William's view is political: he stresses the Church's selection of outside groups that are politically wise to support or oppose (*Rose,* 203), while as a Franciscan he lauds St. Francis' mission to recall the marginal, the outcast (*Rose,* 202). Still, the thrust of the book is toward a Christian Marxism that does not favor violent revolution. Fra Dolcino's violent acts are condemned while instead Adso learns "why Dolcino was in error: the order of things must not be transformed, even if we must fervently hope for its transformation" (*Rose,* 228). We must wait for God to act.

Similarly, William's party at the council pursues what is essentially a socialistic attack on private property, which stresses the poverty of Christ while clearly stopping short of class war as a suitable solution to correct differences (*Rose,* 237). This theme centers most poignantly on the figure of the poor simple girl with whom Adso has discovered physical (material) love and who is condemned as a scapegoat. As William has lamented, "The simple are meat for slaughter, to be used when they are useful in causing trouble for the opposing power, and to be sacrificed when they are no longer of use" (*Rose,* 152). As Salvatore has also confirmed of the persecution of the Jews, "He replied that when your true enemies are too strong, you have to choose weaker enemies" (*Rose,* 192).

Thus, ultimately the book contains a clear political message even if its theology and philosophy remain merely signs for the reader to try to shape, because for William and Adso and, perhaps, for Umberto Eco, the task is ultimately impossible. Therefore, the doubt expressed in the last paragraph and by the final Latin quotation directs Adso (and perhaps by inference Eco and us) to conclude with William's proleptic agnosticism:

> I have never doubted the truth of signs, Adso; they are the only things man has with which to orient himself in the world. What I did not understand was the relation among signs. . . . I behaved stubbornly, pursuing a semblance of order, when I should have known well that there is no order in the universe. (*Rose,* 492)

In William's realization and Eco's final vision, in merely naming not creating the rose, we have neither created nor securely articulated unequivocal truth. Therefore, let us be kind.

4

Welsh Angel in Fallen England:
Ellis Peters' Brother Cadfael

Preceding as well as following *The Name of the Rose* is Ellis Peters' foray into the Middle Ages, the Brother Cadfael series. A scholar herself, like Eco, "Ellis Peters" (the pseudonym of Britain's Edith Pargeter) is a translator of Czech prose and poetry, who has been awarded the Gold Medal and Ribbon of the Czechoslovak Society for Foreign Relations, as well as the Crime Writers Association's Silver Dagger Award. Numerous historical novels have appeared under her own name and nearly as many mysteries under her pseudonym.

Her protagonist Brother Cadfael, like the brothers of Eco's ill-fated abbey, is a Benedictine. His tales are set two centuries earlier, around 1137 to 1140. Though a monk, he is a lay brother; like Sister Ursula and Dr. Mary Finney, he is not ordained. Like Eco's Brother William, he has a colorful past. A Welsh crusader who served against the Saracens and sailed for ten years as a sea captain against the Corsairs, he is distinguished from the more ascetic William by not only approving but also enjoying "pleasurable" "encounters" with the Venetian Bianca, the "Greek boat-girl Arianna," Mariam, the Saracen widow, while his intended fiancée Richildis (to reappear in *Monk's-Hood,* book 3) finally tires of waiting for him and marries a solid yeoman (*Bones,* 6). Now in his late fifties—and early sixties as the series progresses—he has taken "timely retirement" (*Bones,* 7) for the fifteen years prior to the opening of book 1 as herbalist in the Benedictine Convent of St. Peter and St. Paul.

In Brother Cadfael's opening tale *A Morbid Taste for Bones* (1977), Edith Pargeter sets the themes that will characterize the series to follow. In the rough and ready figure of Cadfael she indicts pretension. Far from being a celebration of medieval mystical Christianity, the series seems at times rather an attack on it, representing Cadfael's entrance into convent life merely as a sailor washing up like driftwood onto the shore, the proverbial final "port in the storm." The competition Pargeter depicts between abbeys, which provides the impetus for the action of book 1, is more or less in the spirit of a football rivalry. A nearby Cluniac Monastery has secured the relics of a patron saint and, not to be outdone, Cadfael's abbey must have one, too. So a prefabricated vision takes an abbey delegation off in search of a "spare saint" to Wales "where it was well known that holy men and women had been common as mushrooms in autumn" (*Bones,* 11). Her style, characterized by verbal lushness, minute attention to historical detail, and comic irony, can sober at times into a scathing indictment of hypocrisy:

> "Man," said Cadfael earnestly, "there are as holy persons outside orders as ever there are in, and not to trifle with truth, as good men out of the Christian church as most I've met within it." (*Bones,* 92)

So much for the notion that Christianity makes better people. In fact, the usual run of monks we encounter in the Cadfael tales are ambitious, sanctimonious, superstitious. The few appealing monastics are either naive like Abbot Heribert (whose sting is left for a later book to reveal) or the mischievous worldly Brothers Mark, John, and Cadfael and the worldly wise Abbot Radulfus.

Often the series seems an invective against religiosity, particularly its hypocrisy, with Brother Cadfael's person itself a suitable weapon. A "thickset fellow who rolls from one leg to the other like a sailor" (*Bones,* 6), small, squat, square, and sturdy (*Sparrow,* 46, 59), Cadfael stands as foil to the aristocratic Prior Robert, the sychophantic Brother Jerome, a walking commonsense indictment of all the pretentiousness that monastic life nurtures in the books.

As in this first book, over and over again in the Cadfael series vaunting ambition precipitates murder. God, in *A Morbid Taste for Bones,* consequently is seen as acting through common sense, the stress here being on the common as well as on the sense. Cadfael's responses indicate this truth:

> "God resolves all given time," said Cai philosophically and trudged away into the darkness. And Cadfael returned along the path with the uncomfortable feeling that God, nevertheless, required a little help from men, and what he mostly got was hindrance. (*Bones,* 46)

Usually, of course, the commonsense detection of Cadfael is what helps God along. God's activity in the series, then, occurs, according to Cadfael, "if God aids me with some new thought—for never forget God is far more deeply offended than you or I by this great wrong!" (*Bones,* 145). Therefore, God's activities are often the inspiring of insights and ideas in Brother Cadfael, though God can and does act independently and even miraculously in these remarkable novels.

Like Eco's William, Cadfael has at times a touch of the modern about him. He does not believe all of the superstitions of his contemporaries and like another monk, Mendel, he is a geneticist who gathers poppy seed "and raised and cross-bred them in his own garden, before ever he brought the perfected progeny here with him to make medicines against pain, the chief enemy of man" (*Bones*, 7). Yet at the same time, he lacks William's agnosticism. For Cadfael, and all the monks and parishioners, the dead are alive and conscious of earthly actions. He is as much concerned for the present feelings and wishes of the dead Saint Winifred, whose relics his monastery is seeking, as for those of any of his colleagues or the people they encounter. Further, this first tale turns on an old superstition that a murdered corpse bleeds in accusation against its slayer. Cadfael is comfortable with his time.

Cadfael is a kind of expatriate in England, a sojourner from a Wales where "blood-lines" stand as a superior displacing system to the English hierarchy of power. In countering stratified feudal hierarchy, Ellis Peters has created two Hawthornian spheres whose tension as action shifts back and forth provides one of the most intriguing aspects of the series. Like Hawthorne's old world, the England of the books will be a place of intrigue, duplicity, sophistication, decadence, stratification, a hierarchy that calls out the worst of ambition, pride and false piety in people who wish to rise (a type of Britain in the Arthurian legends). Wales (like Logres) is a homeland (and particularly Cadfael's home-land) of warmth, simplicity, rugged soil and rugged people, straightforward violence and hospitality, a purer land built upon blood ties.

Thus, when England, in the form of a delegation from Cadfael's abbey, invades Wales to usurp a saint, murder results from a devil's brew of pride and ambition that overrules all opposition to the delegation's goals. Even the reli-gious act of worshipping the saint in question is cheapened by the young vision-ary monk who has inspired the delegation into a pseudosexual ecstatic worship that, to Cadfael's disgust, seems to force the Welsh saint into the pagan role of divine mistress (*Bones*, 120). Skillful irony returns the English delegation with what it deserves, the mouldering bones of a murderer, and innocent Wales and its saints are preserved.

From this beginning as backdrop and foil to Cadfael's policing, detecting ministry, Wales looms throughout the series as a haven for all those who flee the conflict. And although we may never arrive at Wales in books like *One Corpse Too Many*, it is continually held out as the refuge of hope to which many of the characters repair throughout the tales. Sanctuary in the Cadfael series is only for the innocent, whether it be the cloistered confines of the abbey's church or the political borders of secular Wales. Though it is held out equally to the guilty, God ultimately allows only the innocent to find it. While the innocents are succored, the guilty are frustrated and slaughtered on the edge of safety. They can find sanctuary only after death and God's righteous ex-actings.

Normally, Wales' function is to stand against the oppression of English laws and practice. Therefore, in *Monk's-Hood*, for example, Wales represents the idea that no one has the right (despite feudal custom) to own another. Such ownership is English not Welsh practice, and the exercise of that practice has robbed a Welsh youth of ancestral rights and motivated reciprocal murder. Again the mere practice of England, the mere hierarchical custom of Britain, is fatal.

Yet when Wales as refuge is approached unworthily, it does not sanction murder. He who has killed for blood to reject law is himself rejected at the gates of the rugged sanctuary, the wild Eden. As in the realization of Eco's Adso, violence is not the proper means of redress, and vengeance is God's. And although Cadfael as lay brother cannot provide absolution, he does assign life-long penance of good action to restore the fallen to grace, duplicating in the guilty person his own path to salvation:

> You want to pay in full. Pay, then! Yours is a lifelong penance, Meurig, I rule that you shall live out your life—and may it be long!—and pay back all your debts by having regard to those who inhabit this world with you. The tale of your good may yet outweigh a thousand times the tale of your evil. This is the penance I lay on you. (*Monk's-Hood*, 207–8)

In the spirit of Father Brown, Cadfael countenances the death of English murderers but sends Welsh murderers out to a life of perpetual penance. The English guilty pay by the law they live, the Welsh live by their blood ties to pay. Cadfael neatly balances this playing off one legal system against another by his parallel eclectic selection of theology and religious obligation. So in *The Sanctuary Sparrow* we learn that the ritual-disregarding Cadfael practices private prayers (*Sparrow*, 159), evidently substituting them for his ceremonial obligations, as he snoozes through chapter or happily skips office. He thus frees himself to minister, herbalist as he is, primarily as a physician of the spirit:

> I know my herbs. They have fixed properties, and follow sacred rules. Human creatures do not so. And I cannot even wish they did. I would not have one scruple of their complexity done away, it would be lamentable loss. (*Fair*, 95)

As he tells a youth, what troubles him is, "There are brews among us that need just as sure a touch, boy, and where to stir and where to let be is puzzling me more than a little" (*Fair*, 95).

As a result his administrations exact justice from the guilty, give succor to the innocent, extend salvation to the repentant. The effect is gauged upon those to whom he ministers, as exemplified in the case of one who, receiving mercy herself, "was deeply preoccupied at this moment with life and death, and willed mercy even to the lowest and the worst in the largeness of the mercy shown to her" (*Fair*, 210).

In *St. Peter's Fair* not only does Cadfael reject the asceticism and mystical trappings of the monastery, but he also jettisons their peculiar ceremonial aspects of faith as well, relying fully upon grace and the salvific disposition of God:

> There has many a man gone through that gate without a safe-conduct, who will reach heaven ahead of some who were escorted through with absolution and ceremony, and had their affairs in order. Kings and princes of the church may find shepherds and serfs preferred before them, and some who claim they have done great good may have to give place to poor wretches who have done wrong and acknowledge it, and have tried to make amends. (*Fair,* 156)

In the best Reformed sense, repentance for Cadfael has far more purchase than any adherence to the strict requirements of church ceremony. His firm reliance on grace gives him a relaxed attitude toward every other aspect of a person's faith and practice, given, of course, assurance of their sincerity.

Thus, Cadfael's commonsense approach to religion will accept with gentle tolerance the psychological benefits of the practice of giving money for masses, later to degenerate into indulgences. He reflects upon one person's offer: "Well, her reserves of money might now be far longer than her reserves of peace of mind were likely to be; she could afford to buy herself a little consolation, and prayers are never wasted" (*Fair,* 63). At the same time, that common sense, even with its tolerance, does not allow churchly superstition to interfere with what seems just. When someone laments of a victim, "He died unshriven," Cadfael corrects firmly:

> Through no fault of his own. So do many. So have saints, martyred without warning. God knows the record without needing word or gesture. It's for the soul facing death that the want of shriving is pain. The soul gone beyond knows that pain for needless vanity. Penitence is in the heart, not in the words spoken. (*Fair,* 63)

Intention is what counts for Cadfael. His emphasis always resists giving priority to any religious practice or ceremonial act. He firmly rests upon the Reformed premise of the "Sovereignty of God," in his particular adaptation as abetted by human activity. So when the abbot questions whether a murderer will gain by his crime, exclaiming, "As God forbid!" Cadfael assures him firmly: "No, Father! But God will forbid" (*Fair,* 118). More than a mere attribute of the holy, "truth" or "justice" for Cadfael is self-admittedly a passion greater even than that for gain (*Fair,* 132). In fact, so great is his reliance upon the sovereignty of God that he actually wonders if prayer can even have retroactive impact on events that have already transpired! (*Fair,* 144). Now that is a nearly heretical reliance upon God. What saves him is that justice is his motivating force, not primarily fatalism, and he will exact justice as firmly as if he were God's avenging instrument. No one escapes confronting one's crime; "But what is justice? If there were two, and one bears all, and the other goes free, is that justice?" (*Fair,* 155). For Cadfael justice will be exacted. And even when the world appears unjust, God will right the scales. As Cadfael informs his assistant Brother Mark:

> Last summer ninety-five men died here in the town, none of whom had done murder. For choosing the wrong side, they died. It falls upon blameless women in war, even in peace at the hands of evil men. It falls upon children who never did harm to any, upon old men, who in their lives have done good to many, and yet are brutally and senselessly slain. Never let it shake your faith that there is a balance hereafter. What you see is only a broken piece from a perfect whole. . . . Such justice as we see is also but a broken sherd. But it is our duty to preserve what we may, and fit together such fragments as we find, and take the rest on trust. (*Fair*, 155–56)

Relaxing, then, within a fixed assurance of God's sovereignty is what gives him his corresponding, at times nearly cavalier, disregard for religious convention. Ultimately he looks beyond religious ceremony of human justification and beyond the legal ritual of human justice to a sovereign rule of God often breathtaking in its implications.

By the last pages of *St. Peter's Fair*, Cadfael can surpass even Calvin to sound like one of the Westminster divines who pushed Calvin's tentative thought into a logical, and to many oppressive, theological system. So assured is he of the centrality of the acts of the Sovereign God that his theodicy presupposes that God is naturally the source of a leper's leprosy as well as the source of his healing: "What God imposed, no doubt for his own good reasons, for reasons as good he has lifted away" (*Leper*, 221). No evil power intercedes to mar God's ineluctable purposes. So irresistible and so determined are God's plans that even the clouds in Cadfael's perception "were not drifting, but proceeding with purpose and deliberation on some predestined course of their own, unhurried and unimpeded, like death" (*Leper*, 222). The traditional "free will" theology of the Roman Catholic Church is certainly submerged in the hyper-Calvinism that terminates the novel. Yet at the same time anachronistically Cadfael maintains a sort of ironic account book system of credits and debits in his actions: "'And God forgive me the lie,' he muttered to himself when he was out of earshot, 'and turn it to truth. Or at least count it as merit to me rather than sin'" (*Leper*, 125).

Putting all into God's hands allows him to fall easily asleep when he knows he cannot act, despite the desperation of the various situations he encounters, increasing, if possible, his personal affirmation of the omniscience of God: "But God, after all, knew where the lost might be found, and it would do no harm to put in a word in that quarter, and admit the inadequacy of human effort" (*Virgin*, 99). Indeed, for Cadfael God does know that human effort, though required, is inadequate, and God can act. But, as we saw in *Leper* when the dark side of God loomed momentarily before us in Cadfael's theology, the question is whether God will act. When a nun is raped and murdered in *The*

Virgin in the Ice, what has God done about it? "'God was taking note of all,' said Cadfael, 'and making place beside him for a little saint without spot. Would you ask her back from thence?'" (*Virgin,* 144). God's evidently self-limited omnipotence allows human evil while actively promoting human good in such a manner that for the hyper-Calvinistic Cadfael, goodness is the gift of God, evil the result of human culpability: "We answer for our own evil, and leave to God our good" (*Virgin,* 110).

Yet such is his theology of human/divine cooperation in justice against the framework of his feudal worldview that vengeance becomes both the domain of God and the duty of the aristocracy in England, though he is equally comfortable with accepting the conflicting way justice works itself out in Wales (*Virgin,* 145). Perhaps, only in this feudal hermeneutic of the avenging lord can the dark side of God, the chastising with leprosy, say, be reconciled with the goodness of God. Despite the atavistic echo of free Edenic Wales, a villein is owned body and soul, property of the lord to be husbanded into a profitable serfdom. The result of this omnipotent priority of God is to free humanity from worrying about reconciling God's two inverse duties or about a semi-laissez-faire divine policy in which catastrophe alternates with periodic (apparently sporadic) though eventually complete correction. Cadfael's advice? "Never go looking for disaster," said Cadfael cheerfully. "Expect the best, and walk so discreetly as to invite it, and then leave all to God" (*Virgin,* 112).

So Cadfael creates a commonsense patchwork theology to try to cover the moral vicissitudes of the world and its people, at times giving us near-fatalism in the name of Providence: "There is no help for it but to wait and believe in justice" (*Ransom,* 124). "'It is God fixes the term,' said Cadfael, 'not men, not kings, not judges. A man must be prepared to face life, as well as death, there's no escape from either. Who knows the length of the penance, or the magnitude of the reparation, that may be required of you?'" (*Ransom,* 183). Essentially he is leaving the ministrations of earthly justice ultimately to the heavenly court. Father Brown, who made the release of killers a regular pastoral practice, would understand.

Like Father Brown, too, Cadfael must finally retreat to a theology that expects life's dilemmas to be solved beyond life's pale: "Surely a balance must be restored elsewhere" (*Ransom,* 55). One reason is that human legal instincts and systems often diametrically oppose one another, as when what is punishable by hanging in England can be seen as a "sacred duty" in Wales (*Ransom,* 56), an insoluble problem for the well-traveled, crosscultural and potentially syncretistic Cadfael. As a result "mortal man," who has one foot in the afterlife anyway, "should be able and willing to delegate at any moment," said Cadfael soberly, "since mortal he is" to the extent that he had "best leave divine justice to its own business . . . for it needs no help from us" (*Ransom,* 34, 54).

Comparing notes with a legendary crusader, Cadfael in *The Leper of St.*

Giles displays a theology that disregards the boundaries of all religions, positing that God selects the faithful out of any cause and rejects the faithless despite the assurances of any church:

> "I have always known that the best of the Saracens could out-Christian many of us Christians." . . . One nobility is kin to another, thought Cadfael. There are alliances that cross the blood-line of families, the borders of countries, even the impassable divide of religion. And it was well possible that Guimar de Massard should find himself closer in spirit to the Fatimid caliphs than to Bohemond and Baldwin and Tancred, squabbling like malicious children over their conquests. (*Leper*, 220)

What probably saved Cadfael from the stake was his atavistic residual hagiology, his merit-based theology, and the fact that the Reformation would not occur for centuries yet.

Creeping into his theology is an all-merciful universalism which can posit that even a murderer dying in a noble sacrificial act is not out of reach of God's hand, "otherwise we are all lost" (*Sparrow*, 222). No wonder he can assure the harried, " 'It's too early to despair. For despair,' he said vigorously, 'it is always too early. Remember that, and keep up your heart' " (*Sparrow*, 26).

In Cadfael's theology of complete dependence on God, one is never too late for grace, even after death. Since Catholicism's tradition of offering prayers for the dead fits his premise, he blithely abandons his incipient hyper-Calvinism for the position that, "Nevertheless, God's mercy is infinite to those who seek it. However late, however, feebly" (*Sparrow*, 211). Whatever theology serves Cadfael's desire to excuse the innocent, condemn and yet redeem the guilty, is amenable and adaptable. Pity and mercy always supererogate from those helped toward their offenders (*Sparrow*, 220).

Perhaps the reason Cadfael must create his own eclectic theology is that whatever insight can be gained by contemplation is obviously negligible compared to that gained by experience. A cloistered life generally serves in Edith Pargeter's view only to produce hypocrisy or naivete. The mystical experience, as we have seen in *Bones*, is at worst sham, at best incomprehensible. In that sense, despite the fact that she writes of those in the mystical tradition, her own stance is prophetic. Pargeter's hero does not follow a religion that takes the worshipper out of the world, that negates images and gifts to arrive at last in union with that imaged, the Great Giver. Her ideal is instead the integrated worshipper who invites through activity the reign of God into the world, who does not invest arduous hours in meditation but rather finds God in the growing of herbs, the healing of saddened hearts, the championing of truth and the ferreting out and routing of evil. Here Cadfael, outside his acknowledgment of the saints and purgatory and particularly in his emphasis on grace and his disregard of ceremony seems to foreshadow the radical Protestant Reformation.

The rest of the abbey—apart from the favored few, Abbot Radulfus, Brothers Paul and Edmund, and, of course, Cadfael—continue to act as "the covey of awed, inquisitive novices" who "broke away with agitated clucking like so many flurried hens" (*Novice,* 51). But meanwhile Cadfael personifies the edenic refuge Wales, succorer of the innocent, until such time as sanctuary delivers the innocent, whether to the devotional life or back vindicated and deepened to the secular world to supererogate a renewed mercy, pity and selflessness, now enabled to shake off the dust of evil (*Novice,* 176).

In essence this series has never satisfactorily come to grips with its theology. Essentially, the weakness of this well written and in many ways superlative series is that, even though it deals with a medieval monk, it has no notion at all of mystical worship. In the history of prayer there are two distinct trends, the prophetic, which invites God into the world of human action, and the mystical, which lifts the worshipper out of the human sphere into the realm of the divine. In the Cadfael series mystical worship is depicted as either a sham or a transport into translated pseudosexual rapture, both aspects located in the initial archetypal figure of Columbanus. Mystical devotion, as an authentic response, is a completely absent element. Eco's book suffers from a similar failing. Neither writer has truly presented a picture of the mystical tradition. For neither writer is mystical worship comprehensible. In Eco's book the cloistered life is cover for the pursuit of sodomy, unbridled power and greed, political ambition and ascendence. For Pargeter it is escape from reality, protection from maturity for a dormitory of cowled Peter Pans, a haven for the hypocritical and for the landless but career-oriented younger gentry. In each case the acceptable monk has his sandals planted firmly in the muck of human affairs and is God's agent there. Cadfael, of course, does not have to buy into the mystical system. He can be an alternative, but someone in the series ought to represent its wholesome aspects! A true "mysterium," depicting the mystical approach to detecting the corresponding, mirroring secrets of God and humanity, has yet to be written. Still, given this ironic limitation, both Edith Pargeter's fascinating and elegantly written series and Eco's *The Name of the Rose* have not only strongly reintroduced us to traditional storytelling but also entertained us with a rich program of philosophies, literary allusions, scriptural themes and references and morality within a plush, dexterous style.

In his whimsical satire *Murder as One of the Fine Arts,* notorious English "opium-eater" Thomas De Quincey blithely describes what mystery writers are attempting when they elevate their whodunits to classic level, as G. K. Chesterton has done by style, atmosphere and paradox, Umberto Eco by thought, bulk and irony, and now Edith Pargeter by developing sociohistorical themes immersed in rich, accurate description and deft human characterization:

People begin to see that something more goes to the composition of a fine murder than two blockheads to kill and be killed—a knife—a purse—and a dark lane. Design, gentlemen, grouping, light and shade, poetry, sentiment, are now deemed indispensable to attempts of this nature. . . . To sketch the history of the art, and to examine its principles critically, now remains as a duty for the connoisseur, and for judges of quite another stamp from his Majesty's Judges of Assize. (De Quincey, 49)

5

From Green Innocence to Brown Maturity:
E. M. A. Allison's *Through the Valley of Death*

If Umberto Eco and Edith Pargeter have provided all but one piece to the contemporary medieval clerical mystery, E. M. A. Allison's 1983 Crime Club offering completes the puzzle.* *Through the Valley of Death* is a tight mystery featuring a monk who knows his mystical worship. What the book recounts essentially is the "coming of age rites" of a forty-six-year-old lifelong brother whom a murder investigation takes from innocence to responsible faith.

Brother Barnabas is the closest of all clerical sleuths in appearance to the archetypal Father Brown. A small (*Valley*, 23) "stocky man, inclining to fat," with "short legs and broad shoulders," "his face was round, giving him a deceptively simple look, and the creases around his mouth betrayed the ease with which he smiled" (*Valley*, 3). Gray haired, out of shape, a good eater, he occasionally gets bled and rested when feeling bloated (*Valley*, 4). "He liked to eat, and his belly showed it. He was getting fat" (*Valley*, 19). As gluttony is apparently a permitted vice in his freezing abbey, he has definitely allowed himself go "running to flesh" (*Valley*, 17). Of peasant birth, the youngest of the eight children of a miller, he was dedicated to the church at eight years of age since there was not enough of an inheritance in the mill to go around (*Valley*, 6–7). He has had no noble learning. He knows no French but simply the English of the people and the Latin of the Church. He is a man of routine who dislikes having his routine disrupted (*Valley*, 11, 14). He is precise, writes in a neat hand (*Valley*, 19), dislikes being hurried (*Valley*, 10, 11). A thirty-eight-year lifetime in the abbey has left Barnabas gentle, kindly and diffident. He has "traveled not at all" (*Valley*, 68), a complete innocent (*Valley*, 98), who "always felt uncomfortable dealing with people," particularly the nobility, who prefers "his facts to be neatly ordered, safely on paper, where they could be

---

*Like such celebrated writers as Ellery Queen and Emma Lathen, author E. M. A. Allison is not one writer but two, a husband and wife team, Eric W. Allison and Mary Ann Allison, who live in Roslyn, New York.

handled without complications" (*Valley*, 100). Barnabas is by no means a rambunctious Sister Mary Helen who practically salivates at the prospect of getting involved in an investigation. Nor is he a Martin Buell, who, while more discreet about it, is equally avid when on the scent. He prefers "avoiding the problem. He had no wish to take on such a distasteful task" (*Valley*, 34).

Barnabas is vulnerable because he is in the wrong job at the wrong time. As cellarer of the Cistercian abbey in Yorkshire, England, in late September of 1379 (fifty-two years after the burning of Eco's abbey, two hundred years after Brother Cadfael was presumably gathered to his fathers), Barnabas is unfortunate enough to have his chief assistant become the victim. As the logical choice to investigate the cause of this catastrophe in his department, the stunned Barnabas uncovers a pit of great evil in the past and present that has culminated in murder. Named from verse 4 of the twenty-third psalm, *Through the Valley of Death* is a book that depicts great evil and great good. Thus, Barnabas must wallow through tales of butchery, unjust war, plunder, rape, sodomy, probable infanticide and murder.

As in *The Name of the Rose,* a snowfall neatly seals off the abbey and its quests for a medieval version of the classic English country house mystery (adding, of course, dozens more "house guests"). In order to conduct his investigation, he must, so to speak, "invent the wheel," since Sherlock Holmes will not be born for five centuries yet. How then can Barnabas discover the Holmesian scientific method? His solution is to apply Aristotelian principles of logic, learned when as a young monk he copied the "Prior Analytics" in the Scriptorium:

> Aristotle said that logic was a method of drawing the correct inferences, and this was what Barnabas needed. Genuine proof results when valid inferences are drawn from true premises. Therefore he needed to learn the facts, the events of the matter, and make these his premises. Then he could apply the two fundamental laws of logic to his preliminary conclusions—the principle of contradiction, which held that a proposition cannot be both true and false, and the principle of the excluded middle, that a proposition must be either true or false. This would give him a set of postulates. From then he should be able to *deduce* the solution, the murderer.
>
> Barnabas clapped his hands. How simple. Careful application of scientific inference and the problem would be solved. (*Valley,* 34–35)

What is significant in this description of method is that the first part assumes induction, inferring from facts to form a theory (what Conan Doyle has been accused of misterming deduction), while the latter part of the method is deduction, deducing from principles (the theory) to the solution. By this means the authors not only provide Barnabas with a method but neatly offer an implicit apology for Conan Doyle and his Holmes which will not be wasted on Holmes' multitudinous admirers. It is well done, indeed. Whether a fourteenth-century monk would term this an application of a "scientific inference" and spend so much time extolling Aristotle rather than his conduit Thomas Aquinas is, of course, open to question. Whether he would proceed, too, to adopt such police procedural terms as "murder weapon," "case," "crime" is also highly dubious. Against these terms jars such antiquated phrasing as "He knew not what to say" (*Valley,* 116–17, cf. 139), a conflict of ancient and modern terminology that Edith Pargeter carefully avoids. Similarly, the constant pausing to explain various obscure terms and practices makes the book read at times like a treatise on monasteries. It breaks the spell being woven by the text and snaps readers back to distant reality. Still this fault has its benefits for it keeps readers' exasperation level with obscure terms and practices on "safe."

Barnabas' down-to-earth common sense is refreshing after the philosophical convolutions of *The Name of the Rose.* Although untested, his is still a commonsense piety. To his cellarer's commercial sense the mystical library of his abbey is a "book cupboard" (*Valley,* 20). At the same time that he possesses such mundane workaday common sense, Barnabas has one quality neither Cadfael nor William displays. He can be overwhelmed with a sense of worship. He will stop in the middle of the investigation, "delighted" to watch the first snowfall of the season (*Valley,* 22). Such a sight can move him to praise: "The beauty of God's creation filled Barnabas's soul. . . . Barnabas felt terribly small, insignificant. What am I? he asked himself. A mere mortal, impure and weak—but a part of God's creation, nonetheless. He fell to his knees and clasped his hands in fervent prayer" (*Valley,* 36). He also prays when troubled by the investigation—a surprisingly rare trait among clerical detectives (*Valley,* 90). The commission draws him near to God: "Rarely before had he felt so close to God, so one with His purposes" (*Valley,* 36). As a result he remains on his knees in contemplation until called to Vespers (*Valley,* 37). Barnabas, cellarer though he may be, is a true devotee of mystical worship. His is a piety that often scorns the kneeling rail to kneel on the floor "as a gesture of greater humility" (*Valley,* 90).

At the outset of his investigation Barnabas has good reason for reluctance beyond his loathing to mix with soldiers and nobles, or his belief that he is not to judge (*Valley,* 3). Barnabas has deep-seated unresolved conflicts in his theology, and these will not stand the tests of reality. He is troubled by Wyclif's charges of abuses in the Church (*Valley,* 72) and tries not to think about the two warring popes currently excommunicating each other until he is confronted with an inept, secularized bishop who needs to be coached in Latin like a novice in order to read a simple service. Violent death shakes his theology, and he finds he has no foundation from which to view it. "Faced with this kind of death, Barnabas found it difficult to think in terms of redemption and salvation. There was no glory, no tranquillity in this death" (*Valley,* 3). Disillusionment follows revelation after revelation of evil in the abbey until Barnabas can do no less than face the overpowering reality of evil head on.

Within this confrontation all that he has believed since childhood crumbles. He enters the abyss. He can either lose God completely and wander or find a new faith, one that can come to grips with reality. Barnabas does choose a new type of faith in God, a faith that matches the fine forensic abilities he displayed in his first encounter with the corpse, checking for plague symptoms and finding the cause of death. It is a faith that takes account of the facts. The clerical detective must approach ministry to the victims and the killer through the crucifix of the murdered savior, the Ultimate Victim, the one who will forgive. As emissary of the Christ who made the eternal difference in human affairs, Barnabas must learn the lesson he does:

> It was no use arguing that one man could not make a difference. If God was to be served, he must make the attempt.
> He looked up at the crucifix on the wall. His faith told him that one man could make a difference. With deep humility he knelt once more to pray. (*Valley,* 185)

To reach that goal, to be able again to pray, he must resolve the tension that has always been seething within him between practical cellarer and mystical monk. That tension turns on whether embroiling himself in human affairs is the proper attitude for a true believer or whether faith should lift him above the cares of the world. Barnabas poses this question to himself at the outset of the novel:

> Barnabas loved the chanting that accompanied the services, and he especially loved to chant antiphony. Antiphons were verses from scripture, or psalms or anthems, chanted in alternation between different groups of chanters. It seemed to him that it must be close to the sound of the heavenly chorus which surrounded the throne of God. He should be making his way down to the church now. It was the hour of Prime, the first of the Little Hours of the day. He should be praising God, not having to deal with Thomas.
> Barnabas stopped short in his thoughts. That was ungenerous; more, it was unchristian. His duty, both as a Christian and as a monk, was to help the afflicted. Besides, he was an official of the Abbey, and it was proper for a brother to bring a problem to him. Thomas was one of his assistants. He had done only what was right. . . . "Where is the body?" (*Valley,* 11)

Later on when he is embroiled in the investigation, that same choice will be hurled at him by another monk: "Barnabas, you must abandon this inquiry. I cannot think that it is the task of such as ourselves, men dedicated to God, to spend our days on mundane matters" (*Valley,* 84–85).

When Barnabas has been assaulted, left for dead, frustrated at every turn, is doubting the existence or the goodness of God, the abbey infirmarer who is treating his body treats his spirit as well, disarmingly presenting his message under the guise of a request for Barnabas' advice on whether or not this lesson is too difficult for novices:

It seems to me that such events as have happened here can easily shake the faith of a man who has never been in the outside world. Such as our young novices, I mean. But those who have always lived here can easily forget that the world is not the perfect place we wish it to be. The fallacy is to blame God for such imperfection. This is where faith can be lost and despair take its place. Am I making myself clear so far, Barnabas? I do not wish to overtax the novices. . . . Good. For, by design, the world is imperfect. Man was created perfect, but God also gave us free will. . . . Without the exercise of free will, there would be no chance of salvation. We would be as the animals of the field. Instead we are given the chance to be tempted and to sin . . . to resist . . . to repent and save the immortal part. (*Valley,* 152–53)

With this truth the mystical Brother Barnabas, whose name—drawn from St. Paul's fellow missionary—means "son of encouragement," must finally come to grips. He decides to reject despair and embrace his own responsibility, to serve God by being ordained. He will "go out into the world, perhaps for a short time, perhaps forever. He would be ordained a priest and then see what good he could do in the world" (*Valley,* 184). He has become a Father Brown in more than appearance only. He has become like his archetype and both their archetypes, Jesus, a minister to the wretched.

6

Father Brown: G. K. Chesterton's Paradoxical, Prototypical Priest

G. K. Chesterton in "How to Write a Detective Story" warns:

> The first and fundamental principle is that the aim of a mystery story, as of every other story and every other mystery, is not darkness but light. The story is written for the moment when the reader does understand. . . . The misunderstanding is only meant as a dark outline of cloud to bring out the brightness of that instant of intelligibility. (Chesterton, "How," 112)

In his article "The Twilight Harlequinade of Chesterton's Father Brown Stories," William J. Scheick points out that Chesterton fleshed out his principle artistically by placing so many of the Father Brown tales in a twilight setting. Alzina Stone Dale, in *The Outline of Sanity: A Life of G. K. Chesterton,* recalls that Chesterton was an artist first; and if he deftly infuses his word sketches with Thomas De Quincey's elements of "Design . . . grouping, *light and shade,*" as well as the required "poetry, sentiment" (De Quincey, 49), he knew, as an artist knows, the value of picturing the idea that lies behind a crafted work. Darkness to set off illumination is his first principle. And Chesterton warns that the secret when revealed (and only a writer who has missed the point thinks baffling a reader is the desired end of a mystery) must be worth the quest. As he puts it, "The climax must not be only the bursting of a bubble but rather the breaking of a dawn." For G. K. Chesterton, "Any form of art, however trivial, refers back to some serious truths" (Chesterton, "How," 113).

Chesterton's second greatest principle is that "the soul" of detective fiction is "simplicity. The secret may appear complex, but it must *be* simple; and in this also it is a symbol of higher mysteries" (Chesterton, "How," 113). Chesterton's appeal to the great mysterium certainly affirms his pivotal place in the transfer (and partial reclamation) of the sacred mysterium to the secular mystery, which in its essence harkens back to its great parent, the quest for the revelation of God.

Third, no what we might call "diabolus ex machina" must appear. As

Chesterton explains, "the fact or figure explaining everything should be a familiar fact or figure" ("How," 114). The criminal must be evident, but, of course, not as a criminal. Realization, the dawn-breaking, comes when what we thought to be familiar is revealed as actually unfamiliar.

For his fourth principle, he counsels the reader to keep in mind that an author is consciously, intentionally arranging all the seemingly haphazard details in the story, and the reader must stalk the author as the real culprit. The story is like "a toy," a "trick," a joke, a dexterous game where anything, even the "love-interest" may be a "blind" ("How," 116–17).

Finally, he reminds the reader "that the detective story like every literary form starts with an idea, and does not merely start out to find one . . . a positive notion, which is in itself a simple notion; some fact of daily life that the writer can remember and the reader can forget" ("How," 117–18). "But anyhow," he concludes, "a tale has to be founded on a truth" ("How," 118).

The result, the reward, is that readers' eyes, perhaps closed like Miniver Cheevy's, will be opened to "the poetry of modern life" ("Defence," 4). Readers will see the beauty and meaning of human artifices:

> The lights of the city begin to glow like innumerable goblin eyes, since they are the guardians of some secret, however crude, which the writer knows and the reader does not. Every twist of the road is like a finger pointing to it; every fantastic skyline of chimney-pots seems wildly and derisively signalling the meaning of the mystery. . . . Every brick has as human a hieroglyph as if it were a graven brick of Babylon; every slate on the roof is as educational a document as if it were a slate covered with addition and subtraction sums. ("Defence," 4–5)

So the search of Sherlock Holmes through minutiae is the quest for the human creator, the "human character in flints and tiles," which is ultimately, of course, his hunt for the human "author" of a crime ("Defence," 5). And the work of the police against crime is the fight against chaos in microcosm, "burglars and footpads are merely placid old cosmic conservatives, happy in the immemorial respectability of apes and wolves." The "agent of social justice" is "the original and poetic figure," whose service to the good is the whole "romance" of humanity since in its rebellion against the relaxation back into chaos "morality is the most dark and daring of conspiracies" ("Defence," 6).

Thus, the ironic Chesterton's vision of order as good's rebellion against chaos, primal good as rebelling against the usurping evil of the "prince of this world," morality as conspirator against the regent immorality of the fallen world mirrors the creator who must come as creation, the commander who dies as a slave, the defeated in whose defeat is the victory. And the vehicle in which he presents these paradoxes is a bumbling little priest with "a face as round and dull as a Norfolk dumpling . . . eyes as empty as the North Sea" (*Innocence,* 5). The Reverend J. Brown, as "The Eye of Apollo" would have his name (*Inno-*

cence, 176)—or is it "Paul" as "The Sign of the Broken Sword" contends? (*Innocence,* 200) or perhaps J. Paul Brown, an ecclesiastical version of the roving sea captain and "citizen of the world" J. Paul Jones—is the epitome of all the eccentric heroes that G. K. Chesterton fabricated in his attempt to flesh out the Scriptural truth that "the preaching of the cross is to them that perish foolishness" (1 Corinthians 1:18a) since, as the King James Bible would put it, "God hath chosen the foolish things of the world to confound the wise; and God hath chosen the weak things of the world to confound the things which are mighty" (1 Corinthians 1:27). Thus, we have Innocent Smith in *Manalive* pursuing with a loaded gun a professor who has preached the weariness and worthlessness of existence and in firing shots demolishes the practicality of his philosophical argument. And we have eccentrics who form organizations against progress in books like *Tales of the Long Bow* and *The Napoleon of Notting Hill;* the oddballs of *The Club of Queer Trades* and the *Four Faultless Felons;* paradoxical mentors like *The Man Who Was Thursday,* or the last great enigmatic detective Mr. Pond, who solves mysteries by exploring their paradoxes in *The Paradoxes of Mr. Pond;* and finally all the poets and lunatics from *The Ball and the Cross* to *The Return of Don Quixote* to *The Poet and the Lunatic.* For Chesterton's vision, the task of the priest and the poet are complementary in their inverse natures, as the childlike Innocent Smith explains:

> "I don't deny," he said, "that there should be priests to remind men that they will one day die. I only say that at certain strange epochs it is necessary to have another kind of priests, called poets, actually to remind men that they are not dead yet." (*Manalive,* 227)

So the childlike, out-of-phase characters of Chesterton, the poets and lunatics and priests, bring home to those they encounter the seriousness and responsibilities of normal adult life. The murderers Father Brown encounters have deluded themselves about the true nature of their actions, as has the professor whom Smith's drastic call to practice what he preaches shocks back to reality. Brown's creed is like Innocent Smith's: "His creed of wonder was Christian by this absolute test; that he felt it continually slipping from himself as much as from others. He had the same pistol for himself, as Brutus said of the dagger" (*Manalive,* 227). Father Brown's "creed of wonder" is that he acknowledges his own culpability so greatly that he can intuit, empathize with and comprehend the culpability of others: "'I am a man,' answered Father Brown gravely, 'and therefore have all devils in my heart'" (*Innocence,* 174–75).

But one would never know this truth from looking at him. At first glance he seems simply "a mild, hard-working little priest" (*Innocence,* 46) from Essex (*Innocence,* 20). He smokes a pipe (*Innocence,* 114) and only "against his common habit" accepts a cigar when agitated, consuming it steadily in silence (*Innocence,* 131). He enjoys wine and beer (*Innocence,* 211) and a fire and ale in a warm inn (*Innocence*, 195), for the inn into which Father Brown retreats is, like the inn into which Lewis' Ransom stumbles at the end of *Out of the Silent Planet*, the healthy center of humanness. He is "very short" (*Innocence*, 5). His voice is high, and he has "all the solemn expectation of a child" (*Innocence*, 75), possessing the "grave stare of a baby" (*Innocence*, 144), appearing to point "awkwardly like a child" (*Innocence*, 217). He bites his finger reflectively (*Innocence*, 196). He carries a commonplace umbrella like that which will later become the trademark of Soeur Angèle (*Innocence*, 5). He changes his ministry quite often as he ministers among "slums and criminals" (*Innocence*, 46). In the first book alone, we are told he is from Cobhole in Essex (*Innocence*, 25), that he is "Father Brown, of the small church of St. Mungo," a suburb north of London (*Innocence*, 117), presumably poor, since in Yorkshire dialect "Mungo" is a personal name built out of the word for milled wool waste used to make cheap cloth, according to Webster's. But in "The Eye of Apollo" he is "attached to St. Francis Xavier's Church, Camberwell" (*Innocence*, 176), while by the last sentence of the last story, "The Three Tools of Death," he seems to have responsibilities at a "Deaf School" (*Innocence*, 226) near Hampstead (*Innocence*, 212). Perhaps he is all priests in all places.

But if Father Brown is transient in ministering base, he is not so transient in theology. He can "paraphrase any page in Aquinas" (*Innocence*, 41) and has no theological doubt where to go for insight, since he prays to God for strength and to heaven for help (*Innocence*, 41). So he can draw on a resource of security and patience from the inexhaustible well of God and be a patient "fisher of humanity": "I caught him, with an unseen hook and an invisible line which is long enough to let him wander to the ends of the world, and still to bring him back with a twitch upon the thread" (*Innocence*, 61). Both his and his narrator's theologies are clearly anti-Calvinist, and within Father Brown's precursory model is firmly established the anti-Reformed strain that will be reinforced in all of the Roman Catholic clerical crime novels. Calvinism is called "morbid" in "The Three Tools of Death" (*Innocence*, 212). "The Honour of Israel Gow" contemplates the "sense of doom in the Calvinist" (*Innocence*, 101). The villainous general in "The Sign of the Broken Sword" has "some of the eccentricities of puritan piety" (*Innocence*, 197), which is not surprising since, because prehistoric Scottish people "really worshipped demons . . . they jumped at the Puritan theology" (*Innocence*, 109). In fact, for Father Brown a Calvinist blacksmith is "a good man, but not a Christian—hard, imperious, unforgiving." The fault lies in his "Scotch religion" which looks down at the world, not up at heaven in humility (*Innocence*, 173). For Father Brown does not believe in "doom" but in "Doomsday" (*Innocence*, 146). Father Brown is also no syncretist and no universalist. He is hostile to Eastern Indian religion whose adherent he sees as claiming that he needs no God and longing for nothingness, annihilation (*Innocence*, 127). Paganism is a labyrinth, and the "sun was the cruellest of all the gods" (*Innocence*, 177). He also defines himself against the "pan-pipe" shaped fairyland (*Innocence*, 140), which is the classic neopaganism that adulterated the vision of so many British writers of the late nineteenth and early twentieth centuries. He allows Flambeau's pillorying of Christian Science as "one of those new religions that forgive your sins by saying you never had any" (*Innocence*, 176–77), adding his own criticism to it (*Innocence*, 206), while for Father Brown the attitude of optimism, of cheerfulness, is a "cruel religion" which will not let one weep (*Innocence*, 225). The one spiritual disease is "thinking one is quite well" (*Innocence*, 177).

If Karl Menninger longs for a cleric who takes the reality of sin seriously, Father Brown is that cleric. He can "smell" evil as a dog smells rats (*Innocence*, 52). He has keen senses (*Innocence*, 50). He has the "knack of friendly silence which is so essential to gossip" (*Innocence*, 142), yet he is not a gossip since he maintains the confidential sanctity of the confessional (e.g., *Innocence*, 136). He is a "commonly" "silent" and "oddly sympathetic little man" (*Innocence*, 142), to whom criminals unburden themselves: "We can't help being priests. People come and tell us these things" (*Innocence*, 22). He queries, "Has it never struck you that a man who does next to nothing but hear men's real sins is not likely to be wholly unaware of human evil?" (*Innocence*, 23). Yet all these confidences do not make him morbid. He is delightfully humorous, though encountering evil can depress him, as at the end of "The Sins of Prince Saradine." To assuage his loneliness he has not a M. Hercule Poirot but a M. Hercule Flambeau, the foremost of his reformed criminals, as his "only friend in the world" (*Innocence*, 131). In some singular manner, the chief of all sinners, he whose crimes could make Father Brown laugh in uproarious appreciation, speaks to the potential depths of Father Brown.

Though Father Brown appears insignificant except for his large grey, ox-like eyes that look outside himself at the world (*Innocence*, 169), his passivity is maieutic in nature, that midwifery that Jesus employed in asking questions of the rich young ruler in Mark 10:18–19; of the Pharisees in Mark 10:3; of his own disciples in Mark 8:27–29, as he prepares them for the great revelation or draws out, particularly in the last instance, the truth already revealed within them.*

In the first tale, "The Blue Cross," in which a master thief disguised as a fellow priest attempts to steal an icon Father Brown is transporting, Father Brown begins his work upon his future Watson, the arch-criminal Flambeau, who is as much an artist of crime as the satiric De Quincey could wish. As Flambeau reflects in "The Flying Stars," "As an artist I had always attempted to provide crimes suitable to the special season or landscapes in which I found

---

*Those interested in further information on the relationship of the methods of Socrates and Jesus may consult the writings of Dr. William T. Iverson.

myself" (*Innocence,* 67). He considers his own criminal performance with critical judgment: "I really think my imitation of Dickens's style was dexterous and literary" (*Innocence,* 67). Father Brown understands this:

> "A crime," he said slowly, "is like any other work of art. Don't look surprised; crimes are by no means the only works of art that come from an infernal workshop. But every work of art, divine or diabolic, has one indispensable mark—I mean, that the centre of it is simple, however much the fulfillment may be complicated." (*Innocence,* 63)

That master sleuth, the atheist Valentin, also accepts this: "The criminal is the creative artist; the detective only the critic" (*Innocence,* 8). But the type of "art," like the dagger in "The Wrong Shape," is evil and must be ended:

> It's very beautiful . . . the colours are very beautiful. But it's the wrong shape. . . . It's the wrong shape in the abstract. Don't you ever feel that about Eastern art? The colours are intoxicatingly lovely; but the shapes are mean and bad—deliberately mean and bad. . . . The lines go wrong on purpose—like serpents doubling to escape. . . . Don't you see it is the wrong shape? Don't you see that it has no hearty and plain purpose? It does not point like a spear. It does not sweep like a scythe. It does not *look* like a weapon. It looks like an instrument of torture. (*Innocence,* 121–22)

Freedom in art as in life is not the ultimate good to be desired; rather, good order is lines going "right" on purpose, and here we see Chesterton's own primal perspective of the detective as agent of order emerging forcefully. By noting the unbridled freedom preached by Flambeau, disguised as a priest in the very first tale, Father Brown is able to penetrate his disguise and bring him to justice, because for Father Brown theology in the microcosm of human affairs consistently reflects the reasonableness of morality, even in the vast physically infinite reaches of stellar space:

> Reason is always reasonable, even in the last limbo, in the lost borderland of things. . . . Reason and justice grip the remotest and the loneliest star . . . the reason and justice of conduct. On plains of opal, under cliffs cut out of pearl, you would still find a notice-board, "Thou shalt not steal." (*Innocence,* 18–19)

Flambeau obviously does not belong to the "family of the priesthood." His opinions are abnormal for a priest, and ultimately, normalcy is the indication of one's acceptance of God's decree and gift of humanness—the human expression of goodness. So every aberration can have a familial referent, as in, "It would be as startling to find a new guest in the hotel that night as to find a new brother taking breakfast or tea in one's own family" (*Innocence,* 49). Chesterton consistently brings home all enigma to such a family referent for explanation and evaluation. As a great family man who loved to be in his home, Chesterton set the familial, the familiar, as a central lodestar of reason and reference in his stories. Agatha Christie's Miss Marple eventually adopted this tactic as she likened all the criminals she met to residents back in her village of St. Mary Mead.* As Valentin observes in "The Secret Garden," "Strange, gentlemen . . . that I should have hunted mysteries all over the earth, and now one comes and settles in my own back-yard" (*Innocence*, 29).

In the second tale, murder claims a guest on Valentin's own grounds. Valentin's secret garden becomes an image kaleidoscopic to all the guests who confront it, and particularly to Father Brown, whose own invitation follows the acquaintance made between Father Brown and the great detective at the arrest of Flambeau in the opening tale. We have already looked once into Valentin's mind to introduce us to the "commonplace" little priest, just as the later Charles Merrill Smith will introduce us to Reverend Randollph as primarily a natty set of clothes to his new co-workers, or Henri Catalan will introduce us to Soeur Angèle as a walking "cornette." And in this we should have been warned that Valentin's naturally arrogant, deprecating perception of Brown resembled the criminal Flambeau's. Now as we scrutinize Valentin's brain within his "natural habitat," against his "secret garden"—which he has constructed as a "subconscious" to his open, public life—we see good and evil meet there as they do in Valentin's brain; just so, Poe's "House of Usher," with its facelike features, its deep "subconscious" chamber, reflects a mind going mad. The sensitive Irish O'Brien intuits it: "The borderland of the brain, where all the monsters are made, moved horribly in the Gaelic O'Brien. . . . A voice older than his first fathers seemed saying in his ear: 'Keep out of the monstrous garden where grows the tree with double fruit'" (*Innocence*, 43). The garden tells the tale: the seemingly wholly reasonable Aristide Valentin is in reality insane in his opposition to the Church. The bumbling, nearly imbecilic Father Brown is wholly reasonable. So who is revealed as the mad one? The person who eats from the tree that would make one the judge of good and evil, the one usurping God's place, not the one who in humility eats from God's provided "Tree of Life." The garden may be a protected Eden, but it is definitely an Eden where the serpent lurks:

---

*On the topic of Chesterton's influence on Christie, the seeds of Agatha Christie's classic acroidal scheme, having the narrating doctor do *The Murder of Roger Ackroyd,* may already have been planted some fifteen years earlier in "The Wrong Shape." Chesterton's doctor writes, "I am a quick man with my hands and in a minute and a half I had done what I wanted to do" (*Innocence*, 135). Christie's doctor writes, *"I hesitated with my hand on the door handle, looking back and wondering if there was anything I had left undone. . . . I did what little had to be done"* (Christie, 304–5). Does there not seem to be an echo here? In that sense, G. K. Chesterton helped begin mystery's overthrow of the security of the commonplace, which Agatha Christie helped further.

> But there was no exit from the garden into the world outside; all round it ran a tall, smooth, unscalable wall with special spikes at the top; no bad garden, perhaps, for a man to reflect in whom some hundred criminals had sworn to kill. (*Innocence*, 24)

In the first tale Father Brown establishes a convention that many clerical detectives will follow after him to varying degrees, putting into effect Chesterton's final principle of the "blind" by deceptively simulating his third principle, the criminal as familiar figure. He thus portrays Father Brown as initially suspected of a crime, vandalism. This motif is repeated and intensified in "The Flying Stars" when he is suspected of theft (*Innocence*, 77). Suspecting the cleric of the crime apparently worked so well for Chesterton that ensuing series regularly used it and augmented it for their initial books. Hence, Rabbi Small, Father Buell, Soeur Angèle, Father Dowling, and even Reverend Randollph are briefly suspected of perpetrating murders before their relationships with the police warm enough to exonerate them automatically when they turn up with their succeeding legions of bodies. But, as each case continually counsels, the appearance of evil is not evil; it is an illusion, just as the appearance of good is not always good. Good and evil are distinct; despite their often initially interchangeable appearances, they are heading toward distinctly different ends and will eventually distinguish themselves and those who are traveling along with them:

> Men may keep a sort of level of good, but no man has ever been able to keep on one level of evil. That road goes down and down. The kind man drinks and turns cruel; the frank man kills and lies about it. Many a man I've known started like you to be an honest outlaw, a merry robber of the rich, and ended stamped in slime. (*Innocence*, 80–81)

How great is the shock when Chesterton reveals a secret criminal among the "good," in a manner Dashiell Hammett will later repeat in his "Continental Op" tales when an attractive young operative turns out to be a criminal. The great detective Valentin, supposed champion of justice, is revealed to be the murderer. Applying rule five, readers realize that if Chesterton in his very second tale will sacrifice a primary character who would have been an excellent foil for the entire series, we can expect him to do anything. There may be no length to which he will not go. As he topples Valentin and Valentin's perspective, which has predominated in "The Blue Cross" and "The Secret Garden," he neatly topples all expectations. Thus, Brown proves that humility frees one to focus not on oneself, on the approval of others or on conquering others' opinions, but on others themselves and therefore upon truth, wherever it might be. And truth is always in the simple and humble, not in the complex and haughty. Again and again at the heart of the Father Brown tales is an illusion, the genuine appearing fake, the fraudulent appearing genuine. A real police officer is bounced around like a Keystone version in "The Flying Stars," just as the genuinely brilliant

Father Brown is given a donkey's head and bears it patiently (*Innocence*, 75), as Chesterton's poem "The Donkey," in the spirit of the old English carol "The Friendly Beasts," tells how the scorned "parody" of an animal bears all, nurturing the secret of its hour of glory, carrying the Christ to Egypt. That humility gives Father Brown "all the solemn expectation of a child at his first matinée" (*Innocence*, 75). And the same humility continues to baffle others, as one worldly colonel indicates when he views Father Brown as "cloistered and ignorant of this world" (*Innocence*, 81), even after Father Brown has caught a thief and restored stolen gems. This conflict creates a sense of paradox that makes a presence as big as an absence (*Innocence*, 26), introduces us to an "elderly young woman" (*Innocence*, 15), lets a young man observe, " 'If you really were mad,' said the young man, 'you would think you must be sane' " (*Innocence*, 88). It lets Father Brown ask in "The Queer Feet," "But why on earth should a man run in order to walk?" (*Innocence*, 51). It presents a dead waiter, "who was there when he could not be there" (*Innocence*, 63). In "The Three Tools of Death," rather than envisioning the usual case of a train giving a shock to a house, it presents a house giving a shock to a train (*Innocence*, 213). The paradoxes, the apparently absurd and self-contradictory statements that nevertheless may be true, are most revealing in the area of faith and Scripture. Father Brown counsels in "The Three Tools of Death" that "men like Armstrong want an occasional glass of wine to sadden them" (*Innocence*, 216), rather than to "gladden" them as the psalmist says (Psalms 104:15a). In "The Queer Feet" the pretentious secular sanctimoniousness of a hotel is "profaned" for about half an hour "by a mere priest" (*Innocence*, 49), while the small shambling priest of Christ has only the victory of truth to contrast him to the false magnificent fair priest of Apollo (*Innocence*, 182). The ironies and the paradoxes make Father Brown suddenly shout with laughter when asked to say seriously what events mean (*Innocence*, 79), for he realizes that the wisdom of truth is to point up the foolishness of this world. Therefore, in this world, "His head was always most valuable when he had lost it" (*Innocence*, 53). Confronting the absurdities that pass for reason in this world, he sees the irony pictured everywhere around him. When a headless body is exhumed, Father Brown observes the lesson in the grotesque illustration: "There are three headless men . . . standing round this open grave" (*Innocence*, 111). Perhaps this is why Chesterton's corpses sometimes lose their heads. For one in "The Honour of Israel Gow" there are two in "The Secret Garden." It symbolizes the lack of reasoning in those heads. Indeed, readers have to keep their heads and wits about them when pursuing his mysteries, for Chesterton deftly paints illusion everywhere in his stories to depict the illusions of life. Illusion is so prevalent and so deceitful that Father Brown himself is continually made humble by it. By his failures Father Brown is continually freed from the exhausting, distracting burden of maintaining pretension and arrogance, humbled enough to relax in the ironies and even use them to further the good: "Never mind; one can sometimes do good by being the right person in the wrong place" (*Innocence*, 142).

Ultimately, then, all the complexities that confront and baffle the detective, as we are confronted and baffled in life, reduce to a simple truth. Every clever crime, like every great enigma, is founded on some simple fact. In "The Queer Feet" the simple fact is that a gentleman's evening dress is the same as a waiter's. The truth in "The Eye of Apollo" is the cruelty of nature, of the worship that deludes one into thinking all is quite well, as "The Three Tools of Death" portrays the cruelty of humorless cheerfulness as a religion in a world that is not cheerful, where only a fool sings songs to a heavy heart (Proverbs 25:20). In "The Sign of the Broken Sword" the truth is the misunderstood fallacy of false piety, "that it is useless for a man to read his Bible unless he also reads everybody else's Bible" (*Innocence*, 206). The heart of true piety is not "me and God" but "God and we." The central truth is always simple, but true humility, perceiving one's place in relation to God, is required to see it. And this truth for Chesterton unlocks the secrets of the universe:

> The modern mind always mixes up two different ideas: mystery in the sense of what is marvellous, and mystery in the sense of what is complicated. That is half its difficulty about miracles. A miracle is startling; but it is simple. It is simple because it *is* a miracle. It is power coming directly from God (or the devil) instead of indirectly through nature or human wills. (*Innocence*, 131)

So the task for Father Brown is to cut through the complex manner to the simple truth, which is also unique and discoverable. As he demonstrates in the perplexing case of Israel Gow, when he easily comes up with creative but invalid theories that will connect all the clues, "Ten false philosophies will fit the universe; ten false theories will fit Glengyle Castle. But we want the real explanation of the castle and the universe" (*Innocence*, 107).

Thus Father Brown relaxes in the paradoxes and employs them, along with his own paradoxical character of having chosen good from a heart that could easily have chosen evil, to bring murderers before the bar of God's justice, rather than simply delivering them up to human authority. Why does he let murderers go? Murderers belong to God and God's justice, and in the revelation of the true tapestry each will see that a fitting place in the pattern has been assigned to all. So he can warn, "No; let him pass. . . . Let Cain pass by, for he belongs to God" (*Innocence*, 189–90). For Father Brown, experiencing salvation begins with the knowledge that leads to repentance, and his task is to encourage that knowledge in the fish he catches with his holy hook. So he exacts a confession from the doctor in "The Wrong Shape" and counsels for hours with the culprit in "The Invisible Man": "But Father Brown walked those snow-covered hills under the stars for many hours with a murderer, and what they said to each other will never be known" (*Innocence*, 100). It will never be known because for Father Brown it is God's business.

Many may be dissatisfied with this reply, just as they may be dissatisfied with some facets of Chesterton's work. However, without a doubt his writing is beautiful, often breaktaking, with such sharp poetic images as "the moon with her scimitar had now ripped up and rolled away all the storm-wrack" (*Innocence*, 28). Here one can see how well he works his verbs, how he infuses the violent energy operant on the ground into the whole fabric and cycle of nature, how with one word he summons up the militant, invoking the Dianan alternative to the Pallas/Cynthia/Chloe/Clair options for lunar imagery while bringing in the oriental ferocity that he has defined in "The Wrong Shape," placing nature at war with its own chaos. He communicates violence, militancy, severe imposition of order in waged war in one succinct energetic sentence. And he has made the integral parts function through his selection of onomatopoetic compound verbs to forestall the need for qualifying adjectives. One can hear the moon's sharp-curved and aptly lunar-shaped sword ri-i-ip up and r-r-ro-o-ollllll away the storm's debris in one swift, flowing action—the action of an expert, graceful martial artist. And, of course, what the mirroring moon images, a nature that has fallen with the lot of Adam, is the saber slash that rips up and rolls away the head of the unfortunate Mr. Brayne.

Still Chesterton has his lapses. For instance, what sort of a Frenchman has he made Flambeau? For that matter what sort of Roman Catholic has he made Father Brown? Brown is certainly a free-floating priest without bishop, pope, Mary, or Rome. He may receive confession and perform the last rites, yet what actually distinguishes him but a few pages of memorized Aquinas from a high-church Anglican, unmoored from office and bishop? The mystery is all about detail, and Chesterton's fourth principle cautions us to see the meticulous plotting of the author's hand in the pages before us. But are the first name changes as careless as Watson's wound altering from his leg to his arm? What of the job changes? Are they intentional or careless, too?

And what of Father Brown himself? Like his namesake Browne in James Joyce's *Dubliners* tale, "The Dead," he is everywhere, with a fluidity of designation and a fluidity of presence that make him seem at times almost omnipresent. In his conscious choice of the good and his service to self-examination as a prelude to repentance, his is the omnipresence of the conscience, the omnipresence of the good, not the ubiquity of iniquity. But if this is the intended conclusion, what of Chesterton's and Father Brown's theological prejudices? Does Chesterton through the vehicle of his creation really wish to exclude from the Christian faith not only the cults but also legitimate parts of the Protestantism he left when he converted from his Methodism *cum* Unitarianism *cum* Anglicanism to Catholicism? Or is this attitude just the blind urban prejudice of the nouveau riche who has just recently left the city? Are any of his villains Roman

Catholic, for example, or are they the protected class? Is this intended to be Flambeau's function? He is certainly more lapsed than the Vicar Wilfred Bohun. This reinforces the prejudice that only atrociously lapsed Catholics commit (nonhomicidal) crimes, while Protestants in good standing commit heinous ones. Harry Kemelman realized he needed a Jewish culprit in two of his books for verisimilitude's sake; did Chesterton, or was apology his goal? But what of perhaps the most serious charge? Explicable lapses are one thing, but telling us "Even Valentin was slightly shocked" (*Innocence,* 29) at the discovery of a decapitated corpse in his garden is cheating. How could the narrator tell us Valentin was shocked in any degree, when he was the calculating murderer? We are not told he appeared shocked. We are told he was shocked. We may have here what Elizabeth Bettenhausen and Linda Clark have pointed out to me as an oxymoron humorously illustrating in the very fabric of the work a tapestry interwoven with paradox, symbolic of the great design of the universe. Otherwise, if this is a lapse and not Chesterton's meticulous intention, then the statement breaks Chesterton's first rule of not simply baffling the reader.

If these are indeed lapses, what they show is that the simple truth at its core is that the mystery for Chesterton is more than his simple rules indicate. It is more than merely an exercise of collecting clues to solve a mystery puzzle, mirroring how we solve the seeming complexities of life. It is a greater parabolic vehicle that concentrates on dealing us its message of fragmentation, culpability, self-deceit, judgment, mercy, justice, punishment, pardon, life and death, good and evil, crime and the security of society, individual sin and the redemption of the individual, corporate sin and the redemption of all humanity.

Today, half a century after his death on June 14, 1936, Chesterton is chiefly remembered for these Father Brown stories, *Orthodoxy* and *The Man Who Was Thursday.* Did he suppose his detective tales represented the pinnacle of his craft? With his penchant for paradox and irony, he would no doubt be vastly amused for, as Alzina Stone Dale reports, he "wrote his Father Brown stories hastily (like almost everything else he wrote), often to finance other projects" (Dale, 158). H. R. F. Keating, creator of Inspector Ghote of the Bombay Police Department, writing in *Twentieth-Century Crime and Mystery Writers,* notes: "Ironically, many of these he regarded as pot-boilers. Told his bank balance had shrunk to a mere hundred pounds, he would say 'That means Father Brown again'" (Reilly, 161).*

And what did Chesterton have to say about his Father Brown tales? In his *Autobiography* he writes:

---

*Keating's assessment is that Chesterton, "a spouting volcano of fire-dazzling words," "appears to have left solely mounds of dead ashes—with one notable exception, his still glowingly alive detective stories about the little, modest Catholic priest Father Brown" (Reilly, 161). Keating exempts *The Man Who Was Thursday* and *The Napoleon of Notting Hill* from his "mounds of dead ashes." The

> As I have said, I have never taken my novels or short stories very seriously, or imagined that I had any particular status in anything so serious as a novel. But I can claim at the same time that it was novel enough to be novel, in the sense of not being historical or biographical; and that even one of my short stories was original enough to do without originals. (*Autobiography*, 332)

In typical Chestertonian fashion he decries his fiction only to end by supporting it. The figure of Father Brown he notes is "a Catholic priest whose external simplicity and internal subtlety formed something near enough to a character for the purposes of this sketchy sort of story-telling" (*Autobiography*, 332). Further, he informs his readers:

> There is also in the conception, as in nearly everything I have ever written, a good deal of inconsistency and inaccuracy on minor points; not the least of such flaws being the general suggestion of Father Brown having nothing in particular to do, except to hang about in any household where there was likely to be a murder. (*Autobiography*, 339–40)

This latter point was picked up by Leonard Wibberley and used to draw a distinction between Father Brown and his Father Bredder and defend Bredder as uniquely active in regular recognizable parish ministry. Taken together, these two quotations suggest a vague sketching in of a character to serve as centerpiece in a rather hastily drawn mystery. But, given Chesterton's affinity to paradox and puzzle, can we believe him? If what he is saying true? Can we take it at face value?

1985–86 *Books in Print* records the following books by G. K. Chesterton currently in print: two editions of *All Is Grist;* three editions of *All Things Considered;* three current editions each of *End of the Armistice, George Bernard Shaw, Orthodoxy, William Blake;* four versions of *The Everlasting Man;* and two editions respectively for *Appreciations and Criticism of the Works of Charles Dickens, As I Was Saying, The Ball and the Cross, Chaucer, Do We Agree?* (with and without the question mark), *The Spirit of Christmas, Thomas Carlyle, Sidelights on New London and Newer New York.* Thirty-one other books are also currently in print, plus eight books coauthored by Chesterton. And this list only catalogues Chesterton's so-called "dead ashes." I have not included the fifteen separate collections of Father Brown tales or the six other omnibus collections of Chesterton's writing. Add to this incredible longevity of works by an author fifty years dead the plethora of references and citations and quotations citing Chesterton on a multiplicity of issues issued yearly in new books and take into account that of the one hundred volumes of Chesterton currently available, twenty-six presses have produced them, and finally consider that what we have listed are only the primary sources, not the wealth of secondary literature pouring out on Chesterton. In sum, the kindest thing one can say about Keating's statement is that he is wrong. Where Keating is right is in his recognition that the three versions of *Innocence,* the three versions of *Incredulity,* the two versions of *Secret* and *Wisdom,* and the reprinting of *Scandal,* plus the reproduction of all or parts of these in the four omnibus collections currently competing to be purchased reveal that Father Brown is indeed "still glowingly alive."

Brief paragraphs later he contradicts the spirited defense he gives of the originality of Brown and the "misunderstanding of the nature of narrative fancy" by concluding that a "character in a novel must be 'meant' for somebody or 'taken from' somebody" (*Autobiography,* 333, 332) and by confessing that he has, indeed, modeled Father Brown on one Father John O'Connor of Bradford. On page 334 he disassociates O'Connor from Brown by arguing, "He is not shabby, but rather neat; he is not clumsy, but very delicate and dexterous; he not only is but looks amusing and amused," yet on page 336 he describes O'Connor as

> a small man with a smooth face and a demure but elfish expression. I was struck by the tact and humour with which he mingled with his very Yorkshire and very Protestant company; and I soon found out that they had, in their bluff way, already learned to appreciate him as something of a character. (*Autobiography,* 336)

How much can we believe of what Chesterton tells us when he has filled his explanation with contradictory information? According to him, his stories are sketchy and full of error, yet original and based, one supposes, on his own rule of meticulous plotting as the intentional arranging of the author, which is his fourth rule. His Brown is a general character not based on anyone, though based on Father O'Connor with a number of striking differences (and striking similarities). Nearly all critics of Chesterton have blithely taken at face value his disarming deprecation of the Father Brown tales and the lively stories he has circulated about their economic nativities, ignoring the web work of qualifications in his explanations that leads a critic deeper and deeper into a judgmental morass. I believe anyone who takes any blank statements of this nature from Chesterton without suspicion has fallen victim to his high humor. G. K. Chesterton has not given us an explanation. He has given us a puzzle. He, after all, delights in being a rumor-monger—about himself. Note this famous example, quoted everywhere in the secondary literature as true: "Of those days the tale is told that I once sent a telegram to my wife in London, which ran; 'Am in Market Harborough. Where ought I to be?' I cannot remember whether this story is true; but is not unlikely or, I think, unreasonable" (*Autobiography,* 335). But is it true? Virtually all the secondary literature treats it as if it were a real event. But does Chesterton make such a claim? He has not confirmed whether the tale is true or not. He has merely, with elfish glee, spread more legend and released more of a smokescreen around his actual character—a misty ambience in which to lurk and spring out at the unsuspecting reader, through which to strut with his inverness cape, his stick, his hunting hat.

But recall the passion and exactitude with which he constructed his two classic essays on mystery stories, which also blaze on as living torches to Chesterton's memory, being reprinted as widely today as in the past. Most of

Chesterton's essays are rambling exercises in word and thought association. He turns on the faucet of his wit, allows the desired measure of intelligence and witticisms to pour out, shuts off the valve, entitles the essay or book with the first thought that set the flow in motion and closes that contribution. But the two essays on the mystery are tight and, for Chesterton, concise. In the same way the Brown stories are usually spare and vivid jewels of wisdom and wit. Perhaps he did wander about in his garden dictating them in batches, but the mind that framed them chipped and trimmed their facets with the subtlety of a master jewel cutter. Milton, too, dictated his work. Those who have been drawn in by Chesterton's disarming and, I believe, misleading deprecation of his Brown stories have stumbled into his protective smokescreen—missing that which they were intended to miss, what his bravado and humor and deprecation were all attempting to protect—the children of his creativity, all of whom were dear to him. How many writers utilize just the same distancing techniques to protect themselves and their dearest expressions from the harsh yellow eye of the predatory critic? Most perhaps beside Ben Jonson and Truman Capote. Not every dictating mystery writer is an Edgar Wallace, writing out the first page in long hand and then tossing off the rest in dictation, yielding numerous books generally judged critically as having one outstanding page and two or three hundred moderate ones. Once when criticizing eugenics proponents Chesterton huffed:

> Of these it is enough to say that they do not understand the nature of a law any more than the nature of a dog. If you let loose a law, it will do as a dog does. It will obey its own nature, not yours. Such sense as you have put into the law (or the dog) will be fulfilled. But you will not be able to fulfill a fragment of anything you have forgotten to put into it. (*Eugenics*, 15–16)

Chesterton obviously put a great degree of sense in his Father Brown tales as he did in his two essays on the mystery, for together and separately they exert as steady and commanding an influence on the genre today as they did over half a century ago.

Having, thus, thoroughly confused and, I believe, deluded and diverted the reader, Chesterton proceeds to give his famous account of interviewing Father O'Connor on "some rather sordid social questions of vice and crime" Chesterton had been considering and of being appalled at the discovery of the "abysses" and "horrors" "this quiet and pleasant celibate had plumbed." Immediately thereafter, upon hearing two undergraduates decry the plight of the same O'Connor, fleeing, as they supposed, the true evil of the real world in his celibate innocence, Chesterton was struck by the irony of the contrast of the priest who fought real evil daily and these two sophisticated Cambridge gentlemen of the world, in actuality as innocent "of real evil as two babies in the same perambulator" (*Autobiography*, 337–39).

That appearance of innocence with the subtle wisdom of the serpent's ways is the chief quality Chesterton has "put into" Father Brown and the one that has determined the subgenre of the clerical sleuths. It is Daniel, the young member of the crowd, speaking up with the force of God's perspicacity and vindicating Susannah. It is Joseph illuminating Pharoah, the canonical Daniel illuminating Belshazzar, the aprocryphal Daniel confounding the priests of Baal. It is every one of the succeeding clerical detectives, dismissed as hopelessly innocent of real evil by their cocharacters, in fact often *being* innocent by their cocharacters' standards, whom God's perspicacity illuminates, shedding supererogated light on the crime. Not for nothing is the messiah known as the dawnbreaker, the bright and morning star, the light of the world.

Three years after *The Innocence of Father Brown*'s 1911 publication date, Chesterton had enough Father Brown tales to issue a second volume, *The Wisdom of Father Brown*, most appropriately titled and most appropriately matched with the preceding title. This new collection draws the lines of the conflict that will demarcate the remainder of Father Brown's battles. In tale after tale he will set a pattern to be followed in *The Incredulity of Father Brown* (1926), *The Secret of Father Brown* (1927), into *The Scandal of Father Brown* (1935). Father Brown will fight the cold calculating tendencies of science to dehumanize people, and in story after story up to the very last moment in the very last uncollected short story "The Vampire of the Village," Brown will fight the matching monster of religious fraud that will seek to enslave the emotions and the spirit of those that dehumanizing science does not subdue.

What point will emerge from the building weight of tale after tale? It is that perception is crucial. The reader has to do in the reading process what Brown does: pierce the innocence of appearance in Brown, find the wisdom in that which is passed off as foolishness, find the evil and foolishness in that which passes for wisdom. Chesterton's aim, we recall, is to have the reader perceive what is significant in mundane things, events, people. He exercises readers by the tales he has them read. And in discovering the depths of attractiveness in the shabby little unattractive Brown, readers find a "man of sorrows" in the priest who has been despised. To underscore this event, Chesterton distances and downgrades the priest by the use of indefinite articles and uncomplimentary descriptions. Chesterton makes him indistinct, as Brown's priestly garb makes him indistinct, a brown paper bag in which the pearl of great price is hidden. Thus, each of these stories introduces Brown in an off-handed, undistinguished manner, letting his service as God's conduit eventually establish his uniqueness. So in the first tale of the second book, "The Absence of Mr. Glass," we are told, "There shambled into the room a shapeless little figure" (*Wisdom*, 230). In the second tale we read, "On the other side of her sat the priest, whose name was Brown" (*Wisdom*, 251). The third tale introduces him simply as "a priest drinking nothing" (*Wisdom*, 266). With the irony of Thackeray slipping his most important statements into brief dependent clauses tacked onto long sentences featuring insignificant events, details, feelings, Chesterton slips the introduction of the most significant character into an afterthought. So Thackeray tacks the death of the main character George in *Vanity Fair* onto a long and frivolous description of a ball. So Father Brown's presence is tacked on as an afterthought to a sentence ostensibly describing the exceptions to the observation that the cafe into which several characters pass is empty. But the nearly ignored pebble in the corner will become the chief cornerstone of wisdom in the ensuing tale. In the fourth story "a figure so incongruous in the scene as to be almost comic. It was a very short man in the black uniform of the Roman secular clergy" (*Wisdom,* 284) serves to introduce Father Brown. In the fifth story he has been reduced to "Flambeau and his friend the priest" (*Wisdom,* 298). By the seventh he is introduced in a newspaper account as simply a "man at the right end of the table . . . as commonplace a person as could be seen anywhere" (*Wisdom,* 335), but later the same reporter recognizes him as "an extraordinary man" *(Wisdom,* 341). In each case Brown has moved from obscurity and disregard to prominence and honor. The effect is cumulative. In three of the last four stories he is introduced by name. The one exception, "The Strange Crime of John Boulnois," detours in order to allow Brown to astonish yet another skeptical and hardened newspaper journalist, so that in future tales the insignificant Father Brown—to his own dismay—could become a newspaper celebrity.

Just as he fails to remain unscathed by the press, so does Father Brown find himself affected by plunge after plunge into the depths of crime, struggling against the attraction of evil. Now we find the Father Brown who reads aloud passages about Vodun "almost with relish" (*Wisdom,* 380). This is certainly the Father Brown who provides the solution to crimes. *The Wisdom of Father Brown* tells of two Father Browns:

> Father Brown was made of two men. There was a man of action, who was as modest as a primrose and as punctual as a clock; who went his small round of duties and never dreamed of altering it. There was also a man of reflection, who was much simpler but much stronger, who could not easily be stopped; whose thought was always (in the only intelligent sense of the words) free thought. He could not help, even unconsciously, asking himself all the questions that there were to be asked, and answering as many of them as he could; all that went on like his breathing or circulation. (*Wisdom,* 385–86)

But there are also two other Father Browns: the one we have come to know is the priest and champion of good who implacably dogs evil ("Vampire," 989), but another who lurks within, the Mr. Hyde, is himself a potential murderer. That darker side of Father Brown has struggled for articulation since the opening of the series. Now in the fourth collection, he emerges fully as the explanation of Brown's detecting style.

The Secret of Father Brown, the fourth book, is set up as a series of reminiscences. The title tale is not a tale at all but the explanation of Father Brown's detecting style. Following it are eight vivid illustrations of that detecting style. At the end Father Brown puts down his wine glass and his recollections, concluding he is "a sort of understudy; always in a state of being ready to act the assassin. I always made it my business, at least, to know the part thoroughly" (*Secret,* 805). The final tale, "The Secret of Flambeau," again is not a tale but the far side of the frame. Father Brown has begun by describing his detecting style as getting inside a criminal, as, in effect, becoming that criminal through empathetic imagination. A skeptical American visitor who has heard of his exploits remains unconvinced that Brown's method is practical. *Why* he doubts is not immediately clear since he has had many examples of the success of Brown's method. What he means, of course, is not that Brown's method as a detective does not apprehend criminals but that it encourages tolerance of crime, confirming crime through his identification with the criminals. No criminal, the American claims, thus pursued, would ever reform. At that, Flambeau—retired and posing as the gentleman farmer, M. Duroc, rich in children, comforts, and livestock—discards his alias by way of final illustration, throwing himself on the mercy of his visitor. When the American recoils that no one could imagine being so shameless as to expose a host, Brown neatly caps his method by murmuring, "I could try" (*Secret,* 811). What exactly is this secret of his detecting style?

> "The secret is. . . . You see, it was I who killed all those people. . . . You see, I had murdered them all myself. . . . So, of course, I knew how it was done. . . . I had planned out each of the crimes very carefully," went on Father Brown. "I had thought out exactly how a thing like that could be done, and in what style or state of mind a man could really do it. And when I was quite sure that I felt exactly like the murderer myself, of course I knew who he was. . . . I mean that I really did see myself, and my real self, committing the murder. I didn't actually kill the men by material means; but that's not the point. Any brick or bit of machinery might have killed them by material means. I mean that I thought and thought about how a man might come to be like that, until I realised that I really *was* like that, in everything except actual final consent to the action. It was once suggested to me by a friend of mine, as a sort of religious exercise. I believe he got it from Pope Leo XIII, who was always rather a hero of mine." (*Secret,* 637–38)

He goes on to contrast his method or "Absence of method. . . . Absence of mind too, I'm afraid," as he murmurs (*Secret,* 636), with so-called scientific deduction:

> Science is a grand thing when you can get it; in its real sense one of the grandest words in the world. But what do these men mean, nine times out of ten, when they use it nowadays? When they say detection is a science? When they say criminology is a science? They mean getting *outside* a man and studying him as if he were a gigantic insect. . . . When the scientist talks

about a type, he never means himself, but always his neighbour; probably his poorer neighbour. . . . I don't try to get outside the man. I try to get inside the murderer. . . . Indeed it's much more than that, don't you see? I *am* inside a man. I am always inside a man, moving his arms and legs; but I wait till I know I am inside a murderer, thinking his thoughts, wrestling with his passions; till I have bent myself into the posture of his hunched and peering hatred; till I see the world with his bloodshot and squinting eyes, looking between the blinkers of his half-witted concentration; looking up the short and sharp perspective of a straight road to a pool of blood. Till I am really a murderer. (*Secret*, 639)

As Brown has explained his technique earlier, "I can always grasp moral evidence easier than the other sorts. I go by a man's eyes and voice, don't you know, and whether his family seems happy, and by what subjects he chooses—and avoids" (*Wisdom*, 272). Sister Mary Helen and her police will later adapt this analysis of the eye. Brown has already explained he tends toward what is "psychologically possible" (*Wisdom*, 273). Now we know what he means: what is psychologically possible for him, himself, to commit. And no crime seems too heinous for one who honestly searches the depths.

His detecting, human and flawed though it may be, is brilliant precisely because of its human imperfection. Hunting for the humanly imperfect, he seeks a low enough level, for the lodestone of his own human imperfection drops him down in a moral plumbline measure that swings across the suspects until it centers over the current depth of wickedness. Brown, as a plumbline, is held by no one less than God. His detecting is a holy calling. In the depths his perspicacity is illumined by God's light, for Brown's theology posits detecting as service to the true God. His is a theological task to explode mysteries and expose deceptions:

"I know the Unknown God," said the little priest, with an unconscious grandeur of certitude that stood up like a granite tower. "I know his name; it is Satan. The true God was made flesh and dwelt among us. And I say to you, wherever you find men ruled merely by mystery, it is the mystery of iniquity. If the devil tells you something is too fearful to look at, look at it. If he says something too terrible to hear, hear it. If you think some truth unbearable, bear it. I entreat your Grace to end this nightmare now and here at this table."

"If I did," said the Duke in a low voice, "you and all you believe, and all by which alone you live, would be the first to shrivel and perish. You would have an instant to know the great Nothing before you died."

"The cross of Christ be between me and harm," said Father Brown. (*Wisdom*, 344)

All dispelling of mysteries that impede growth in goodness and communion with God are Brown's purview. And these stem from the Satanic. As he explains to the plagued Admiral Pendragon, suffering beneath his so-called family curse, "Do you know that in my business you're an exorcist almost before anything else?" (*Wisdom*, 361). And Brown the exorcist exorcises Satan whether the great deceiver be hiding in scientific atheism, bogus miracles, predatory religious cults, or in the seven sinful vices that cause murder, theft, extortion, false witness and true scandal.

Therefore, all of the Father Brown tales seem to comprise a great thematic circle, exposing religious and scientific evils that block out true faith. Appropriately, the final Father Brown collection will end precisely where the first tale began, with a theft not a murder, and, pointedly, a theft of a precious religious relic. But this time Father Brown will not be alone, nor does he have to rely on the atheistic police. He has as companion the first great thief now shriven and redeemed, Flambeau. If Father Brown were to look back and assess his life, he would see, if he counted all else for naught, he would still have this one great gain. The striking coincidence of the two thefts of religious relics by clever and blasphemous opponents compels us to ask if this is intentional. Did Chesterton perhaps suspect this was his last Father Brown book and arrange the tale to bring the saga full circle—with one exception: the gain of Flambeau? Chesterton did leave one last known uncollected Father Brown story, "The Vampire of the Village," but the coincidence of the correspondence of "The Insoluble Problem" and "The Blue Cross" is thought-provoking.

If it were worthwhile for us to write a detailed biography of Father Brown, we could, perhaps, approximate one by following the career of Flambeau from thief to thief catcher to retired landowner. Why he must still live under an alias, hiding from the "police of two hemispheres" (*Secret,* 810) after a long period strutting about openly as a private investigator is anybody's guess. Probably Flambeau simply summoned up that dramatic announcement in "The Secret of Flambeau" for the effect of surprise. After all, he was ever the actor. At any rate we do learn in his confession that he stole for twenty years (*Secret,* 810). Brown was already an active parish priest with a long association with criminals when he attracted Flambeau. We could classify Brown's activities into the pre-Flambeauian period, the Flambeau-as-thief tales, the Flambeau-as-investigator tales, the Flambeau-as-gentleman-of-leisure (and perhaps this category would subdivide into before and after investigator periods), and the Flambeau-as-family-man period, yielding a post-Flambeau Father Brown. Chesterton would probably be appalled if we did, for as we have speculated, the undefinable "all priests one will ever meet" has been written into Brown's character and it must be maintained. Still, we have learned quite a bit about this supposedly sketchy character in these fifty-one stories, and a bare bones biography might look like this: Born to a "rustic" family and "grown, with other turnips, in Essex" ("Vampire," 987), about three-quarters of the way through the nineteenth century (1870, for example, would make him forty-one at the time of *Innocence,* enough time to have traveled widely and picked up all his obscure knowledge, and sixty-nine at the time of "Vampire"), J. Paul Brown entered the Roman Catholic secular priesthood at an early age and mixed the vagabond restlessness of youth with the callings of his vocation. After a stint in North

America ministering to inmates of a Chicago prison (*Wisdom,* 299), his vocation took him to impoverished and rural missions all over England, serving the poorest level of the British industrial society. Particularly in these industrial cities, ministering among those from whom Britain's blue collar criminal classes are drawn, he became, as a by-product of his counseling ministery, an expert in such exotic flim flam confidence techniques as "the Donkey's Whistle," "the duplicate brown parcel," and the infamous "spots." None of these curacies lasted long, Brown shifting with the fluidity of the uprooted itinerant laborers he served. Interspersed were various missionary posts around the world, but Brown kept returning to minister in England. After a career serving and salvaging lower class criminals, he began encountering and ultimately convicting and converting the infamous "Colossus of Crime," M. Hercule Flambeau. Their relationship matured as Brown continued following a succession of callings that took him all over England. While Flambeau was seeking an honest occupation and after he opened his now famous private investigation firm, in the spirit of his legendary predecessor Vidocq, founder of the Sûreté, Brown and Flambeau would coordinate their various activities to work as much as possible together. Meanwhile despite the fact that he was a poor sailor and got regularly seasick, Brown continued his restless traveling all over Great Britain, Europe, North and South America, often serving in brief curacies or accepting invitations to travel by those who had learned of his fame as an amateur detective through the extensive and enthusiastic newspaper coverage this seemingly diffident cleric regularly attracted. Brown himself seemed ambivalent toward the attention and adulation he was receiving. His first publicized triumph, the arrest of Flambeau, was followed rapidly by another masterstroke abroad, the exposure of the noted Aristide Valentin, Chief of the Paris Police and rumored to be "the greatest detective alive" (*Innocence,* 22). Returning in slowly burgeoning honor to England, Brown began to act as consultant to the now rehabilitated Flambeau, after Flambeau's release. Eventually Brown worked with the police when an "able amateur" was needed (*Scandal,* 896). In this capacity as part-time consulting detective and semi-retired cleric, he responded all over England and the world to particularly complex and perplexing cases. After a long, meandering ministry, expanding his consulting services to many who sought his aid, officially and unofficially, Brown became legendary, the subject of magazine stories, numerous articles, symposiums and discussion groups. Despite semi-retirement he did not lessen his activity with age but continued to the end to score his remarkably astute, inductive victories. Active through 1939, when the case dubbed "The Vampire of The Village" was recorded in a Chicago Tribune short story, Brown survived his creator by four years. Regularly, his life has been extended through the medium of motion pictures and eventually television to relive some of his more celebrated adventures. Surviving even the actors who portrayed him, Father Brown continues a long and active career both in the fifteen versions of various collections of his stories currently in print in the 1980s and in the flourishing secondary literature being created in Canada's *The Chesterton Review*.

How has Father Brown been regarded? As we can see from the few quotations I have gleaned from the wealth of literature written on them, the Father Brown stories have been generally roundly praised. The praise has also been tempered with criticisms ranging from hasty production to Leonard Wibberley's criticism of the amorphousness of Brown's actual ministry. One critic, no less than the great Dorothy Sayers, cast her imperious eye on Brown's lack of follow-through to ensure justice. As she sees it:

> The sprightly amateur must not be sprightly all the time, lest at some point we should be reminded that this is, after all, a question of somebody's being foully murdered, and that flippancy is indecent. To make the transition from the detached to the human point of view is one of the writer's hardest tasks. It is especially hard when the murderer has been made human and sympathetic. A real person has then to be brought to the gallows, and this must not be done too lightheartedly. Mr. G. K. Chesterton deals with this problem by merely refusing to face it. His Father Brown (who looks at sin and crime from the religious point of view) retires from the problem before the arrest is reached. He is satisfied with a confession. The sordid details take place "off." (Sayers, *Omnibus,* 38)

The normally astute Dorothy Sayers has, I believe, missed the point here. Father Dowling may wrestle with this problem, seeing the need for both earthly justice and heavenly mercy, but God's bar is the bar that Father Brown recognizes. After his activity in "The Blue Cross" and his possible disenchantment with the police beginning with "The Mistake of the Machine" back in his Chicago days and continuing through his further disenchantment when the great police chief Valentin proves criminal, Brown simply begins to alter his method of ensuring justice is done. He does not merely retire from the problem and leave the sordid details to be performed "off." Rather, like Brother Cadfael after him (while, in quintessential Chestertonian form, also before him), he brings the culprit before God's bar, himself serving first the role of prosecutor, then defense attorney, passing judgment and giving penance. He is arresting officer, prosecution, defense, judge, jury and jailer, incarcerating his convicts in the prison of God's mercy, sentenced to a life of repentance. In this he is truly God's vicarious representative on earth, the role of the priest. He will and does cooperate with the official police when they are worthy of cooperation and when the crime fits the earthly punishment for it. But Brown appeals to a higher penal code in determining how to correct the guilty he apprehends. And this apprehension and sentencing of penance summarizes Father Brown's pastoral response. Father Brown is not, after all, a Peter Wimsey who has never made a Christian commitment. Wimsey, we know, would feel such an action to be mildly indecent.

Instead, Wimsey deals with the here and now of human justice. But Father Brown's here and now deals with divine justice, meted out by God through Brown and God's other earthly agents in God's time, as Brown himself and Brown's apprehended stand before that final bar. Wimsey's, then, is the arraignment court from which there is trial and appeal. But Brown's is the one Great Supreme Court where only one voice can ultimately argue for defense—the Book of Hebrews' great attorney, Jesus. As for Father Brown, he is content to his end to bring his charges to that final court where justice is always done and mercy always poignantly available. Apparently, Brown's solution satisfied the many, for his influence has permeated all of literature. His books sell widely. His example is continually cited when a new cleric notes another bite out of the forbidden fruit of good and evil and sets out after the biter.

We have already noted his commanding impact everywhere in both the secular and the clerical crime novel. Imitation may be the sincerest form of flattery, but pervasiveness of influence is marked by parody. The caricature of Father Brown in such pastiches as Leo Bruce's *A Case for Three Detectives,* where he has been elevated in rank to Monsignor Smith, assures his fame. In fact, G. K. Chesterton himself has been fictionalized by John Dickson Carr as the brilliant but eccentric Dr. Gideon Fell in twenty-three novels published over a thirty-year period from *Hag's Nook* and *The Mad Hatter Mystery,* both of 1933, to *Dark of the Moon* in 1967. Indeed, Chesterton's impact has been felt as far afield as in what Alyona Kojevnikov has called the "religious renaissance going on in the Soviet Union" (Buxbaum, 14b). Chesterton's books have become bestsellers underground and overground. As Kojevnikov notes,

> One group bought a photocopier and began printing prayer books, Russian Orthodox and other religious texts—including the works of C. S. Lewis and G. K. Chesterton—and sold them "quite openly, at very low prices," she said.
>
> "As the demand was so great, a distribution network of willing volunteers sprang up from the farthest reaches of Siberia to the southernmost regions of the Ukraine," she said. "It was the sheer scope of the operation that brought about its downfall, for in order to even partly satisfy demand, too many people had to be drafted to simply keep up volume of production.
>
> "The result was inevitable. The initiators of the enterprise . . . were all arrested in April, 1982, and brought to trial in December of that year."
>
> Articles in one Russian paper accused the conspirators of having been motivated by greed, at the same time claiming that religion was dying among the Russian people.
>
> "If religion is on the way out, why was it possible for the sale of religious books to be such a profitable enterprise?" Kojevnikov queried rhetorically.
>
> Religion, she says—Russian Orthodox, Baptist and a variety of underground churches such as the True Orthodox and Eastern Rite Orthodox—is emphatically not on its way out. (Buxbaum, 15b)

And neither is Father Brown "on his way out," despite the death of his creator some fifty years ago. His conversion to other media such as the television episodes with Kenneth More and films like 1979's *Sanctuary of Fear* with Barnard Hughes cements his continuance in time.

Perhaps the most fitting observation one can make about the irrepressible eccentric G. K. Chesterton and his equally outrageous priest is to apply to these droll murder-and-mayhem-mongers Chesterton's own words about illness, that disrupter of all comforts, that old strict schoolmaster who lectures in severe illustration about the need for health, both temporal and eternal:

> There is in the world a very aged rioter and demagogue who breaks into the most refined retreats with the dreadful information that all men are brothers, and wherever this leveller went on his pale horse it was Father Brown's trade to follow. (*Innocence*, 48)

And now this lifelong celibate's children also follow.

7

Sister Ursula: Wise Woman

The first clear successor to Father Brown was created in Chesterton's lifetime. *The Crime at Diana's Pool* (1927) introduced the brilliant but brief career of an Anglican priest, Canon Whitechurch's Vicar Westerham. But the first Roman Catholic successor was not a priest at all but a nun who appeared nearly a decade after Chesterton's death: "This was no otherworldly innocence before him, but a lively, sensible, and wise woman" (*Nine,* 138). "The force lost a wonderful policewoman when you decided to take the veil" (*Rocket,* 26).

In comparative folklore there are a number of stock characters that serve like common denominators in the popular tales of numerous nations: the handsome valiant prince, the beautiful distressed princess, the cruel old king, the wicked stepmother, the noble warrior, the ambitious scheming servant, the wise woman. George McDonald in his children's fantasies drew on the wise woman to create such fierce, feminine images of power and deity as the Grandmother/ Servant Girl of the Princess and Curdie tales, the North Wind of *At the Back of the North Wind,* and of course, the Wise Woman in *A Double Story* (often entitled *The Lost Princess*). The classification goes as far back as Old Testament times to that wise woman who saved a city by tossing a rebel's head over the wall to his pursuers (2 Samuel 20:14–22), and the wise woman who, taking an upper millstone in hand, swiftly and neatly terminated a siege by simply locating the enemy's commander and, essentially, dropping a brick on him (Judges 9:53). H. H. Holmes' Sister Ursula is in every aspect a wise woman. The amorphic quality her habit gives her prompted this remark by Michelle B. Slung in *Crime on Her Mind:* "During the mid-forties, the younger women were edged out and replaced by wry, sexless, ageless female sleuths such as H. H. Holmes's Sister Ursula and Matthew Head's medical missionary Dr. Mary Finney" (Slung, xxviii). Actually, Sister Ursula is archetypal. She is true to the paradigm she represents, the category of all wise women in a present incarnation.

Sister Ursula is the voice of reason and sanity in her brief career of two locked-room novels (*Nine Times Nine* and *Rocket to the Morgue*) and five short stories. Author H. H. Holmes, a pseudonym for William Anthony Parker White, invested more time and energy critiquing music, science fiction, and mysteries for the *New York Times* and, under another better known pseudonym, Anthony Boucher, creating numerous adventures for detectives Colonel Rand and Fergus O'Breen. But Sister Ursula is among his most appealing creations, and her two novels deserve to be better known today than they are. Perhaps since *Rocket* first appeared in paperback on the eve of World War II, its fate can be attributed to the vast literary fallout as well as the recycling of paper engendered by the war. Jacques Barzun and Wendell Hertig Taylor preemptorily dismiss the Holmes books on two counts:

> *Rocket to the Morgue.* . . . The main interest of this poorly contrived and poorly told murder story is the presentation of science-fiction writers, interspersed with discussions of their craft. . . . The L.A. lieutenant and his friends are not convincing, and the victim and plot not engaging. (Barzun, 69)

And

> *Nine Times Nine.* . . . This early story introduces several of the characters that we find again in *Rocket to the Morgue,* and in the same unsatisfactory way. Apart from elements extraneous to the plot (e.g., good theorizing references to Sherlock Holmes), the story is messy, and the motives weak and hard to credit. Domesticity and calf love take up space and leave Lieutenant Marshall little chance to shine. It is Sister Ursula who does the work of explaining a locked-room murder arising out of a Los Angeles "cult." Why the author borrowed the name of a murderous American maniac of the nineties is hard to fathom." (Barzun, 240)

But these judgments are as unwarranted as they are ungracious and essentially sexist. In addition to dismissing the main detective, Sister Ursula, entirely for her male foil, Lieutenant Marshall, they overlook the charm, wit and painstaking ingenuity that created these two conscious variations of the locked-room puzzle (and lest we miss what White is up to, he has his police lieutenant's wife neatly reprise John Dickson Carr's list of possible solutions ostensibly as an aid to her husband). Although the *Catalogue* does not find the characters or their domesticity "convincing" and "engaging," they are entertaining, regardless of the question of whether mere verisimilitude provides their raison d'etre. White has put into practice the advice of one of his characters: "Fiction is basically about people" (*Rocket,* 51). And the novels can be reread for their characters and literary wit as well as for their contributions to the locked-room genre. Like John Canaday's, William White's characters seem to step out of P. G. Wodehouse's England, and White's writing, while lapsing at times into soap-opera and lacking the vivid spark of Wodehouse's Mulliner tales, still transcends Canaday's ponderousness with a lighter freshness.

But the real charm here is in the delightful Sister Ursula, whose celestial wit steals into the earthy lives of her cocharacters with heaven-honed perspicacity. Of course her gifts have a strong earthly basis, explaining her talents in locating the convent's missing sacramental wine and exposing the slasher of Sister Perpetua's illuminated manuscript. As daughter of a police captain, she was heading into a career in law enforcement when a long convalescence deflected her into a religious order (*Nine*, 137). So she is not a woman easily frightened (*Nine*, 140). As might be expected of a woman once seeking a career with the police, she is not nonviolent, though she warns against needless violence (*Nine*, 142). Like Wisdom in Proverbs 9 she can be almost childlike, both delighted and delightful. Yet her mind sears unerringly, penetrating the entanglements of a locked-room puzzle like a knife through cord.

Her ministering experience along with her resolute trust in God give her a larger, wiser perspective on death than those of her fellow characters: "Death isn't so horrible after you've worked in a charity ward, Doctor. And besides, I'm so much more certain than you are that death is swallowed up in victory" (*Nine*, 75). Her theology also gives an acute ministerial reason for solving crime in the first novel: "I do not want what now seems a miracle of evil to go unsolved" (*Nine*, 138).

Evil in that first novel is strikingly contemporary, cultic evil. Although written in 1940, *Nine Times Nine* could have been written today. The title signifies a curse laid by a cult on its gadfly, rich investigator A. Wolfe Harrigan, whose campaign to expose religious rackets is in essence religious—a defense of the Catholic Church. He sees himself as "a lay crusader" "fighting heresy" (*Nine*, 34).

When Harrigan is slain in his locked study, the cult leader, a mystical yellow-robed character calling himself Ahasver, the wandering Jew, head of the Children of Light, takes credit. When another cult leader calling himself a Swami turns out to be Jewish, the novel appears for a time anti-Semitic, yet this appeal to prewar Nazi-inspired anti-Semitic consciousness is generally a ploy and is eventually fifty percent exploded.

Matt Duncan, the normal everyday protagonist with whom the author probably intended the reader to identify, finds himself out of his W.P.A. writing job and idly reflecting on his last assignment, covering services at the dedication of the new chapel of the Sisters of Martha of Bethany (*Nine*, 3). In a highly charged, theologically romantic mood he senses religious significance everywhere. As Matt reflects on his dismissal during spring when Christ's passion is celebrated, White constructs a parallel between Christ's passion and any individual human catastrophe. There is no pathetic fallacy. Nature can laugh in sun or cry in rain regardless of humans' feelings. He sees, for example, rain-glistening Los Angeles revealed in "gleaming miniature" and muses: "One thing I do understand in the Bible," he said, "is the temptation on the mountain. To see the kingdoms of the earth spread out before you. . . . That was before electricity, too. If Satan had had neon, he might have won" (*Nine*, 15). "Neon" is what the bogus cult does have. And the glittering iron pyrite of the "angel of light" temporarily deceives even Matt. As in all the clerical mysteries, appearances in this one are deceiving. Sister Ursula begins as a female counterpart to Father Brown, first appearing to Matt to be evil. Ahasver he finds initially attractive, while he accuses Sister Ursula of aiding a conspiracy to railroad a young girl Maria Monk-like into a convent. The foolish Matt soon discovers Ahasver's normal midwestern "ordinary, wholesome, salt-of-the-earth" (*Nine*, 47) congregation hissing out a deadly curse while to his embarrassment Sister Ursula has been talking the young woman *out* of religious life.

Both the nun and the prophet, after all, are difficult to discern in their religious garb, Ahasver bearded and robed in yellow, Ursula enveloped in her habit. But Ahasver's is the formlessness of evil while Sister Ursula's is the primal quality of generality that allows her to represent the archetypal category of the saintly wise woman. Deciphering this difference is what the novel is all about—the separation of true religion from the predatory bogus cults. Sister Ursula knows the difference, fleshing it out in her own actions. The determiner is coercion of choice and seduction rather than invitation to adherence and persuasion.

Thus, *Nine Times Nine* seems eerily contemporary to the current reader. Its strikingly methodical separation of true religious conversion from proselytized manipulation through the hermeneutic of coercion is a position to which the church is just returning. How did we lose this 1940s clarity? Where is the continuity of our historical gains? One wonders.

Nine Times Nine in its depicted cultic theology, too, substantiates the claims about originality made in Ecclesiastes:

> "That modern Christianity results from a conspiracy of Paul and Luke, who twisted the true facts of Christ's life to suit their own purposes. That the only true Gospel is the Gospel of Joseph of Arimathea, which Ahasver claims to have found in Tibet and himself translated from the ancient manuscripts. That Christ, Joseph of Arimathea, and Ahasver were all members of the ascetic Jewish order known as the Essenes. And that Ahasver's immortality—for he does lay literal claim to being the Wandering Jew—was imposed on him by Christ, not as a punishment, but so that he could carry the spark of truth on through all the ages when the false Christianity of Paul and Luke would be in the ascendant.
>
> "He asserts—and makes out a fair case for it—that Paul-Luke Christianity is in a bad way today. The time has come at last, after these nineteen centuries, for him to step forward and teach the truth. The old order is on the way out—
>
> > et antiquum documentum
> > novo cedat ritui,
>
> as we sing at Benediction. So Ahasver is giving people The Truth, and making a very good thing of it."
>
> "Sounds harmless enough," said Matt. (*Nine*, 42–43)

Compounded from a mix similar to *Holy Blood, Holy Grail*'s updated reserving of *The Passover Plot*'s rewarming of David Strauss' moldy nineteenth-century conspiracy theory with a sauce of camp black magic, curses, incantations, astral projection, the turkish taffies of sickeningly sweet but nutritionally thin cultic nourishment steam away before the spiritually hungry in Ahasver's syncretistic theological cafeteria. The mystical avatars preside in his pantheon of guiding deities, writing revelations before his eyes as mediumlike he preaches from an empty book.

Similar to Mr. Moon's shifting the conspiracy theory to encompass John the Baptist, Ahasver rediverts it through Paul to Luke. Prophetic of "New Age" syncretism, Ahasver receives a new scripture which is similarly "equal parts of Christianity and theosophy, with liberal dashes of Dale Carnegie and the Republican National Committee" (*Nine*, 49). It is fervently anticommunist. Add the *I Ching* and we have a kind of counterfeit Unification. Ahasver's syncretism unifies in the grand manner in his Nine ancients presidium of aeons: Jesus, Guatama, Confucius, Elijah, Daniel, Saint Germain, Joseph, Plato, Krishna (*Nine*, 51–52). His magic incorporates the theory so popularized by Robert Graves and others that Jesus spent time in ancient India or Egypt or Tibet, in Ahasver's case as an Essene ambassador, learning ancient secrets. So Gnosticlike, the hidden truths must be carefully revealed to the initiates. But the end result of Ahasver's mix is a "mystery of hate" (*Nine*, 52) with an ulterior (occult?) avaricious aim that stands in diametrical opposition to true religion. In magic the goal is to command the deity, in this case the ancients, by gaining the secret knowledge to exercise their power over them, in effect to say, "My will be done." In religion the goal is humble submission to the deity, "Thy will be done." The vertical difference in divine power direction dictates the horizontal difference in attitude toward converts. The initiate who seeks to enslave the deity does not pause at enslaving the converts. In magic initiation is secondary enslavement. As the deity is ultimately bound to the unlocking of the secrets of its power, so are the initiates bound to that power transferred to their wizard. In religion the leader has modeled surrender and the convert emulates. Elevation in honor healthfully counterbalances self-negation in humility. The deity becomes the central mediator, and the faithful become familial. Coercion, then, is the life's blood of the first. Submission is the heart of the second. And when these systems clash, deferment to the deity, the greater power, pits that greater power against the lesser human gnostic to the inevitable defeat of the latter. In this case Ursula as a conduit for the wisdom of God opens up a floodgate of perceptions to the baffled police. By the second book the police come begging to her for her insights. Sister Ursula is the celestial policewoman who ultimately brings the culprit before God's bar of justice in spiritual arrest. And before her, God's approved vehicle, the wise woman, both murderer and cult leader bow exposed and defeated. In her submission Sister Ursula triumphs.

Thus, God honors the wise woman whose obedience to God is self-commanded, and in God's magnanimous fashion the hand-maiden is exalted. Certainly, police detective Lieutenant Terence Marshall calls her blessed. If any seed of self destruction lies in the figure of Sister Ursula, it is in this very strength. Slowly her archetypal quality undermines her distinctive personality.

By the time of "Coffin Corner" (published in 1942 in Ellery Queen's *The Great Women Detectives and Criminals: The Female of the Species*) Ursula has become fully the archetype:

> But there was nothing astonishing in the appearance of Sister Mary Ursula, O.M.B., when she came into the patio to greet them. She seemed—no, not just like any other nun, but like the ideal of a nun such as you conceive but do not always find. Quiet, simple, human, with the unobtrusive but intense inner glow of the devotional life. ("Corner," 227)

And consequently she passes from Sherlock fully to Mycroft Holmes, simply receiving visitors in the abbey, hearing their stories, exhibiting a flash of vestigial elfishness, and delivering the truth. Still, Ursula's gift to see sense in apparent senselessness is what remains.

8

Soeur Angèle: Defender of the Innocent

Saint Vincent de Paul (ca. 1581–1660) accomplished much in his long life. Cleric to kings and queens, this Gascony-born son of peasants survived capture and enslavement by Turkish pirates to found numerous mission works among the French poor, a vast ministry that took him all over France to care for galley slaves, to establish the Congregation of Priests of the Mission (Vincentians) whose instructions to clerics and those preparing for ordination have often been credited as the beginnings of the modern theological seminary, and in 1634 to establish what was to become the Sisters of Charity, an order of women dedicated to serving the poor. This last order provided the impetus in the mid-1950s for French novelist Henri Dupuy-Mazuel under the pseudonym Henri Catalan to create the Sister of Charity *par excellence* Doctor Angèle Persent d'Ericy, graduate of the Medical Faculty at Paris, late intern at Baudelocque, winner of the Honorable Mention by the Academy of Medicine for her doctoral dissertation on the origin of mental deficiency in children, and renowned clerical detective for her work in such illustrious cases as that of *The Embarrassed Ladies* (1955), the singular affair of *The Ghosts of Chambord* (1956), and the preternaturally tinged case of *The Bell Ringer's Niece* (1957).

Sister of Charity Soeur Angèle involved herself in these sordid affairs—and among clerical crime novels the activities of those she encounters are among the most complexly immoral—with the purely Vincentian goal of saving the innocent. For her that goal becomes nearly a compulsion. Though she begins with anonymity in the first chapter of each book, reminiscent of her two predecessors Sister Ursula and Father Brown, a brief bout with Sister Ursula's spiritual curse, pride, and an oversized umbrella like Father Brown's, her single-minded goal to serve the innocent soon distances her from both. Like Father Brown (and later occasionally Father Dowling) she is more than ready to allow a murderer to escape if that murderer has come before the bar of God's justice, but unlike even Father Brown, if she can free the innocent by *not* discovering the murderer, she will willingly do so. She has no interest in usurping the place of the police, but solely in securing the safety of the innocent:

> "You'll tell Superintendent Fortin?"
>
> "That Juliette is innocent, yes. It is not my business to catch murderers, my sole interest is in the protection of the innocent. As it happens I cannot clear Juliette without making it obvious who the murderer is. But I must clear her." (*Ghosts*, 161)

So dedicated is she to this mission that at times even an agnostic police superintendent must remind her that there is more to a full theology than love and mercy:

> "I'll be praying for him."
>
> "Praying? For that little swine?"
>
> "The worse he is, the more he needs it. I'll pray for his poor soul. St. Therese's prayers won grace for Pranzini, who was a far more hardened sinner."
>
> "Have it your own way, Sister. But I'm glad juries are not composed of Sisters of Charity. There'd be an end of justice. And I seem to remember in my catechism that God isn't only merciful, He's just, too."
>
> "You quoted that before. . . . But it doesn't mean what you think. God's justice and men's have a different measure." (*Ghosts*, 186)

Perhaps Soeur Angèle emphasizes God's mercy to what might seem excess because of her point of reference. With the incredibly depraved people she encounters in her series, how could one emphasize justice? What would they do?

In the first book, originally entitled "Le Cas de Soeur Angèle" and rendered into English as *Soeur Angèle and the Embarrassed Ladies,* those ladies are embarrassed by the affair each has had with Angèle's own roguish cousin the Baron d'Orchais. When the baron is bludgeoned in his boudoir, codiscoverer of the body Soeur Angèle just has time to pocket the piles of photographs and billets-doux before the police arrive. Her intention is to visit each of the baron's paramours in turn and return these damaging letters, but to her surprise only a few of the correspondents appreciate her efforts. Some simply do not care; some wish she had left the compromising letters in place for the welcome scandalous publicity. When the baron's valet and his cousin, a maid, are arrested, Soeur Angèle must find the murderer to exonerate them, but so tangled have the machinations of her dead cousin been that when she does find the murderer, she identifies that culprit as one of the "innocent victims" and allows the guilty one to escape across the border before informing the police. This is an act worthy of Father Brown, but in Soeur Angèle's world, where immorality has become so prevalent that it has dulled people into amorality, it is difficult to tell who is the culprit and who is the victim. In this case Soeur Angèle believes that the murder victim is more the culprit than the murderer.

Needless to say the police are far from happy with the results. What has become of Saint Thomas' respect for civil law as an extension of God's law? But when they attempt to remonstrate against Soeur Angèle's unorthodox interpretations, they are in for an unpleasant surprise, for she sees such a flaunting of human convention as her mission:

> "You may get out of it this time without any serious consequences. Only don't do it again."
> "But," said Soeur Angèle, "I *might* do it again, you know. . . .
> "Yes, I might easily do it again. Charity, monsieur, knows no limits. St. Paul says that if you have all the other virtues but have not charity you have nothing. And charity shows itself everywhere and in all sorts of forms. Charity is not simply a matter of relieving the body's suffering, it must be ready also to relieve moral suffering and heal the wounds of the soul. You see, I'm a daughter of Charity. Our founder St. Vincent de Paul was Chaplain to galley slaves. . . . St. Vincent helped the convicts with all the resources of his intelligence, which was remarkable, and of his heart. There were no limits to the trouble he took and the risks he took to get the innocent released. Do you imagine that he never broke any regulations? And justice was not the loser but the gainer. Well, gentlemen, I am one of his sisters." (*Ladies*, 141–42)

Though the results may be the same, surely there is a hermeneutic other than St. Thomas' operating here.

So adept is Soeur Angèle at serving her innocents by ferreting out guilt and so consistent is her method with the program outlined above that by the third book one policeman is warning another: "'This promises to be quite a case. . . . But you've got Soeur Angèle,' he added mischievously. The superintendent looked gloomy. 'And keep your eye out for the Corinthians.' 'Corinthians?' 'Yes—the first epistle, thirteenth chapter'" (*Niece*, 36). However, the same charity she turns to victims and criminals she turns toward the police. To her crusty old instructor in legal medicine Professor Robin she allows: "'Oh I know you like to call yourself an unbeliever,' said Soeur Angèle tranquilly. 'But deep down you love God, I'm quite certain of it'" (*Ladies*, 18).

And in the same way she turns that charity of faith to the participants, she turns the clarity of faith to the detection itself:

> "Thank you, Inspector, and in return I'll pray for you."
> "Thank *you*, Sister, but I prefer proofs."
> "Quite so. I'll pray for proofs." (*Ladies*, 25)

In fact, all her dealings are marked by the certitude that her faith is an effective factor. As she observes to the secular authorities with whom she works, "I've been mixed up in this affair by what you call chance and I call Providence" (*Ladies*, 24), and for Soeur Angèle Providence is an inexhaustible and intrinsic resource for her detecting method, which she simply describes as, "I studied the affair, thought about it endlessly, and prayed a lot" (*Ladies*, 124).

There is one more factor Soeur Angèle needs to add to this checklist. More than many other clerical detectives, she works through intuition. We are continually told she has "the strongest feeling" (*Ladies*, 48), or "she could not shake off the feeling that somewhere in the house the key to the problem was to be found" (*Niece*, 129). And like all the clerical detectives she does not trust appearances: " 'I don't believe things are as simple as you seem to think. Don't forget that often the innocent seem to be the most guilty!' " (*Ghosts*, 52). Thus, departing from the Poe/Conan Doyle Anglo-American legacy of calculating scientific detection, Soeur Angèle's stories, like Maurice LeBlanc's Arsène Lupin tales, are more intuitive and emotionally oriented, more psychological perhaps, though they still contain detection.

Further, in contrast to most of the clerical sleuths, who follow in Father Brown's jaded train that the clergy above all people know the abysmal depths of the human heart, these novels' view is that Soeur Angèle is somehow protected and childlike and her mentor Professor Robin is the one who has "seen far more of the realities of life, especially in the seamier side" (*Ladies*, 30). She is continually shocked by revelations about the lives of others. Thus, when we are told, "But in the old days you smoked like a chimney" (*Ladies*, 102), and " 'You probably didn't know,' said the nun, 'that I was supposed to have the steadiest head in Baudelocque' " (*Ghosts*, 36), a place that knows no limit of decency (*Niece*, 161), and further that this hard-drinking, chain-smoking survivor of a worldly environment is shocked by people's sexual peccadillos, we have cause to wonder. We also wonder when we are told that this doctor, who currently serves an orphanage of one hundred and eighty-two children in the Near East (*Ladies*, 70) and presumably has seen many children die, reacts to the quiet death of one:

> In the nun's heart there was sudden rebellion: it was too unjust, too cruel: where was the infinite goodness of God? It was the first time since she became a nun that her faith had been clouded by a doubt. Then she began to recall the things she had seen these last two days, and bowed her head in acceptance. (*Ladies*, 84)

Dupuy-Mazuel cannot have it both ways. Either she is the resident doctor of an orphanage in Bethlehem whose ability to smoke like an expectant father and drink like a derelict suggests a streetwise past, or she is a young sheltered innocent whose presence makes an onlooker draw a comparison between nuns and children (*Ladies*, 70), and who in league with Professor Robin carries on her children's crusade on behalf of God's innocents.

Unique to the Roman Catholic clerical crime novel is the hostility and disrespect to which priests and nuns are subjected in the Soeur Angèle tales. As in the Don Camillo stories, local politicians such as the mayor in *The Bell Ringer's Niece* tend to be hostile free-thinkers. The mayor is even so gauche as to suggest Soeur Angèle may herself be involved in the murder. His sneering evaluation of religion is:

The bell ringer was a simple-minded poor devil. He swallowed all that religious rubbish. But his brother is an intelligent man. He sees through the whole business. He has no time for priests and nuns and all their flummery. You observe that none of it was able to save the poor old wretch from being murdered—and in what they call the house of God. Can you beat that? (*Niece*, 16)

Recalling the Sebastian series, religion in general or Soeur Angèle in particular is often brusquely insulted, jostled aside, caricatured by a nun's cornette being placed on a goose christened with her name, or called bloodthirsty for probing through a crowd to aid one injured (*Ladies*, 72).

In view of such ridicule, she needs multiple resources to function in an environment like the France reflected in the books, replete with so many hostile to the Church, a France where proximity to the scene of a crime or circumstantial evidence is enough to justify arrest, and a France where the general valuing of humanity is presented as low:

"But don't forget that this village, like every other village in the country, is one mass of rumours and rancours and old hatreds. It looks so serene, with its fields lying under the open sky. But I'll bet there are plenty of people here who will seize on this crime as a heaven-sent chance to dig a knife into a neighbour's back." (*Niece*, 44)

Among her resources Soeur Angèle counts her ability to knock out a man with one blow of her umbrella (*Ladies*, 31), and to command a whole pantheon of saints to pray to, including St. Mary Margaret, for guidance (*Ladies*, 28) and particularly Our Lady, Mary Queen of Heaven. Though she speaks of Providence (*Ladies*, 40), her real devotion seems to be to Mary, as evident in *The Bell Ringer's Nice*. In a comic moment a boy responds to her catechizing that God the Father is Creator and that Baby Jesus gives us

"Toys for Christmas. He gives them to good children."
"He does indeed. He gave you some?"
"Lots and lots."
"Good. And the third Person, the Holy Ghost, what is He?"
The boy stayed silent, then cried triumphantly, "He's a pigeon." (*Ladies*, 60)

One wonders if the people's theology ever climbs above this level.

Certainly that question is central to *The Bell Ringer's Niece*. Immediately after the murder of a poor bell ringer, the deceased's niece reports an appearance of the Virgin Mary. The faithful flock in from everywhere, property values zoom upwards, and strangely there are but two hold-outs. " 'It seems crazy to me,' said the photographer. 'Everybody in the village believes that our Lady appeared, except the priest and the nun!' " (*Niece*, 55). Soeur Angèle, now Mother Superior of a hospice for the elderly, her enormous slate-grey umbrella of the first book (*Ladies*, 3) converted to a slate-blue umbrella (*Niece*, 9), comes under fire for her skepticism from the populace. The conflict is a continuous one in the Roman Catholic Church. As recently as September 19, 1985, according to a news story in *U.S.A. Today*, worshippers at Chicago's St. John of God Catholic Church insisted that their statue of the Virgin Mary "wept real tears" in May of 1984. Crowds of up to 6,000 visitors a day have since flocked to the statue. As one woman explains, "I've come three times. . . . Not only has she cried here but elsewhere. She's cried for us because we have sinned. She's crying for Chicago." The lone hold-out? The Archdiocese of Chicago after a year-long investigation concluded there is "no evidence" to substantiate parishioners' claims. According to *U.S.A. Today*, "church officials don't accept their miracle" ("Church," 3A). Out of this kind of holy skepticism has come Angèle's faith.

When she looks for wisdom she follows this sage advice, "When you have a really serious problem of conscience, go for advice to the humblest priest you know. The simplest souls are the purest and therefore the nearest to God. It is the rule I follow myself and it has never failed me" (*Ghosts*, 72–73). Thus, she consults simple country priests and keeps her resolve while others doubt her.

In *The Bell Ringer's Niece* we have the best puzzle of the three books and correspondingly the best writing of the series. Truncation has been the greatest failing plaguing the series, as indicated by Dupuy-Mazuel's waste of the promises of drama inherent in Soeur Angèle's conflict with the Church over the extent of her vocation as detective. One does not expect a multivolume conflict as in the Rabbi Small series, but a mere thirteen pages of chapter 6 is hardly enough to do the theme justice. There have been snatches of good writing, such as the neat connecting up of the quoted "pigeon" catechism on page 60 of *Ladies* with the visual vignette thirty pages later, "Two white pigeons flew low over the nuns, and their white wings seemed to mingle with the white cornettes" (*Ladies*, 90), or the flapping of bird's wings to help remind Soeur Angèle of the presence of the Spirit and ease the child's death (*Ladies*, 84). And again, though rare, there have been artful turns of phrase such as this one from *Ghosts:* "The loud-speakers magnified and multiplied announcements of every degree of dullness" (*Ghosts*, 151). But despite their humor, the first two books seem only minor achievements.

In *The Bell Ringer's Niece*, the puzzles, the characters' interaction and the writing seem to have finally congealed into a thoroughly exciting and finally harrowing mystery. Here the amorality of the characters goes beyond simply the sexual indiscretions of the first two books, which have led to a cheapening attitude toward the value of human life and thus to murder. Now the sexually indiscreet are among the victims, for the evil are so depraved that they would exploit sacred religion and even sacrifice the sanity of their own children for gain. Murder is but a thoughtless removal of an obstacle, and against this kind of depth of depravity that knows no faith, no restraints of parental love, no compunction to stop the sacrifice of the innocent, Soeur Angèle's perspicacious goodness shines forth like a votive candle. Christian charity has been ironically called her hobby (*Ghosts*, 94), but in her reluctance to accept even the miraculous if humans are not fully beneficially served we see the depth of her calling.

To her predecessor Sister Ursula a similar remark was once directed, "'You missed your vocation,' he said with a touch of irony. 'What a detective you'd have made'" (*Ladies*, 124). But Soeur Angèle, defender of the innocent in the footprints of St. Vincent de Paul, has not missed her calling. She serves the poor, the prisoner, as St. Vincent did the galley slaves. If that service dictates she solve crimes, then solve them she does, no matter how much her style may dismay or outrage the professionals of the field, for, as the clerical detectives continually assure us, nothing is as it seems, even the apparent capabilities of these seemingly benign and ineffectual detecting clerics themselves. So her exploits let her answer the most mocking queries with shocking strength:

> "Okay. Tell me where you've go to. You've pursued inquiries, no doubt interrogated masses of witnesses, interviewed your highly virtuous ladies, made brilliant deductions, fooled the police, redressed the scales of justice, and discovered the murderer all by yourself."
>
> "Yes," said the nun calmly, "that's exactly what I've done." (*Ladies*, 131–32)

9

What Is Duty?
Margaret Ann Hubbard's Sister Simon

Why with so many women writing the ministerial mystery are not more feminine clerical detectives created by women? Margaret Scherf, Ellis Peters, and Barbara Ninde Byfield all created male clerical sleuths. Matthew Head, H. H. Holmes, Henri Catalan all created female clerical sleuths. Few women until the recent authors Dorothy Gilman, Isabelle Holland, and Sister Carol Anne O'Marie created female clerical detectives. But an exception and anticipator of the current trend is Margaret Ann Hubbard, whose trailblazing mysteries featured women and murder.

Beginning in 1950 Hubbard introduced the first of her tight, swiftly paced theological mysteries. Built, as are all her succeeding mysteries, on the theme "be sure your sin will find you out," it featured a past adultery whose lethal hand reached into a quiet New Orleans women's college and began picking off students. Helping the police solve these crimes were a succession of wise nuns, serving as saintly sidekicks. This saintly sidekick pattern held through three mysteries over the sixteen years from *Murder Takes the Veil* (1950) to *Murder at St. Dennis* (1952) through her last book, *Step Softly on My Grave* (1966). All of these active nuns attempted, with varying degrees of success, to aid potential victims, reprimand apprehended culprits, and indulge in a bit of detecting.

But if Margaret Ann Hubbard's participating nuns are strikingly reminiscent of Vicar Whitechurch's meddling clerics, she does have one Vicar Westerham in these excellent action-packed gothic mysteries. Sister Mary Simon is a "young" and "pretty" (*Case*, 24), white-garbed (*Case*, 182) hospital supervisor with a "peckishly strict" attitude who is a "peevish disciplinarian" because she is "very little older than the students" (*Case*, 24). Overworked by sixteen-hour days, she is normally fatigued. She cannot remember the last time she had recreation (*Case*, 89). Bending wearily over her desk at the hospital (*Case*, 24), bent on saving the world or at least her patients, she is on a collision course with a nervous breakdown. But murder intervenes. Severe, feeling "the burden of her youth and inexperience," she becomes an example of the fulfillment of proleptic guilt, a performatory utterance when she begins the tale by refusing to pass on a desperate telephone message to someone she supervises (*Case,* 24). Her perfunctory adherence to the rules becomes a manifest contradiction when that adherence to the very rules that are made to preserve life allows the caller to lose life. Stalked by a killer, the fugitive makes one frantic telephone call which is imperiously blocked by the harried Sister Simon. Challenged with her part in the catastrophe, the nun flings up her hasty barriers of defense and denial. She holds up her code of duty. Sister Simon is so brittle she needs to change. And she will have her opportunity in this powerful and delightful tale.

In *Sister Simon's Murder Case,* as in them all, a past crime produces present murder, so the past evil tradition has to be ended, the murder solved and laid to rest, in order to insure continuing life. But in addition to this regular feature, we find now that even good traditions from the past in the form of convent rules have come to straightjacket those living in the present until even these traditional rules have to be somewhat altered.

Thus, Sister Simon's clerical sleuth's tale is like Westerham's—a tale of beginnings. Like Westerham, Hubbard's clerical sleuth is no seasoned professional, but is, of course, fraught with potential. Her very weakness comes from her devotion to God and others. She loves children. She is "never in the least confused as to her religious vocation." But "she had allowed the human irritations of supervising to beat her down" (*Case,* 25). Perhaps, one could argue, this pre-Vatican II stringent enforcement of ecclesiastical rules and the dehumanizing pain it inflicts provide the reasons why later writers like Andrew M. Greeley allow adherents of their religion to break the rules blithely. Like Margaret Hubbard, they see the strict rules of traditional Catholicism as too restrictive to allow living. To her very colleagues, "that nun thinks being a supervisor is saying no all the time" (*Case,* 30). When Simon staggers under this burden of rules, her underlings reprimand her roundly. One of them realizes, "'She had said a lot of things to the nun. Too many. But Sisters were human. If they made human mistakes, why shouldn't they bear the consequences?'" (*Case,* 36). They jeeringly call her "Sister Simon, the immaculate" (*Case,* 39). So driven is she that she continually dashes from place to place in an habitual haste that sends her stiff skirts clattering (*Case,* 133), a haste that rides her, except when she is trying to avoid "the things that were waiting for her to think about" (*Case,* 43–44): whether her enforcement of the rules has permitted someone to die. Still, she justifies her actions continuously, blaming others for her failure: "The woman had no business being where she was at such an hour with such a request. I couldn't foresee what would happen! I have to keep order" (*Case,* 44). But deep inside she feels the urge to cry when treated kindly and she flees to the safety of her convent and her thirty house sisters (*Case,* 126). Under her toughness lies pain. Like Sister Ursula, she is the daughter of a policeman. But unlike either Ursula's father or Claire Aldington's district attorney father, Simon's died in duty:

> Her father had been killed by a murderer he and another policeman were trying to apprehend, and she had promised herself then and there that she would become a detective and avenge all murders. At thirteen, there had been nothing impossible about that. Her father had taught her to shoot "from the hip," that is, without using the sights. She could hit a moving target at fifty feet with a pistol—a skill you seldom needed in the convent. (*Case,* 60–61)

The frame of that memory lies around her vocation. That skill bequeathed sleeps in the person she was, lying dormant in the woman who has become Sister Simon. But what is her duty? As the tale commences, she believes it is strict adherence to the rules of her order, to the rules of the hospital. She appeals to St. Augustine's dictates:

> Lizette, I was reading St. Augustine tonight. About duty. He says, "In doing what we ought we deserve no praise, because it is our duty." And the reverse is also true. In doing what we ought we deserve no blame. (*Case,* 108–9)

Yet, she is full of self-reproach. She is beset by a lingering sense of guilt (*Case,* 134). She lasts as long as she does because she has a great capacity to rationalize St. Augustine's and the convent's rules. When she grows up, she will be a Sister Mary Teresa, adept at the art of reinterpretation:

> St. Augustine, it seemed, had the answer. She had read it this evening. "Let the superior be obeyed like a mother, with all due honor, so that you offend not God through offending her." But how could Mother be offended through a short friendly conversation she would never hear about? (*Case,* 111)

Further, she will lie to comfort an old nun (*Case,* 163), absolving the elderly sister from an omission similar to hers. But her argument will not serve for herself. Still blamed by herself and those she supervises, in desperate straits, ridden by guilt of that adherence to duty which caused her to ignore the plea for help of a woman in mortal danger, she reaches finally to desperate measures to save at least one of the witnesses' lives.

In the spirit of her reckless poker-playing peers and mother superior, Sister Simon concocts a bold plan to flush out the killer. Unfortunately her student confederates ruin it by impetuous action. With so many characters in this novel doing amateur detecting, and with Sister Simon's incredibly busy schedule, she almost does not have time to solve the crime. Thus, this is nearly not a clerical crime novel. Simon only steps in as the tale progresses, when persistent guilt will not let her alone. With so many others doing the spade work, the novel makes it into the subgenre by the barest margin. As it is, Sister Simon, like Claire Aldington, overhears a pertinent bit of information about an unusual talent that suddenly tells her who the killer is. Without that information, her plan would have simply been a general play at flushing out the predator by use of a decoy goat, hoping the hidden hunting party of police can bag the killer before the killer silences another witness. Further, if anything else in the story is implausible, it is the incredibly flimsy reason given for a stupid action by an otherwise intelligent character that precipitates the ending. But desperately guilt-ridden people do commit incredibly thoughtless actions—though this one stretches one's willing suspension of disbelief (*Case,* 160–61). So Sister Simon must respond equally outrageously. And she does:

> Sister Simon was amazed at herself, really. When she took the veil she had put off her identity as a policeman's daughter. Mother Richard would never approve. St. Augustine might get a kick out of it, but not Mother. (*Case,* 156)

Yet, she has to act when the rules give out:

> There was no rule, no precedent to cover the situation of a soggy nun stranded on a street curb while, two miles away, a murderer made away with a victim she had delivered, although unwittingly, into his hands. (*Case,* 173)

So, desperately praying directly to the "Lord" (*Case,* 154), no "middle-man" saints for her busy schedule, she races through the rain to apprehend the killer. The police are too slow for her. Descriptions of movement provide some of the finest moments in this novel. Not a witty writer like Margaret Scherf or a plush one like Ellis Peters, Margaret Ann Hubbard is primarily an action writer, and she does particularly well with movement. Her description of a freight elevator, for example, has a sliding, sibilant sound, "The second floor slid down from above and slipped away below" (*Case,* 34). The narrative takes it in one continuous movement. Sister Simon, too, is purely a woman of action. Her theology is a bit sketchy. Her view of life is stripped down to the barest essentials:

> The only answer I can give you, Lizette, is that we aren't in a position to judge the fairness of life. There's an old story, you must have heard it, about a man who stood watching a nun scrubbing a floor, and he said, "Sister, I wouldn't lead your kind of life for a million dollars." And she smiled and said, "Neither would I." The purpose is what counts, you see. (*Case,* 131–32)

In this light she does not foist her own sixteen-hour days on others. In this she really does portray an authentic representation of a hard worker. With similar authenticity, she does not prescribe asceticism for others. To one who complains her life is too blessed compared to others, Simon replies sensibly, "Much more will be expected of you. So take your happiness and be thankful for it" (*Case*, 132). Of course, when she supervises her charges on the floor, she works them hard in the line of duty. But when their time is over, she lets them go. Culminating her own life of action, she slugs the murderer and holds him and an accomplice at bay at gunpoint in a pure action ending—no sitting around for eight pages of explanation for Margaret Hubbard. The story hits climax and finishes in a matter of a few racing paragraphs. If Dorothy Gilman's nuns are not nonviolent, what of Sister Simon? A crack shot, she warns, " 'If you move, either one, I'll shoot the two of you' " (*Case*, 181). And "she would indeed shoot him without the slightest hesitation" (*Case*, 181).

What has happened here simply is that Sister Simon has changed the rules. She has resalvaged skills supposedly left out of the convent when she traded her old life and her old identity for her new one. Like Sister Joseph, who can fan shuffle a poker hand, Simon has entertained her colleagues with some sharp shooting at the last nurses' picnic (*Case*, 61). But the skills of a former life must be more than anomalies, remnants that somehow slipped in through the convent door. These are skills that were developed for survival on the outside. The problem is that these nuns do not live cloistered. They work outside the convent. Therefore, the conflict and its resolution reveal that convent rules are inapplicable in the real world or in real ministry to the world on the outside. If she is going to rescue victims and uphold justice, she will need to resummon the skills her detective father bequeathed her: a love of justice, a steady nerve, a firm hand, courage, and a deadly aim. Without these, the victim she sought to save and probably Sister Simon herself would end the book dead. They might be seen as martyrs but more likely simply as victims. If she wants to stay a ministering servant, she had better be prepared to shoot. Had Sister Simon lived in Detroit, *The Rosary Murders* of twenty years later might never have piled up as many bodies as they did. "Assailant Shot by Nun," the headline might have blared. If they could only have gotten her attention and she could only have scheduled it in, she might have snuffed out that case as readily as she did this one once she turned her attention to it.

What, then, does *Sister Simon's Murder Case* illustrate? The picture will be expanded, probably far beyond Margaret Ann Hubbard's taste, in Andrew M. Greeley. But the outline is here. Duty is more than dead convent rules. Further, if one is going to serve real people with real life and death problems, a champion of God might have to fight physically to wrest victims away from Satanic predators. The world does not play by the convent's Queensbury rules. The true minister has to be true to the gospel of comfort, while armed with justice's big stick.

10

Leonard Holton's Father Bredder:
The Priest That Roared

*Now I'm not fond of bashing people around or shooting them,
and casual sex I disagree with. On the other hand I have no great
talent for the threads of detail which form the smooth and satisfactory web of the detective story as written by women writers.
It occurred to me then that I had to devise a nonfussy and nonviolent sort of detective—a detective with an entirely different personality and motivation from the usual private eye; although on
reflection few of them are usual. This decided me that if I made
my detective a priest I could give my stories a background and
quality others lacked—a spiritual quality. I reasoned that from
the point of view of a priest, a crime is not merely an offense
against the laws of Man. It is (infinitely more important) an
offense against the laws of God. "Thou shalt not Kill," "Thou
shalt not Steal" are not, after all, reckoned man-made laws in
their origin. When a criminal is caught and brought to justice,
nothing at all has been achieved from the priestly point of view
unless the offender acknowledges his offense against his Creator
and repents it. Indeed, if the crime is murder and the culprit is
executed unrepentant, he faces a sentence of eternal damnation.*
Leonard Patrick O'Connor Wibberley

The above writer is author of, among dozens of books, the contemporary classic
novel *The Mouse That Roared*. In that famous novel and each of its successors,
which feature the plucky success of the tiny neomedieval Duchy of Grand
Fenwick as it muscles out a place among the superpowers of the world, Wibberley championed the small and weak against the prominent and mighty.

In the Father Bredder mystery tales he attempts the same goal, raising a
meek Father Brownish cleric up from the supposedly slumbering irrelevancy of

a local parish convent chaplaincy to astound the police with his uncanny ability to track elusive murderers across the complex spiritual landscape of fraud, dissemblance, and self-deception to the lair of the guilty soul. Leonard Wibberley himself fervently denies the resemblance to Chesterton's archetypal transfer of the Daniel of *Susannah* to the cleric of the twentieth century:

> Now when an author devises a detective series with a priest as a hero, it is immediately assumed that his inspiration was Chesterton's Father Brown. Although I had certainly read a couple of the Father Brown stories, I wasn't particularly struck by them. Chesterton spent much of his life battling the Dragon Paradox, and Father Brown isn't, in my view, so much of a priest as he is a Paradox tamer. I'm not an expert on him, but I was never particularly struck by his spiritual depth. I don't recall him ever visiting, as a priest, the inmates of seamy flophouse hotels, or trying to explain to children the mystery of the Christian Trinity. Father Bredder does all that appertains to the priesthood while examining bodies and diving on sunken barges for evidence which a "spiritual fingerprint" has suggested should be there. There is not in all this a whit of criticism of the classic Father Brown. I merely hope to point out that Father Bredder isn't in the slightest degree related to Father Brown. I don't suppose I will succeed. (Penzler, 29)

Wibberley's hope is partially achieved. We have seen the dismal task involved in trying to reconcile Brown's itinerancy, his excessive freedom to go gallivanting off after mysteries. At times he does hurry back to duties at a deaf school or arrive to give the last rites, yet his complete absence of accountability to a superior is hard to reconcile with any form of the Roman Catholic priesthood with which we are familiar. Brown, after all, is a shadowy character to nail down precisely because in his all-engulfing flexibility he does represent all priests in all places. Yet Wibberley might "protest a bit too much." To disregard the constant ministry Brown enjoys with the lowest classes and to make his cleric the precise inverse of Brown in stature, large where Brown is small, begs the comparison. And in comparison we note they share the same essential meekness, Father Brown's celebrated childlike innocence. They also share a method that takes into account the spiritual over the scientific, though Bredder is not as belligerent as Brown is in this respect. Even in regard to the taming of paradoxes, the first tale flings Bredder against enigmas that threaten to be paradoxes. "How can a devil doing evil do a great good?" is the riddle the murderer poses. "How can one who honors John the Baptist commit a murder similar to John's—a beheading?" questions the priest. If Leonard Wibberley has followed Chesterton in anything in his opening tale, he has followed him in resolving enigmas that border on paradox. Yet Holton is right in wishing to separate his creation from Father Brown.

Father Joseph Bredder, O.F.M., is neither simple copy nor simple inverse of Father Brown. He is a unique creation, one of the most consciously devotional and theological of the clerical sleuths, and his approach to the grace of the sacrament of mystery solving originates in his theological outlook. For him finding the murderer is a holy task, the highest calling of a priest:

> Murder is a crime which cries, not merely for vengeance, but far more important, it cries for repentance. And I must do what I can in any way I can to find the murderer and bring him or her to repentance for the salvation of his soul. . . . In that this crime is a mortal offense in the eyes of God, it is a matter for all Christians, and especially for a priest. I am not concerned with the trial and execution of the murderer, which concerns the lay authorities. I am concerned only with the salvation of his soul. That is a charge upon me which I cannot ignore. (*Saint Maker*, 71–72).

> Man might execute the murderer, but forgiveness lay with God. And forgiveness was all important, for without forgiveness the punishment was eternal damnation. He, Father Bredder, must try to avert that infinitely more awful sentence being passed on the murderer. It was a charge upon him, a grievously heavy duty, which he must perform. (*Saint Maker*, 27)

And Father Bredder is well equipped to handle that duty. As an ex-Marine sergeant decorated by three countries (*Secret*, 5), he cites his traumatic war-time experiences killing "terrified men who had been brought up pagans and did not know what they were doing" as the "why and when and how he had decided to become a priest" (*Saint Maker*, 102).

Now he is in another kind of war. Like little Grand Fenwick, the minuscule bantam rooster in the barnyard politics of international competition, Father Bredder, too, must claw away at a power that dwarfs him in its sinister potency. He recognizes that his has become a war against no enemy less than the Great Monster. He is Walter Wangerin, Jr.'s Chanticleer to the Worm Ouroboros, St. George to the Great Dragon, Frodo against the Dark Lord of Mordor. And each of these images is only a pale reflection of the final enemy he has drawn:

> Satan was abroad in the mean and cluttered streets of his parish, and what he was engaged in now was not the solution of a murder, but the combat to which he had devoted his life as a priest—the combat against the forces of darkness which he was sure spoke through the blasphemous note he held in his hand. (*Saint Maker*, 120)

The police recognize his task as well:

> For a moment Lieutenant Minardi reflected on good and evil, the two great forces which contend with the world as a battleground and the population of the world as the prize involved in the fray. For the first time he saw the priest in a strange light—a sort of policeman, a policeman of God, and the thought astonished him with its aptness. The criminal code and the code of God; he, Minardi, operated from one and the priest from the other, and both worked to the same end, the prevention of evil, though in the case of the priest the fate of a human soul was at stake. He, the policeman, was concerned only with life and property. (*Saint Maker*, 136–37)

If Septimus has left the force to become an "ex-copper" upon joining the Anglican priesthood, ex-Marine Bredder has in effect joined the force upon becoming, in effect, a "celestial copper." And as God's policeman, he is a strange
warrior, an oddly matched David to take on the great Goliath, ex-Marine hero
that he is.

To his advantage, he is big, a six-foot-one-and-a-half (or two, according
to *Flowers by Request*), two-hundred-pound (*Saint Maker*, 3) strong man whose
feet hurt from supporting him (*Secret*, 81). With his thick black hair sheared
into a butch, his long legs (*Saint Maker*, 166), and his cheap rough-cut black
Carolina tobacco (*Saint Maker*, 155–56), he looks like an ex-prize fighter (*Saint
Maker*, 6, 7). As a matter of fact, he has been a Golden Glove boxing champion
and contender for the middleweight championship (*Jonah*, 29). At forty, big
and awkward, he is yet, despite appearances, generally free of the killer instinct
that makes champion boxers and warriors do what they do. Instead, he is
compassionate and easy-going. He speaks Spanish in his ministry (*Secret*, 110),
while he is a gentle giant bred in Twin Forks (near Toledo, according to *Wolves*,
4), Ohio, with a strong conservative instinct. Though poor, he is generous (*Saint
Maker*, 100). Guilt-ridden that he is not humble enough, burdened with a sensitive conscience (*Saint Maker*, 5), and diffident in his dealings with women,
"like an uncouth giant among so many dolls" of the convent (*Saint Maker*, 6),
he is thoroughly henpecked by his housekeeper, the mother superior of the
convent he pastors, and even by the girls attending the convent school.

Entering middle age, he is already at a dead end in a large squalid parish
(*Saint Maker*, 39), so poor in its living that when he travels he cannot afford a
hotel but must seek out a shabby room (*Saint Maker*, 119). Like television's
short-lived Father of Hell Town, he allows drunks to sleep in the pews of his
church, since "what they seek they will find in the church"—eternal rest (*Secret*,
83). He believes even "God the Father" "didn't quite approve of him" (*Saint
Maker*, 6). In all he allows himself to be bullied by those with whom he works,
for he is a "kindly man . . . and he inclined always to forgiveness" (*Saint
Maker*, 2). He is chronically misunderstood and his views are chronically rejected by his coworkers (*Secret*, 84). Yet even while they bully him, the nuns
around him recognize his strength. He is so big that one nun fantasizes that, if
there were another persecution, Bredder would either strengthen all of them to
accept martyrdom or perhaps drive the lions off (*Saint Maker*, 69–70). In this
one aspect he is determined and implacable: he is absolutely resolute in following his priestly duty as he sees it, whether it suits the expectations of others or
not. He turns the opinion of his bishop from questioning his involvement in
detection to support (*Saint Maker*, 107). He is equally resolute with the Mother
Superior and the parents of the convent girls whose complaints she conveys:

I'm sorry. I quite understand the position of these parents, though I don't agree with it. It's not a Christian position, but a position based on what is called "society." Sometimes I think these concepts of society or social prestige are contrary to true Christianity. We would all be better Christians if we did not have them. (*Saint Maker*, 71)

Far from being cowed into compliance by others, he is deeply disturbed by their complaints, by his parishioners' suspicion of wrongdoing, by the hate mail he has received:

All this evil mail provoked by the murder depressed Father Bredder, and it hurt him deeply that after nearly two thousand years of Christianity and Christian teaching, the minds of so many men and women should be so deeply steeped in evil and that the pleasant faces of people passed in the streets might be masks for the thoughts of witch doctors. (*Saint Maker*, 39)

In his human struggle with guilt and depression he fulfills the intentions that all clerical detective writers seem to hold for their creations—to show the clergy as human. As Bredder argues, "Priests are human, just like bus drivers. . . . We are consecrated to God, but we are not angels. Not even saints. Just humans" (*Saint Maker*, 17).

Out of Father Bredder's humanness comes his pity for both the victim and the murderer, for Cain fleeing from God. To Bredder the Church must always be vulnerably available to those who sin:

I feel that the doors of God's church should never be closed . . . I think about it this way. If a man must steal, it is because he is, or thinks he is, in desperate need of money, but has no way of getting it. Again, if a man steals in a church, he is stealing in the presence of God and will, even in the act of sin, be reminded that his Creator knows of his misdeed and so may repent it. (*Saint Maker*, 18)

Challenged, he returns, "'It isn't an old point of view,' said Father Bredder. 'It is a Christian point of view, and if it strikes you as odd, it is only because Christianity has become odd'" (*Saint Maker*, 18). Indeed, he injects that "odd" viewpoint into every contact he has in the novels, and he stops those he encounters, stalling them into reflection: "The other two looked at him as if remembering something important which they had forgotten in the press of business" (*Saint Maker*, 24). The roar of the mouse is startling. It astonishes and provokes reaction.

Father Bredder brings a unique communal view to Los Angeles, vintage 1959, a California before federal civil rights legislation had teeth, when "immigrant Orientals" were prohibited by state law from "owning property" (*Saint Maker*, 94), when decayed mansions of nineteenth-century entrepreneurs still stood shakily as rooming houses. His associates rival even Simon Templar's and Peter Wimsey's for their variety. He numbers among his exotic circle of friends a film star, a millionaire, a Buddhist priest, a Turkish World War I veteran, a prize fighter, a juvenile delinquent, and very shortly a homicide detective. When, like most of the clerical detectives, he is initially suspected himself of the murder (*Saint Maker*, 80–81), these friends peel off rolls of bills, ready to send him off to China, to Cuba, to Haiti. Far from being offended, Bredder is amused: "Father Bredder chuckled. His most loyal friends were sinners, and plainly they thought him a sinner like themselves" (*Saint Maker*, 91). Bredder is providentially blessed that he can chuckle. His humor will stand him in good stead since he will experience a repetition of suspicion that no other clerical detective will be forced to undergo. Unlike the others, Father Bredder will be resuspected of murder in the third book, *Secret of the Doubting Saint* (*Secret*, 121), the sixth, *Out of the Depths*, (*Depths*, 61), and even the eighth, *A Problem in Angels* (*Angels*, 64), a completely unprecedented repetition. He knows what it feels like to be hunted.

Gentle with others, he has a compassionate definition of sin:

> You must remember that primarily sin is a conscious matter, a willful disobedience of the commandments of God or the church, or a willful neglect of duties required by God. So I would say that since you did not intend to sin, then there is no question of sin involved. (*Saint Maker*, 58)

But sin is also by his statement secondarily an unconscious matter. He does recognize "sins of omission" (*Saint Maker*, 104), and this second category comes back to haunt him when a crazed murderer, who in a warped way intended no sin, feeds back all of Bredder's advice in twisted form (e.g., *Saint Maker*, 170).

In eerie parallel, the murderer and Bredder operate on the same principles with drastically different results. While the initial tale, *The Saint Maker*, is a rather fantastical murder mystery full of improbable events, it sets up a neat series of juxtaposed oppositions that set a continual zig-zag journey for the reader between faith and lunacy.

Following a fanciful notion that a ferocious depiction of the archangel Michael in the church's stained glass window is pointing at the statue of John the Baptist, we are taken into a tale where the severed head of John is contrasted with the severed head of deer and elks and bears, trophies of the hunt. When Bredder comes up with a severed head left in his church, he must discover how anonymous notes involving the beheading of John and the slaughter of the innocents in the biblical incarnation account explain this contemporary execution. To do that, he must confront the Devil, who has entered his church via an unknown parishioner, by employing a spiritual police procedure that will ferret out guilt, arrest the dupes of evil, and resecure his parish as a precinct station of the good. But the police procedure he must adopt is not the normal one. That fails him miserably, and he begins to question whether he is "going about the exposure of the Devil in the right way?" (*Saint Maker,* 120):

> Suddenly he realized he was not. He had confined his detective work to the methods of the laity, and that had crippled him in his approach. He had found a woman who had known Mrs. Marsh, though casually, and a fictitious address, and had come up against a dead end. That was because his approach was wrong. It was the approach of a policeman and not of a priest. It was the approach of someone who searched for a person and not for a soul. And his business was souls. (*Saint Maker,* 121)

So he turns to another Roman Catholic church for help, and there in the baptismal records he finds the information he needs, for no responsible Roman Catholic mother will lie on the christening forms for her baby!

Once Bredder has struck the proper approach for "a policeman of God" (*Saint Maker,* 136), "the spiritual approach," he proceeds by applying the hermeneutic of what seems to him to be spiritually right (*Saint Maker,* 137). Thus, when the police come up with a suspect, Bredder pauses to consider if that conclusion seems spiritually correct. In a sense he is searching for what Wibberley has called a "spiritual fingerprint" (Penzler, 29). Would that person, spiritually speaking, be likely to be the murderer? After eliminating two of the police's prime suspects, he himself discovers the "spiritually right" person (*Saint Maker,* 137), a crazed, faithful Roman Catholic. As will be repeated fifteen years later in Smith's *Reverend Randollph and the Wages of Sin,* the most apparently sanctified of parishioners, the most guilt-ridden and sin-obsessed (whether in this case obsessed with one's own sin as well as others' or, as in *Wages'* case, obsessed with the sin of others) commits the murder. No wonder Martin Buell is so skeptical of Christians in his series. No wonder Eco's Brother William ends up in doubt and possibly despair. The motives here, as in these other books, are twistedly spiritual. In *Wages* the killer desires to purge God's sanctuary of sinners, in this case to make saints out of sinners. *The Saint Maker'*s eerie theme can be found again in Flannery O'Connor's haunting short story "A Good Man Is Hard to Find," wherein a pathological killer places victims at the penultimate moment of their lives so they will experience their finest moment of self-authenticity and honesty. Likewise here, after taking victims to confession so they will be purged, the murderer sends them to heaven so that, shriven, they will become saints. The murderer is the "Saint Maker." As the crazed murderer explains about one of the victims, "'Still, I have prayed for him every night, and you yourself told me, Father, that prayers for the dead are never wasted.' The priest gave a look of agony" (*Saint Maker,* 170).

The agony of Minardi, the secular policeman, that we have seen throughout the tale has become the agony of the priest. As the policeman explains, "I'd sooner let the guilty escape than convict the innocent" (*Saint Maker,* 139). But

Bredder's agony is greater than this. He feels the agony of responsibility. He himself has fed the murderer the theology that has in its perversion precipitated the recent murder.

In the secular policeman's reflection on this deadly irony the point of this moral tale is made clearly and forcefully. In contrasting the two principals of the tale, Father Bredder the priest and the murderer, the police lieutenant recognizes that Bredder had found the love and grace of Christian theology, while the murderer had learned only its rules, having "attended to all the outward signs but lost the inward grace, and so had produced vice out of virtue" (*Saint Maker,* 179). One thinks of the same lesson that Father Bredder drew from the tale of the villainous Bible reader in "The Sign of the Broken Sword": "Minardi was no theologian, but he wondered how many people, sticking to the letter, turn good into evil and kill or main or hurt or persecute others in the name of good works" (*Saint Maker,* 179).

Thus, his quest for Satan ironically takes Father Bredder back to his own teaching. The work of Satan turns out to be a perversion of Bredder's own gospel! Horrified by it, he finds his eyes welling with bitter tears (*Saint Maker,* 180). And in his distress, the forceful "henpecking" women around him firmly guide him back to perspective. A "Sister Ursula," another wise woman, helps him out of his despair by criticizing it as "pride": "We mustn't judge the acceptability of our work in God's eyes. . . . All we can do is try. The assessment belongs to God. To try to judge ourselves is to usurp His position. It's pride" (*Saint Maker,* 181). The lesson is well taken. It is the requirement of the "watchman" in Ezekiel 33:1–9. The true minister is not responsible for results, only for delivering the message. This is a vital lesson every city minister must learn if he or she is to continue. To take responsibility for more is to usurp the place of the Lord of the Harvest. Comforted, Bredder survives to take on Satan for another set of rounds through ten more adventures, exploding such enigmas as the "Jonah Man" myth, the existence of werewolves, and vengeance by the dead.

Fantastic though some of these stories are, there is no denying that they contribute some of the most intriguing thoughts and one of the more attractive of the clerical sleuths. What impact have they had? According to their author, from the start their financial path was difficult. Despite the heritage of Father Brown, of Sister Ursula, of Whitechurch's clerics, of Soeur Angèle, despite such trailblazing predecessors, they had a dour reception:

> To backtrack a little: the first book was of course rejected by several publishers. Nobody understood it. It wasn't a simple murder story. It wasn't a beat-'em-up-and-love-'em story. The motive for the murder was queer, to say the least. And of course the rules of detective-story writing properly outlawed any trace of insanity on the part of the criminal.
>
> I happened to be in New York when the last rejection came in and my agent (who didn't

understand the book either) suggested I might have a chat with Ed Bond who was then in charge of detective fiction at Dodd, Mead. I had at this point rewritten the manuscript to play down the spiritual content of the book, following the well-known motto, so different from that M-G-M, Pecunia Gratia Artis. I explained to Mr. Bond what I had been trying to do—write a book in which the real crime was against God, not Man.

"Put that back into the manuscript," he said, "and I'll buy it." And he did. That was the first of ten Father Bredder stories published by Dodd, Mead.

Right now it would be nice to say that they swept the nation, but the fact is that they didn't even sweep half a block of Madison Avenue. Nobody had any explanation for this, for everybody at Dodd, Mead loved Father Bredder. I think it was based in the religious trauma that had seized the whole of the Western world and centered around the proposition that God may be nothing more than a psychological response to an unfaceable fate—death. Father Bredder is not worried about this trauma. He goes on mediating as best he can between God and Man. (Penzler, 31–32)

Perhaps this lack of response explains why the quality of the series flickered after the sixth volume and only raised to a flame again with the final two books before being permanently extinguished. Most series seem to have off books, but this series gets more and more careless in its plots, more and more sloppy in its details. Perhaps Leonard Wibberley lost heart. The economic woes of Father Bredder certainly provide a plausible explanation. We might contrast this to a series with a similar number of volumes, Ellis Peter's Cadfael novels. None of her books has fallen near the depth or suffered the lack of public recognition of these under discussion. Instead, her books move from strength to strength as she wins Silver Dagger awards for them, each new one better in quality and reception than the last. If small sales and lack of interest really did scar the Bredder series, what a vast and deadly influence lack of encouragement has on literary output and merit. Why did Wibberley not simply give up sooner? Unlike the small variety of dinosaur, the great gargantuans took quite a while to realize they were dead. Sadly, when Bredder finally succumbed in 1977, it was to a mere muffled plop in the tarpit of public taste. Few apparently noticed his going under. When he did, we lost a major figure in the clerical crime genre.

Surveying the books as a whole, we notice the Bredder series is remarkable for several factors. First is Bredder's thorough development of the "spiritual fingerprint" approach to his work as a "policeman of God." Second, there is the plot structure of paralleled images that contrast authenticity with fallacy. Third, and least, there are a remarkable number of errors in the series, particularly inconsistencies of names and dates, unparalleled in the genre.

For those, like the Inklings, whose theology of art posits art as subcreation in the image of the Great Creator, slovenliness is a mild form of blasphemy, a sin against one's own reflection of heaven. Nobody likes a shirker or a cheat. In the Bredder stories carelessness in detail becomes indicative of carelessness in theology as the series progresses. Bredder begins, as we have seen, by providing wise and workable interpretations of Roman Catholic theology, but as the books disintegrate, he begins fatuously dallying with horoscopes, denigrating prayer, condoning promiscuity, tossing off numerous ill-thought-out remarks.

The major theme for the series forms the spiritual counterpart to that of *The Mouse That Roared:* that God uses the simple, insignificant things in this world to confound the wise and powerful. Some might suppose before examining the subgenre that such a theme would characterize the entire clerical crime novel, yet it does not. Randollph, Bede, and Alington's Archdeacons are not small, insignificant, meek clerics who astound others. They are powerful ecclesiastical demigods who stoop to participate in the affairs of common humanity. But in Bredder we see a clerical version of insignificant Grand Fenwick roaring away.

In that sense, deny it as he will, Leonard Wibberley has placed on Father Bredder's broad shoulders Father Brown's small but weighty mantle. And Father Bredder has generally worn it well and passed it on. The fact that eleven of these books were published in hardcover and sold to book clubs and paperback houses should mean something, as does the fact that they can still be found everywhere in active lending libraries. To normal authors, that would be a smashing success. The point of reference of a writer who is in the rarified atmosphere of producing an international bestseller, which launched a pair of major motion pictures starring Peter Sellers, is understandably higher than most. Further, a 1971 television pilot movie, *The Badge and the Cross,* starring George Kennedy, initiated a thirteen-episode Father Bredder series called *Sarge.* The demise of *Sarge* as a series is part of a pattern affecting highly successful detective series which have not been able to transfer to television. In the clerical crime genre Rabbi Small's conversion to *Lanigan's Rabbi* was short lived. Fans of written series tend to have firm, if radically conflicting, pictures of protagonists in their minds. A single actor has difficulty satisfying a majority of them. Consider all the incarnations of Miss Marple from Helen Hayes to Angela Lansbury to Joan Hickson. Perhaps the least Miss Marpleish to judge by the books, the incomparable Margaret Rutherford, proved ironically the most successful. Further, the relentless pace of a week-by-week production schedule immediately uses up the original material, and staff or script writers often do little more than produce a shabby counterfeit of an author's style and content. True fans soon spot the *faux pas* and spurn such series. So television success is not a true judgment of a printed book's worth. Sale of books may arguably be, but perhaps even that does not reveal a series' worth or the final extent of its influence, though it certainly describes the effect of its immediate impact.

Beyond all these factors the Holton books have their own fictional credentials. During the difficult years of the apathetic fifties and the anti-institutional sixties before the early seventies Jesus movement, when theology became respectable again, into the late seventies and the eighties neoconservative reclamation, when the clerical crime novel along with the institutional church was again flourishing, the Father Bredder tales kept the Roman Catholic crime novel alive. It was the major series being produced. During these years of self-effacement, of neglect, there was one small fictional Roman Catholic voice that thundered.

11

The Scholastic World of Ralph McInerny's Father Dowling and "Monica Quill's" Sister Mary Teresa

Roger Dowling

Is scholastic Roman Catholicism still viable in this rationalistic, pluralistic, relativistic time in which we live? Has even the Roman Catholic Church after Vatican II left traditional Roman Catholic thought behind, largely ignoring Pope John Paul II and opting instead for a new liberalized conscience-oriented departure from the past and with it a new openness to the theologies of the future? The writings of William Kienzle seem to sway back and forth between the two sides of that issue, and the novels of Andrew M. Greeley weigh heavily upon the newer side.

In contrast, Dr. Ralph M. McInerny, a midwestern Roman Catholic philosopher, is concerned in all he writes that traditional scholastic thought not be lost along with the faddish rejection of some varieties of Thomism that has occurred since Pope John XXIII's call for "aggiornamento" (an updating and renewal within the Roman Catholic Church). In 1966 he wrote a defense of the Church's charge to philosophers to follow Thomas as a guide for philosophizing in which he claims that Thomism should serve as a base from which Roman Catholic philosophers begin and not an end for their thinking. Rather than seeing Thomism as a straightjacket for the religious mind, McInerny observes, "Indeed, I shall argue that the very spirit of Thomism requires an endless openness to whatever philosophizing goes on; Thomism, in short, is not a closed system" (*Renewal*, 18). Admitting "most philosophers who lay claim to the title of Thomist are pretty miserable thinkers, not exactly electric in the classroom and painfully narrow in their interests and information" (*Renewal*, 16), he proceeds to lampoon the faddists who reject all Thomism simply to be modern, concluding, "What is pardonable, at least as a passing phase, in an undergraduate is reprehensible in those who may seem to the uninstructed to be speaking with something resembling authority" (*Renewal*, 20).

McInerny recognizes the profound "distaste" for Thomism that exists in this post-Vatican II age of the Church. He observes that many have come to regard Thomists as if they "constituted a kind of international Mafia or Cosa Nostra" (*Renewal,* 24), locking the Church up in a tight protective "Brother-hood" of the mind. Thus, they reject all Thomist thought for freedom to philoso-phize within all the new systems.

But for Ralph McInerny, "We must learn to distinguish between St. Tho-mas and the Thomism that has too often obtained in our colleges and seminaries" (*Renewal,* 30). This concern he has recognized to be his calling and it is reflected in the bulk of his philosophical endeavors. In addition to serving as coeditor of *The New Scholasticism,* he has compiled and edited papers on Thomas, hosted symposiums, and authored such works as *The Logic of Anal-ogy, Studies in Analogy, Thomism in an Age of Renewal, St. Thomas Aquinas,* a study of Thomas' life and thought, and *Ethica Thomistica: The Moral Philoso-phy of Thomas Aquinas.* His own admiration for Thomas is unmistakable. In volume 2 of the textbook *A History of Western Philosophy,* employing the metaphor of a mountain range to depict the various medieval philosophers, he writes, "Quite unabashedly we will find the highest peak on the medieval terrain in the thirteenth century, particularly in the thought of Thomas Aquinas" (*His-tory,* 8). He considers the philosophers preceding St. Thomas as a kind of "praeparatio thomistica," whose thought ended in "Thomas as the telos of this development (*History,* 8). His own life has been given to scholastic thought as he has served for years as Michael P. Grace Professor of Medieval Studies and director of the Medieval Institute and the Jacques Maritain Center at the Univer-sity of Notre Dame in Indiana. Indeed, in the preface of *Ethica Thomistica* (1983) he refers to St. Thomas as "a man who has been the author's intellectual mentor for over thirty years" (*Ethica,* ix).

Thus, Ralph McInerny by his own statements—e.g., "I am a Thomist, or try to be" (*Renewal,* 21)—is convinced that Thomas' thought is not hopelessly antiquated and should indeed guide Roman Catholic philosophy today. In point of fact he rates Thomas' writing as one of the bases of philosophy, along with tradition, under which he recognizes doctrinal tradition of the church (*Renewal,* 32) and tradition of philosophy (*Renewal,* 35) and reason (*Renewal,* 30), cer-tainly a basic and heady company for one single philosopher's work to occupy. Small wonder, then, that for Ralph McInerny St. Thomas is, indeed, "a man who for some seven hundred years has been a major influence in philosophy and theology" (*Thomas,* 9). And, clearly, from a survey of McInerny's scholarly activities the goals for his *St. Thomas Aquinas* are the goals for nearly all of his writing: "I wanted to make the thought of Thomas Aquinas attractive, but attractive for the right reasons" (*Thomas,* 9), and "Most important, I have tried to present Thomas in such a way that my reader would quickly leave me and go to the works of Aquinas himself" (*Thomas,* 9).

Ralph McInerny is, indeed, an eloquent apologist for the relevancy of St.

Thomas' thought in Roman Catholicism today. But outside the walls of the Jacques Maritain Center or the philosophy classes of Notre Dame or even the courts of the Vatican, is Thomas any longer relevant in today's society? Certainly his secondary works claim he is. But McInerny realizes the limits of declaration in a way not many thinkers outside of Plato and Søren Kierkegaard have. To go beyond the limits of mere syllogistic proclamation—hardly the potent tool in this media-oriented relativistic age some preachers and apologists still seem to think it is—McInerny has fulfilled the tentative promise of Dorothy Gilman and the preceding Roman Catholic clerical crime novelists' first faint prophecies by writing nearly a score of philosophical volumes that seek to demonstrate by extended parable that Thomist thought is still relevant. What makes his approach so interesting is that he, too, has chosen to write these philosophical volumes as clerical crime novels. And McInerny takes his parables seriously, crafting them with levels of meaning and fleshing out within them the religious and liturgical forms of contemporary Catholicism. His mysteries are in the mode that some call "psychological thrillers." In them he is less interested in the subtleties of detection than in the anguish his characters experience as moral agents whose choices invariably involve them in what their Church (especially since taking its stands on abortion and birth control) brands the greatest of mortal sins—the taking of human life.

His major creation and vehicle has been Father Roger Dowling, former alcoholic during fifteen frustrating years of helplessly watching the human anguish he was forced to cause while practicing canonical law on the Archdiocesan Marriage Court. Dowling is now farmed out into redemptive exile as parish priest at end-of-the-road St. Hilary's Parish in Fox River, Illinois. Dowling's excursions into sin, justice, mercy and repentance well articulate McInerny's own views of the direction Roman Catholic life and thought under "aggiornamento" should go, is going and must go in North America. In all his novels, general fiction as well as suspense, and particularly in the Father Dowling stories, Ralph McInerny has fleshed out his understanding of the views of St. Thomas and the scholastic theologians and offered them by parable as a mirror image of our world. Why has a professor chosen to join the ranks of the mystery novelists? Why has a philosopher chosen to demonstrate his convictions in this way? One might ask why Plato wrote much of his philosophy as conversations between Socrates, his students and his colleagues. An answer might be to give readers a sense of participation in the discussion, to let us argue along. McInerny's verisimilitude invites participation plus something more. His technique gives us the opportunity to judge whether, indeed, the world we see created reflects our world. If so, then we agree that the Thomist thought upon which the mediation of justice, mercy, and consequence rests and the Thomist concepts and concerns he presents are not only continually relevant but also essentially the exercise of our human responsibilities and the understanding of the working of God. Ralph McInerny's defense, then, has much to gain if we see his novels as correct depictions. He gains a positive judgment for his defense and proves by parable what *Thomism in an Age of Renewal* seeks to prove by argument.

How does he go about this fleshing out of scholastic thought? He does it through the moral dilemmas he depicts in the modern landscape he sketches and the human reactions and solutions he provides, predicated upon his own Thomist assumptions. In authenticating his tales, we authenticate his premises.

In the first Dowling story *Her Death of Cold,* published in 1977, eleven years after *Thomism in an Age of Renewal,* McInerny gives us such a human dilemma. Elderly Sylvia Lowry is a devout and fearful Roman Catholic widow. Estranged from her children, she turns to the Church to give her a sense of security in this world and the quickly approaching next one. When she is found frozen in her freezer cabinet, McInerny turns a number of perspectives upon the true nature of the crime that took her life and its meaning for the killer, the law of God, and the law of society. Chief among these perspectives upon this human condition are two. The first is represented by a secular foil, Phil Keegan, formerly a candidate for the priesthood in the seminary class behind Father Dowling, currently the dropped-out, widowed, child-deserted chief of detectives of the Fox River police force. Keegan represents what could be called a modi-fied contemporary perspective, devoutly Catholic yet pluralistic, fragmented, filled with a nostalgic nodding to the past which has been knocked about so as to emerge as an uneasy reliance on the mechanized exigencies of the post-Christian period. As McInerny depicts him:

> His lids veiled his eyes, giving him the look of a doubter, the look of one who has seen too much, a man for whom Diogenes with his lamp has too often turned out to be a Peeping Tom or an arsonist. Anyone is capable of anything. And everyone must pay for what he has done. That was elementary. That was justice. Without justice, life would be a mockery. (*Cold,* 41)

Keegan could be called, in one use of the term, a realist because he sees the chaos of society and superimposes law upon it to give it coherence, order and meaning.

The second perspective is that of Father Roger Dowling, and his interests in contrast are clearly, consciously Thomist. Dowling, too, is interested in the law, but in the law as a tool of divine providence, not simply as an end for ordering in itself. As the book's promotional sales pitch assures us, Father Roger Dowling is the "veteran of years of exposure to his fellow creatures. Inured as he is to human folly, philosophically detached and quite unshockable, Father Dowling yet has a passion for seeing clearly. And where crime is concerned, he *must* see clearly: the intent behind the crime is his utmost concern" (*Cold,* dust jacket). In fact, if a thematic impetus could be discerned for the novel, this would be it. If G. K. Chesterton's Father Brown solved crimes by entering the mind of the murderer and then doing what the murderer would do and going where the murderer would go until he arrived at the murderer, Dowling takes the process one step further. He discerns *the intent* of the murderer. Why is the intent behind the crime his utmost concern? Because the intent behind a human action appears to have been Thomas' concern.

If as a later book *Second Vespers* tells us, "the *Summa theologiae* of Aquinas" is one of Father Dowling's three favorite books (*Vespers*, 38–39), the very world that Father Dowling and his cocreations occupy is one steeped in and ordered by scholastic thought. It exists from these first characters' general assumption of human relationships within the framework of the chain of being:

> Sylvia drew vitality from the man, moon to his sun. She was vibrant, energetic, a real force in the city. And then he died and she became, well, what she became. A whining old woman, sniveling in church, afraid of everything. (*Cold,* 85)

> Keegan did not like that. A man should stand up and answer for his deeds. There was no need to drag his wife through this, no matter how willing she might be. (*Cold,* 134)

And it proceeds through their assumption of the trustworthiness of the law, since human law, as we know from St. Thomas, proceeds from natural law, which itself proceeds from divine law and eternal law: "So you have nothing to fear. The law, Mendax, is sometimes a recalcitrant bitch, but in the end, over the long haul, she proves ever faithful" (*Cold,* 156–57). Their first tale centers to a great degree upon the symbol of the rosary, which, we are told, "goes back to the thirteenth century, to Dominic, the founder of the Order of Preachers, the Dominicans. The rosary is the prayer Our Lady urged upon Dominic and his new order of mendicant friars in their struggle against the Albigensians" (*Cold,* 112). St. Thomas was, after all, a Dominican.

But the impetus is in the book's emphasis on intent, motivation, and responsibility. Over and over again Dowling voices the concern that the responsibility of the crime be brought home to its perpetrator so an examination of his or her intention and motivation can be conducted. When at the climax Father Dowling finally faces a murderer, the priest's concern turns fully to the intention. After hearing in the confessional how a thief was surprised by the victim and struck her without meaning to harm her, Dowling makes his ruling:

> After a moment Dowling nodded, though he doubted Hospers could see this. "No, perhaps not. Your sin was not murder. . . . You have confessed a sin of the flesh. You confess to intending to steal some money. And, in striking Mrs. Lowry, you had no intention to harm her, to kill her? Is that right? . . . All right. I am going to give you absolution." (*Cold,* 205)

Still, the unintentional murderer must make restitution of what he stole, pray for the soul of the dead, and confess to the police. Human law must still be served:

> And then, as he recited the formula of absolution, Father Dowling felt his sense of the irony of this situation leave him. How often the deed we mean to do turns into something else, something we did not really intend. A relatively innocent action, an instinctive response, can look to the outsider like a criminal deed. It was the outsider's vantage point that Phil Keegan must adopt, but it was different in the world of the confessional, where the Divine Comedy was somewhat less enigmatic and more mysterious. A priest learns how frequently truly sinful deeds can wear an innocent public face. The outward consequences, the observable effects of what we do are seldom commensurable with the true nature of our acts. (*Cold,* 206)

As it turns out confusion as to when exactly the death occurred—a question of whether the blow by Hospers or her interment in the freezer by her son-in-law was the cause of death—handcuffs the law's ability to bring judgment. But God's judgment has been sought and satisfied.

What makes the solution work in the context of this book is the fact that all the characters agree with the worldview expressed. Only Keegan, the failed novitiate, holds out unsatisfied. Complaining about the failure of the district attorney to prosecute, Keegan fumes:

> "The ass is telling me that because I have two murderers I don't have any."
> "Or that you have no murder."
> "A woman was killed, Father. Society cannot be maintained if things like that go unpunished."
> "Society is built on unpunished crimes."
> "You don't believe that."
> "Oh, but I do." (*Cold,* 210)

Father Dowling recognizes a world where, indeed, society is built on unpunished crimes. So apparently ultimately does Ralph McInerny.

In that sense Dowling's concerns seem outside of reason, particularly to the orderly mind of Phil Keegan, who obviously agrees with Thomas' teaching that law is a kind of practical reason that directs our actions to a good end. But is this because our actions are indeed unreasonable or because they are beyond reason? For St. Thomas the domain beyond reason is that of faith, for reason, though it can tell us God exists, cannot apprehend the divine nature. Here in the realm of faith one can begin to glimpse the design of God for the world. Society is, after all, a preparatory school for heaven, and it employs as a schoolteacher human law, but the essential point of its curriculum is restoration to the Creator. So what achieves reconciliation is Father Dowling's aim, despite its general inadequacy in the here and now.

Thus, Dowling, not the police, is the one who succeeds in solving the crime and in dispensing God's mercy, even though he insists the perpetrator must still accept society's exactments, such as they are able to be levied, since it is important to try to maintain order, another Thomist precept. Thus, Dowling generally succeeds within the genre of the story, but do this story and its successors succeed within the context of the world we know and see?

Those of us outside scholastic Roman Catholic thought may regard traditional chain-of-being hierarchical anthropology as a curse rather than an asset to male/female Christian relations. Similarly, we may wonder if terming malignant evil a privation of good or a deprivation of being (or a vitamin deficiency, as Dorothy Gilman's nuns would have it) is strong enough for the malicious cruelty that plagues us after Auschwitz. We may wonder if the edifice of scholastic thought, like one of the great gothic buildings, is more a monument to the past with its lofty towers and its drafty hallways than a snug shelter within which to survive the crazed technological future. We ask whether its just-war theory is even a rational possibility against the prospect of a no-win nuclear holocaust. We question the utility of Thomas' proofs—which demonstrate the logic of God's existence, given the premise of a rationally ordered universe with an ordering center—when many thinkers no longer seem to accept the premise and care little about the outcome. For a contemporary Protestant like myself in the Reformed tradition, what value does Roman Catholic tradition distilled through these fictional exercises provide? What Ralph McInerny offers is what every good storyteller and ultimately every good theologian offers: a parable by which to interpret life. Jesus taught in parables. St. Thomas himself often argued by analogy, particularly about the essence of God. And what is a story really but a modern parable? What is a parable, at times, but an extended analogy? Ralph McInerny's stories are potent parables.

What makes the Dowling mystery series succeed is the verisimilitude with which it depicts contemporary dilemmas and its refusal to truncate these dilemmas by aptly isolating axioms to interpret and solve them. Dowling's confusion and dismay at the tragedies of the marriage tribunal echo some of the actual tragedies recorded by the North American Conference of Separated and Divorced Catholics (NACSDC). Participants like Joe and Luisa White, interviewed in the September 1, 1983, issue of *The Boston Globe* (pages 69 and 73) tell of years of struggle for annulments, removal from the sacraments if they remarried without approval, and conflicting messages from priests. Some advised a form of sanctified extramarital cohabitation termed "sacramental marriage," which included unpublicized "underground wedding(s)" in rectories of neighboring parishes, while other priests felt obligated to remove them from advising Catholic Youth Organizations, counseling them that their only recourse was to pray. This anguish McInerny does not mute in tale after tale where murderers escape, the innocent suffer, and the good are hounded by frustration and loneliness.

What makes Ralph McInerny and his stories succeed besides this assiduous adherence to reflecting reality is that McInerny brings to St. Thomas, Thomism, and the people that comprise the Roman Catholic community today a compassion that lifts him above cant and helps him discern motives and cures. His astute ability to separate Thomas from Thomism and by this means to forge a new practical Thomism that opens rather than closes doors in the Church also reflects his ability to discern the human component within each issue of canon law and what human needs need to be served. This hermeneutic of compassion has let him discover the human Thomas and find a Thomism humane in its concerns. This compassion also lets him mirror the true people who comprise Catholicism. Thus, his parables accurately articulate both the successes and failures of the Church to serve them.

Mary Teresa

While Father Dowling was seeking to adopt a scholastic view that adapted the solid philosophical foundations of traditional Roman Catholic thought to the new perspectives, patterns, problems and possibilities of living in the contemporary world, another clerical sleuth spent her waking hours in a scholarly voyage through the twelfth century, emerging only to solve a series of murders. Her first excursion back to the present occurred in 1981, when Ralph McInerny's company, Vanguard, issued a book credited to one Monica Quill and entitled *Not a Blessed Thing*. It was soon followed by other volumes. Although the first volume recorded its copyright in the name of Monica Quill, its Library of Congress data omitted its author entry. By the third volume apparently the secret was out, for under the Monica Quill copyright, the author listed on the Library of Congress catalogue card was Ralph M. McInerny.

Not a Blessed Thing was so successful that volume 2, *Let Us Prey*, was at publication already a selection of both the Detective Book Club and the Catholic Digest Book Club. The opening sentence tells us why. It is a near-classic opening line for what The Crime Club was wont to call a "favorite sleuth" mystery: "Kim had promised Joyce she would keep Attila the nun out of the kitchen that afternoon, so she took Sister Mary Teresa into the sun porch of the old mansion on Walton Street where she could glare at television" (*Blessed*, 5). This marvelously compact sentence tells us everything. Compare it with Hawthorne's opening pages for *The Scarlet Letter*, where his subtle distribution of light and dark shades begins to depict the ambiguities that the story will reveal. But this is the modern age. Where Hawthorne had the leisure of paragraphs and pages, the contemporary writer must be content with sentences, and, normally, with as few of these as possible. The opening sentence of *Not a Blessed Thing* with journalistic compactness introduces us to who, what and where: three women, one, at least, a nun; in an old mansion, on Walton Street. Then with two jests, one a noun and one a strong verb, it focuses in on one of the women and sketches in her character: Attila the nun glares. We can already see that Kim and Joyce defer to Mary Teresa, who even maintains, along with the tribute of their attention, two names to their one. As they kowtow to her in the opening sentence, so will they in the following series. Kim will become Archie Goodwin to Mary Teresa's Nero Wolfe. Small wonder, then, that the publisher has chosen to advertise H. F. Heard's development of Mycroft Holmes mysteries on the end cover, for Sister Mary Teresa is a clerical/religious reflection of Conan Doyle's classic armchair detective, on which all the subsequent armchair detectives, including those in the clerical crime novel, are based. Appropriately, this includes—increasingly in *Rocket to the Morgue* and nearly completely by the time of "Coffin Corner"—Mary Teresa's predecessor Sister Ursula. But, as we have been warned in the opening sentence, against Ursula's airy diffidence is set the irascibility of "Attila the nun," Mary Teresa. As Mary Teresa sits muttering at the television, Kim, sunk into half-oblivious exhaustion before the first novel even begins, is attempting to recover "after a truly hectic day spent running errands for Sister Mary Teresa" (*Blessed*, 5). And we meet a no-nonsense ecclesiastical addition to the armchair genre who brooks no excuse or deception on her way to the truth of things.

Doctor Mary Teresa Dempsey—nicknamed "Emtee" by her students as a semi-acronym (*Blessed*, 7)—has been for over a half a century a member of the Order of Martha and Mary—nicknamed the "M&M's" (*Blessed*, 9). Aged about seventy-eight, she is older even than Sister O'Marie's Sister Mary Helen, who is seventy-four. At about five feet in height and nearly two hundred pounds, she strikes people as a "fat little nun behind the desk busy writing her daily quota of pages" (*Prey*, 7). Though she still wears her traditional habit (*Blessed*, 6, 7), her order is far from traditional. With fewer students in their college and fewer novitiates in their order, the sisters have chosen to go out in a blaze of glory. In a last glorious "lark" the local chapter sold its assets and distributed the profits in plump envelopes to the poor. Three sisters, Mary Teresa, Kim, and Joyce, are all that remain of the midwestern region of the order (*Blessed*, 9), having moved to a house designed by Frank Lloyd Wright (*Blessed*, 29) in Chicago (*Blessed*, 25).

What happened to the rest of the sisters?

The M. & M.s had moved to Walton Street with the notion that they would minister to the lay people among whom they would live. Long before the community was whittled down to three this hope had been dashed. The laity proved to be remarkably disinterested in nuns who looked like other women and, in any case, what did the M. & M.s know that could be of help to their neighbors? The bulk of the nuns had swiftly joined the supposed object of their new apostolate and, in the end, it was Joyce who had come to know and befriend their neighbors. (*Prey*, 33)

The series, therefore, becomes an interpretation of the lives and faith of those who chose to stay, providing an appealing apology for a nun's life. As Sister Mary Teresa explains, "It is a matter of calling. Married people see our life as impossibly burdensome. And so it would be if one did not have a vocation. 'Each has his gift from the Lord'" (*Blessed*, 64). According to Sister Mary Teresa:

> It is easy for a woman to dedicate herself. . . . Nothing comes easier to us. The only question is to what, more importantly to whom, will we dedicate ourselves. In the end, God alone is the supreme object of all human dedication, but for most He is an indirect object. The religious tries to make Him the direct object of dedication, the point of her life, taking the role of husband. Did you know that the nun is called the spouse of Christ? (*Above*, 93)

These nuns are enlightened, tolerant, gentle with others' understanding of the faith and with others' weaknesses:

> We nuns have so many more opportunities to reflect on our lives, to pray, to ask God's help, yet we are forever falling short of our ideal. It keeps us humble. It certainly prevents us from feeling sanctimonious or superior to those who have fewer spiritual opportunities than we do. (*Above*, 57)

They have grown tolerant through their contact with the people of the neighborhood. Many things still offend them, but they have learned to accept others, as did the brittle but awakening Sister Simon. And they themselves are slowly accepted, Mary Teresa's habit, their nunnery right in the center of the neighborhood, their chapel and offices, matins and lauds, their celibacy, ol' Uncle Tom Cobley and all.

Among the things Mary Teresa still regards with distaste are psychiatrists (*Prey*, 183), cigarette smoke (*Nun*, 51) (though she refrains from mentioning it and keeps ashtrays around for guests), the term "Ms." (*Prey*, 37), and interruptions as she works on her "opus magnum" (*Blessed*, 16) on twelfth-century French monasticism (*Blessed*, 20). Dr. Dempsey's research is by no means the frivolous meanderings of an old religious through the past, whiling away the waning hours of a long fruitful life of service by dwelling back in the days of the glory of the religious life. Like her creator she is a renowned scholar. Formerly a brilliant professor of history at the order's erstwhile women's college (*Blessed*, 10), where she was a "stingy grader" and "demanding teacher" (*Above*, 8), she now puts in two four-hour stints of writing every day, including Sunday (*Blessed*, 33). She holds both her earned doctorate and a half dozen honorary degrees (*Blessed*, 41). With her conservative outlook, which admires President Ronald Reagan (*Above*, 156), writing longhand at her cherrywood desk, her neat notes organized as stringently as her thought, she champions gradation and hierarchy (*Blessed*, 50, 156), somewhat like "a dinosaur in Lincoln Park" (*Blessed*, 14). Leaving the mass to one Father Rausch, who thought-fully supplies it in Latin (*Blessed*, 177), she invests her time in her scholarship, her impact on others and the careful coddling of her legend, and, of course, her detection. Impervious to irony (*Blessed*, 53), she pursues whatever course she thinks advisable, considering the opinions of others or the directives of the police as negotiable and surmountable as problems in research. Besides closing her eyes for a twenty-minute morning meditation after she says her little office, matins and lauds, from which nothing short of an earthquake can arouse her (*Blessed*, 30), she is constantly pushing ahead on problems.

In her research, scholarly and constabulary, she is a breath short of unscru-pulous. Though she does not lie (*Blessed*, 38), she has mastered the priestly art of casuistry. Having "extremely nuanced notions of truth-telling" (*Blessed*, 41), she does so much truth-twisting that we can practically hear truth pounding the floor, shrieking "uncle!" (cf. *Blessed*, 52). As she contends, "You are not responsible for the inferences people make when you utter perfectly innocuous remarks" (*Prey*, 123). As her assistant Kim squirms with stricken conscience, Sister Mary Teresa conducts her many deceptive interviews, pumping witnesses for information they do not know they are giving:

> Kim did not know how long she could go on deceiving him as to why she was here. Emtee Dempsey would have had a complicated argument purporting to prove she had a moral obliga-tion to deceive Tom Moran. (*Above*, 73)

When Mary Teresa justifies what she wants to do in regard to the truth, Kim, her assistant, is convinced "there was a fallacy lurking" in her reasoning (*Prey*, 124). But that fallacy is the necessary struggle for normal existence within a rigid system of stringent rules. The ancient rabbis would certainly understand and laud her as being skilled in Halakah.

But a good deal of the time, Sister Mary Teresa does not appear to wish to be understood. She is not averse to being thought of as outrageous in her actions (*Prey*, 159). She likes to pack a World War II German luger for emer-gencies (*Blessed*, 18, 19), feeling with Sister Simon that a good aim (and a lot of noise) is a good defense. And Sister Mary Teresa does not mind making a lot of noise. Thumping along with her cane, she is a formidable sight. But in reality, she is "not half the curmudgeon she seemed" (*Blessed*, 32). She can be smug. Unlike Martin Buell, she cannot be smug about her cooking. She is a poor cook who achieves "painful" results (*Prey*, 179). This is not because she does not like to eat. She enjoys buttering and marmalading her toast one bit at a time (*Blessed*, 46) and shoving it in with her "fat little fingers" (*Prey*, 196). What she can be smug about is the fact that, as annoying as she is to Kim's brother Richard, a captain of detectives, she is "capable of seeing something others did not see, not even with the trained eye of a policeman" (*Blessed*, 35).

Convinced that "Sin is what's wrong with the world" (*Blessed,* 32), she resists being told, "But you are not an instrument of justice" (*Prey,* 147). An instrument of justice is precisely what Sister Mary Teresa is in this series. With her flair for the dramatic—she can "make a simple phone call seem the dramatic equivalent of a declaration of World War III" (*Nun,* 52)—her nerve of a burglar, her ability "to maneuver others into situations where she herself was the dramatic center of things" (*Nun,* 52), she employs the house on Walton Street as her own personal central bureau of investigation to which she draws the police, the victims, the suspects, and in which she makes her dramatic announcements solving crimes. Her technique is to ask "cui bono?" Who profits or gains from an act (e.g., *Blessed,* 121, 123, 151, 180, 182)? She may be accused by the exasperated police of detecting chiefly by intuition, but intuition for her is as rigorous and responsible a process as the police's procedure:

> There are hunches, insights, intuitions. And they do seem to come out of the blue. They don't. They are the fruit of half-conscious connections being made by the mind, swift inferences, seeing what a combination of things already known entails. You knew among innumerable others things A and B. When they are juxtaposed in your mind, you realize that C must be inferred from them. Take any intuition and you will find it is a species of deduction. (*Blessed,* 171–72)

As she contends:

> The police mind is a professional mind and is not immune to the familiar dangers of narrow expertise. . . . We become the victims of past success. A method that has worked well before tends to be trusted blindly and we resist anything that calls it into question. Progress in science is made by those who thumb their noses at received opinion and narrow orthodoxies. . . . The point is that police procedure is just that, a procedure, a method, a trusted modus operandi. By and large, it deserves that trust, but it must be employed with a skeptical eye all the same, for who is to say when the exception will arise? . . . People are always exceptions. Theories about human behavior must take that into account. This applies with special force in the investigation of a murder. (*Prey,* 89–90)

Before the first story begins, she has already assisted the police in a number of cases (*Blessed,* 35) and is already known by reputation (*Blessed,* 130). The police have certainly come out the worse for wear from this assistance. Richard, for example,

> was confident he would be spared purgatory in the next life because of what he suffered from Sister Mary Teresa in this one. . . . It wasn't simply that she wished to help the police. In many instances she seemed to want to take their place. Worse, far worse, the old nun had on too many occasions seen to the bottom of cases that interested her long before the police investigation was done. (*Nun,* 23)

Her motivation is that which drives all the clerical sleuths at one time or another:

> Sister Mary Teresa took it as a religious obligation to hunger and thirst after justice and she had no patience with those who became sentimental on the subject of punishment. She had a little lecture on capital punishment to counter maudlin denials of the moral responsibility of the human agent. (*Prey*, 197)

Her excursions into the twelfth century have certainly left her with a firm scholastic theology that brooks no modern softening of the concepts of responsibility and consequence. Sister Mary Teresa believes in capital punishment. As she explains:

> Anyone who strangles people in cold blood for his own trivial advantage should be repaid in kind. . . . Murder is a capital crime. . . . The rule of law reposes on a social system of stability and justice. Like our own. . . . You and I—society—do not have the power to forgive a murder. God does that. And the death penalty does not interfere with God's mercy. It may be an instrument of it. (*Above*, 127)

Her scholastic theology also lends her a certitude beyond the frailties of human justice, a confidence she shares with Roger Dowling. When Richard urges, "Leave this to the police, Sister. We've done our job, justice will be served," she replies:

> I'm delighted to hear that. I never doubted it for a moment. The fact that so many criminals go undiscovered and their crimes unpunished does not disturb my certainty. God is justice. He is also mercy. You and I are merely human. (*Prey*, 52)

As one fan of hers, her newspaper contact Katherine Senski, applies this concept, "If there were justice in the world, she would be president" (*Blessed*, 56).

Sister Kim Moriarity, Richard's sister, does most of the legwork to bring about these feats of inductive analysis. In case we did not miss McInerny's obvious modeling on Mycroft Holmes, we might wonder if the choice of Kim's name marks his attempt, like Nicholas Meyer's, to salvage that old reprobate, Sherlock's arch villain, Professor Moriarity. Kim, however, is an aspiring professor, working on her own long-term doctorate in history at Northwestern (supposedly to succeed Emtee Dempsey but now, with the termination of the college, emptied in prospects).

Yet, despite all the frustration she causes for Kim, as well as for all the characters in these novels, Mary Teresa, traditional habit and all, is "a reassuring symbol in a world that seemed to change with such dizzying rapidity" (*Nun*, 13). As Archie to Nero Wolfe, Kim clings to the rock of Emtee Dempsey, while often mentally berating her. And there is something more: "As she often had before, Emtee Dempsey surprised Kim by the compassion she showed toward a person caught up in one of the social ills the old nun condemned so roundly in the abstract" (*Nun*, 13). Beneath the gruffness there is a compassion, and a compassion with the power to do something to right a wrong. The protector with a heart is an image that has made Parker's Spenser so popular. Pierce the cynicism of Marlowe and you have a code. Look under the crooked reputation that is good for business in Sam Spade and you have honesty and a distaste for guns. Look beneath the sneering self-sufficiency of the early Simon Templar and you have a loyalty to the memory of a friend that rivals Damon's and Pythias'. Beneath the gruffness of Mary Teresa, beneath her theatricality, beneath her forbidding bark is compassion. And this is the message of the mysterium. Beneath the might and power and vengeance against evil, the exacting of justice, the toppling of the oppressor wells mercy for the repentant, comfort for the grieving, succor for the oppressed. In the house on Walton Street lives its image.

12

Mrs. Pollifax Gets Ordained:
Dorothy Gilman's *A Nun in the Closet*

Two years before Father Dowling's fictional demotion to St. Hilary's launched the first of his novelistic expositions of contemporary Thomism, a more moderately scaled presentation of Thomism, with a correspondingly harsher indictment of the Reformation, anticipated his apologies, while taking a step he did not take, defining itself against Reformational Protestantism. Dorothy Gilman's 1975 adventure *A Nun in the Closet* is a clerical crime novel reminiscent of the tradition of the Rabbi Small tales while eventually departing from them by opting for a syncretistic theological blending unthinkable to Rabbi Small. Thus, while it is like the Father Brown tales in defining Catholicism rigorously against Reformed Protestantism, it is unlike most of the other offerings in the subgenre of the Roman Catholic clerical crime novel in that it eventually opts for a syncretistic blending of Roman Catholicism and Eastern thought.

Author Dorothy Gilman is best known for her Mrs. Pollifax spy novels. A widowed, gray-haired, garden-clubbing churchwoman from New Brunswick, New Jersey, home of Johnson & Johnson, Rutgers University, and "the banks of the ol' Raritan," Mrs. Pollifax does volunteer work with the C.I.A. that has led her around the world to adventures in Central America, in Africa, behind the Iron Curtain. Interestingly, it has also led her over the years into Eastern meditation, which by her most recent book she practices regularly along with the martial arts. The link between the martial arts and religious meditation is, of course, well established, Tai Chi flowing sinuously into Tai Chi Chu'an.

Dorothy Gilman, too, has traveled frequently, her own restless life reflecting the constant movement in her books. Starting, like Mrs. Pollifax, in New Jersey, she is, by the time she writes *A Nun in the Closet,* "living in Nova Scotia and raising medicinal herbs on a saltwater farm" (Gilman, back dust jacket).

A Nun in the Closet (1975) begins with an interesting travel premise. The Abbey of St. Tabitha has inherited a property in New York state. Two sisters, John and Hyacinthe, are sent to examine it. Their trip out of the cloister into the "real world" becomes a multilevel journey into outside consciousness as they encounter in kaleidoscopic array the hitherto unknown worlds of syndicate crime, the oppression of the migrant worker, hippiedom, small-town politics, and Eastern mysticism.

Like Mrs. Pollifax before them, the two sisters move from innocence to experience. Like all the clerical sleuths, they must learn the standard lesson of the deception of appearances: "Of course I understand *now* that things are no longer what they appear to be, but Mr. Armisbruck, although a Lutheran, is always what he appears to be, and he's been the extent of our experience until Monday" (Gilman, 105). One is reminded of the unintentionally comic way in which St. Teresa of Avila closed her classic *The Interior Castle:* "I ask that each time you read this work you, in my name, praise His Majesty fervently and ask for the increase of His Church and for light for the Lutherans" (Teresa, 196). Unlike Mrs. Pollifax at the outset of her tales, the sisters come equipped with an amazing array of resources, pietistic and practical. Sister John, cheerful and optimistic, can fix machinery, defy the mafia, and take on a town. She is a community organizer in a habit. Sister Hyacinthe, dark and brooding, is an Appalachian hill child who can extract from nature banquets and poultices. For her a forest is a hospital or a restaurant. A walk in the woods can yield her enough food to feed a household and folk remedies sufficient to bring a grievously wounded mobster back to life. The sisters are hardly the stereotypes of cloistered nuns. Like Soeur Angèle and Sister Ursula before them, they are interestingly enough not nonviolent. When pursuing a mysterious thump upstairs in their ramshackle new mansion, they arm themselves with a heavy iron skillet and a carving knife (Gilman, 25–26).

Naive as they might be about the current ways of the world, the sisters are theologically sophisticated. And the security of their sense of calling puts them into direct conflict with others, usually triumphantly. When they discover a hunted man with a gunshot wound in their closet, Sister John reflects, "'Sister Hyacinthe, it's a grave responsibility, sanctuary. . . . We're under God's laws, not man's, and this poor soul has appealed to us for help'" (Gilman, 29). Secure as they are in setting aside the laws of society, they are equally so in correcting the worldly people they meet: "'There's a good deal to be said for letting God judge such matters,' Sister John told him serenely, 'and His are the rules we live by here'" (Gilman, 52). The sisters' boldness is not limited simply to talk. Gilman's sisters take initiative, beginning by harboring a fugitive and ending with one of them in jail for disturbing the peace. They are the ones who endure the rough and tumble action.

Thus, Gilman's tale can be read in one dimension as anticipating the interests of feminist criticism. For these, the mystery genre is certainly an appropriate place to turn. Since its inception women have figured prominently in its arena. Elaine Budd notes in her article "Women of Mystery":

From its beginnings, crime writing has been an Equal Opportunity Employer. Ever since the mystery began to assume a definite shape in the nineteenth century, it has admitted women to all its precincts. In Victorian England Arthur Conan Doyle augmented his income from a meager medical practice with his Sherlock Holmes stories; at the same time, on this side of the Atlantic, Louisa May Alcott fleshed out her own slim fortunes from *Little Women* with anonymous chillers like *Behind the Mask*. The golden age of the mystery began just after World War I, when in England such women as Dorothy L. Sayers and Agatha Christie began their stories of Lord Peter Wimsey and Hercule Poirot, followed in the thirties in this country by Dorothy B. Hughes (at 79, still writing from her home in New Mexico) and Charlotte Armstrong.

Today we are in another golden age, with women such as Mary Higgins Clark, Dorothy Uhnak, and P. D. James turning out the taut, tight, tense books that make the best-seller lists. Always strong when writing novels of psychological suspense, some women have added another dimension to the genre with tough new realism. One of the strongest: Dorothy Uhnak, whose latest book, *False Witness*, is a shocker dealing with the rape, sodomy, assault, and attempted murder and dismemberment of a famous woman television personality. "I write from fourteen years of service as a police officer and the only female in an all-male unit," Uhnak says. "Though fiction, my books deal in reality. My degree is in criminal justice—not literature." (Budd, 122)

Jacques Barzun and Wendell Hertig Taylor in their massive, authoritative, though at times cavalier, *A Catalogue of Crime* observe:

> The *roman policier*, long, improbable, and marred by courtroom rhetoric, was adapted into English by a number of gifted woman writers—Anna Katharine Green, Mrs. Belloc Lowndes, the Baroness Orczy, Mary Roberts Rinehart, Isabel Ostrander—who filled the years between 1880 and that great transformation of the 1920s of which, a decade earlier, E. C. Bentley, G. K. Chesterton, and R. Austin Freeman were the neglected pioneers.
>
> The greatest masters of the twenties and thirties were in fact mistresses. Christie, Sayers, Allingham, Marsh, and Heyer rose with the triumph of feminism and deserved the plaudits they received from both sexes. They wrote true detection; they fashioned unsurpassable models. (Barzun, 12)

As a result "feminine" has come to be a category of criticism in this genre, as have such terms as acroidal to depict the technique of having the narrator as murderer (as introduced in Agatha Christie's classic *The Murder of Roger Ackroyd*) and the letters HIBK to denote the "Had-I-But-Known" school of introducing nonprofessionals as protagonists,* both categories created from the trailblazing contributions of women in the field. On the term "feminine" as a category of crime fiction criticism, clerical crime novelist Leonard Holton (Wibberley), creator of Father Bredder, has elaborated:

---

*As coined by Ogden Nash in his poem "Don't Guess, Let Me Tell You," which has been collected in his *The Face Is Familiar*. Maryruth C. Clanton credits Mary Roberts Rinehart's 1908 *The Circular Staircase* as beginning this school.

The detective stories written by men these days are usually full of tough talk and tense action and casual sex. Women on the other hand tend to deal with minutiae of appearance, of habit, of thought, or dress, weather and surroundings; of remarks or absence of remarks. These form a truer but quieter picture of life as life is. As a result women in my view are far superior to men in writing detective fiction. Indeed, when I think of the great detective story writers of the twentieth century, I don't think of Edgar Wallace (remember him?), Dashiell Hammett, or Ian Fleming, or the magnificent Ross Macdonald. I think of Dorothy Sayers, Josephine Tey, Agatha Christie, and (a recent find for me, but certainly a writer of the first water) Emma Lathen. (Penzler, 27)

With women so dominant in the field, one would suppose women would be well represented in the clerical crime novel. But although Ellis Peters, Margaret Scherf and Barbara Ninde Byfield all created male clerical sleuths, between Margaret Ann Hubbard and Sister O'Marie, Dorothy Gilman appears to have been the only prominent female writer who created a feminine clerical detective and solely in *A Nun in the Closet*. As we have seen, that does not mean Sister John and Sister Hyacinthe were in their time the sole feminine clerical detectives. Predecessors Dr. Mary Finney, Sister Ursula, and Soeur Angèle all had sustained series of their own, but all had been created by men.

Professor Joyce Erickson in a perceptive article about applying feminist criticism to books written by women observes:

Of course, all human beings have the capacity to make *others* of human beings who are not part of the group they consider definitive, but no distinction has been so pervasive in human experience as the distinction between men as the norm and women as the *other*, nor has it been the case that the asymmetry has been universal as it is with males and females.

Thus it is that some feminists see the oppression of women as the model for all other oppressions—caste, class, race—which perceive the less powerful as *other*. (Erickson, 66)

Now, this is exactly where Dorothy Gilman focuses her book. She begins with the most marginal "other" of society, the cloistered nun, she who is hidden away upon the fringe, who knows nothing of feminism, hippies, yippies, the plight of the migrant worker, and has only heard in faint rumor of muggings and inflation—yet is strangely conversant in horse racing tips, hangovers (Gilman, 119), the sophisticated cartoons of James Thurber (Gilman, 110), and renting safe-deposit boxes (Gilman, 131). As Sister John explains in her prayer to God, "As you know, we've been living very simply at St. Tabitha's and we lack worldly experience" (Gilman, 124). In that sense the novel might be seen as an intensified version of "Mrs. Pollifax Gets Ordained," though (despite the lapses noted) Mrs. Pollifax began as Mata Hari compared to the sisters. Beginning, then, as "other," the nuns are presented as increasingly familiar to us. They share our fears, joys, concerns. In one nice juxtaposition near the end of the novel, Sister John is enlightened by the "new liberated" nun Dominican Sister Isabelle Irwin, as they sit not in a cloister cell but in a prison cell. Meanwhile at the mansion they intend as the new abbey, "Sister Ursula," the incognito name of the gangster found wounded and sheltered by Sister John, sits not in a prison cell but in an impoverished cloister, having been liberated from the subworld of criminals and prison cells by hippies who have come to visit him in his convalescence.

Interesting also to underscore is that "Sister Ursula," who is the "nun in the closet" of the title (Gilman, 31, 50, 53), is not a nun at all but a fugitive from the mafia. Taking a cue from Poe's "The Purloined Letter," the sisters eliminate his "otherness" by swaddling him in the habit of their order, symbolically "re-birthing" or "baptizing" him into the protective perimeters of their acceptance. Truly, the sisters do act as caretakers of the world. This universal openness, however, will later on undercut the distinctiveness of their theological identity, when a yellow-robed eclectic guru (who quotes the Sufis, the *I Ching*, reads auras, and alludes to reincarnation) proves not inauthentic as in *Nine Times Nine* but authentic (Gilman, 69). But here their flexibility serves them in extending their ministry to all the needy.

The legendary St. Ursula herself, of course, whose feast is celebrated on October 21, seems hardly a fit subject to inspire mystery fiction, she being more a victim than anything else. Ursula, from a legend of about 975, was reputedly a British king's daughter who, vowing to preserve her virginity, refused a marriage to a pagan king's son and set sail with an escort of 11,000 virgins, eventually being martyred by an arrow wound (an appropriate phallic symbol) after turning down a second less civilized suitor, a Hun prince. Her legend inspired another Saint, Angela Merici, to found in 1535 the oldest Roman Catholic teaching order for women, the Company of St. Ursula or the Ursulines.

While the appearance of the name in *A Nun in the Closet* may easily be traced to a salute to Holmes' Sister Ursula, Holmes' original appropriation from such an inappropriate place as a legendary saint noted less for her brains than for her beauty is a little less clear. This depiction of Ursula not as victor but as victim may, however, shed light on another possible source of origin, a nun named Ursula who was both victim and victor in a homosexual British diplomat's classic gothic precursor to the modern mystery, *The Monk*. Matthew Gregory Lewis' late eighteenth-century novel of dark doings in an Italian nunnery and monastery is set in the tradition of Horace Walpole's classic horror thriller of thirty years before, *The Castle of Otranto,* and Anne Radcliffe's more recent 1794 smash *The Mysteries of Udolpho*. While not clearly a mystery novel, this indictment of personality ministries does contain a certain amount of indirect interrogation of witnesses to the kidnapping of two women—interrupted periodically by their beloveds' bouts with that eighteenth-century fictional scourge "brain fever," triggered whenever bad news is delivered. While not our kind of clerical crime novel, though a novel of clerical crime since the prioress of a nunnery and the abbot of the monastery are the criminals, this supernatural horror tale does contain one memorable nun, Mother St. Ursula, who suspecting her prioress of nefarious deeds, secrets herself behind a curtain and witnesses what she supposes is the administration of poison to one of these unfortunate victims. Ursula then engineers by stealth and by means of a secret message her own arrest and that of the prioress, thus breaking the case wide open and bringing the evil deeds to light:

> "Betrayed?" replied St. Ursula, who now arrived conducted by some of the archers, and followed by the nun her companion in the procession: "not betrayed, but discovered. In me recognize your accusor: You know not how well I am instructed in your guilt:—Segnor," she continued, turning to Don Ramirez, "I commit myself to your custody. I charge the prioress of St. Clare with murder, and stake my life for the justice of my accusation." (Lewis, 338)

Though Ursula here is a material witness not a detective, still this is the rousing stuff of which models of fictional behavior are made. While, as we have noted, this extravaganza does not contain a detecting clerical sleuth but a witnessing cleric, it does contain a guest appearance of the Devil, whose retributional ending harkens back to that of the avenging angel's in *Susannah*. It also contains an attractive figure of Sister Ursula who is at first victimized and later whose cleverness serves justice, thereby obliquely if not directly providing the model for both the Sister Ursula to be developed by William Parker White under the pseudonym of H. H. Holmes and the "Sister Ursula" of *A Nun in the Closet*.

At any rate, Gilman's "Sister Ursula," not being a true nun and being a member of the marginal criminal class of society, serves as a neat foil for two nuns whose marginalism and distance from society is that of innocence. Through their interaction with him and with the others they meet we begin to see the basic humanity of the two nuns. And as the sisters' "otherness" drops away, their concern becomes focused on another group of marginal but not voluntary outcasts, the migrant workers. Sister John's campaign to bring these dispossessed into society provides a central motif that produces the book's tensions. Ultimately unity is achieved on all levels: the cloistered nuns unite with their liberated sisters and society; the various competing denominational ministers in the town join with each other and with the mayor and his government; the migrant workers align with the hippies and finally with the larger society of the town; and the hippies come into communication with a representative of the most aberrantly, conservatively fascist faction of society, the mob. That is, unity in this book of "oriental Thomism" is reached with all but the flagrantly hypocritical, boorish "Presbyterian" sheriff, who represents all that is evil. A crook himself, he lacks even the dignity of the mafia, choosing rather hypocritically to run drugs in secret, cheating both his constituents, the decent electorate of the town, and the Hemingway-quoting mob (Gilman, 185). Such an anomaly in the unsympathetic portrayal of the sheriff makes this book nearly unique among the clerical crime novels in that the enforcer of law is continually hostile to the clerical detective (even Father Brown won over Valentin). In this unredeemed image the book becomes anti-Reformed, the sheriff emerging as theologically representative since no other Presbyterian is introduced to annul or even to temper his evil, Presbyterians being conspicuously absent among the Roman Catholic and Episcopal priests, the Baptist minister and the Rabbi who come to the nuns' aid (Gilman, 154). Instead, Buddhism becomes the sole complement to the nuns' post-Vatican II syncretism.

In regards to the scholastic underpinnings of the nun's theology, Sister John is a firm advocate of the priority of order:

> "I like a firm base. . . . A sense of order, a stable background in which to place events, which I must say appear to be accumulating rapidly. I like to see how things work. . . . What we're speaking of," said Sister John gently, "is divine order." (Gilman, 51)

As we have seen in the sanctuary discussion recounted earlier, the sisters have a clear grasp on how that order mandates priorities that can set aside lesser decrees, as those of the civil law, in favor of higher divine ones.

Similarly, their approach to evil is thoroughly Roman Catholic in the Augustinian/Thomist tradition. "Evil is, after all, only a deficiency of goodness" (Gilman, 90). With St. Thomas they consider it a privation, but the terms they use are modern ones. Evil is "like a vitamin deficiency" (Gilman, 90). There is "very little nourishment" in the world (Gilman, 33). Still, their Catholicism is firmly post-Vatican II in outlook. "Pope *John* would have understood, I'm sure of it, God rest his soul" (Gilman, 58), and:

> "Sister John, we're not detectives, we're nuns. . . ." "If we can grow vegetables and print a newspaper and raise goats and live in the presence of God, and bake bread and butcher a cow, I don't see why we can't solve a few finite mysteries as well, Sister Hyacinthe." (Gilman, 57)

Their relaxation of the tight standards of the pre-Vatican II church allows them, like the Hebrew midwives, to relax the truth in favor of a higher good. While not "lying"—"Oh, we can't lie. . . . Absolutely not" (Gilman, 54)—they do adopt a form of "situation ethics": "It's only a very small rearrangement of the truth for compassionate purposes" (Gilman, 37).

This relaxation extends to doctrinal religion as well. With the flower children they embrace Lamaism, a form of Mahayana Buddhism of Tibetan guru Bhanjan Singh, just as the hippies have done (and interestingly similar to what Mrs. Pollifax has also done in her increasing practice of Hindu guru Maharishi Mahesh Yogi's Transcendental Meditation). Roman Catholic faith is natural to them but excitement comes from discovering the *I Ching*. Thus, the sisters are always learning from the guru while the guru never learns from them, Sister Hyacinthe always having felt something was missing until the guru came along. Bhanjan Singh, however, clearly observes the difference between his Buddhism and their Christianity (e.g., "Your Ecclesiastes says" or "If I may quote the I Ching"). The book emerges finally more Buddhist than Christian in scope and flavor of presentation. The sisters, in particular Sister Hyacinthe, move in the same direction as Mrs. Pollifax has gone theologically, toward the enlightenment of Eastern religions. Thus, while the book is Roman Catholic in base and is characterized by a firm rejection of Reformed Protestantism as a legitimate approach, it ends strangely in a capitulation to Buddhism.

On the penultimate page Sister Hyacinthe goes so far in forgetting the certitude of her doctrinal Catholicism, which has sustained her throughout the book, as to encourage fortunetelling, practice oriental meditation, and to confess that she had not known completion until her encounter with Bhanjan Singh. So finally, improbably:

> Over by the van Sister Hyacinthe was pressing a bouquet of herbs into Bhanjan Singh's hand. "There's rosemary for remembrance, and comfrey for healing, and yarrow for divination, and after meeting you I shall never feel lonely again." (Gilman, 190).

The guru on his side makes no similar confession, merely tossing off a few parting "fortune cookie-ish" plaudits: "'A lamp has no rays at all in the face of the sun,' he said, 'and a high minaret even in the foothills of a mountain looks low.'" He finally ends the book, "For we are waves whose stillness is non-being. We are alive because of this, that we have no rest" (Gilman, 191). St. Thomas would have cringed. The Catholicism the book presents as so potent in its earlier pages is compromised. It is added to but does not itself add, ultimately proving itself to be but a step towards and not a parallel to the final happiness and fulfillment of Buddhism. Thus, the book in value is Buddhist not Christian, its Christianity merely pointing the way to the enlightenment and fulfillment of Buddhism.

There is, however, another way to read what Kathy Kelley calls this "Buddhist Soaked Melodrama":

> Our nun friends are seen eager and open to change but with too reckless an abandon. Sr.'s Hyacinthe and John are typical of their contemporaries in real life in the late 1960s and early 1970s. There is seen to be a syncretistic blending of beliefs. The scene closes with Sr. Hyacinthe saying her usual night prayers on her knees, then dropping to the floor with crossed legs under her trying a tentative mantra. Indeed the Catholic Church threw open the windows to the wind. The author does well to make a strong point for the risks of change and reinforces in the character of the nuns a parody on their naivete. (Kelley, 4)

Further, in light of her perspective that Catholicism has opened its "windows to the wind," Kathy Kelley interprets the secreting of the fugitive in the nun's habit thus: "The good sisters have chosen to become actively involved with the outcasts, identifying with them each to whatever lengths seemed appropriate. All members of the case involve themselves in one another's lives" (Kelley, 6). How in return does this involvement affect the sisters? Kathy Kelley comments on Sister John:

> One wonders just how much she has gained from all her new experiences when at the height of jeopardy, facing a hit man's gun point, she resorts to a Latin prayer to the Blessed Mother Mary. Ah, but these Mafiosa are would be (or should be) Catholics no doubt. A nun in an old habit, praying to Mary in Latin was just too much for the hit man and she disarmed him without so much as lifting a finger. (Kelley, 7–8).

Thus, Ms. Kelley concludes:

> There were some attachments made and Sr. John dares to talk of corresponding with them. She went so far as addressing and stamping envelopes for such. Not a notable gesture? On the contrary! Cloistered nuns do not correspond with those outside their walls. Sr. John has indeed made a great deal of progress. (Kelley, 8).

Seen in this perspective, the attraction to Buddhism is the "growing pains" of an infant awareness. Our critique of *A Nun in the Closet* need not end on such a dour note, however. As was stressed earlier, the book's major contribution lies in its sympathetic presentation of the marginal: the nuns, the migrant workers, the hippies, even the mafia, the federal police, and eventually the townspeople.

Thus, *A Nun in the Closet,* from this perspective, becomes a good starting place for the feminine clerical crime novel in its elimination of the concept of "other," and its emphasis on the immanence of God. Particularly, its implications for creating an entire subgenre of feminine clerical crime novels are theologically intriguing. Such a movement would necessarily define itself against the Barthian tendency to see God as the Wholly Other. Instead a view of God as immanent becomes the focus, potentially threatening perhaps to reintroduce the natural theology of witchcraft or, as we have seen here, abdicate to an Eastern mystical blending with the Divine All. This is not, of course, to say that the excess in the Barthian, perhaps masculine, mode does not end as its telos outside Christianity. Movement from deism to Barth's wholly other to Tillich's ground of being to a theological absentee-landlordism (as in H. P. Lovecraft's chilling theology of the complete absence of the good Gods and the escape from celestial restraints and supplanting by malevolent deities) to the God-is-dead movement that takes us back full circle past deism is equally undesirable from a Christian standpoint.

In moderation, the emphasis on the feminine serves to eliminate the concept of "other" in humanity, just as emphasizing the immanence of God is complemented by a healthy recognition of God's transcendence. This true Christian perspective flows from the authentic image of God as female and male, whose full expression in humanity could only be achieved by God's creation of both faces of the human mirror: "Let us make the human in our image . . . male and female God created them." Therefore, the transcendent God's justice corrects all, the oppressor and the oppressed, while the immanent God's mercy provides redemption equally in a soteriological and in a social sense.

The feminine clerical crime novel, aware as any "colonial" literature emerging from oppression is aware of the concerns of both "the rulers" and "the ruled" has, thus, the unique potential to create itself as a mirroring fiction that does not truncate the image of either God or humanity.

13

Sister O'Marie's Sister Mary Helen:
Detective or Detective Novel Directory?

If Eco's Brother William seems Sherlock Holmes in a tonsure, Sister Ursula the wise woman personified, and the nuns of Dorothy Gilman Mrs. Pollifax ordained, Sister Mary Helen of *A Novena for Murder* seems at times all of these and Agatha Christie's Miss Marple besides. She is also none of these since the book's dedication reveals a "real Sister Mary Helen, whose inspiration caused it to happen" (*Novena,* v). If she had no other distinction, the fictional Mary Helen at seventy-five (*Novena,* 110, 183) would clearly be one of the oldest of the clerical sleuths. She is second only to seventy-eight-year-old Sister Mary Teresa.

Author Sister Carol Anne O'Marie is a nun herself, a member of the Sisters of St. Joseph of Carondelet who took her vows in 1954, the same year as ex-priest William Kienzle and his fictional priest Father Koesler. Like Kienzle, too, she worked as associate editor on a diocesan Sacramento *Catholic Herald,* but has also worked in parochial education as a teacher, principal, religious superior, and the director of development at Carondelet High School in California. Her creation has spent an "entire religious life," an impressive fifty years in teaching (*Novena,* 17), suggesting, if the story is supposed to take place in 1984, the year of publication, that she began teaching back in 1934. This would move her vows back twenty years before her creator's. Sister Mary Helen may now be frail, but she certainly proves to be a handful for a police officer who has "trouble dealing with strong women" (*Novena,* 46). Well-plenished with mercurial Irish emotion, the former Sally O'Conner (*Novena,* 110) has slightly overlapping front teeth (*Novena,* 135), "old hazel eyes" which "hadn't missed a trick" (*Novena,* 61), and an eye that still appreciates a "handsome hunk" (*Novena,* 59). A "little nun with the touch of brogue" (*Novena,* 61), she can fire off a few choice "damns" when heated (*Novena,* 99) or detonate a bit of caustic wit. Her dry quips, usually self-directed, leave most characters she encounters open-mouthed.

Sister Mary Helen is a virtual stand-up comic. When asked if she anticipates staying at her new post, the fragile little nun replies, "My next change, Inspector, will probably be to Holy Cross Cemetery" (*Novena*, 29). Her view of life is a running monologue of one-liners, and these provide some of the most delightful moments in the book. When an exasperated sister queries what the students will think about a murder on campus, she waits until the sister is "safely out of earshot" to reply, "They probably think it is the most exciting thing that's happened around here in years" (*Novena*, 27). A passion for mystery novels requires that she wrap up her "St. P. D. James" in tooled leather devotional bindings, explaining, "Late afternoon . . . old gray-haired nun . . . sitting alone with book in lap. Everyone expects a prayer book. Right? . . . Then, why blow the stereotype?" (*Novena*, 15). When her superior of the order initiates several meetings, Mary Helen, who has now "begun to lie a little about her age," promptly dubs them "Senility Sessions" (*Novena*, 17). She even turns her ironic eye on the convent itself. When pedantic Sister Therese (who insists on pronouncing her name "trays") wants to start the novena of the title—a nine-day prayer vigil calling on a higher authority to clear up the murder mystery—Sister Mary Helen mugs, "Never underestimate her clout. . . . Put yourself in Dismas's place. What would you do if, out of the blue, right in the middle of enjoying a peaceful eternity, Sister Therese got on your case?" (*Novena*, 25).

When Sister Mary Helen gets on the murderer's case, she is as relentless in plaguing the police and pursuing the murderer as Therese is in hounding St. Dismas. Farmed out to Mount St. Francis College for Women, a green pasture for her declining years, Sister Mary Helen, who has been eluding retirement for at least five years (*Novena*, 17), is understandably less than enthusiastic. But the pattern set by her superiors for the rest of her life is about to alter. As the book opens there is an earthquake, and a star falls in the night sky—the ancient symbols of predestined fate being surpassed, of a change occurring in the fixed plan of life. The sudden shaking of the set world planned out for the inhabitants of the college will change their pattern forever. When the earth stills, a professor who a short while before interviewed Mary Helen, lies dead by a fallen statue. Had this remained an ancient piece of literature, the gods or fate might assume the blame, but in the modern mystery, the D. A. calls it murder.

Mary Helen, that devotee of P. D. James, is quick to plunge into her very own murder case, announcing, "I am an avid mystery fan and I read recently, in one of my books . . ." (*Novena*, 58). One might suppose that nothing communicable to an elderly, white-haired nun would be evoked from the police, but fortunately the detective, unique in the genre, confesses, "I read the same mystery books she does" (*Novena*, 59). The police also follow Sister Mary Helen's prejudice for reading suspects' eyes. One of them dismisses a potential suspect because she has "innocent eyes," while three speeches later dismissing Sister Mary Helen as "a real eye nut" (*Novena*, 154). Apparently the police in this novel work by a modification of Sister Mary Helen's approach, which is detection by intuition, despite their scientific facade:

> When lined up beside motive and opportunity, nice eyes and instinct were hardly a logical argument. Mary Helen realized that. Yet she knew, as surely as she knew the sun would rise in the east, that Leonel was innocent. (*Novena*, 43)

She works not by reason, but by senses, smelling evil out, like Father Brown, sensing it. The police realize this and categorize her style: "It's her intuition" (*Novena*, 91). Foil to Sister Mary Helen in a refreshing innovation for the feminine clerical crime novel is police inspector Kate Murphy. Like Sara Paretsky's V. I. Warshawski, Kate is the daughter of a cop. Unlike Sister Ursula, Kate has gone into the force and is shacking up with "handsome hunk" Jack Bassetti. A "sharp," "good cop," "Homicide's token woman," young, red-headed, fiery-tempered Kate Murphy (*Novena*, 21–22) seems the ideal foil for gentle, puckish, celibate, aura-of-innocence, silver-haired Sister Mary Helen. Yet, Mary Helen is not about to let her past define her since the earthquake and falling star have freed her; and she has pitched her habit for "a smart, navy blue suit, her gray hair styled in an attractive feather cut" (*Novena*, 28). Two things she cannot dismiss are her nun's eyes, sweeping the suspects like two Alcatraz searchlights behind her bifocals. As one appropriately Irish cop recalls, "Those peaceful, piercing eyes he remembered from grammar school, eyes that seemed to be able to read minds" (*Novena*, 28).

If her detecting style is rather disorganized and tenuous, so is her basically simple theology:

> "If God is for you, who can be against?" St. Paul's letter to the Romans. And Paul was so right. Furthermore, whose side could God possibly be on but hers, especially when she was trying to help vindicate an innocent man—one who kept losing his temper and seemed in no way concerned about disproving his own guilt? (*Novena*, 66)

Beyond this, her theology leaves much to be desired. If *A Nun in the Closet* pointed the way to creating a fiction that truncates neither God nor humanity, *A Novena for Murder* only partially achieves that goal. Theologically, Mary Helen's elimination of the otherness of God and her emphasis on immanence precipitates a rather obnoxious familiarity with a Good Ol' Boy in the Sky. God is as sprightly and colloquial as the nuns:

> Immediately, she began to reason with God. Dear Lord, think of poor Therese. She's on the seventh day of her novena, the one she began to catch one murderer of one victim. Now look what You are letting happen! Two murders, and now maybe two murderers! How, in heaven's name, can You do that to poor, high-strung Therese!

Mary Helen was glad God seldom talked back, because she was pretty sure she knew what He would say. "Hold on! People murdering one another is not exactly the way I plan things! But relax, old dear, and stick with Me. We'll work it out!" And she knew He was oh, so right. (*Novena*, 140–41)

Not content with treating the God of the universe as a recalcitrant eighth-grade boy in one of her former classes, Sister Mary Helen, like Sister Therese, keeps right on badgering the deity. Jeremiah might take her correspondence course:

"Don't You know this is the eighth day of Therese's novena?" She felt a bit presumptuous asking God if He knew what day it was, but they did say there was no such thing as time in eternity. "You are supposed to find the murderer, not more people who have been murdered!" (*Novena*, 165)

Now the nun is telling the deity what to do. If this were not written by a nun, we might suspect some disgruntled survivor of the parochial schools was venting anger against the presumptions of the religious.

As superstitious as all the nuns in her new assignment, Mary Helen throws salt over her shoulder for good luck (*Novena*, 66). Apparently, her weak and familiar God is not powerful enough to solve the murders without a little super-natural aid, even with the advice of St. Dismas. As Mary Helen prays, "'And if You have half a chance, God,' she prayed earnestly, 'please, end it quickly'" (*Novena*, 107). Weak as this is, it is superior to her prayer a few pages earlier, "'Dear God, make all this go away,' she had prayed. But of course, nothing had gone away" (*Novena*, 97). The "of course" here seems to typify her attitude. Perhaps, these California murders are too tough for God to handle. (And this is a classic California-school murder where, as Mary Helen bluntly puts it, "every murderer is someone somebody knows" (*Novena*, 31).) What saves the book and the reader, since the deity is obviously incapacitated, is its humor and Mary Helen's plucky intuition. As the investigation unfolds, there are quintessential moments of high humor. One policeman, outraged that the second murder should take place in the chapel, exclaims, "Goddam, no place is sacred any more!" as "His curse rang through the chapel" (*Novena*, 87).

If *A Novena for Murder* fails theologically to provide a fully elaborated view of God and theology, it nevertheless realizes the portrayal of the clergy, the humanizing of Sister Mary Helen and her sister nuns. If a goal of the ministerial mystery has been to present the cleric as fully human, as not-other to the rest of the characters and by reference and reflection to the rest of humanity, the nuns in *A Novena for Murder* are charmingly human. For portraits of nuns they are refreshingly unpredictable and offbeat. Sister Anne, the campus minister, meditates in lotus position, arousing Sister Mary Helen's skepticism rather than the kind of arduous approval found in *A Nun in the Closet*. If Sister Eileen is superstitious and Therese confuses folk wisdom with Scripture, these are human failings. So we have nuns sporting Mickey Mouse watches (*Novena*, 69), nuns believing, as Mary Helen does, old sayings like "Death always comes in threes" (*Novena*, 35), nuns wearing Paiute moccasins (*Novena*, 12) and practicing T.M., and all the nuns outraged together at the evil that has invaded their turf (*Novena*, 97–98). If any character has not been realized, it is the cardboard, chip-on-her-shoulder, pseudo-feminist Kate Murphy. Kate has converted Sam Stack's verbal counterfeit feminism into action. The mockery of marriage, blithely dismissed as, "So far, Kate was having her cake and enjoying every bite of it" (*Novena*, 48), is presented as somehow alluringly better than marriage itself. The same enigma can be found in William Kienzle's earlier books with the hot, idyllic relationship of his two reporters. What is the point of Sister O'Marie's narrative approval? Her characters reduce to some kind of post-teenagers bubbling over with libido but incapable of commitment. Sister O'Marie's and ex-Father Kienzle's attempt to be relevant comes off as faddish and shallow, ultimately infusing the toxin of superficiality into the deep meaning of relationships. This is not to say that live-in relationships would not exist in these specific situations. It is simply to criticize the way they are presented. For example, the sex scenes are real juvenile panters. Jack is already yelling, "'Hurry up, hon'" while Kate is in the bathroom (*Novena*, 126). She wants to chat a bit before enjoying the primal scene but Jack is groaning away, "'If you love me, for God's sake, hurry up.'" To this she thinks inexplicably "'Good God, the man was patient!'" (*Novena*, 128). Patient? He finally explodes with an oath and gets tangled up in her granny gown. There are techniques, after all, to aid guys who suffer from premature ejaculation. Jack's case certainly seems rather severe if Kate has not even emerged from the bathroom when he is already in trouble. And she, the poor innocent, thinks him "patient"? The clincher is that the text would have us believe that Kate and Jack have been living together for a while now. From whence this atavistic teenage panic? The portrayal is more of the stuff of fundamentalist teenage sex manuals ("the boy can't help it, girls") than of real conjugal love. The failure to portray convincing sex in this novel, in the early Kienzle, and in the torrid and sadistic lust scenes of Andrew M. Greeley's scorchers suggests that the cloistered life, if nothing else, certainly gives one a cumulative lifelong case of the hots, as well as a second-hand (presumably) and unrealistic picture of what enjoying sex is really like. Celibate writers who want a truer picture of sex can find it in Charles Merrill Smith's pacing, where love is less frantic and more peaceful, building to its torrid moments like a warm, swelling tropical storm. First the closeness, then the warmth, then the humidity and the heat before the appropriate celestial fireworks for a good hearty long storm, and finally the warm sun bathing all with afterglow. They might also consult Edith Pargeter, who portrays the killer not the hero of *The Virgin in the Ice* as having that frantic back-of-the-auto sexual style. Sex is a fundamental quality of human nature. Abused, it leads to murder in *The*

Avenging Angel. Denied, it apparently avenges itself with lifelong preoccupation. Fulfilled, it creates a deep committed oneness that reflects the triune God. Connubial unity reflects the united God. And at the right hand of this united God are pleasures here and forever, as the Psalmist assures as (Psalm 16:11). But if this one aspect of *A Novena for Murder* is inadequately innocent, other emotions are not. Particularly poignant is the superb portrayal of the nuns' expressions of grief at the presence of death:

> Mary Helen fumbled for a Kleenex. "Almost new." She handed her friend two crumpled pieces of tissue. Eileen bent over and began to sob. Clapping her hands over her ears, Mary Helen let her weep. (*Novena*, 84–85)

Mary Helen's own heroine P. D. James, in an excellent interview by D. C. Denison in *The Boston Globe Magazine*, commented on the relationship between writers and their characters:

> I think [the mystery is] moving much closer to main-line fiction and a bit outside the rather trite conventions. Certainly modern mystery writers care more about their characters. In the old days, as I've said, the puzzle dominated the whole book, and everything else was rather perfunctory. Now I think they're more ambiguous in the sense that in the old days, the villain was always totally villainous, and the police were always totally uncorrupt. Now, I think we've realized that there isn't so much black and white, only shades of gray. Now they have some of the moral ambiguities of true novels. (Denison, 18, 20)

Though her villains are certainly purely villains, perhaps another way to read the character flaws of her protagonists is as Sister O'Marie's way to present true ambiguities. Even if the experienced sexual responses of her lovers could be deepened and matured in technique, perhaps they ought to be left juvenile in emotion to depict lack of growth that comes without commitment. On the other hand, those of us who remember struggling along with Audrey Hepburn through her *Nun's Story* are relieved and delighted by the sprightly, refreshing nuns we find here.

A further refreshing aspect of this book and of the entire genre is that the mystery is one body of literature that does not suffer from ageism. Sister Mary Helen and Sister Mary Therese are but two of the strong cadre of able and astute senior clerics who include sixty-year-old Brother Cadfael, mid-fifties Martin Buell, Robert Koesler, and toward the end of his series Father Bredder. Septimus, we recall, is a retired bobby. Bede has a grown son. Alington's Castleton, Warriner's Toft, and even Head's two missionaries, Emily and Dr. Mary Finney, are all mature leaders.

Mary Helen is retiring from a fifty-year teaching stint, and all her reading has apparently prepared her for detecting. In fact, her reading seems at times to get in the way of the story. In addition to P. D. James (*Novena*, 14, 15, 18), we find references to Miss Marple, Nero Wolfe, Perry Mason, Sherlock Holmes and Watson, Wilkie Collins' *The Moonstone,* Charlie Chan and Number One Son, "whodunits," and Mrs. Pollifax, as well as Shakespeare, Humphrey Bogart, *The Odd Couple, The Spy Who Came in from the Cold,* Cinderella, Robert Frost, Mother Goose rhymes, Alfred Hitchcock, Gerard Manley Hopkins, *The Streets of San Francisco,* Rodin's *The Thinker,* Samuel Butler, Plato, Cervantes, and Horace as well as numerous quotations, maxims, proverbs. The book is such a web-work of literary allusions that perhaps Sister O'Marie should have made her nun a retired teacher of literature rather than history. In fact, so full is *A Novena for Murder* in its allusions to other mystery novels that at times it seems more a celebration of the genre than a novel itself. Watching the allusions pile up and threaten to crowd out the story, we might suspect that Sister O'Marie has written a book about mystery novels rather than a novel itself. Sister Mary Helen is more a walking directory of what detectives would do, of what fictional detectives have done, than a detective. Take, for example, her depiction of the finding of the body. Discovering the body, of course, represents different things to different mysteries. For Chesterton the body is solid evidence for the grotesqueness and paradoxical quality of life. So his bodies are bizarrely twisted to appear as anything at first glance but what they are. Confronting the enigma, one discovers a dead human. For Dorothy Sayers, exemplified in *Have His Carcase,* the discovery is a clinical, forensic one, cold, evaluative and eventually chilling in its affirmation that all humanity has been stamped out by murder. Here we have only the nausea to give us any emotional sense of what the body means. Perhaps that is why Sister Mary Helen must keep fighting down her sense of elation in doing detection by a reminder that it is "oh, so serious."

Still, Sister O'Marie's nuns live and breathe. Even their innocence is attractive and ultimately convincing. Maybe the failure of the other characters is a testimony to Sister O'Marie's own purity. She doesn't portray sin well. Illicit sex is on a par with a naughty overindulgence in chocolates. Blasphemy is cute and "in." Murder is a noble act—like Lily Tomlin's "Rid-a-rat" in *Nine to Five.* Breaking a coroner's seal, lying, and theft are all cute. We are cued to react with horror when one of the nuns heaves. But ultimately, if sin is an unknown commodity for Sister O'Marie—and its sordidness will be a nasty surprise for anyone inclined to think otherwise—innocence is certainly not. Maybe there is no true goodness in this book, no option to do the right when weighing the cost of the wrong. But there is certainly a heady supply of three-dimensional salutary innocence, and this is the book's finest facet. How many writers are truly capable of making innocence live and breathe? Most of the time innocence is just waiting to be sullied and only with a Roman Missalian/John Hickian fall from grace can the innocent character come alive. But Sister O'Marie's delightful nuns make innocence fashionable, attractive, alive. And this is a delightful accomplishment.

14

"Mass" Murder in Kienzle's Koesler Series

Carnage in the clerical crime novel sometimes runs from average to slightly below average compared with the rest of the mystery genre. The Father Brown stories and the Whitechurch novels alternate between tales of theft and murder. C. A. Alington's and Stephen Chance's series do not feature any murders, while most other examples of the subgenre feature either a single corpse or, as in Charles Merrill Smith's *Avenging Angel* and *Holy Terror,* two or three connected killings. The extreme of the genre, however, is the Father Koesler series by William X. Kienzle.

Interestingly, Koesler's dates are William Kienzle's dates, Koesler's experiences are Kienzle's experiences. Like his detective, William X. Kienzle was ordained to the priesthood in 1954 and served for twenty years as a parish priest, fourteen of these as editor-in-chief of *The Michigan Catholic,* a "religious house organ," as his creation snidely observes. Indubitably, if Ross Macdonald, who observed the affinity between detectives and their creators in his essay "The Writer as Detective Hero," had reviewed this information and learned that Kienzle himself was born in one of the hospitals used in *The Rosary Murders,* he would have been content to lump Kienzle/Koesler together in his list of fictional authorial clones. In fact, Kienzle himself comments:

> He is—as I was—a Detroit diocesan Catholic priest, past editor of a weekly Catholic paper, and pastor of St. Anselm's, a suburban parish. We are the same age, height, and build. We have a similar philosophy of life. I know him well. (Reilly, 530)

Yet, unlike Koesler, Kienzle left the priesthood and married, while stranding his character in celibacy, a situation which has left his creation feeling increasingly more desperate about his celibacy as he ages (e.g., *Sudden,* 26, 30, 32). Still, despite ogling women and savoring ribald jokes, Koesler appears a psychologically mature single person, on good terms with himself and relaxed to be who he is in relation to his calling and the world. In this Koesler is a major accomplishment. He and his fellow priests more than any of the other characters in these books live and breathe. If the police and the reporters might tend at times toward stereotypes, Kienzle's priests are certainly thoroughly three-dimensional. One expects to meet any one of them at the next parish one visits. Father Robert Koesler (pronounced Kessler (*Rosary*, 28)), is an Irish and German (*Shadow*, 188), tall, thin, blond, six-foot-three-inch (*Hat*, 17, *Mind*, 19, *Rosary*, 7) cleric, who is priest-editor of the *Detroit Catholic*, a diocesan paper (*Rosary*, 2), and in residence at St. Ursula's parish (*Rosary*, 2). By the next book he is calling his own parish St. Anselm's in Dearborn Heights (*Mind*, 19), presumably not a sister to the St. Anselm's New York Episcopalian parish that Isabelle Holland's Reverend Claire Aldington serves. The child of traditional Catholics who died a year apart from each other (*Kill*, 189, 190), Koesler was ordained in 1954 (*Shadow*, 106). He habitually daydreams through the mass, though by the fifth book the problem is becoming acute (e.g., *Shadow*, 21, 107). For him the mass's "routine had a way of dulling concentration" (*Shadow*, 24). A sports lover who is average to slightly above average (*Shadow*, 170–71), he is no aging ascetic-in-training but a "gregarious" though "not garrulous" (*Shadow*, 233) man who likes his bourbon manhattans and has been known to be the life of the party. In *The Rosary Murders* he is a chain smoker who will have stopped smoking for five years by the time of *Shadow of Death*, placing the action of the three books intervening between *The Rosary Murders* (1979) and *Shadow of Death* (1983) into a five-year span. A mild civil libertarian, he has "an active dislike" for "most of the 2,414 laws in the Code of Canon Law" (*Hat*, 47) and only believes in the pope "sometimes" (*Hat*, 48): "In practice, Koesler bent Church law as far as he feasibly could to serve the needs of individuals" (*Hat*, 135). Like few other clerical sleuths he enjoys writing sermons, for he sees reconciling the assigned Scripture readings as a kind of mystery puzzle, deciphering why the liturgist thought two readings produced one message (*Hat*, 135). He is in his mid-fifties (*Mind*, 19) and wears glasses (*Shadow*, 67). Active, he has the reactions of a high-strung greyhound in his opening novel. Aptly, he drives a yellow Cheetah (*Kill*, 224). A nervously fast eater, he tears through his food "like a starving European child" (*Rosary*, 1). He does not believe in dessert, nor can he make good coffee (*Kill*, 243). This nervousness and its swift reactions will stand him in good stead later when his life is continually threatened throughout the series. He is, like so many of his peers, briefly suspected of murder (*Hat*, 91–92). A bit ashamed of his job on "what was little more than a religious house organ," he wishes he "belonged to a somewhat more legitimate news medium" (*Rosary*, 4). He has a "characteristic humble manner" (*Kill*, 223). Though he prefers "peace and quiet in church" (*Rosary*, 11), since we have already learned he is gregarious, we suspect he is the one who likes to make the noise. He is, like Sister Mary Helen, "simply a mystery buff. He read mystery novels like some priests read the Bible. He loved a mystery" (*Rosary*, 3), which is a good attitude to have for a clerical sleuth, because he will have plenty to solve.

His first mystery comes along immediately after he begins wondering who pulled the plug on an elderly hospitalized priest and ends having him running for his life. Ironically, his hobby of collecting rosaries—"You can never have too many rosaries, he thought, though he was coming close" (*Rosary*, 13)— unearths a deadly source of supply when simple black rosaries are left on the battered bodies of priest and nuns.

What is the motive for these murders? Koesler, who is a good counselor, adept at reassuring, finds out in a marvelous theological *cul de sac*. As father confessor he learns the killer's motive but cannot share it with the police because of the seal of the confessional. Full of common experiential knowledge, Koesler is the kind who encourages confidence:

> He'd learned long ago that when people tell a priest—or, he supposed, a minister or a psychotherapist—something shocking, they knew damn well it was shocking and they needed no response, not even a raised eyebrow, to confirm their conviction. (*Rosary*, 11)

Eerily, the motive for the murders involves pastoral counselors not taking their parishioners' problems seriously enough. Righting disorder is a primary priestly function for Kienzle. If priests will not deal with the world's disorder, *The Rosary Murders* argues, they will fall victim to it. Like Agatha Christie's *The ABC Murders* and the many similar thrillers that followed it, *The Rosary Murders* is a superlative example of the nonclassical mystery. Here we do not have a gathering of people cut off in a drawing room, on an island, in an airplane, snowed in, locked in, or otherwise isolated. Nor is the killer a familiar character. Instead, the killer is an unknown psychopath into whose mind, as in *The ABC Murders*, we peer, a malevolent paranoid, whose "calling" is to slaughter priests and nuns and leave black rosaries in their hands. In that sense the tale is more a thriller or a tale of suspense, closer to the classic melodrama or horror tale, than a mystery that reveals a secret, unless the secret here is the insane motivation of the killer.

All of this thought, action and argument is borne along in a paratactic staccato style that is fresh, journalistic and full of humor. Short humorous vignettes continually pepper the narrative, lightening its horror, as for example, the brief vignette of the five-year-old boy, who, told to be quiet in church since God is present, greets Koesler with, "Hi, God" (*Rosary*, 9). If the classic "Ah! Ah-h-h-h-h . . ." structure of the original gothics, before the term became synonymous with modern romance, can be found anywhere in the ministerial mystery, it is certainly here in the earlier Kienzle books. In these unnerving tales of homey clerical scenes interspersed with swift and violent death, the clerical population of Detroit significantly declines. *The Rosary Murders,* when it exploded on the literary world, opened the way for Koesler's immediate reappearance.

Its sequel, *Death Wears a Red Hat* (1980), proved to be another tale of mass slaughter but from a completely different perspective and featuring a wholly different set of victims. After a two-book interlude, *Shadow of Death* (1983) provided an unexpected sequel to *Death Wears a Red Hat,* the inverted sequel to its own predecessor, *The Rosary Murders.* In *The Rosary Murders,* we recall, a crazed killer wantonly slaughters priests and nuns until he is finally apprehended. He leaves at the scene a simple black rosary as his sinister sign. In *Death Wears a Red Hat,* set two years after *The Rosary Murders* (*Hat,* 18, 45), conversely a vigilante leaving small statuettes thins out Detroit's leading thugs, pimps, conmen, and pushers who have managed to escape the justice of the courts. In the extra symbolic gesture, he leaves their severed heads grotesquely propped in prominent places—tucked in a cardinal's red hat, suspended from a cathedral roof, or replacing the stone heads on top of statues. The statues selected are indicative of the crimes being punished (*Hat,* 126). Never apprehended, the suspected vigilante, a black civic leader who is a Haitian immigrant, is an ordained deacon of the Roman Catholic Church. His motive seems to be, as Koesler conjectures, "A statement on sin. Sin as the using and misusing of people" (*Hat,* 273). In contrast, *Shadow of Death* again features the slaughter of the leading clergy, attributed to a version of the Jamaican Rastafarian movement. Koesler's own theology—which had already begun to crack in *Red Hat* with the realization that "his personal theology and conscience had been formed with a blindness toward an alien but legitimate culture" (*Hat,* 288)—opens him to the possibility of the syncretism of Christianity and Vodun as an acceptable form of worship. He does not consider that Vodun, called by its popular name Voodoo, is already a syncretistic melding of African animism and ancestor worship with Catholicism or that sorcery has been condemned since the ancient eastern Old Testament. Uncertain and confused, he finally retreats to dependence on the syncretistic Roman Catholic/Vodun vigilante's own conscience as the final determiner: "Koesler knew that according to Catholic doctrine, one's conscience, unless hopelessly pathological, was the supreme personal arbiter" (*Hat,* 294). He will bring that confusion into the next few books and be forced to deal with it again when *Shadow of Death* reintroduces the syncretistic dilemma. At any rate, in a grotesque eucatastrophe of an ending, a wave of good works sweeps Detroit, inspired by terror of the avenger. A hardened newspaper editor puts the cap on the tale with a sinister, if telling, eisegesis of Proverbs 9:10: "The beginning of wisdom is the fear of the Lord" (*Hat,* 298). Proverbs' sage might have implied reverence with the word *fear,* but in the Detroit of *Death Wears a Red Hat* the word means terror. Whether the theology of such a rendering is more Christian or Vodun is certainly a subject for speculation.

However, the sheer amount of slaughter in the tale is truly something unique in the genre. The cumulative victims of the abortionists, the drug dealers, the vigilante, and the thugs who rub out competitors and pin it on the vigilante become too numerous to count. There are over a dozen and nearly a score of shot, tortured, knifed, or butchered dead or maimed bodies of pharmacists, saleswomen, thugs, pimps, teenagers, abortionists, drug addicts and on and on. "Mass" murder is certainly the main mechanism that moves the narrative along, as the butchered swing eerily from the ecclesiastical ceilings or stare grotesquely from the Golgotha of sacred statues. And yet, despite the slaughter, in this book Kienzle achieves the goals that nearly every crime author seeks: to invoke pity for the victims, regret for the victim/culprits, and satisfaction at the apprehension or destruction of the most sadistically evil of the predators.

Multiple murder attempts continue in *Assault with Intent,* and *Shadow of Death* drops the main characters like so many September flies. Rafael Sabatini, meticulous author of such historical studies as *The Life of Cesare Borgia* and *Torquemada and the Spanish Inquisition* as well as such famous costume adventures as *Scaramouche, The Sea-Hawk,* and *Captain Blood,* is said to have kept miniature representatives of his characters on his desk, knocking each one off as they were slain in order to keep track. William Kienzle might well do something similar since his carnage runs so high. In *Shadow of Death,* as in the earlier *The Rosary Murders,* a "poor nun" is raped, tortured, twenty-seven crosses carved into her flesh" (*Shadow,* 15); two cardinals are stabbed to death before us; a main character is beaten nearly to death, with all ten fingers, seven ribs, and nearly every bone in his body fractured; series regular Inspector Koznicki is shot; and even Father Koesler himself suffers a multiple-injury car accident. The carnage, as in *Red Hat,* becomes quite nauseating, while the book thoroughly summarizes all the volumes that have preceded. If terror comes from witnessing in minute detail how many ways humans can be butchered, Kienzle is a master of terror. Andrew M. Greeley, who will exceed Kienzle's detailed horrors, wrote drolly in the promotional blurb to *The Rosary Murders,* "I want twenty-four-hour police protection" (*Rosary,* back dust jacket).

The volumes in this series seem to follow a regular pattern of mass murder by an individual, mass murder by an individual, and contemplated individual murder by a mass in the first triad; and in the second triad, mass murder by a group, attempted mass murder by a group, and contemplated individual murder by a mass, this time with the real murder of an individual by another. This mass-mass-single, mass-attempted mass-single pattern graphs the series like a morse code signal. So much slaughter must and does have theological significance:

> The essence of the Bible, at least for the Christian, occurs when Almighty God allows His Son to be brutally executed. In fact, the execution may be said to be the fulfillment of the Father's will.

> When you move back into the Old Testament, killings multiply. And, not infrequently, they are in response to God's will. It starts with Cain killing Abel. Moses kills an Egyptian. God takes the firstborn of each Egyptian family. God wipes out the entire Egyptian army in the Red Sea. Whole cities are destroyed at God's command. And—in perhaps the most touching instance—to test his faith, Abraham is ordered to sacrifice his only son. Then, there is that rather obscure woman in the Book of Maccabees who encourages her sons to die under torture rather than sin. (*Sudden*, 250)

But this reasoning belongs to the religiously twisted killers, not the priests of this series.

Against such strong evil and twisted religiosity, Koesler needs to summon up a strong responsive theology. Unfortunately, his bout with syncretism in his second outing has left him so confused that he seems to stumble through the first five books before finally forging a potent pastoral theology in *Kill and Tell*.

The slow formulation of Koesler's theological perspective provides one of the most fascinating dimensions of these books. He begins by reacting against the compulsive-obsessive religiosity of traditional credit-book Catholicism. This he slowly dismantles and replaces with reliance upon one's own conscience and on God:

> "Our early impression of God," Koesler continued, "was heavy with vengeance. We could lead decent lives in the state of sanctifying grace and then maybe slip and eat one pork chop on a Friday and if we died before getting to confession God would zap us into hell. And, while that oversimplifies things a bit, it is pretty much the way we were taught.
> "Now, I think, we tend to view the morality of a life as a whole rather than consider its individual episodes. Not that an act of theft is good. But that the act of theft flows from a lifestyle where an individual act of thievery might be more a mistake than typical of the way that person would ordinarily operate. . . . But Henry has been judged by God . . . by an all-loving and forgiving and understanding God. We mustn't lose faith that Henry has found that God can find ways unknown to humans to forgive. We leave Henry to our Father in heaven with great confidence and hope. It's all we can do." (*Sudden*, 197)

Fueled further by encountering such hostile views toward traditional Roman Catholicism as that of the Rastas, who Koesler is told "are of the opinion that the Pope is the Satan of Babylon" (*Shadow*, 125), he continues to strip his theology down to a slim, lithe, workaday pastoral outlook, ultimately concentrating on two factors, the power of the individual conscience to determine right and wrong and the efficacy of God's gracious forgiveness. The implications he works out best in the confessional. So through the series, in scene after scene, we accompany the good Father in some of the most delightful glimpses into pastoral care in the entire subgenre. In being set up for the big one, we watch Koesler conducting a number of confessions in both pre- and post-Vatican II styles, hearing and absolving everyone from child to adult. With children Koesler's cumulative experiential rules are as follows:

But Koesler, in confessional matters, lived by two rules: Don't interrupt a child's laundry list of sins—the list is probably memorized and if it is interrupted one may reap prolonged silence. Followed by a starting over. And secondly, don't use the confessional for teaching. (*Kill,* 59)

By allowing the confessional to become the place where human conscience meets itself and God, Koesler can permit the conscience to become for him the rule within the rule that allows a faithful believer to set aside the rules. With this as a basis he can now redefine his own theology, as he does in *Kill and Tell*. Finally opposing Eastern mysticism, Unification and Hare Krishna (*Kill,* 215), reading his breviary in Latin (*Kill,* 145), constantly praying for his parishioners' problems and reading devotional books on prayer (*Kill,* 110), he can reappropriate the best of Catholic tradition. As an essential plot element, he even confirms a belief in demon possession (*Kill,* 146), adding to an earlier defense of New Testament miracles (*Shadow,* 166). Attempting to balance the best of the old with the best of the new, he strictly refuses to adopt the old school liberal idea that, since God has reconciled the world to Godself, the job of the cleric is to inform people they have been redeemed and to charge them to begin acting as redeemed people. For Koesler's confessional theology, there can be no absolution, no forgiveness without repentance. Father Koesler holds fast here to the full message of the Christ, "Repent for the reign of God is at hand" (Matthew 3:2, 4:17). In this credo for Father Koesler, as for all the clerical sleuths, all the issues meet: the responsibility for sin, the access to forgiveness, the claims of the civil courts, the penalty for civil crime, the claim of the celestial court, the penalty for sin.

Once repentance is exacted, Koesler is thoroughly optimistic:

Who knows? After death, who knows the immense power of God's forgiveness? We believe that after death there is a judgment. And, aided by Scripture and tradition, we think we know the rules under which we will be judged. But we don't really know how much God can and will forgive, nor how much He will not. All prayers after death, no matter how holy or sinful the deceased's life, presume nothing. They only ask mercy. (*Sudden,* 251)

Mass carnage may abound as it will, but Koesler can relax at the end of each book in the healthy consolation of faith:

As far as he was concerned, it seemed to bring everything full circle. It all started last Sunday and it was all over this Sunday. It thoroughly satisfied the priest's deep-felt need for symmetry in life.

God's in Her heaven; all's right with the world. (*Sudden,* 257)

His final trust in the balance of life and its hint of a feminine pronoun for God will be expanded and expounded in Andrew M. Greeley's book of the same year, *Happy Are the Meek*.

For now, Koesler ultimately rests within the assurance that life is so structured that no matter how vast and heinous the crimes he must confront, good will balance all; a symmetry will be restored to life in heaven's providence. This attitude has become habitual with him and perhaps rightly so, for in these books sheer slaughter is a metaphor for the seriousness of habitual acts. What one does directly affects whether one ultimately lives or dies, whether one heals or kills or whether one ultimately finds peace or does not. Books are collections of metaphors and images that tell us something by creating a running series of word pictures that connect like so many celluloid stills into a flowing parable. Extravagant as its proliferation may be in this series, murder here, precipitated by sin, reveals that habitual evil acts are malignant and ultimately spiritually terminal. Through depicted death those acts literally wreak destruction. Like the extravagant Old Testament prophecies of Joel that Peter saw fulfilled at Pentecost (Acts 2:14ff.), a "visual" message warns of something invisible going on within that is still authentically deadly. If sin is leading humanity to eternal damnation, then as a warning sin leads many representative characters in the stories to death. Inversely, habitual acts of contrition and confession lead others to wholeness and ultimately to peace and salvation. Finally, in addition to sin and redemption, the essential indistinguishable humanity of the priests that are God's vehicles to dispense God's means of dealing with these realities are Kienzle's concern. And few, except for Andrew M. Greeley, have demythologized and humanized the priesthood to the extent William Kienzle has done.

15

God as Lover/God as Sadist: Andrew M. Greeley's Blackie Ryan Series

"No one resists grace, Nick. It's a combination of mist and quicksilver. It sneaks in through the cracks and the crannies, fills up the interstices that our plans and programs and personalities leave empty, takes possession of the random openings we give it and then, when we least expect it, when we've done everything in our power to stop it, BANG! there's the big surprise."
          Andrew M. Greeley, *Virgin and Martyr*

To judge by the number of defensive prologues and afterwords Father Andrew M. Greeley has appended to his immensely successful bestselling novels, a good part of the "surprise" of "grace" in his works is how a leading and respected sacerdotal statesperson of the North American Roman Catholic Church can write such racy and violent novels, filled with priests fornicating, torture murders, multitudinous adulteries, vulgarities, blasphemies, and a general pessimism in regards to the effectiveness of the leadership of the higher echelons of the Vatican. If Leonard Holton found a thin and unsupportive audience for his Father Bredder thrillers in the 1960s, twenty years later Father Greeley's tales, from his first bestselling novel *The Cardinal Sins* have been enthusiastically received by an immense reading public. In fact, he has been so successful that after several books he was able to pledge one and a quarter million dollars to fund a chair of Catholic theology at the University of Chicago (*Garcia*, 63). Whether *The Cardinal Sins, Thy Brother's Wife, Ascent into Hell*, and *Lord of the Dance* looked like a clerical rendering of *Peyton Place* or not, whatever it was that Father Greeley was supplying, the reading public was buying in quantity. The three novels following *The Cardinal Sins* Greeley called *The Passover Trilogy*, closing the set with *Lord of the Dance*. As the first volume in a new series entitled *Time between the Stars*, *Virgin and Martyr* used the characters of the earlier trilogy but introduced a new one, a detecting priest named Father Blackie Ryan, plunging Andrew Greeley into the clerical crime novel. Beguiled like so many others by the clerical sleuth, in 1985 he also published a second book, a paperback original featuring the same clerical sleuth and purporting to begin a clerical crime series. But *Happy Are the Meek,* despite its claim, does not begin a ministerial mystery series; it merely scales down the quantity of pages and immensely complex structural delights of the superlative *Virgin and Martyr. Virgin and Martyr* is a major work, a theological and structural peak in Greeley's novels, a *tour de force* through the new theologies of the Roman church. Ultimately opting for moderation in religious fervor, it fulfills one of the four mottos that introduce it, an inscription on a bell at Holy Trinity Church, Cambridge: "Glory to God in the highest and damnation to all enthusiasts" (*Martyr,* vii).

Although a substantial contribution to the subgenre, *Virgin and Martyr* is only one-half a clerical crime novel, because while Blackie Ryan does detect throughout the novel, he only becomes ordained as Father Blackie Ryan a bit more than halfway through the novel. However, since the novel is set up as a series of thoughts, conversations, and letters, adapting the epistolary style of such writers as Samuel Richardson, it is framed beginning and end by an ordained Blackie Ryan. Along with Alice Walker, whose *The Color Purple* demonstrated how immensely effective this narrative structure can still be, Greeley employs it to tell a moving story of a devout and troubled woman whose struggles with faith reflect the struggle of the entire contemporary American Catholic church.

The book opens with the struggle over the will of Catherine Collins, heiress to seven million dollars and martyr in a revolutionary war in the small and troubled fictional Latin American Republic of Costaguana. Cousin Blackie Ryan and devoted would-be-husband attorney Nick Curran are unsatisfied with the vague reports of her martyrdom. The quest for proof and Blackie's ordination turn the book into a clerical crime novel. The unfolding of the tale of Catherine is a work of art. The basic structure is right out of the Old Testament. Catherine, like Israel, spends her life running away from her true lover, Nick, who like the Lord waits patiently for his errant lover to return. His complaint is similar to the prophets', anguishing for the marriage supper of Revelation. In its wheels within wheels the young Catherine is introduced to us theologically in several vignettes of religious prophecy and fervor. Her mother interrupts a teenage party on New Year's Eve, the beginning of a year, a new age, to announce the Fatima letter recently opened by the pope prophesies that, rather than beginning a new year, Catherine and her friends will see the end of the world. The prophecy, fraudulent as it is, eerily describes Catherine's subsequent life: new beginnings that mark only repetitions of old failures and deeper and deeper personal catastrophes. As Blackie observes at the end of the tale, "You show us that it is possible to do what we must spend most of our lives doing, neutralizing horror and beginning again" (*Martyr,* 407).

In another early scene an ecstatic pentecostal priest seeking to convert a seven-year-old child, recently dead of tuberculosis, into the first Chicago saint triggers the clouding over of a mirror and a miserific vision for Nick Curran, unseen by his classmate Catherine (*Martyr,* 58–59). The seeking is led by fervent Father Ed Carney. Hundreds of pages later the same Father Ed, now a liberation theologian and radical activist priest, has lured the same Catherine to a small, troubled country where again he leads a group to seek an encounter with God, this time a politically revolutionary beatific vision. But again in the face of Catherine, encountering the experience that has made her St. Catherine, Nick sees only horror, the face of hell looking out in her "terrifying revelation" (*Martyr,* 328). Like the false pentecostal vision and the false existence of her patron saint, Catherine of Alexandria (tossed out of the Church's register of saints), Catherine's martyrdom and reputation as a saint are fictitious. When everyone's would-be saint Catherine Collins appears in a flickering candlelight, the light goes out (*Martyr,* 401). As St. Catherine was struck from the register (*Martyr,* 64–65), the contemporary "St." Catherine is proved to be not a saintly martyr but the victim of the maniacal messianic delusions of religious enthusiasts like Father Ed Carney. And yet, unmartyred and uncanonized though she may be, the true martyr of faith, the witness Catherine Collins, not St. Catherine of Chicago but simply Cathy Collins, witness for Christ, triumphs with Nick: "Against the combined wonder-workers Nicholas and Catherine, the forces of evil traditionally have been no match" (*Martyr,* 437). Greeley will add St. Michael to this new human register of saints in *Angels of September* (*Angels,* 344). Pursuing Catherine and Nick and all the characters of the book is an Old Testament theophany, scaled down appropriately to fit this bleak modern age. A pillar of cloud leading the people in the Old Testament, God is now reduced to wispy quicksilver mists pursuing people. At the first chink in human despair God whirls in and envelopes with love. Having but a few thin chances to envelope in *Virgin and Martyr,* God all but makes up for it with an orgy of enveloping in the sequel, *Happy Are the Meek.*

As we noted, *Happy Are the Meek* consciously launches an entire series of clerical crime novels based on the Beatitudes. In its structure, *Happy Are the Meek* appears at first blush to be a reworking of H. H. Holmes' first Sister Ursula novel, *Nine Times Nine.* Greeley's Wolfe Quinlan, like Holmes' A. Wolfe Harrigan, is found dead in his locked study (*Meek,* 38) after having angered the leader of a cult. Both books are "a classic locked-room puzzle" (*Meek,* 2). There is even a reference to St. Ursula, but as a parish (*Meek,* 11). In the place of Ahasver is one Louis Connery, a cult leader who, like Ahasver, assumes an alias, "Father Armande de St. Cyr." He is a defrocked priest ejected for the stipends he was charging for working miracles (*Meek,* 11) and for excessive familiarity with the mothers of the children in his parish. Both Holmes' and Greeley's cult leaders are suspected of killing their victims while simultaneously appearing before a crowd of their followers. Both claim the ability to "bilocate" (*Meek,* 12) by astral projection (Holmes, *Nine,* 84). The worship of Greeley's Angels of Light cult not only sounds a lot like the demonically cursing syncretistic Children of Light cult of Holmes, but also adopts a monotheism that blends in the sun in a manner reminiscent of the robed and flowery Apollo cult of G. K. Chesterton's "The Eye of Apollo":

> It wasn't like much—white robes, candles, processions, chants in a language I was told was Babylonian (why Lucifer would understand that better than English was not clear to me), a flowery sermon by Father Armande about "life forces" and "sacred energies" that seemed devoid of religious content, bowing and kneeling before an image of the sun—in front of which Father Armande stood in white gown and red cloak as though he were the Angel of Light's grand vizier. (*Meek,* 48)

Reinterpreting, as does Holmes' cult, and blaming in place of Paul "Jewish and Christian leaders" for distorting the "true" gospels, the cult claims:

> Lucifer was not a wicked angel. Some Jewish and Christian leaders made that all up. He represents the life force in nature. He's the light of the world. He's preparing the way for the return of Christ, the real Christ, not the weak character we read about in the Bible. Our new faith is dignified and intelligent. (*Meek,* 47)

It proves to be exactly as dignified as was Holmes' stolid midwestern congregation, hissing out the "Nine times nine" curse, their faces distorted with hatred. Followers of Father Armande are fortunate to escape with their lives. Wolfe Quinlan, like investigator Wolfe Harrigan before him, does not. While nodding to Holmes and Chesterton, the book also appears to nod subliminally at Leonard Holton's *A Pact with Satan,* opening with a wife's claim that her dead "husband's ghost haunts the house" (*Meek,* 1) and letting Blackie Ryan observe that she is "blundering toward self-immolation" (*Meek,* 4). Indeed, the wife is nearly immolated like the troubled wife in *A Pact with Satan,* before this truly harrowing tale is over. The cult leader, like the crazed Father Bill Spaeth of *Grenelle* and Father Ed Carney of *Virgin and Martyr*—who has not progressed as far as demonism by the novel's end but is certainly on the way—has begun as an activist priest and ended up a devil-worshipper (*Meek,* 80). One might believe from reading *Meek* and *Grenelle* that social activism leads to devil worship. Flying around the book come poltergeist manifestations right out of Steven Spielberg's movie; objects whiz around the room and crash on walls. But the explanation eventually threatens to take the book over the boundaries of the mystery into the supernatural thriller: one character is psychic and the husband may have indeed indicated from his troubled grave that he wants a consecrated Catholic burial. Whether these lame developments cause the book to become a hybrid—a supernatural thriller—must be put in question. If so, it is one of the few in the genre since *Susannah,* discounting Matthew G. Lewis' *The Monk,* which some list as a mystery, though I do not. Even Father Bredder's supernatural puzzles always have a suitably empirical explanation, which the mystery genre normally demands.

While *Happy Are the Meek* rides the thin line between mystery and fantasy, positing equally plausible natural and supernatural explanations for events, Blackie Ryan's sequel to *Virgin and Martyr* in the *Time between the Stars* collection, *Angels of September,* takes the psychic tinge of telekinetic powers in *Happy Are the Meek* a step further. That book crosses the line into supranaturalistic horror with the potent image of a psychically charged painting of hell that lays supranatural claim to a troubled woman. Although Blackie Ryan detects, he concludes that strange occurrences in an art gallery are caused by preternatural phenomena, producing a supranatural adventure reminiscent of the spiritual power that Charles Williams put into his "theological thrillers." Ryan's favored explanation—that a painting is charged with a double set of emotions that create a new evil being of kinetic power—could be considered natural. Still, Ryan, skeptical though he may be of the supernatural, arms himself against this apparition with a squirt jar of holy water, cross, rosary, and the ritual of exorcism before venturing off to do battle.

Andrew Greeley has created a powerful image of guilt in his picture—a focal point for love and hatred, guilt and forgiveness to meet, bringing the war that the God of love wages in heaven visually, symbolically to earth. In this, the potent fantastical image of the picture, the intervention of the supernatural into the natural, culminates the progressively overt supranatural manifestations in Greeley's prior work, such as the miserific vision in *Virgin and Martyr* and the poltergeist manifestations in *Happy Are the Meek.*

Unlike *Angels of September* with its crossover elements of billowing smoke, crashing explosions, diabolical laughter, attacks of unearthly cold and heat, centered upon the dancing, psychologically changing picture, *Happy Are the Meek* maintains a slightly more natural explanation for its extraordinary phenomena, though this point is arguable in the case of the poltergeist manifestation and produces an interestingly composed mystery.

Andrew Greeley is a good writer whose sentences have bite. They seize readers and pull them into the story. The content shakes readers roughly, then tosses them to the next sentence, like a bulldog worrying a bone. And there is enough here to worry anyone, as wife beating piles on religious torture, adultery on incest, brutality on brutality. But Greeley's style, apart from the inflammatory content, is enough to ignite interest. He is one of the most facile writers in the genre. Like Margaret Scherf he can summarize a character in a strong illuminating phrase. At times he sounds like Raymond Chandler. But Father Greeley's priest is not a hard-boiled Chandler antihero. He can cry when moved, as when he rushes from the closing courtroom scene to hide his tears in *Virgin and Martyr* (*Martyr*, 437), or when he feels "odd, stinging reactions behind my eyes" upon hearing a pathetic tale of "tragedy and despair" in *Happy Are the Meek* (*Meek*, 184). When he solves the crime in *Meek*, he is so appalled by the solution that he has to vomit (*Meek*, 147), a regular reaction by Greeley characters to emotional scenes. Rather than Chandlerian, he is Chestertonian or Dickensian.

The Reverend Monsignor John Blackwood Ryan, A.B., S.T.L., Ph.D., prefers to be called "Blackie." In fact he insists on it:

> There are a number of theories as to why Katie Ryan—God rest her wonderful soul—gave him that middle name. One is that she had made a Blackwood convention at bridge the night she conceived him. Another is that one of the ancestral Collinses was actually called "Black Blackwood" when he led an eighteenth-century group of Irish revolutionary Whiteboys. You can never be sure with the Ryans, but Blackie seemed to want to be called nothing else. (*Martyr*, 19)

He is "a round little priest" (*Meek*, 242) whose nieces and nephews accuse him of cultivating the appearance of G. K. Chesterton's Father Brown. In fact everyone, even outsiders, sees the resemblance:

> Blackie looks like a modern Father Brown, short, pudgy, cherubic, with curly brown hair, apple cheeks and an expression of impenetrable composure. He is the kind of utterly unimportant-appearing person that you wouldn't even notice if he was on an elevator when the door opened and you walked in. He is also the brightest man I know, ruthlessly loyal, and as much a pixie as his cousin, though he hides that last attribute behind his guise of mordant cynicism. (*Martyr*, 64)

Even Blackie Ryan calls himself "the poor man's Father Brown" (*Meek*, 5) as his nearsighed eyes blink their way through the text (*Martyr*, 64). In fact, he is described as "pathetically nearsighted" (*Meek*, 5) which, he contends, produces a "bumbling, nearsighted incompetence" (*Meek*, 10). While he would like to think of himself as Dickensian, and receives a promise from the women he aids to help turn his office into a quaint Dickens setting, his sister calls him "The Punk" (*Meek*, 2). Like Sister Mary Helen, he is well aware of the image parishioners have of the cloth and will find himself doing things to fulfill expectations, such as "trying to sound the way incense smells" in his speech (*Meek*, 18) or "folding my hands piously, as Monsignors used to do in the old days" (*Meek*, 5), or piling "up the old baptismal books on my desk because that seemed to be the sort of thing monsignors ought to do" (*Meek*, 4). But his family, nearly all of whom have remarkable nicknames, laughingly consider him a "crazy little leprechaun" (*Martyr*, 36), a faerie child, a little changeling left to them. Irish, of course, and still familiar with Gaelic (e.g., *Meek*, 122, 135), he is likely to hum the Irish folk tune "The Whistling Gypsy" as a sign to others he is thinking intently (*Martyr*, 243, 359, 367). For fun he adopts "a phony Irish brogue" (*Angels*, 115). As a child Blackie was already different. While other teenagers drifted off to neck at parties, Blackie would secret himself in the libraries of various homes, reading *Goodbye, Columbus, Goldfinger* or Teilhard de Chardin's *The Phenomenon of Man*. The older teenagers recall, "We didn't mind Blackie, who even then was a strange little kid, because after a few minutes he seemed to become quite invisible" (*Martyr*, 25). To his sister, the famous psychoanalyst, he "knows more about women than most men, but he can't cope with the sexuality" (*Martyr*, 44). High-powered characters like the activist priest Ed Carney tend to forget his name. "But then," as Blackie Ryan explains, "I am quite insignificant in every imaginable way" (*Martyr*, 7).

But like the Father Brown whom he resembles, Blackie is ignored to others' detriment. A natural detective, he has "a superb gift for intrigue" (*Martyr*, 351), and "loves the mysterious" (*Martyr*, 367). He is also an intellectual snob (e.g., *Meek*, 2, 4, 7), who calls himself in jest (or half in jest) "Blackwood the Magnificent" (*Meek*, 133). This helps him in his role since childhood as a debunker. When Catherine's mother makes her dramatic announcement of the end of the world, then blesses all and glides out, Blackie begins a caricature of the pope misplacing the Fatima letter and then gives alternate theories of its content, such as: "'Actually, when he opened it,' Blackie continued, 'he found it was a bill for the Last Supper and he said he wouldn't pay because Jewish catering services always charged too much'" (*Martyr*, 33). His debunking can get protectively vicious when he tears a professor apart after class for persecuting his cousin Catherine (*Martyr*, 189). As in all Greeley's tight Irish families, Blackie takes care of his own. His debunking lends him a clearsighted view of other clergy, whom he considers often full of envy (*Martyr*, 186), and lets him doubt such accepted Catholic doctrines as fire in purgatory (*Martyr*, 167). Later he will turn that searing perspicacity on traditional church institutions full of "Great Silences and Little Silences and all kinds of damn-fool silences" (*Martyr*, 149), as well as radical new theological institutions he considers no more than "Communists with clerical collars" (*Martyr*, 311). While he can turn some of that withering fire on himself, he is more likely to conclude, for example, "I am accounted an excellent preacher, not that that is a great accomplishment in the present state of the art" (*Martyr*, 407).

For him the true Christian is not an enthusiast who chases the newest religious fire, but a hard-working moderate who works on mastering a simple faith, namely, the good Christian believes only a few things, but those very strongly. No ascetic, he likes huge meals at lunch (e.g., *Meek*, 96), can eat voraciously or fast assiduously, and exercise vigorously or not at all without changing even slightly in appearance, measurement, or in any other noticeable way (*Meek*, 96). Brother of another famed sister, a science fiction writer, he reads devotionally from the patristics right after dinner (*Meek*, 96), awakening after two hours of patrology "refreshed and invigorated and resolved to resume his investigations" (*Angels*, 207). His doctorate is in philosophy (*Meek*, 163); he has taught classics at the seminary level for eight years and authored two books, *Salvation in Process: Catholicism and the Philosophy of Alfred North Whitehead* (1980), which sounds suspiciously like his dissertation, and *Truth in William James: An Irishman's Best Guess*, published in 1985, the year of the story. One thing he does not claim to do is administer his "large and variegated parish" well; in fact he believes he administers "badly" (*Meek*, 7). A monsignor of the archdiocese of Chicago, working under long-time Greeley protagonist Cardinal Sean Cronin, he is based around Hyde Park and the University of Chicago (*Meek*, 12) at Holy Name Cathedral, 732 North Wabash, Chicago, Illinois 60611 (*Meek*, 255)—where doubtless a harried postal department will soon begin receiving letters from readers who confuse verisimilitude with real life.

A flashy car buff like Father Buell and Reverend Randollph, he has fixed up his "father's antique gull-wing Mercedes, with a brand-new engine" (*Meek*, 233). His reputation is that "I am supposed to be skilled with puzzles . . . and that I have a reputation for being fair, especially to women" (*Meek*, 131). Both of these characteristics will stand him in good stead when he takes on the problem of *Happy Are the Meek*, a plot that turns on the oppression of the meek, in this case the oppression of women by men. Motive and means are known; as in many classic locked-room problems, the puzzle is the opportunity (*Meek*, 108). As far as motive is concerned, any of the characters who comprise Quinlan's family or business associates have reason to kill this drunken, brutalizing oppressor. The means is derived from Oscar Wilde's reflections at Reading Gaol. As Ryan quotes him, "We all kill the one we love. The coward with a cruel word. The brave one with a sword" (*Meek*, 144). Wolfe Quinlan is killed by the thrust of a medieval sword when a suit of armor topples on him. Blackie Ryan must discover whether it was suicide or murder.

Blackie Ryan has been playing detective, we have seen, since the days of *Virgin and Martyr*, when, as he says, "I had cast myself in the Holmes role and Nick as Watson" (*Martyr*, 365). By now he is introducing himself comically as "your friendly parish priest detective" (*Meek*, 164). Clearly, however, he dissociates himself from the police, stating firmly, "I'm not a policeman" (*Meek*, 164). And with the intellectual snobbery we noted earlier, he disdains the police:

The Long Beach Police, I decided, pushing aside the clippings Larry Burke had left for my perusal, were a thoroughly modern, professional small-town police force.

That meant that they had some skill in harassing teenage beer consumers on the beach at
night, but were of no use whatsoever in a murder case.
And the State Police were precious little better. (*Meek*, 15)

This does not prevent him from teaming up for consultation and for his required
leg work with his cousin Mike Casey, a retired deputy superintendent of police,
author of "two very sensible books on detective procedure," and Ryan's "occasional Watson and Lestrade combined" (*Meek*, 11). When he is not aiding Ryan,
he paints professionally (*Meek*, 10). Mike Casey, we might add, was forced to
retire for political reasons, another cause of Blackie Ryan's disdain for the
institutional police. As we recall, Ryan, like all Greeley's positive characters,
defends his own. That is, no doubt, why he does not feel himself compelled to
turn suspects over to the police. As he reassures one character, "'As to your
concerns, I have no evidence to suspect Mrs. Quinlan of murder, and even if I
did it would not follow that I could consider myself bound to turn over such
evidence to the police'" (*Meek*, 94). He asks, "Am I an employee of the police
department of Chicago or Elmhurst or Long Beach? Am I an agent of the
LaPorte County prosecutor? Am I even a licensed private detective?" And his
parishioner must answer, "You're my pastor" (*Meek*, 94).

Despite the fact that he is not a "licensed private detective," his approach
is like Nero Wolfe's (*Meek*, 67), though he is also like a number of amateur
detectives as well. Like the Sister Ursula of "Coffin Corner," he conducts
interviews in his office, and through these interviews he solves the crime. The
model was Mycroft Holmes', before it was Sister Ursula's or Nero Wolfe's.
The Sherlock Holmes, Terence Marshall, or Archie Goodwin who does the leg
work is Mike Casey (*Meek*, 67). Like Hercule Poirot's Captain Hastings,
Blackie Ryan makes charts of the suspects (*Meek*, 107). He seems to be the
only major clerical sleuth who does. His detecting philosophy appears to be
drawn from Michael Polyani's views. He believes detecting is comprised of
"faith that there is a solution, hard intellectual work to search for it, and then a
moment of blinding illumination" (*Meek*, 147). When seeking that blinding
illumination, Ryan is relentless. As he notes about the locked-room puzzle,
once his curiosity has been engaged, "It would have, in fact, required several
angry archangels to keep me away from it" (*Meek*, 10). With his clear conscience (*Meek*, 146) balanced by a dissembling manner that disdains "candor"
as "a strategy" (*Martyr*, 171), Blackie moves into the ambiguous and often
deadly theological world where commitment, guilt, and the influence of exhortation are often used by predators to enslave the meek. In dealing with both the
dilemmas of *Virgin and Martyr* and *Happy Are the Meek*, he makes use of the
second part of his earlier declaration, his "reputation for being fair, especially
to women."

Blackie, at the outset of *Happy Are the Meek,* expresses in a conversation with Cardinal Sean Cronin his views on the oppression of women:

> Men have oppressed women in every society the world has ever known, a situation that is thoroughly unsatisfactory from a woman's viewpoint and, if the truth is told, less than rewarding for a man too. . . . For while it may be advantageous and amusing to push them around and collect them like jewels or cattle, they are only fully rewarding when they are treated like equals. . . . Even in our so-called civilized world . . . a stranger, a friend, a madman, a father, even a husband, can hurt and humiliate them as a matter of male right. A stroll fifty yards down the beach at night may become a walk into hell. A few serial rapists who get special kicks out of last-minute decisions whether to kill their victims can terrorize all the women in a city. Your Polish friend in Rome does not help when he says they can't be priests. (*Meek,* 8–9)

He soon runs into Quinlan's wife, the Suzie he remembers as a little classmate when he was in his parish school. Her plight is that of victim of her husband and her church:

> We were taught by our parents and by the Church that the finest accomplishment for a woman was to have a husband and a family. Nothing else mattered. If we were too intelligent or too good at something, like art or music, that might even be bad because men didn't like bright or talented women. A woman's task was to raise her children, keep the husband happy, and help him become a success in his career. If he was a success, then she was too. . . . He wanted a dumb little bunny. My family told me I should be a dumb little bunny. My church seemed to agree that I was most pleasing to God when I was a dumb little bunny. So I acted like one. (*Meek,* 172–73, 187)

Dealing with Suzie's plight takes Ryan into a deep theological reflection on the point of Christianity, centering particularly on the Beatitudes (which we have been told will characterize the coming series). As Greeley has told us as preface to the series:

> The Beatitudes represent, if not in exact words, an important component of the teachings of Jesus, but they should not be interpreted as a new list of rules. Jesus came to teach that rules are of little use in our relationship with God. We do not constrain God's love by keeping rules, since that love is a freely given starting point of our relationship (a passionate love affair) with God. We may keep rules because all communities need rules to stay together and because as ethical beings we should behave ethically, but that, according to Jesus, is a minor part of our relationship with God. (*Meek,* v–vi)

This Christianity he sees as standing against its pernicious counterfeits, represented by both the institutional and the new revolutionary doctrines and practices of the Church. He sees the one oppressive system simply developing into the second:

It would be nice to have some sisters who didn't know all the answers. The ones who taught me in grammar school knew all the answers about religion. . . . And now sisters have all the answers about feminism and identifying with the poor and peace and justice. I would like, just once before I die, to hear a nun say, "I don't know." (*Martyr*, 113)

From the unbending hierarchical conservative church comes an unbending hierarchical revolutionary church, as unthinking and dogmatic as its predecessor:

They are characterized by the following: A fierce hatred of the United States. An innocence of the complexities of international economics. A bland assumption that Marxism has been validated as a solution to social problems. A poverty of serious theological reflection. And the pretense that no Marxist society exists anywhere in the world by which Marxist "praxis" (their word, if you say "practice" you are horribly out of fashion) could be evaluated.

Their basic argument was as follows: Christians must be committed to the elimination of social injustice; Marxism eliminates social injustice; therefore, Christians must be Marxists. (*Martyr*, 311)

Ryan sees this syndrome as typified by one arrogant North American seminary which featured itself as the "Seminary of the Oppressed." Scholars there divided between the "Augustines," who worked on their *City of God,* and the attacking "Visigoths." According to Ryan:

At Assembly, the generic Visigothic theology went something as follows: I am a Visigoth and hence a member of an oppressed group. I speak for the million people of my group. I theologize out of our experience of oppression. We are a holy people because of our oppression and indeed the only holy people. All other peoples have no right to claim holiness or even Christianity. They must listen to our theological pronouncements on their knees and abase themselves for what their ancestors or their society have done to us poor Visigoths. (*Martyr*, 258)

Yet Blackie Ryan is not about to replace Christianity with an alternative. And traditionally, he maintains the right attitude in the face of the occult—fear. He finds it "scary" (*Meek*, 79) and has not "resolved yet" what "wrestling with principalities and powers" means (*Angels*, 372), reserving for religious lunatics belief in a hell of literal flames, typified by the attempted immolation at the end.

What, then, does he offer in place of the old and the new Church, the old conservative and the new revolutionary faith? Ryan's theology is very interesting and, eventually, very disturbing. In his quest for symmetry on the very last page of *Sudden Death*, William Kienzle had his Father Koesler refer to God as being in Her heaven. Where Koesler ends, Blackie Ryan begins. From the outset Blackie refers to God in the feminine. If the book is about the oppression of women, the feminine God of Blackie Ryan is certainly not the author of that oppression—or so we would at first believe. When one character, whom Ryan is maneuvering into returning to church, asks suspiciously, "I don't have to stop being angry at God?" Ryan returns blithely, "A matter between you and Her in which I would not dream of being involved" (*Meek*, 5 cf. 252, 227). What do we know about this feminine God of Ryan's? Well, She enjoys contention. She creates people to fight with each other: "Laurel and Sue would continue to fight. That's the way God designed mothers and daughters because, I suspect, She enjoys watching a good fight now and again. Nonetheless, their love would endure and flourish" (*Meek*, 252). When Ryan uses the feminine pronoun for God, he becomes so familiar that he tells God off: "God be good to her and if She isn't She's going to hear about it" (*Meek*, 148). Casting God in the feminine obviously means for him immanence. But casting God in either the feminine or the immanent is surely not license for disrespect. He also slides in a few lower case "he's" and several upper case "He's," suggesting a full picture of God, a reality whose nature is only expressed in both the feminine and masculine. But his anthropomorphic God is hardly the great victor pictured in the Scriptures. Rather, his is "a God who is pathetically eager to forgive at the slightest hint of any emotion that can be called compunction" (*Meek*, 203). Again, "God absolves, Sue, with scandalous ease. Confessors, with more caution perhaps, absolve in his name" (*Meek*, 204). According to Blackie Ryan:

> Are there minor tangles and details to clean up, like murder and adultery and devil worship? The Lady God sniffs disdainfully. Why else do I have people like you, Blackie Ryan the Priest, save to dispose of such matters while I cavort around the cosmos, pursuing the needs of my insatiable passions?
>
> I anthropomorphize and metaphorize, you say? Certainly! How else can we deal with the Absolute? However, the metaphor is not greater than the reality, but less.
>
> So Blackie Ryan the Priest had better dispose of the mess before the Lord God comes back and requires an explanation. No one wants to explain to an angry lover. (*Meek*, 206)

As he explains further:

> The problem in which I was involved was, as surely the reader will have perceived, God's fault. He is a notoriously unprincipled character, which presumably is not objectionable, since He made up the principles to begin with. The Lady God dances around us through most of our lives, desiring us with an obsession that makes Larry Burke's hunger for Suzie look mild and waiting for those occasional moments of meekness that permit Her to intrude and possess, to seize and to transform.
>
> The two of them are together at the side of the pool; they begin to engage in routine human behavior. The Lord God is lurking there, prancing around them with unseemly delight; perhaps there will be a slim chance to steer them both in His direction, a flicker of an eyebrow, a touch of a hand that will open them both up to a more demanding Lover than either can imagine.
>
> Then Suzie, perhaps in a weariness that approaches despair and under the impulse of sexual needs she hardly recognizes, abandons her life-long mask of submission and momentarily replaces it with surrender. In those same few seconds Larry perceives her not as an object to be used but as a woman to be cherished. . . . That is all the unprincipled Lady God needs. Their love affair is now a ménage à trois. God's delight is infinitely greater than the orgasms

of the two lovers, who may understand dimly at the fringes of their consciousness that they have been trapped by the Great Voyeur. . . . Hooray for the Lord God! Love triumphs. Right? Right! (*Meek*, 205–6)

This wanton God of Ryan's is a development of the God of process theology, "God, the fellow pilgrim who suffers with us, to quote Professor Whitehead" (*Meek*, 14). As he summarizes the position in response to the query, "Who's Whitehead?" "Process philosopher. God is process. Fellow pilgrim who suffers" (*Meek*, 243). For him, "God tries" (*Meek*, 5), appearing about one level above the protagonist's conclusion in Woody Allen's *Love and Death* that God is not evil, but simply an underachiever. Rather than preferring the pompous failure God of *Love and Death*, Ryan praises comedian George Burns' portrayal in the film *Oh, God* as "splendid" (*Meek*, 5). Against this God are arrayed the fierce deities of strict traditional Catholicism and bloodthirsty, ferocious liberation theology. But Ryan's God is a lover who longs for a love affair with humanity. And Blackie thoroughly prefers "God's love affair" to such "gibberish" as salvation history (*Martyr*, 196). This God is delighted to set aside the sexual rules of the Bible in the interest of promoting love, for, as we recall from the quotation on the Beatitudes, rules are human conventions to rule human behavior.

This is the same argument Greeley has employed in such earlier books as *Thy Brother's Wife* to correct such primary characters as Blackie Ryan's present boss Cardinal Sean Cronin. After Cronin makes love to his stepsister in disregard of his priestly vows and her marital vows, she reproves his first qualms of conscience with:

I refuse to think that any of this is wrong. We're not committing sin, and I won't have you stirring up your goddamned conscience. . . . Neither one of us is going to give up our commitments, Sean. I'm going back to Paul. You're going back to your Church. This is just an interlude. Paul doesn't own my body, and the Church doesn't own you . . . I'm sure God doesn't think it's wrong. You know that yourself, Sean. It's just your clerical conscience that won't let you admit it. . . . No, I'm not saying anything about rules. This has been a time when the rules don't apply. They'll start applying again as soon as I leave for Chicago. This has been a good thing for both of us and I won't let you say otherwise. (*Wife*, 200)

Cronin gets a second dose of this advice from the Italian Angelica in Rome: "Bah, you Americans are such terrible prudes. . . . Welcome into the human race" (*Wife*, 205). Some television evangelists may feel the same way. For Ryan, God, who makes the rules, blithely sets them aside for the sake of love. This rather extreme situation ethics philosophy does not appear at first to apply to murder, about which Ryan says, "I could not easily condone the violation of that right [to live] save in the most direct and essential self-defense" (*Meek*, 95). Yet, hearing the catalogue of offenses Wolfe Quinlan has committed against his wife, he eventually concludes whoever dispatched this loathsome creature has done "a very good piece of work indeed" (*Meek,* 186). No struggles for Blackie Ryan comparable to those of Hercule Poirot in *Curtain.*

But legitimating illicit sex and possibly going soft on murder are not the only lapses in his ethics/theology. There may be a darker side as well. To glimpse it, we must put clearly before us the extent and significance of all the sexual activity through which God communicates in these torrid potboilers. First of all, we have to understand that despite all his assurances, Blackie Ryan is not totally convinced of his position. Watching Lawrence Burke pursue another husband's wife, Ryan nods benignly, "I did not tell him that the most he could accomplish between sweaty sheets with my former fellow parishioner La Suzie, should he finally manage to achieve such a position, was a minor venial sin" (*Meek,* 6). Ryan has not closed the door to the possibility that an act of indiscretion is still sin. In his counseling we can see his ambivalence as he presents an ambivalent Church to confused would-be confessee Anne Marie O'Brien Reilly of *Angels of September,* who has asked how "grave" is her sin of adultery:

> "Are you willing, Anne, to live with a Church that lays down principles and then says that in practice it's impossible for us to make judgments about individual cases?"
> "That's not the Church in which I was raised."
> "It's the Church now. . . . Look, I don't approve of adultery, for the very good reason that innocent parties are often hurt. Who is being hurt in your love with the Senator? Not your husband, God knows. And not his wife, either. Doesn't that diminish the sin somewhat, even in your moral system?"
> "Are you saying that it was not wrong?"
> "Leave aside the rules you learned from Healy's *Moral Guidance* at Mundelein College. . . . What kind of a God would it be who sends a lover to hell?" (*Angels,* 287)

What kind, indeed? The God of the Old Testament would, as witness God's anger against adulterous Israel.

Further, Ryan maintains many of his traditional Roman Catholic doctrines. In a pinch he admits, "I prayed all the way to God, Mary, and all the saints and angels of whose existence I was aware (*Meek,* 237). He also believes in Purgatory (*Meek,* 111) and is quite prepared to perform an exorcism. In point of fact, he has benignly misjudged the depths of the passion of a character like Lawrence Burke. Burke himself reflects, "My desire to excel him [Quinlan] with his wife was, as I have said, quite mad. But that did not stop me from coming perilously close to putting Tancredi's sword into his body a half hour before someone else actually did it" (*Meek,* 38). Ryan in playing with human passion is indeed igniting an inferno. Only the pressure of rules and responsibilities seems to save Greeley's fornicating clergy from ultimately degenerating like John Updike's Tom Marshfield in *A Month of Sundays,* whose sensible parishioners have placed this antinomian, satyromaniac cleric in a sanitarium.

Greeley's are clearly stories of grace, and in these tales God usually is symbolized by a female character, such as Nora in *Thy Brother's Wife* or Maria, Greeley's acknowledged voice in *Ascent into Hell:*

> Nor should it be assumed because Hugh Donlon is a priest and I am a priest that his voice is my voice. Only Maria speaks for me. Moreover, like God, I refuse to assume responsibility for the moral behavior of my creatures. (*Ascent,* ix)

As Maria stands naked over priest Hugh Donlon, she lectures:

> "Now, I hear that you love me, but you still are obliged to go back to the priesthood because you must do penance for your sins and your family expects it and if you don't Peggy will have another heart attack. Go ahead and say it." She folded her arms. "I don't believe a word of it. And neither do you." (*Ascent,* 355)

Through their sexual ministrations these women bring to the bleak lives of unhappy priests a God of love in contrast to the God of justice beneath whose stern yoke the priests have been suffering. In *Happy Are the Meek* this truth is revealed physically to the simpler characters Suzie Wade Quinlan and Lawrence F. X. Burke but by inference to the clerical sleuth, who is the main interpreter of what is happening. But what makes this all Christian? Is it not as much bacchanalian? Is it not really, essentially, Valentinian Gnosticism? The priests' God of justice is the Demiurge, the God of the Old Testament. Christ, as the God of grace, takes pity on humanity as Christ took pity on the Demiurge's sibling Enthymesis, from whom has come the matter, psyche, and pneuma with which the Demiurge created heaven and earth and all its creatures. Here is conflict between a God of the Old Testament and a loving Christ of the New: a choice between justice and love. And, as we all know, a strain of gnostics under Isidore and the extreme escapades of Carpocrates translated the advent and ministry of this new God of love into reveling in sexual promiscuity (cf. J. N. D. Kelly, *Doctrines,* 22–28). Is this the telos of Blackie Ryan's developing theology?

Further, juxtaposed against this free-wheeling sex that the dancing deity distributes is an equally detailed and appalling catalogue of torture scenes. Against page after page of intimate love-making is stacked page after page of ritual torture, sadistic dismemberment, serial murder, police brutality, and a shocking catalogue of humiliations and sexual degradations, particularly in *Virgin and Martyr* and *Happy Are the Meek.* The opening pages of *Happy Are the Clean of Heart* are comprised of an all-night sadistic torture of a woman, painstakingly tracing the planning, the ruse for entry into her apartment, and the first several acts of bashing, burning, and battering.

Why is there so much illicit sex in Greeley's mysteries? Why is there so much sadistic violence? In Greeley's vision there are only two options in human contact between the sexes: acts of physical love and acts of physical hate. Therefore, both are catalogued in painstaking detail. The love affairs of dancing grace are contrasted with the sadistic bondage of evil. These would seem to be the two options, particularly in a universe where God is limited in power to a well-meaning deity.

When in *Angels of September* Anne wonders about "the New God and the Old God," Cardinal Sean Cronin announces of past priests and nuns who harped on God's condemning justice, "Those teachers were wrong. . . . A proper portrait of God's justice would picture him dragging all of us into heaven by the skin of our teeth" (*Angels*, 2). Blackie Ryan chimes in, "By Her own admission, God is horny" (*Angels*, 2). For Ryan, "God is an implacable lover who will not be put off. He even cheats on us sometimes and breaks his own rules, the way lovers do" (*Angels*, 73). This new God fills an erotically spiritual kind of human loneliness that makes St. John of the Cross' Lover seem indeed as sexual as spiritual:

> There were two kinds of loneliness. The first, a loneliness of boredom and emptiness, did not bother her. Her life was busy and challenging, too much to do rather than not enough. Perhaps River Forest and grandchildren would make sense if she did feel bored and empty.
> The other kind of loneliness could be filled only by a man who loved her. Or a God who loved her. (*Angels*, 49)

This new God struggles in contrast against the old God of the Church's teaching. That was the God who created a hell of fire. When the now sexually/ spiritually liberated Cardinal Cronin is asked if there is still a hell, he replies, "I doubt it." But Blackie counters, "There has to be the possibility of refusing the offer of God's love. . . . God doesn't torment those who don't love Her back." For him, hell is "A place where God puts people until She figures out a way to give them a second chance." Asked if God cheats on Her own rules, Blackie replies, "All the time" (*Angels*, 7). To Ryan, "Each of us creates his or her own hell" (*Angels*, 441) and again, "Hell is not responding to God's love" (*Angels*, 73). Blackie's sister Mary Kate observes:

> If women who believe in hell are honest with themselves, they'll admit that the worst possible eternal punishment would be endless sexual exploitation. Those fears are built into our bodies, I think. (*Angels*, 411)

As the main character Anne fantasizes, *"This is what hell is like for women,* she thought—*sexual degradation that never ends, always exciting you and never satisfying"* (*Angels*, 339). And this vision she experiences in great and terrifying detail. Mary Kate's prescription is to "block out" this terrifying fantasy of hell "with images of a God who says that He—or She—is Love" (*Angels*, 411).

But what if there is a disturbing dimension to this dichotomy? What if these are two sides of one coin? The age-old theodicy questions, trying to account for the world's evil, query: If God is the source of all, can God be all good and not all powerful? Can God be all powerful and not all good? Can evil have another origin? Is God not the source of all? Traditionally, Christian theologians who struggle inadequately with the answer affirm that God is all good and all power-ful and that evil exists. God's goodness burns like a purgative fire, and the terrible goodness of God can burn away human evil, yet sadistic evil cannot be equated with God. God has self-limited power to allow human (and angelic) activity, and in this power void both acts in God's will (good) and against God's will (evil) can be done. But what if there is a sinister answer? By contrast, hyper-Calvinists and process theologians like John Hick with his so-called Ire-naen view in *Evil and the God of Love,* in which he adopts the Old Roman Missal's view of a happy fall, pose the theodicy of a dark side of God. Despite opening assurances by Blackie Ryan, what if the act of love and the act of torture are two parts of each entity? each relationship? even of God? Blackie's reflections at the end of *Virgin and Martyr* seem to suggest this truly miserific conclusion, when he says of the incredible torture Catherine the heroine has suffered:

> "It seems to have facilitated her maturation," I said pedantically. "Most people don't grow up, no matter how high the cost. Maybe it was a *felix culpa.* . . . A tortured and adult Cathy is better than an untortured and juvenile Cathy," I said, persisting in my defense of the crooked lines of God. (*Martyr,* 431)

James Johnson's Ray Sebastian has said continually that his ministry is making the crooked lines straight *for* God, but Blackie Ryan posits the crooked lines are *of* God.

If this is Blackie's authentic position, there is a new and horrifying dimen-sion to his capricious God and the capricious priests and salacious parishioners who follow. Since the rules of marital sex do not apply when the capricious God dances by, are we now to believe the rules of not hurting others are also suspended when the God who has created mothers and daughters to fight wants to see some blood? If the female God enjoys a good fight between mothers and daughters, has the lower-case "he" God created boxers? And does the upper-case "He" God then create ax murderers? Is there actually no order at all in the universe that this capricious "absolute" has imposed rigidly on humanity and has also imposed on himself? If they help us grow, are love and sadistic violence really part of God's will? Was the Inquisition, then, actually wrong? Essentially, is God lover or sadist depending on our limited process God's capricious mood?

If so, we have a new and chillingly sinister interpretation for our now terrifying opening quotation. H. P. Lovecraft and the secular mystery's father

Edgar Allen Poe in their miserific vision would clearly understand:

> No one resists grace, Nick. It's a combination of mist and quicksilver. It sneaks in through the cracks and the crannies, fills up the interstices that our plans and programs and personalities leave empty, takes possession of the random openings we give it and then, when we least expect it, when we've done everything in our power to stop it, BANG! there's the big surprise. (*Martyr*, 13)

What exactly does Blackie Ryan mean by "BANG!"?

Part Three

Ministers and Murderers

16

First and Lost:
Viar Whitechurch's Vicar Westerham

The common word in writing circles is that characters survive their authors. A writer who wishes to be remembered must create a character that will be remembered. If one is not mother to Scarlet O'Hara, Jane Eyre, Pollyanna or father to Ebenezer Scrooge, Long John Silver or Tarzan, one's work will be forgotten, while often work less competent will live on, embodied in a colorful character. In the mystery story, longevity comes with a memorable series character. The incomparable Dashiell Hammett may have been able to create characters so full and satisfying that one book has the impact of a series, as he did with Nick and Nora Charles in *The Thin Man*, but the tendency is to do what film makers later did with the Charles family—make them into series characters and thereby ensure a history to be remembered. So the great fictional detectives who have lived on, from Dupin through Holmes to Hercule Poirot, Jane Marple and the Saint, are series characters.

Canon Victor Lorenzo Whitechurch is a writer largely forgotten today. He is not listed in the new edition of the massive *Twentieth-Century Crime and Mystery Writers*. His work is not found in the latest authoritative compilations of classic and contemporary mystery tales. And yet Whitechurch's works were respected and widely circulated in his day. Howard Haycraft in his 1941 history of the genre, *Murder for Pleasure: The Life and Times of the Detective Story*, wrote:

> Canon Victor L. Whitechurch (1868–1933) is another outstanding representative of the cloth. In the early years of the century he wrote several impressive semi-detective stories with railroad backgrounds. He returned to the lists in 1927 with *Shot on the Downs* and contributed several other technically competent novels before his death. (Haycraft, *Pleasure,* 156)

To Haycraft, *Thrilling Stories of the Railway* was "a remarkable and inexplicably neglected book" (Haycraft, Art, 471).

Victor Whitechurch was one of the select cadre of "Certain Members of the

Detection Club" to compile that legendary composite novel, *The Floating Admiral* (1932). His companions included G. K. Chesterton, Dorothy Sayers, Agatha Christie, Father Knox, Freeman Wills Crofts, Anthony Berkeley, the Coles and others of the cardinal mystery writers of the opening half of the century. In fact, the canon was given the honors of opening the novel (Chesterton's prologue, according to Dorothy Sayers, was written last). He was the one who set the scene, wrote the first chapter, (though, unfortunately, in one of his more "purplish" moments), established the principal characters, characteristically filling the lists full of vicars and constables, equipping even the corpse, that infamous "floating admiral," with "a round, black, clerical hat, such as Mr. Mount, the Vicar, usually wore" (*Admiral*, 15).

Dorothy Sayers included his short story, "Sir Gilbert Murrell's Picture," from *Thrilling Stories of the Railway* (1912) in her "Specialists" section in her landmark premier volume of the three-volume *Great Short Stories of Detection, Mystery and Horror,* which appeared in 1929 in the United States as *The Omnibus of Crime.* Three years later in *The Second Omnibus of Crime,* she included his espionage tale, "How the Captain Tracked a German Spy" from *The Adventures of Captain Koravitch.*

But what happened to Whitechurch? His work, which appeared "impressive" and "technically competent" to as sage an authority as Howard Haycraft, has virtually disappeared today. Canon Whitechurch, I believe, was lost in the congregation of his creations. Rather than having created a clerical detective, Whitechurch created a roster of sometimes-detecting, often-meddling clerical sleuths of all sizes, shapes, ages, and capacities and matched them with a department of occasionally appreciative, often exasperated police detectives. Had Whitechurch centered his energy on his major clerical creation, young Vicar Westerham in *The Crime at Diana's Pool,* he might have created a character attractive and memorable enough to have survived, gently handed down like an heirloom in his delicate, finely wrought porcelain novels. But by overpopulating his roster with such bores as the inept Canon Fittleworth, the shady Reverend Howard Ross of *Left in Charge,* or the innocent, studious and somewhat colorless Dean Lake, Whitechurch lost poor Westerham in the noise of the solemn assembly. Whitechurch also mixed numerous mainline romances and adventures so thoroughly among his mysteries and filled them with such antiquated ecclesiastical customs, regional dialect (the bane of all modern readers), and Edwardian social and political concerns that they have, like the majority of George MacDonald's Victorian adult novels, aged into senility, passing on to entombment in library archives. His few mysteries, with their kaleidoscopic personnel, have not built for him a stable enough craft to weather the sea of succeeding clerical novels and reach the future as they ought to have done. They are well enough built ships and could stand up to modern competition, for Whitechurch knew how to write a mystery, but their captains are eminently forgettable. In the introduction to his academic/police procedural, *Murder at the College* (1932), Whitechurch himself lectured:

> It is, perhaps, unfortunate that the "Detective Story" is so often confused with the "Thriller," for it does not at all follow that they are one and the same thing. . . . The true "Detective Story" is a "problem," the problem of how some particular crime was committed and who committed it, a problem which, while often demanding smaller problems, should not deviate from the main question in hand. "A crime, and its solution." That's the description of the real "Detective Story." (*College,* 5)

Earlier in *The Crime at Diana's Pool*, Whitechurch outlined his particular approach to the craft:

> If it is permitted to dignify what is merely a detective yarn with a preface I should like to tell the reader a little secret about the method in which the tale is constructed. In most detective stories the author knows exactly what the end is going to be, and writes up to that end from the beginning. But in reality, the solver of a problem in criminology has to begin at the beginning, without knowing the end, working it out from clues concerning which he does not recognize the full bearing at first.
>
> I have tried to follow this method in construction of the following story. To begin with I had no plot. When I had written the first chapter I did not know why the crime had been committed, who had done it, or how it was done. Then with an open mind, I picked up the clues which seemed to show themselves, and found, as I went on, their bearing on the problem. In many respects the story appeared to work itself out to that inevitable conclusion about which, to begin with, I was in entire ignorance.
>
> A speculative reader may, if he chooses close the book when he has read the first chapter and try to evolve a plot from what he finds there. It would be interesting to know if his conclusions resemble, in any way, what follows in the book. (*Pool,* v)

That Whitechurch's method was successful in creating satisfying detective stories was affirmed by Jacques Barzun and Wendell Hertig Taylor's positive assessment of his work in *A Catalogue of Crime:* "According to him, he wrote without plan or premeditation. The verdict must be that he was the greatest improvisor in the genre—all but one of the stories have distinctive merit" (Barzun, 434). They identify six of his novels as detective stories, beginning with *The Templeton Case* (1924), *Shot on the Downs* and *The Crime at Diana's Pool* (both 1927), *The Robbery at Rudwick House* (1929)—though I question whether this novel is more a crime novel than a true mystery—*Murder at the Pageant* (1930), and *Murder at the College* (also published as *Murder at Exbridge* in 1932). Several surrounding novels are worthy of note, particularly *The Dean and Jecinora* (1926) and *First and Last* (1930), while motifs introduced in such earlier books as *A Bishop out of Residence* (1924) or any of the Downland collection provide the skeletal structure later fleshed out in the mysteries.

One of Whitechurch's favorite motifs is the incognito presence of the notable cleric, who for reasons vacational or ministerial prefers to conceal his identity and later dazzle the unsuspecting citizenry. Dean C. A. Alington will develop this motif more fully in one of many tributes he apparently pays to his predecessor, Whitechurch. His first archdeacon novel set his detecting clerics afloat on a Mediterranean pleasure cruise. Perhaps it is that same Mediterranean pleasure cruise that the dean of Frattenbury gives up to his fugitive brother in *The Dean and Jecinora.* Alington used for a pseudonym S. C. Westerham, perhaps in tribute to Whitechurch's archetypal Anglican detecting cleric Vicar Westerham. Thus, appropriately, Alington's archdeacons benefit from the pleasure cruise the dean missed, as their creator obviously benefited from the Anglican clerical detective novel that Canon Whitechurch launched. *The Dean and Jecinora,* as well, lays a foundation for the succeeding mysteries. It is a crime novel concerning a swindle, a favorite motif. Unfortunately, the book features a *deus ex machina* in lieu of detection, a regular failing of Whitechurch's work.

The Dean and Jecinora also provides one of the finer glimpses of humanitarian thought, which passes for theology in Whitechurch's earlier work:

> Do you know I am glad of the experience. I have been learning much. . . . You see, I have lived a rather secluded life, with my books and in a quiet little parish. My friends have been those of my own calibre. I can't say I have mixed with the world very much. Certainly I have had no striking adventure—until now. But there is one thing that has been borne in upon me impressively. . . . The extreme kindness—kindness of judgment, perhaps I should call it—of people whom I have not, I suppose, had the opportunity of understanding before. . . . I trust I have always tried to exercise a humane judgment myself. But I know now that I shall return to my work at Frattenbury with a wider outlook than—than—I should probably have gained had I taken my projected trip round the Mediterranean. No, I do not regret my enforced holiday here—not for a moment! (*Dean,* 260–61)

Such reluctance to go deeper into a theological interpretation of experiences seems to characterize all of Whitechurch's clerics. One begins to feel that the earlier clerics, struggling to throw off their Victorian restraints, consider speaking of God as hopelessly antiquated, or perhaps as enlightened modern gentlemen they consider it mildly offensive. Still, they can be stung into theological riposte, as is the Dean when someone questions the viability of keeping up his cathedral:

> I think, that there is something in ascribing glory to God by means of a beautiful building and its services. . . . And you will not find very much glory in humanity, I think, unless you keep the glory of God in due perspective as a living entity. And that is what, in a measure, a cathedral serves to do. (*Dean,* 145)

This is not to say that Whitechurch's clerics *never* wax theological. One argument in *A Bishop out of Residence* (1924) may raise a few North American eyebrows, but it is nevertheless theological:

"I know," he said, in a restrained voice, "we all of us are in danger of being mesmerised by the spirit of the age and of forgetting the spirit of the Master. The spirit of the age is democracy. And the democracy of this world is only a form of individual selfishness voiced under the guise of resolutions passed by majorities. And the Master was *One*—and showed us the only way." (*Bishop,* 312)

Again, Whitechurch puts in the mouth of an incognito bishop who has just stumbled through an internship impersonating a country vicar:

"I don't mind confessing to you, George, that I shall hesitate in future in saying that the parson of a small country parish has nothing to do and nothing to occupy his mind. I was expected to manage smoky church stoves, to light the lamps when I had an extra service, to do a hundred and one things with the schools—I'd no idea what it meant to act as correspondent—to haul recalcitrant hobbledehoys out of bed in the morning, to—oh, I could go on half the night telling you." (*Bishop,* 309)

"We're too highly organised in the Church, George. I'm thinking of these country folks and their ways. I'm afraid—yes—I admit it—that we put our trust too much in reports of committees, and try to inaugurate and run all sorts of complicated machinery—and talk—and talk in conferences and councils. And, all the time, it's the personal touch that tells. We're out for winning souls," and he sighed once more, "but, somehow, the original way laid down for winning them doesn't mean organising them into batches." (*Bishop,* 311)

A similar and very poignant plea for the plight of the poor country cleric can be found in *The Robbery at Rudwick House.* As one true veteran of the country parish remonstrates in *A Bishop out of Residence,* " 'A *comfortable* life! A country parson for thirty-seven years, and a *comfortable* life! My *dear* fellow! But, thank God, I've got through somehow' " (*Bishop,* 96). His late novel *First and Last* also contains a poignant plea for the rustic cleric, and finally in this novel, a vague and unsystematic theological thinking can be found. Mainly, it is a theology of denial, denying that the ten commandments are regularly broken by parishioners, denying that God monitors our religious "*p*'s and *q*'s" above acting sensibly. Whitechurch's clerics, when pressed by inquiry or when under strain, can wax theological; but they do not by any means normally provide a running theological interpretation of life, as does Father Brown, Father Dowling or Reverend Randollph. We are fortunate if they drop any theological observations in the course of a novel. Peter Wimsey would have felt comfortable around them. In sum, they seem to act almost as though a good Anglican Christian is the sporting thing to be, as if Jews or Hindus are somehow not fairly playing the game. This is the theological legacy Whitechurch's clerics bring to his mysteries.

The first clerical participant in the first of Whitechurch's novels universally recognized as a mystery is Canon Fittleworth. *The Templeton Case* is set, as is the bulk of Whitechurch's fiction, in the mythical southern cathedral town of

Frattenbury and its environs. An ancient city with medieval ruins, Frattenbury boasts a theological college, a cathedral close, and a nearby shoreline. Canon Charles Fittleworth is one of those clerics who is as much a nuisance as an assistance to the police, earning such epithets as "that idiot of a parson" (*Templeton*, 138) as he pockets evidence, embarrasses the police at the inquest, and generally muddles up the case in the first half of the book. Mercifully he forgoes active for sporadic assistance in the latter half, finally figuring in the finale.

But the one cleric who is very much appreciated for his mixing up in police business and Whitechurch's crowning clerical achievement as well as his major contribution to the subgenre is Vicar Harry Westerham. As *The Crime at Diana's Pool* opens, Westerham has only been vicar of Coppleswick for a little over a year. Like Rabbi Small, he is a young man in his late twenties, and he owes his position to "assiduous work as a curate in a large town parish where he had made a name for himself" (*Pool*, 75). Unlike Whitechurch's many failed vicars, such as Vicar Frimley of *The Robbery at Rudwick House* or Alan Crawford of *First and Last*, Westerham is in comfortable enough means to maintain servants (*Pool*, 266). "Capable, a gentleman and possessed of a stock of good all round common sense" (*Pool*, 76), Westerham has taken a country parish "partly because he wanted more time for study, and had some idea of writing" (*Pool*, 77). He is a scholar like Whitechurch's monograph-writing archdeacon, the Venerable Cyril Osborne Lakenham, the liturgy expert of *The Robbery at Rudwick House*, but he is unlike the archdeacon in that he is also a person capable of regularly acting decisively.

An active pastor, he pauses during his investigation to give services (*Pool*, 88), a confirmation class in which he tries to explain the catechism to a half dozen youths (*Pool*, 90), and a parochial committee meeting to arrange a fete and sale for church funds (*Pool*, 118). His busy schedule confirms the Reverend Whitechurch's standard requirement for all his fictional clerics that a parson's exacting week's work is "more than simply preaching, a thankless burden for which the parson is rarely given credit" (*Pool*, 121). Westerham does, however, let his preoccupation with the case take over some of his sermon preparation time, making him push Bible and prayer book aside (*Pool*, 229). Still, his confirmation classes pay off: " 'If you've told lies, George,' he said, 'you must ask God to forgive you. And, as I've told you all, you can make your confession to me or to some other clergyman, if you want to' " (*Pool*, 263). A higher church variety of Anglican, like all of Whitechurch's clerics, he is not Docetist, being a seasoned drinker and smoker who can serve up a fine whiskey and soda. In appearance, he is described as "a clergyman, wearing a dark grey suit and straw hat, a man of about thirty, not very tall, squarely built, clean shaven, with a good-humored, pleasant face—dark brown eyes with an occasional twinkle in them—the Vicar of Coppleswick" (*Pool*, 10). He is "not particularly musical" (*Pool*, 14). A true follower of Holmes, he "despised" cigarettes, enjoying a "quiet pipe" (*Pool*, 14). In fact, he more than enjoys his pipe: "The Vicar, hardened smoker as he was, lighted a fresh pipe and watched him" (*Pool*, 51). His addiction is milder than Holmes'.

Chief among his attributes is his keen quality of observation:

> Apart from being an energetic parish priest Westerham was a particularly shrewd and capable man. And it was no idle boast of his that he had made a habit of observation—many of his parishioners little guessed how closely and clearly he had summed them up by observing those ordinary idiosyncracies which escape the notice of most people.
>
> But the Sergeant would have been considerably more impressed could he have looked within the note book which Westerham took from a drawer he unlocked in his study table. In it he had noted down, and commented upon briefly, every detail and incident that he had observed or remembered in connection with the crime, from his first arrival at the garden party to the present moment. To these notes he proceeded now to add the information which Ringwood had just given him, sprawling back in his chair, smoking vigourously, and, every now and then pausing with his hand holding his fountain pen, stretched out straight in front of him, another characteristic posture of his when working out a thing in his mind. (*Pool*, 72–73)

This talent for observation weds his pastoral work with his detection.

> He had made it a habit of practicing registering things in his mind, a useful habit, as every parish priest knows who has tried it. Over and over again in the course of house to house visiting in his parish some object, lying on the table, or mantlepiece, would bring back to his mind in a flash the recollection of a former visit, and he would be able to ask, by association of ideas, whether Mary was getting on in her new place, what had happened to Tom since he had joined the army. . . . Now he tried to reverse the process. (*Pool*, 24–25)

Further, despite his remarkably disciplined gifts, Westerham manages to maintain a certain amount of humility, and he keeps in perspective that the aim of his work is ministry and the pursuit of truth:

> I don't claim to be a Sherlock Holmes, my deductions are only commonplace—there's no brilliance in them. Beside, I was activated by a motive all the time. I wanted to get hold of poor Nayland's murderer, and I also wanted to get someone out of rather a trying ordeal. (*Pool*, 291)

Of course, the ministering here is not entirely selfless. That "someone" he wants to extract from "a trying ordeal" is someone female to whom he wishes to be engaged. At the same time, truth appears in itself to be a strong motive for him, for we are assured that the vicar has a strict regard for the truth (*Pool*, 167). Westerham "had a habit of doggedly getting to the root of things and overcoming obstacles" (*Pool*, 167). As a detective, the vicar solves crimes "because I'm a man who always wants to get at the reasons of things. I suppose I've a logical turn of mind. But I want to observe a bit more before I form any theory" (*Pool*, 68).

At the same time that he has the regulation issue of humility so necessary to equip the true cleric, he has no overwrought false veneer of modesty or pseudohumility concerning his gifts. In point of fact, he has a good opinion of himself:

> Now, I'm not a detective, Ringwood, but you were good enough once to give me credit for observation. Well, I am observant. And, not only that, but I'm a bit fond of finding out where my observations lead me. (*Pool*, 268)

As a superior detective, he cannot help but amuse himself by discovering clues and then returning them, for "he wanted to see if the police would notice it" (*Pool*, 27). As a result of his detailed record of new details observed and remembered in regard to the crime (*Pool*, 72), the police ask for his notes (*Pool*, 294). And Westerham earns the accolades of everyone he meets. His parishioners, as well as the police, exclaim, "Gad! Padre. You're pretty observant, What!" (*Pool*, 22); "You're an observant man" (*Pool*, 141); "Ah! Sharp fellow that padre!" (*Pool*, 150); "We look upon you quite as an assistant in the case, sir" (*Pool*, 104). "You ought to have been one of us, sir," summarizes Sergeant Ringwood, the police detective. "As it is, I may be glad of your help" (*Pool*, 33).

Ringwood, though a shade less astute than Westerham, is clever and crafty enough to appreciate Westerham's finely tuned acumen. Affecting a childlike guise, he acts "lethargic" around people, never letting others see into the "whole of his character and temperament" (*Pool*, 34), just as Westerham is clever and crafty enough to get a suspected murderer's imprint on glass by having him taste a wine (*Pool*, 261). All of this astute observation pays off as Westerham solves the murder by observing a man roll a cigarette (*Pool*, 284) and throw darts (*Pool*, 290).

Unlike many of his Whitechurchian contemporaries (particularly unlike the inept, muddleheaded Canon Fittleworth) and unlike many succeeding clerical sleuths, Westerham has no difficulty in cooperating with the police. Indeed, like Septimus and Sister Ursula, he might have been one of them. When an inquiry begins to stall and would be aided by his divulging what he knows to the constabulary, he believes "it's the duty of a citizen to help the police in a murder case" (*Pool*, 202). "Again even if Westerham had made any new discoveries he would not have acted as the amateur detective of the story books usually does—kept them to himself and triumphantly have proved the official police to have been in the wrong" (*Pool*, 107). Indeed, he has no hesitation in fingering suspects for the police (*Pool*, 16).

The tension between the cleric and the confessional versus the police and the courtroom is constant in the clerical crime novel. In one sense, the murder mystery itself can be viewed as a literature of revenge. Perhaps, along with the antecedents of the medieval romance, frontier literature and the western, nineteenth-century Darwinian and Freudian naturalism and the ancient confessional literature and its secular offspring, the biography and autobiography, one could turn to the great Oriental theater of revenge for insights into the nature of mystery literature. In such a perspective the mystery represents society taking its revenge on a criminal for disruption, for destroying one of its component parts, for flagrant rebellion against its mores and its laws.

The clerical crime novel experiences a certain tension in relating to these claims of society for vengeance. Clerics usually recognize a higher claim. Certain clerics are like Father Brown, who after turning his first captive over to the police, eventually begins pocketing confessions of guilt himself, taking murderers for strolls over the moors, submitting cases solely to the Divine Judge. Some are like Father Dowling, a former judge himself of a sacred yet earthly court, the Roman Catholic Church's marriage tribunal, who seems to have one blindfolded eye turned toward earthly justice and the other toward its heavenly counterpart. Dowling wonders how one can forgive a multiple murderer here on earth, unhesitatingly turning that culprit over to earthly legal retribution. Yet he believes as well in the justice and mercy of heavenly justice in a separate trial and penance. "Ex-copper" Septimus and the rather secularized Reverend Randollph, on the other hand, seem to believe firmly in earthly justice. Septimus, like any policeman, wants prosecution, and Randollph, when the law cannot touch a culprit, as happens in *The Unholy Bible,* wants to level at least some kind of penance even if it is only terminating "an undetected murderer" from "the church's ushering corps" (Smith, *Bible,* 190). Obviously the murderer is *not* undetected. Randollph has discovered him. But since the police have not, and earthly vengeance has not been exacted, to Randollph he remains undetected. Vicar Westerham would seem to fit firmly in this final category. To cement matters, we learn he believes in capital punishment (*Pool,* 89).

Theologically, Westerham's views are as sketchy as are his Whitechurchian peers' views. Perhaps his views are similar to those of the skeptical Basil Grant in *First and Last,* who when asked, "'Suppose you *knew* the world were coming to an end—say this afternoon—what would you do?'" replies, "'Have lunch first . . . because it's a sensible thing to do, and I don't think God is down on fellows who do sensible things. And that's religion, to my mind'" (*First,* 40–41). Perhaps, "that's religion" to Westerham's mind as well. As for the rest, perhaps his worship experience is similar to that of *First and Last*'s Reverend Philip Merston, who is "rather typical of the times in which he lived" (*First,* 21):

In church he was inordinately severe of expression—matching things there in general. . . . As for his sermons, these, too, were typical. Dry discourses, punctiliously written and unemotionally read, discussing the meaning of words, explaining parables and making them seem

uninteresting by taking away all imagination from them, detailing and analyzing Old and New
Testament characters, interspersed with doctrinal subjects—the efficacy of faith, the awfulness
of sin, the musical delights of heaven and the torments of hell. All very correctly preached,
with a total absence of enthusiasm. (*First*, 21–22)

True, Westerham is no longer a Victorian like Merston, and as a "modern"
presumably has reinforced that "enthusiasm" back into his message, yet we
never see such a transfusion take place. In fact, Whitechurch's novels provide
us with a parade of "moderns," archly smoking flappers, upwardly mobile
young male financiers, newly liberalized doting and lenient parents, all shep-
herded by enlightened clerics who think "modern." Whitechurch's theology
seems to have slipped down into a crevice between the changing of the eras and
thus has not managed to provide an operating theological basis for the actions
of all these clerics. We know they align with "Providence." We know they
eschew outdated Victorian rigidity. We know they are modernly in vogue. We
just do not know what they believe. We do not know why they are clerics. We
do not know what sets them apart as clerics. Perhaps *they* do not know why they
are clerics. Perhaps Whitechurch does not know why they are clerics. Rather,
Whitechurch's writing seems to take its greatest pains in establishing that clerics
are really regular fellows. Such is the case with his portrayal of Westerham:

Westerham, to the external world, was an energetic, capable parish priest, a good organizer,
and a plain, sensible preacher. Therefore, the ordinary external world labelled him as a parson
and pigeon-holed him accordingly. Most people have the extraordinary notion that a clergyman
is something different from an ordinary man, that he lives entirely apart from others in a
theological atmosphere and only looks out on life from a religious standpoint. It is ludicrous,
at times, to notice how, in society, the host or hostess will try to talk shop to a parson, the
latest utterance of a bishop, ecclesiastical architecture, Sunday School treats, Mothers' Meetings, when, all the time, they would certainly not attempt to talk to a surgeon about his
operations, or to a lawyer about conveyances of leasehold properties. In nine cases out of ten,
also, that parson doesn't want to talk shop at all—only, as has been said, they have labelled
him and stuffed him into a mental pigeon-hole—and won't let him get out. (*Pool*, 71–72)

But there is another more pagan dimension to Westerham. As in the classical origins and resultant nature of both the ancient Greek and Oriental theaters
of revenge, there is a latent paganism in the figure of the avenger, despite his
clerical collar and seminary refining. Potentially, Westerham the avenger is a
primitive. In a moment of stress, the veneer of civilization drops off him as if
he were one of Edgar Rice Burroughs' thinly civilized primitives, the Eternal
Savage, Jimber-Jaw, or John Clayton, Lord Greystoke:

Afterwards Westerham used to say he was ashamed of himself at the recollection of that
moment. Just then, parson or no parson, he was tasting that terrible exuberance born of a man

hunt, the latent savage, call it that if you like, that lurks beneath the veneer of polished civilization. (*Pool*, 279–80)

In such moments, his categories, too, are classical, not biblical. "'Nemesis!' exclaimed the Vicar, as he suddenly realized that they were standing almost upon the spot where the murder had taken place" (*Pool*, 278). And he is not recognized by those he runs to earth as the avenging angel but as Apollyon, the accuser, the destroyer. "You devil!" screams the murderer at the vicar (*Pool*, 280):

> "No wonder he called you a devil, Mr. Westerham," exclaimed the detective, and there was admiration in the tone of his voice. "I'm beginning to think you're uncanny myself." (*Pool*, 291).

In another kind of passion, too, his veneer of civilized Christianity drops away as the vicar and his beloved meet "under the auspices of the little blind God" (*Pool*, 265). At least we are spared the meager fare of syncretism and positive thinking that might have comprised his sermons and are fed instead on the rich full feast of his inductions.

His adventure, *The Crime at Diana's Pool*, in the classic British tradition, opens with a crime at a large country house fete that throw suspicion on a number of characters. Felix Nayland—like his near namesake and Dr. Fu Manchu's nemesis, Sax Rohmer's Nayland Smith—"was in the Diplomatic service for a time—then he went abroad on his own account—fond of exploring" and has been on expeditions in such exotic places as Central Asia and South America (*Pool*, 40), Now he has retired to a country house at Coppleswick. As his first (and last) major social event, he throws a fete for his neighbors, a festive celebration that features "The Green Albanian Band and Western Glee Singers" (*Pool*, 5). During the party one band member disappears. When the vicar and chief constable of the county, Major Challow, are leaving the event, they stumble across a body clothed in the bandsman's jacket, lying in the garden pond called Diana's Pool. It is Nayland's body in the bandsman's coat. The resulting quest for the killer yields a tale of international intrigue that, ignited in San Miguel, just a little north of Brazil, has exploded in the quiet English countryside. On the way to the solution, the narrative marvelously mocks straightlaced country conventions and provincial expectations.

Spoofing the stereotypical local constabulary, it presents to us

> Froome the local constable. . . . He saluted the Vicar gravely, and immediately produced note book and pencil, moistening the latter with his lips before he began to write. Froome knew the routine that was required of him. . . . "But we'll get him, never fear," the policeman went on oracularly. (*Pool*, 28)

British snobbery takes a good drubbing, too. Nayland's new neighbors are insufferably provincial, as evidenced by this "witty" exchange, comparing Albanians and albinos:

> "Jove, though," went on the major, adjusting his monocle as he spoke, "one of 'em's a foreigner, apparently, even if he isn't a pink-eyed white rabbit, Miss Garforth."
>
> "I see," replied Miss Garforth, "the man whose coat doesn't fit him—it's a bit too big. Oh, yes—he doesn't look English, does he?" (*Pool*, 8)

Opposed to Alington, the foreigners in the tale are given a dignity that equals (e.g., *Pool*, 119–20) and ultimately surpasses that of the British when we learn that the worst traitor in San Miguel is an Englishman (*Pool*, 22). Still, with adept detachment, Whitechurch can make Westerham quail in his essentially stiff-upper-lip Anglicanism at a pure display of otherness: "The Vicar shuddered—it was such an essentially foreign action" (*Pool*, 228).

Women, too, have an attractive dignity in Whitechurch's tales and earn such handsome salutes for their cool professional actions as Westerham's "She's behaved like a heroine over it" (*Pool*, 233). In *The Robbery at Rudwick House*, an American woman is the financial wizard who secures the dean's brother's fortunes, and in *The Templeton Case* the police detective's wife is essentially the one who gives the key insights that lead toward solving the case.

Not so far away from his Christian clerical calling, too, is the principle on which Westerham operates and by which he eventually solves the crime. As he observes, "Let us go further on the assumption of St. Augustine, 'credo, quia incredibile est,' and assume that the apparently unbelievable is true" (*Pool*, 143).

Yet, with all its assets, *The Crime at Diana's Pool* does have mechanical flaws along with its theological ones. Its ending is a bit too melodramatic, which perhaps accounts for its inabiity to bridge time into the present. A puff of wind blows a key letter into a drawer (*Pool*, 122), where it remains until conveniently discovered at the appropriate time.

Dorothy Sayers has leveled further charges in her preface to *The Omnibus of Crime*, observing that Whitechurch commits the unforgivable sin of keeping clues discovered by the detective secret from the reader (Sayers, *Omnibus*, 32–33 n.1). As she explains his "crime":

> The writer keeps this clue to himself, and springs the detective's conclusions upon us like a bolt from the blue. . . .
>
> For many years, the newness of the genre and the immense prestige of Holmes blinded readers' eyes to these feats of legerdemain. Gradually, however, as the bedazzlement wore off, the public became more and more exacting. The uncritical are still catered for by the "thriller," in which nothing is explained, but connoisseurs have come, more and more, to call

for a story which puts them on an equal footing with the detective himself, as regards all clues and discoveries. (Sayers, *Omnibus,* 32)

The same charge can be leveled against *The Templeton Case,* in which we were not told that a character has used his *left* hand in pouring from a decanter.

Still, the flaws are those of a first novel in a series and could have been easily rectified by such a gifted writer as Canon Whitechurch. Had Whitechurch been of the persuasion of Ross Macdonald or Robert Parker, he could have molded Westerham in his dream image and given him a superb series of tales, bestowing him as a legacy upon his struggling future parishioners and clerics. As it was, Westerham happily exonerated and married the girl of his fancy, and deep in marital bliss was shouldered aside by the grim parade of Whitechurch's guardians of justice: Detective Sergeant Ambrose of the Exbridgeshire police, Superintendent Chuff of the District Division, Superintendent Kieth, Detective Sergeant Howe, Superintendent King, Inspector Fraser of the C.I.D., Detective Sergeant Mirfield, Chief Inspector Ferguson of the C.I.D., Major Renshaw, Detective Sergeant Robert Colson, Superintendent Walters, Detective Sergeant Ringwood, and so on. Archetypal as the first Protestant clerical detective might have been, Vicar Westerham fell out of step and was left behind in the march of that vast host of competent, tight-lipped professionals who staffed the remainder of Whitechurch's mysteries.

17

Archdeacons Aground:
C. A. Alington's Archdeacons Series

The mystery genre has counted some outstanding clerics among its perpetrators from the days of Monsignor Ronald A. Knox down to the Reverend Charles Merrill Smith and Sister Carol O'Marie, but perhaps the most distinguished of all was one cleric who was all but buried under titles and honors such as Head Master of Eton, Chaplain to H. M. The King, Honorary Fellow of Trinity College, Oxford, Sometime Fellow of All Souls College, The Dean of Durham, The Very Reverend Cyril Argentine Alington, D.D. While other writers might recruit a prominent author or critic for their forewords, C. A. Alington's *Elementary Christianity* claims no one less than The Lord Bishop of London, and his Old Testament introduction, The Archbishop of York. Therefore, readers will not be surprised to discover that his clerical sleuths are no mere football heroes cum professors cum pastors like Randollph, or farmed-out fathers like Dowling, nor do they sport mere meager doctorates as titles like Mary Finney. No, his heroes are no less than the Venerable John Craggs, the Archdeacon of Thorp, and the Venerable James Castleton, Archdeacon of Garminster. Further, neither of these two supervisors of pastors has had to earn his rank book by book like C. S. Forester's Horatio Hornblower, painstakingly gathering promotion after promotion. Rather, they arrive with theirs full blown in their very first book.

Alington adorns his archdeacons' debut, *Archdeacons Afloat*, with a quotation from the priest in *Don Quixote*, chapter 32: "This is done for the diversion of our thoughts," and that is just what his book is—a diversion. Alington is well equipped for thorough scholarship and proclamation as the wide range of his theological output reveals through topics ranging from the Old Testament exegetical survey in his *A New Approach to the Old Testament,* to church history in *Christianity in England: An Historical Sketch,* to theology in *The Life Everlasting.* He has also written primers like *Elementary Christianity* (1927) and *Christian Outlines: An Introduction to Religion* (1932). Unfortunately, Alington does not tap these resources in his premier fictional volume. When Alington sets himself to divert, he stays steadfastly to that program.

Archdeacons Afloat, therefore, is a somewhat lazy travelogue of the Mediterranean islands, basically a holiday-paced adventure with a mild little mystery peering diffidently out at the end. His archdeacons are traveling incognito, to avoid the bother of that peculiar style of deference lay people adopt around labeled clerics, with a boat-load of substantially racist and thoroughly provincial English tourists who inveigh against the inhabitants of the various islands they visit—including Greeks, Spaniards, blacks, Americans, and Scottish thrown in for variety—in short virtually everyone who is not English. While the archdeacons do not strike a reader as particularly bright—one of them nearly blows his cover by blithely beginning a sentence, "One of my clergy said he hoped to 'contact me' the other day" (*Afloat,* 51)—their traveling companions are even duller, affecting surprise when his identity is finally overtly revealed (*Afloat,* 117). Many such lapses that riddle the text are doubtless intentional since Alington peppers his "Dear reader," overbloated, sermonic style of writing with a droll sense of humor. Thus, his archdeacons are terrified of women: "Really, there ought to be special measures taken to protect the clergy from the female sex" (*Afloat,* 28). When they need to prevaricate for convenience (like Dorothy Gilmman's Sisters John and Hyacinthe, they never lie), they legitimate it by labeling it "Pecca fortiter" (*Afloat,* 34), baptizing it in the ecclesiastical wash of Latin. Captured ashore by a band of Greek brigands, one of the archdeacons bargains for a group-rate ransom, taking the concept of Mediterranean haggling to absurd lengths. The brigand chief, however, attaches a surcharge in place of tipping.

At the climax of their at-times tedious sojourn, Alington has one archdeacon code a cryptic message into the ransom note that the other archdeacon solves by suggesting various Old Testament passages as keys. To this clerical teamwork another passenger pays the accolade, "Castleton, what a thing it is to be a Biblical scholar! I really believe you've saved the situation" (*Afloat,* 122), no doubt an irresistible climax for the author of *A New Approach to the Old Testament* to graft onto his mystery novel. Together his archdeacons earn this final handsome tribute:

> I may remark that the events of this evening have permanently raised my opinion of archdeacons as a class. I know not whether the ingenuity displayed by the Archdeacon of Thorp in composing his letter, or the patience and erudition shown by the Archdeacon of Garminster in contributing so greatly to its solution is worthy of the higher praise. Gentlemen, I give you the toast of the Archidiaconate of the Church of England! (*Afloat,* 122)

The ending, however, is marred when Alington suddenly ceases the action in favor of a long-winded orator's florid account of the outcome of the tale—a most infelicitous decision on his part.

One thing primarily is missing, however. One would expect archdeacons to pray at the very least when in life-and-death circumstances, such as capture by brigands. But outside their evident biblical prowess, when the chips are down, Alington's archdeacons are a secular lot, indistinguishable from the nonecclesiastics around them. While theologically Alington's archdeacons are certainly not Anglo-Catholics in any sense, his archdeacon of Garminster bristles when suspected of wearing an alb (*Afloat,* 45) and experiences an "inward shiver" (*Afloat,* 47) when confronted with the apparently loathesome prospect of hearing a confession, they at times hardly seem even Anglican clerics at all. Like Charles Merrill Smith's Reverend Randollph, they appear to have reduced Christianity to a set of ethical mannerisms, a kind of etiquette that allows a certain amount of breaching (the convenient lies, the dissimulation of true identity, the avoidance of assisting people who need to unburden their hearts) while holding the line on more flagrant social gaffs. Why a man who would argue so rigorously for incarnated Christianity in such books as *Elementary Christianity* would serve up such theologically anemic heroes is a matter for conjecture. Alington does display a self-deprecating knee-jerk obeisance to the skepticism of science in his nonfiction books, and perhaps this timidity in the face of now outmoded vestigial nineteenth-century rationalism is the reason. At any rate his archdeacons in this first book in sum total are little more than grown Eton schoolboys who, like Bertie Wooster, happen to have won the Scripture knowledge prize. As champions of the faith, they would have earned the disgusted flat of Sir Galahad's sword. Unlike nonfiction, fiction, of course, need not instruct, but neither ought it to jettison an author's stance. At any rate, when Alington chooses to divert and beguile, he certainly empties out his other intentions.

This raises a more serious question: Where is God in his books? Instead of Christianity, the motivating force cited is Fate, with a capital "F." "But the Fates had decreed otherwise" (*Ashore,* 158, 159), we read, and "the malice of Fate inspired" (*Ashore,* 160; *Gold,* 168). Like so many other British writers of the late 1800s and early 1900s—from such light examples as Elizabeth Goudge's *Linnets and Valerians* and Kenneth Grahame's *The Wind in the Willows,* where Pan appears, to the dark celtic neoclassicism of James Joyce's Icarian *A Portrait of the Artist as a Young Man* or his pillorying of Christianity in *Ulysses*—Alington nods to the neoclassical, actually neopagan, literary climate of the turn of the century. Perhaps a way to read his opening two books is to see in their Grecian mountain beginnings a moving from the Olympiad heights to the modern plains of England, specifically to the terrain of "Blankshire," which will figure as the foundational setting of the remaining books of the series. Here "Fate" decrees and humans work out their destinies, beneath those determining and rather malicious forces, with the strong atavistic mountainous crags of Craggs and the bulwark fastness of "Castle-ton" providing whatever human security the church can give them.

By *Gold and Gaiters* the neoclassical cast of the ecclesiastical eccentrics comprising the cathedral staff parades before us a dean who, in his adulation for the Greeks and the patriarch of the Orthodox Church, is off climbing Mount Athos, a suffragan bishop who is always gone, and Archdeacon Castleton, now nearly seventy, who devotes a great portion of his time to curating the cathedral library, where the precious Roman coins, whose theft comprises the crime of the book, are housed. Added to these for spice are a bishop who, reminiscent of the "Red Dean of Canterbury," reputedly keeps a framed picture of Stalin on his desk, and a canon who believes the cathedral should sell its treasures to aid the poor and use its building for evangelical work, to produce a light social comedy with a clerical zoo. In this respect, in the remaining books the tribute to P. G. Wodehouse, the pinnacle of twentieth-century British light social comedy, becomes increasingly overt as Alington appropriates such Wodehousian names as "Emsworth" and "Bertie" for a new set of primary characters and sets his action in "Blankshire" (Blandings?). Like his namesake Lord Emsworth, Alington's Mr. Emsworth is "an enthusiastic novice" gardener (*Gold,* 18). And Alington peoples his books with uncles and aunts in the Wodehousian mode. *Gold and Gaiters* nods also to a number of other authors in its style, topics, and construction from Dickens to James Hilton in *Good-bye, Mister Chips,* and catalogues a salute to numerous amateur detectives from Holmes to Wimsey to Miss Marple, Reggie Fortune, Poirot, Inspector French and others (*Gold,* 165–68). The Dean of Durham further slyly incorporates a reference to Dr. Johnson's whimsical evaluation of Durham Cathedral (*Gold,* 27–28).

By the last several books, the archdeacons, and particularly Archdeacon Castleton, who is "one of those people who dislike crime in the abstract as much as in the concrete" (*Gold,* 153), have completely abdicated the role of detective to such previously supporting characters as former villain Sir Michael Mohun and the comedy duo of schoolmasters Emsworth and Birtley. But while the archdeacons may be fading in *Gold and Gaiters,* God finally makes an oblique appearance on the penultimate and ultimate pages, as Providence at least replaces malicious Fate in returning the stolen coins and providing a pleasant betrothal for Archdeacon Castleton's favorite niece: "All these combined to throw him into a kind of bewildered happiness at the proved goodness of Providence," though this happiness is qualified slightly by "Providence (in the midst of its general beneficence)" choosing for the eventual marriage as "distant a site" as the Sudan (*Gold,* 206).

Why should the archdeacon be so bewildered by the beneficence of the Christian deity that he, as a senior cleric and supervisor of clerics, has presumably espoused for so many years? Because this deity has become closely identified with the Greco-Roman Fate. And the capricious and often hostile actions that are the characteristic modus operandi (m.o., as the police procedurals have it) of that deity have colored and to a great degree recast Castleton's Christian faith. Still, if the final pages return to us a glimpse of the revelation of the goodness of the Church of England's true deity, we might be content.

Catherine Aird in her article "The Devout: Vicars, Curates and Relentlessly Inquisitive Clerics" in *Murder Ink* has noted, "Evensong never seems to clash with a dénouement when the amiable Archdeacons of Thorp and Garminster, creations of C. A. Alington, D.D., are solving a gentle mystery" (Winn, 468). As we see, theology, violence and the overwrought intricacies of the cerebral puzzle also do not seem to interfere. Obviously the good dean did not keep Dame Agatha awake at night worrying about his encroachment on her domain. And if Chesterton did not live to see this challenge to Father Brown's primacy, his defense would probably not have been needed anyway. These stories are gentle, if plodding, generally verbose, and often rather dull, and yet as often they are light and pleasant, with a good ironic insight into human behavior and relationships. Wodehouse once whimsicaly recommended his Mr. Mulliner stories not be given to invalids in too large doses. Maybe Alington's are the proper strength.

Nevertheless, their hesitation to incorporate theology, their general abdication as far as divine speculation is concerned, is what takes the ultimate depth and satisfaction out of both their mystery and their mysterium. Ultimately a mechanistic Fate as determiner is no more than that—mechanistic. How much better and deeper and satisfying could those potentially fine books have been if the Very Reverend C. A. Alington in his fiction had only practiced what he preached in his nonfiction.

18

Margaret Scherf's Misanthropic Minister
Martin Buell

Curiously, the denominational distribution of the clerical detectives seems on the surface to determine how theological and how personally pleasing a particular detective is likely to be. The two rabbi Daniels of *Bel and the Dragon* and *Susannah,* as well as David Small, are all thoroughly theological in outlook. Only the first seems to have a particularly pleasing personality, in order no doubt to provide the basis to duplicate the canonical king's concern, when heaved, like the canonical Daniel, into a lions' den. After all, if Rabbi David Small were suddenly catapulted back in time and tossed to the carnivores, how many of his synagogue board members would be likely to help Hugh Lanigan and Mariam bail him out, and how many would merely breathe a sign of relief? The Roman Catholics tend to be theological and generally lovable. Father Bredder is beloved by all, while Father Brown is admired and becomes the object of the deep devotion of former adversary Flambeau. Blackie Ryan, Brown's Elisha, as he seems to have caught his mantle, is admired and known affectionately as "The Punk." The pixie-like Sister Ursula is lovable, as is the delightful Sister Mary Helen. Hippies as well as townspeople fall in love with Dorothy Gilman's Sisters John and Hyacinthe. That occasional life of the party Father Koesler has his cadre of fellow priests while even Father Dowling has his Phil Keegan.

But the Protestants are not particularly likeable and the Anglicans not even very theological. Of course, there are exceptions, such as the Reverend Dr. C. P. Randollph, who is nearly admirable and theological enough for the entire genre. Simon Bede may not be theological, and his status and influence may be lowered by his illicit affair with Helen Bullock, but he still has his personal charm to salvage the affection of his peers and his nonprofessional relationships. Vicar Westerham, snob though he may be, at least garners the admiration of his parishioners and the affection of his own beloved. Still, nobody likes Ray Sebastian until the end of his series, when he begins to win grudging respect, even if his colleagues continue to attempt to knock him off. And he finally wins at least the love and loyalty of the magnificent Barbara Churchill. Dr. Mary Finney is acidic with everyone. Hooper and Emily take a good deal of guff in their enlightened admiration. The Reverend Claire Aldington does not seem to like anyone outside of her son Jamie, a plump, freshmouthed child whom she adores. Characters would like to like her, even love her, if she would allow the possibility. Most of Vicar Whitechurch's clerics are an unpleasant, snobbish, and priggish lot, disregarded by the police and almost everyone else. C. A. Alington's archdeacons are also an unpleasant lot, though Garminster is passed off as pleasant and Thorp manages to marry, proving Cupid is, indeed, a blind god. Septimus has his dogs, the dean's son and one or two parishioners, and the camaraderie of his ex-police mates, which puts him high on the list. But apparently Martin Buell has chiefly his dog Bascomb, the only one among his circle with whom he does not trade insults. None of these last few clerics is particularly theological. A reader could suffocate in the thin theological stratosphere of the Anglican/Episcopalian books. And apparently on the surface the least amiable and most misanthropic of them all is Father Martin Buell.

Buell's acidic gruffness is reminiscent of Mary Finney's. Being a westerner, as she is, his idea is apparently to say the exact opposite of what he means. His insult in his declaration of affection. Thus, he is as comfortable as an old shoe to his equally taciturn and deflating far western fictional peers. As they jibe, criticize, and play nasty jokes on one another, spreading vicious rumors and shirking responsibilities, they forge an apparently perverse but ultimately caring community. They accept one another, the more idiosyncratic, the better. As the far extreme of the untheological, unamiable clerical sleuth, Buell is a sheer delight in his perversity. For cathartic therapy the Martin Buell books are a necessity for any cleric, religious worker, or active lay worker. Every acidic, sarcastic, unloving thought that could ever be levied at the church, fellow believers, or the work of ministry is here in exquisitely comic prose. Immediately edifying? Not particularly. Entertaining? Absolutely. Ultimately edifying? Perhaps.

Buell is the creation of Margaret Louise Scherf, who also created pathologist Grace Severance, Emily and Henry Bryce, Lieutenant Ryan, and a host of one-shot detectives in her twenty-five mysteries, among other books, published and retitled and republished between 1940 and 1978. From a varied career which spanned multiple occupations, from publishing house work with Robert M. McBride, the Campfire Girls magazine, and the Wise Book Company to secretarial work with the naval inspector at the Bethlehem Steel Shipyard in Brooklyn to activity in the Democratic Party, culminating in a stint in the Montana state legislature, Margaret Scherf sharpened her style into one of the most jaundiced and original in the subgenre. Her irony even extended to patterning a murder victim on herself for *The Corpse in the Flannel Nightgown* (1965), published the year Margaret Scherf's career peaked in the Montana state senate. Selma

Colfax, imperious matriarch, is in numerous ways like the Margaret Scherf of 1965, accomplished, renowned, authoritative. She has a home at Flathead Lake (*Nightgown,* 10) and runs a "lucrative cherry orchard" (*Nightgown,* 13). According to the end flap of the non-Buell mystery *The Beautiful Birthday Cake* (1971), Margaret Scherf "and her husband own and manage a cherry orchard on Flathead Lake near Kalispell, in western Montana, and they spend their winters in an old mining town in Arizona" (*Cake,* end flap). Selma Colfax is a forthright dowager: "She was as meek and humble and self-effacing as General De Gaulle, and she wore people down until they were glad to give in just to stop hearing her voice" (*Nightgown,* 10). Buell finds her irritating: "You could not, in fairness, say she was an enemy, except in the sense that all parishioners were the enemies of all parsons, but she was a hair shirt he was glad to defer putting on" (*Nightgown,* 14). He never does put this one on because she is murdered before he arrives. (Thus, author Scherf disintegrates her mirror image in what will prove to be the final Buell book.) This jaundiced outlook becomes characteristic of Buell.

Martin Buell, who was introduced in *Always Murder a Friend* (1948), where, of course, he is suspected of murder, managed to star in seven mysteries from 1948 to 1965. At the outset of his series he is already a big man, weighing some one hundred ninety-five pounds, which will climb to two hundred ten by the last book. He is an expert chef who can make even the worried eat (e.g., *Overshoes,* 45, 148). He has an aversion to lettuce and jello (*Overshoes,* 69) and makes "damn good coffee." He loathes hunting and fishing (*Overshoes,* 133–34), preferring the food he prepares to be already off the hoof. He also has the appearance of sloth: "Father Buell got a taste of walking at the age of ten months and never tried it again" (*Elk,* 40). Slugged once when he happens inadvertently to be on foot, he remarks, "This showed the folly of going anywhere on foot—awful things happened to people who walked" (*Elk,* 178).

But if Leonard Holton wishes his cleric to be active, Buell is his dream fulfillment. Buell has to do four services, two in Farrington, one in Stoner in the afternoon, and one in Meade at eight in the evening. Farrington is located in the series in Sweet Grass County, Montana. While there is no Farrington listed in Sweet Grass County, Montana, which is in the southern region of the state just above the border of Wyoming and Yellowstone National Park, there is a Big Timber, the place where Buell keeps cattle. Buell's Farrington is a small town where the local doctor still makes house calls (*Overshoes,* 8).

Buell claims to write his sermons on Friday morning (*Elk,* 50). This will slip as the series progresses. He can be diplomatic, letting an elderly parishioner cheat at cards because "some people just have to win" (*Elk,* 52), and using "strategy" to divert people's plans into courses he considers desirable (*Elk,* 54). Like Randollph's bishop, he knows when to be silent:

> There had been a time when silence made him uneasy, when he felt responsible for keeping the air filled between himself and other people. Now he let things take their natural course, and if a fellow didn't want to talk, Martin didn't talk either. (*Elk*, 63)

Though he growls "unchristian remarks" at anyone who disturbs him before his coffee in the morning (*Elk*, 44), he can suppress himself when he does not like somebody. Sheriff Hunnicut says he looks "like a very patient mad bull" (*Elk*, 82). And despite his often cavalier attitude, he is at heart concerned about his standing with his congregation: "I shudder to think what will happen to me if I'm mentioned [in connection with another investigation]. . . . A clergyman is never so solid that a few well-chosen misstatements won't toss him sky-high" (*Elk*, 84). His services draw "a handful of people," though, of course, he holds a number of them in several towns (*Elk*, 85). He is being compared with his predecessor, the "perfect Dr. Dobson" (*Elk*, 129). He expects little of his parishioners theologically and is amused by a reply to his question, "'What would you do if you wanted to test someone's character?'" The person whose character Buell wants to test replies, "'I'd ask her if she understood the Trinity. If she said yes, I'd know she was a little careless with the truth'" (*Elk*, 51).

As for Buell's detecting style, Sheriff Hunnicut rules,

> It's the damnedest assortment of unlikely facts I ever saw, Buell. But whenever you get into something it immediately becomes highly improbable. You do something to these cases. (*Elk*, 117)

Indeed, he has fully adopted his view of himself as a detective from Hunnicut's quips: "Everybody knows I stumble around in these things and cause a lot of uneasiness in the bishop's study, but I'm harmless, really." To this someone replies, "That depends on the point of view" (*Overshoes*, 126). Those who review his interpretation of pastoral duties will tend to agree. Buell feels his pastoral duties include matchmaking (*Overshoes*, 147). For him, a minister's occupation is defined as "a professional concern with other people's morals." Further, in ministry his theory and practice do not always agree: "In theory he felt it was downright dastardly to read other people's mail, but in practice it sometimes proved interesting and informative" (*Overshoes*, 124).

Well suited to his joint calling of ministry and detection, he can go two or three days without sleep (*Toothache*, 23), avoiding exercise "like a snakebite" (*Toothache*, 31), careening in his fiery red Packard around the Montana mountainsides while smoking a big cigar and crouching beneath his black stetson. Buell's interest in these mountains is clearly academic rather than aesthetic, since Buell is big and likes to feel big:

> Bishop Kingsley's idea in holding the convention in the park had been communion with nature. He wanted to give his clergymen a few days in the open, along with the dose of diocesan

business. It was a nice thought, for those who liked nature. Martin did not, although the mountain across the lake wasn't bad, as mountains went. Not too unfriendly. Not too severe. Mountains took a rather disdainful view of man, he thought, and he didn't see why people felt happy looking at a mountain. It made them feel small, they said. Who wanted to feel small? (*Toothache*, 4)

And in these mountains he is introduced to a series regular, his consistent comrade and dearest friend, Bascomb the Chesapeake Bay retriever: a cleric and his dog. Naturally, in keeping with his character, Buell first turns down the offer of the puppy, but finally reluctantly rescues Bascomb from a derelict life. Bascomb's cheerful equanimity becomes a foil for Buell, who considers the dog more hopeful about the future of the human race than he is.

Buell has a right to be depressed by humanity's general outlook, for a pall of suspicion hangs over him from the first book, when an audacious murderer tries to incriminate him. This suspicion is only partially dispelled by the apprehension of the true killer and is pervasive as the series progresses. Buell is the first one the doctor suspects when another body is found. Buell's neighbor, housekeeper, and doctor kindly, if improbably, destroy evidence, and the sheriff looks the other way at the hint of foul doings in order to protect Buell from becoming embroiled in another murder. Naturally, for this series, their solicitation is carefully disguised. As Sheriff Hunnicut drily notes, "Farrington used to be [a trusting town] . . . until the Reverend Martin Buell arrived and began finding a murderer in every nightshirt" (*Toothache*, 127). Buell's small-town parsimonious vestry also effectively disguises its concern, having him heat with three wood stoves in lieu of allowing him an oil furnace (*Overshoes*, 18).

Perhaps this kind of parishioner attitude explains why Buell, on his side, maintains himself basically by his droll sense of humor. When his bishop suggests he looks "liverish" and needs a tonic, he growls, "The best tonic for a cleric at this time of year would be a complete turnover in his parish" (*Overshoes*, 38). Indeed, in Pastor Buell's jaded view, "The Church . . . was limited to the people best able, by reason of long familiarity with its forms, to resist religion" (*Toothache*, 27). Among the parishioners of Farrington's churches:

Mrs. McCoy came to church, Martin knew, for two reasons. One was to please Helen, the other was to see if anybody made a mistake during the service. It was her great hope, he felt sure, that some Sunday the altar boy would trip going down the chancel steps with the cross. He did not mention these reasons to Hattie, who had gone back into the church and was crossing the sanctuary with a brisk nod of her head. She made a trip every Sunday into the vestry to see if anyone had been nipping at the communion wine. She made a mark on the bottle, and Martin usually moved the mark upward during the week so as not to disturb her convictions about the wickedness of man. (*Toothache*, 29)

Of the doctor's wife he muses, "Mrs. Crabbe had been to the eight o'clock service and was feeling so virtuous you couldn't touch her with a ten-foot pole" (*Toothache*, 113). Buell observes of his dog, "He's very trusting. Never knew any Christians until he came to Farrington." For himself he claims, "When a man tells me he's a Christian, I grab my wallet with both hands" (*Toothache*, 36). Buell frankly assesses the value of the coin of his parishioners' moral state after announcing "the parish was in the clear financially":

> I'm not so sure we're in such a satisfactory state as far as our souls are concerned. This parish has always been sounder in the pocketbook than in the conscience, but I'll talk about that in church. (*Elk*, 17)

Such low opinion is by no means restricted to Buell: "A good many people in Farrington left their keys in their mailboxes, but Fred's long association with church members had made him cautious" (*Elk*, 174–75). Beyond parishioners, Buell finds the prospect of meeting with other clergy fills him with doom and discouragement. Because of all his tribulations he firmly keeps his herd of cattle "as insurance against the sudden parochial and diocesan storms that sometimes swept away an unsuspecting clergyman" (*Overshoes*, 31). If Buell feels ill, he blames it on "an excess of virtue" (*Overshoes*, 8). In a general observation, he concludes, "There are times when I could entirely dispense with people" (*Toothache*, 7). Against his share of the verbal blitzkrieg of others, Buell allows himself an "ounce of gratuitous malice" "once a week" (*Toothache*, 48). Toward his superiors he turns a jaundiced eye, particularly on his archdeacon, who rewards Buell's suspicions by sticking him with the guardianship of an unwanted infant. No sane man or woman in any local town will take the infant until Buell leans on a woman who entertains the thin hope of being the second Mrs. Buell. Buell takes his superiors' idiosyncracies as givens, filling up on breakfast so as to look uninterested in food later on in the day in a nod to their asceticism (*Toothache*, 12). Toward his peers he has "a great contempt for men who kept diaries" (*Toothache*, 3). As for such activities as keeping up with the clerical times, Buell subscribes faithfully to *The Churchman*. His purpose? When he cannot sleep, he merely takes out the latest issue and falls asleep immediately (*Toothache*, 50).

But one activity that rivets Buell's interest is investigating murder, despite the best attempts of the sheriff, his friends, and his housekeeper to keep him free of its taint. We have seen many different reasons given to justify the clerical sleuth's involvement in a murder investigation. Another character provides Buell's rationale, which turns out to be the simplest. Why does Martin Buell detect? "'You also like a bit of excitement, Reverend'" (*Toothache*, 59).

Along the way Buell can nonchalantly dip into a corpse's pack of cigarettes, thereby unearthing a clue, worm his way into someone else's attic to look for compromising letters, and poke through other people's personal photographs. For Buell invading everyone's privacy is second nature; it is his definition of ministry: "Running a church is mostly poking your nose into private affairs, Jude. In that respect it's a lot like the law" (*Toothache*, 76). Buell's sage connection between the function of civil and spiritual justice neatly paves the way for Septimus, who comes the nearest of all clerical sleuths to uniting them.

One would suppose the solving of all these crimes would be seen as keeping Buell's mind from stagnating. But his investigating is an activity that does not charm others and is not credited to him by his congregation as a sophisticated form of continuing education. For Reverend Randollph it is good publicity; for Rabbi Small it is one of his saving graces, as he bails accused Jews out of trouble and pinpoints the culpable Gentiles; congregations like Dowling's seem to be indifferent to it if the cleric keeps delivering on the pastoral contract. But for Buell's, "If the more militant members of his parish found he was interested in another criminal case, there might be a great deal of unpleasantness" (*Overshoes*, 106). Buell even receives the scorn of other members of "the Ministerial Association" for his pains. Particularly, the obnoxious Presbyterian minister in town takes every opportunity to needle him:

> "Parish business, I presume?" Emerson was really nasty this morning. "Really, Buell, I don't understand how you become involved in these things. Nothing like that ever happens to me." (*Overshoes*, 116)

Buell began solving murders for the excitement and might well have dropped detecting given the reaction of his parishioners. But he continues for pastoral reasons:

> It would be expedient to withdraw, there was no doubt of that. But he knew he would not withdraw. There was a brutal nature still at work, and for the safety of Diana, and perhaps of other persons, it had better be revealed with all possible speed. (*Overshoes*, 106)

The reason Buell continues is not because of his excessive virtue. He would seem more likely to favor the sermon text of Henry Fielding's dubious minister in *Shamela*, "Be not righteous over much." Buell, ruminating on sermon material from his experiences, notes:

> "Beware of the good deed"—there was a text. . . . Fortunately he didn't have to post his weekly gems of wisdom on a bulletin board for the other clergymen to criticize. He wouldn't go so far as to say good deeds were dynamite, but he would recommend a little forethought as to the effect on the Good Deedee, and less concentration on the polishing of the Good Doer's halo. (*Overshoes*, 23)

But Buell is, after all, a minister and despite all impatience with his charges, bordering at times on downright loathing, he is compelled to detect periodically in order to deliver them from the taint or the clutches of evil. And what Buell wants most to guard his commonplace flock against is fanaticism:

> "A fanatic will do anything to promote his ideas," Martin reminded him. "The world right now is full of people who don't give a hoot in harrah for the present—so long as they can see their own ideas triumphant in the future. How do we know what tomorrow's men are going to want? We keep fighting and dying for the future of mankind, and if we fight and die enough there won't be any mankind in the future. What wouldn't I give to hear somebody speak up for the here and now!" He glared at Sir Wilfred. "And don't tell me this doesn't tie in with Christian theology." (*Pie,* 134)

While this is laudable, he goes overboard in confusing zeal with fanaticism, and in a peculiar bit of misogynism he attacks church-minded women, attempting to keep them off the vestry by arguing, "Once let 'em get the upper hand and you're sunk, Yates. They begin to treat you like a Pekingese on a string and you have no more to say in your own church than the janitor" (*Pie,* 170). He goes so far in attacking his zealous parishioners as to snort, "'Women,' Martin grumbled to himself. 'You can't make Christians of 'em and you can't run a Christian church without 'em'" (*Pie,* 159). So Buell zealously attacks all forms of zeal, whether superstitious, religious, humanitarian, or political, dishonest or honest, selfish or selfless. He reduces all to a humble common denominator by the application of scorn.

This equalizing eye characterizes author Margaret Scherf's outlook and style, laying, with nearly biblical zest, every raised hill low and every crookedly narrow path painfully straight, or at least fully berated. Apparently this approach characterized Scherf's whole outlook on life. During World War II she took a job as secretary to the naval inspector at the Bethlehem Steel Shipyard in Brooklyn. This she did when she was already a published author with several books to her credit. In characteristic self-effacement she made her patriotic pitch for buying war bonds and stamps in this delightful Ogden Nash-like poem, printed in the opening pages of the non-Buell mystery *They Came to Kill* (1942):

> The author of *They Came to Kill* comments: "I don't want to tell anyone else what to do with their money. This is a note to myself":
>
> What do you mean,
> Walking around in Nylons without runs
> When MacArthur needs guns?
>
> You've killed a lot of people, Scherf,
> But what have you done
> To hustle Adolf under the turf?

Oh, you bought some ten cent stamps?
Well, well.

An occasional dime
Isn't going to construct a griddle
For Goering's middle.

You'd better fork over to your Uncle Sam
Or you'll be sitting in the Nazi stables
Writing publicity for Goebbels.
(*Kill,* iii)

Her work against Hitler's master race certainly illuminates Buell's attacks
against utopianism and fanaticism.

Her contained, controlled, but steady acetylene torch which she had the
grace to turn on herself as well, went on past the Church and its adherents and
detractors to scorch sacrosanct civic organizations as well. As we can see, there
is a deeper social function for her deflating, equalizing eye and its cathartic
gaze, turning as it does to expose an evil underside in apparently normal living
that might give Father Brown pause.

In tale after tale Margaret Scherf's technique is to have the murderer revealed as a normal everyday intimate whom no one has really known despite
constant contact. Along with her fondness for popping the murderer out of the
tight closet of a victim's intimates, Scherf also enjoys letting the body (or parts
of it) topple out of some everyday container for household use. In *The Elk and
the Evidence* it is in freezer paper for holding meat, in *Never Turn Your Back* it
is in a packing crate for a grandfather clock to be set up in a leading Presbyterian
churchwoman's front room. Perhaps this is why she turns her particularly acidic
eye on everything about day-to-day living. She sounds like Garrison Keillor
after a bad night. Thus, the baleful eye discovers "Charlie Russell's bony
drawings of the last of something—General Custer or a buffalo" (*Elk,* 32); the
motivation of hunters: "They go out there to conserve the wild life. Nobody is
more earnest about the preservation of wild life than a hunter" (*Elk,* 48); "professional" westerners: "a westerner you could slice and serve with lettuce. Full
of picturesque stories, songs, flapjack recipes, rope tricks" (*Elk,* 48). When the
narration is not turning Farrington into Lake Wobegon after a mudslide, Buell
is carrying the caustic banner and waving it at the well-intended:

In bed he reflected that there was no end to the trouble you could get into when you thought
you were doing a noble deed. It reminded him of the time he had felt sorry for Miss Hattie's
sister Susan, chopping wood with a dull ax, and had taken it off to be sharpened. Miss Susan
was delighted and nearly chopped off her foot. Miss Hattie accused him of a desire to see Susan
crippled. The more people involved in a Sir Galahad action the worse the consequences,
generally. It was not exactly a subject for a sermon, but he had often wished he could make

one on it. There seemed to be a direct ratio between one's assurance of saintliness and the extent of the damage that resulted. He still shuddered when he recalled the six days of Shakespeare-aloud which Mrs. Jerome had inflicted on him during his last bout with lumbago. Lumbago was enough for man to bear without the addition of Mrs. Jerome as Richard II. (*Elk*, 107–8)

Buell uses it, too, to endure his tedious and generally hostile church activities. Only Kemelman's Rabbi Small has anything to measure against the daily contact Buell has with his parish:

He seldom attended a meeting of Christ Church Guild, but he was determined to suffer through this one. It was only a week after Thanksgiving and the wrangling over Christmas had already begun. The Sunday-school teachers were quarreling over the children's party, Mrs. Jerome threatened not to give a tree this year because someone had said last year's was scrubby, the vestrymen had taken a stiff-necked attitude toward a dance in the parish house, and Miss Hattie Kettlehorn had cooked up a rumor about the rector and a certain lady in the parish. The fact that the lady had all the appeal of a second-class vulture seemed not to diminish the eagerness with which the story was circulated. It promised to be one of the most difficult Christmas seasons Martin had ever experienced. . . . He wondered sometimes what the reading of the minutes and the pansy notes and the rummage sales had to do with the life of Christ. But if you let yourself become too analytical you'd be useless as a working rector. Everything in this world, Buell, he told himself, is a compromise between what it ought to be and what it can be, with human beings running it. (*Elk*, 14,16)

Even the unchurched are included in Buell's thrusts:

"My father went to church twice every Sunday and he was the meanest man I ever knew."
"I suppose he wore pants and ate meat?" Martin asked. "You ought to give up everything he did, to be consistent." (*Elk*, 68)

Further, as a good Arminian-based clerical detective, he reserves a few choice jabs for the Reformed. When his housekeeper, Mrs. Beekman, asks, "Who would do such a disgusting thing?" as tucking a toe in his elk roast, Buell quips, "No Episcopalian. Some demented Presbyterian, probably" (*Elk*, 45). He also likes to bedevil his Roman Catholic counterparts. When asked if he minds being mistaken for one, he replies, "No. Especially when I'm doing something they think a Roman priest should not do, such as talking to a pretty girl" (*Elk*, 140–41).

As one might anticipate, in response to Buell's complaints, the best intentions of his parishioners to improve his comfort and safety lead to some harrowing living conditions for Buell. In *Elk* he is refused an electric blanket, elsewhere he is refused a furnace and his manse is even torn down in his absence to be replaced by a prefabricated box house. With all that has been inflicted upon him, we understand why he is not more surprised that a free gift of an elk roast produces a severed human toe. We can only lament that Buell lived too early to have taken solace in the therapy of *The Wittenburg* [*sic*] *Door*.

The great contribution of the Buell series is to put a pin in the bloated dignity of Protestants. The exhilaration here is in having a cleric who, to the despair of his more socially minded members and to the anxiety mixed with amusement of his bishop, proceeds to muck about with murders, blithely running to seed, sporting a pot belly, a loud car, and a soiled reputation for propriety. When on the scent, Buell thinks nothing of breaking and entering (*Elk*, 176) or pumping false positive rumors into the gossip mill to counteract equally false malicious ones (*Elk*, 123). Buell has come to terms with himself, his comforts, and his limitations. As he sums up his philosophy:

> I could threaten myself with a diet, but after an acquaintance of over fifty years I know it would be no more than a threat. So I just enjoy my weaknesses wherever they manifest themselves. (*Elk*, 97)

For Margaret Scherf, we can see, humor is essential to all humanity and human interaction. She has Buell conjecture:

> Perhaps there was a comic aspect to all human beings, even murderers. This was a possibility no reformer would admit—a reformer liked to think of his villains as of a constant, pure and ominous black. (*Elk*, 88)

But for Buell, "I allow for human frailty" (*Elk*, 114).

Thus, for Scherf and her character Buell the only two elements of society that are unacceptable are those which do not allow for human frailty. The first group, less detrimental but greatly annoying, is comprised of those who regard their fellows with censuring looks, "rather like Martin Luther or Cromwell or some other disagreeably moral human being" (*Elk*, 28). As her examples reveal, such people usually have a theologically Lutheran or Reformed perspective. In the nonmystery, *Wedding Train* (1960), she takes off the gloves and slugs some straw Presbyterian clerics she creates:

> Was there anything so dull as a clergyman? . . . Nothing went on in these but a weak struggle against the lusts of the flesh, which had plenty of time to rise like dough in their lazy frames. None of them had a farm, probably didn't even have gardens. Just went around eating up other people's hard-earned corn and potatoes. (*Train*, 150)

These clerics set a framework for the obnoxious, condescending Emerson, Buell's Presbyterian counterpart, who slithers into the series like the accuser into the Garden.

The other undesirable element is composed of the killers. Summing up *Elk*'s murderer, Buell reflects:

> Even in defeat the man was obnoxious, insolent. The rot that had appeared externally was only a fraction of the total decay. . . . A man should take what he wanted in the world. Get yours while the getting is good. If you don't take it, someone else will. God deliver us from the realists, Martin thought. (*Elk,* 188)

Buell seeks to separate himself from Father Brown, who could smell evil as a dog smells rats: "'You're frightened, Buell,' he told himself. 'You can't smell evil.'" Still, "Again he had that crawling sensation that evil was close to him, that the air was thick with the smell of it" (*Elk,* 173). Given his views, naturally, Buell believes totally in the reality of evil:

> Martin was aware of evil—he believed firmly the church's astringent doctrine that evil was in all men, in varying intensity. But having settled comfortably into the parish at Farrington and conquered or held at bay the most virulent enemies of Christianity in his own church, he had come to think of evil as prevailing in places like Chicago. . . . With the finding of Emmons' mangled body he was convinced that the evil was not unintentional, not remote. It was fundamental, pervasive, a necklace of planned and hideous deeds. (*Elk,* 141–42)

Despite Scherf's antipathy to the "disagreeably moral," she uses a morality in little things as in big things to counteract pervasive evil. A character's cheating at cards is the main indicator of a moral vacuum within. His cheating is its outer rim. Buell abhors moral laxity in those he encounters, apparently opposing it to the acceptable human frailty which we have just seen extolled. Ironically, in the philosophy of the comfort-oriented, easygoing, breaking-and-entering Buell, an easygoing attitude toward morality leads to eventual disaster: "Nobody ever gets excited about a man's soul until he's all through with it. Then I'm supposed to come along and give him a ticket to heaven and a few kind words of introduction to the Almighty" (*Elk,* 20–21). Moral slovenliness also provides the reason why a killer in the microcosmic worldview of Scherf's mysteries always gets caught:

> "The trouble with a murder," Martin observed, "is that there's always something left over. If it hadn't been the toe, or the key, it would have been something else. And a murderer hasn't much chance to practice his trade before he puts it to serious use." (*Elk,* 188)

Since Buell's books succeeded even with their flaws and under the usually selective imprint of the Crime Club, Margaret Scherf is clearly providing other benefits: her affirmation of the reality of evil and the need to oppose it, her humorous portrayal of church life and its holy hot water, and her gift of a noninflated Episcopalian rector. Scherf once commented, "My theory is that mysteries appeal to people because the central problem is soluble, unlike most of the problems in the real world" (Reilly, 793). Her central problems and their solutions may be particularly artificial, but there is a certain comfort in the knowledge that they are constructed inevitably to be solved. Buell may have his limitations, but he will not let us or the innocent down.

With Buell's blithe dismissal of Reformed thought, of Roman Catholic theology, of much else, what does he put into his own sermons that leaves his parishioners so little enthusiasm for them, as evidenced by sparse attendance and no desire for repetition? The hunt for Buell's theology in his books is more difficult than the one for the murderer—the murderer is discovered. A compendium of Buell's theological thought gleaned from the entire series yields little material. One wonders just what that doctorate of his is in. About the only thing he does with any gusto is cook, and he is a superb chef who draws grunts of admiration from the other characters in the book. At the needling of another minister he does break out a copy of Herodotus "for self-improvement" to make sure his mind does not "stagnate." Besides,

> The chapters were wonderfully short. He finished up the war between the Argians and the Lacedaemonians, a war which definitely settled an issue. The Argians, who had worn their hair short, let it grow, and the Lacedaemonians, who had always worn theirs long, cut it off. (*Overshoes*, 144)

What little theology can be found is usually given in response to point blank questions that his attitude toward truth will not let him dodge. With Septimus' ease he may prefabricate a loose tale to worm information out of the unsuspecting (e.g., *Toothache*, 93), but, unlike fellow Anglican Septimus, he does not lie when asked a straightforward question (e.g., *Overshoes*, 121). Yet when asked point blank, "Do you really believe in hell?" Buell evades, associating hell with Reformed doctrine: "'That's a question you'd better take up with your own parson,' Martin said, resolved not to get into the Presbyterian hell this early in the morning if he could help it" (*Back*, 117–18). He likes nothing better than to confront the challenges of an atheist: "Few people these days were interested enough in God to deny his existence. A genuine unbeliever was something to get your teeth into, he reflected" (*Toothache*, 30).

We have evidence that he believes in God, and that he believes the doctrine of the Trinity is difficult to understand. We do not have much evidence that he relies on God or doctrines. In fact, a good deal of what passes for Buell's pastoral counseling is simply home-spun commonsense advice. For instance, Buell growls at a discouraged would-be football coach whose dreams are spoiled by a lost leg:

> "We're all amputees, in one way or another, Smith. . . . By the time we reach your age, sometimes long before, some precious dream has gotten into the buzzsaw of reality. . . . Let's look at the coaching business. You get a nice job, good salary, everybody welcomes you to town. You're a hero, until you have a couple of years of losing teams. Then you're as welcome downtown among the great athletic wizards behind their clothing counters as a blizzard the

Saturday before Easter. Man, you've got no imagination. Get into the paying end of football—
sell the supplies." (*Back,* 44)

And Buell's gruff approach is like a cold dose of water. It revives by shock.
The drawback of such an approach is impatience: "He was a poor nurse, feeling
impatient with the ailing and hating confinement" (*Back,* 76). But it works well
with certain personalities. Dr. Buell might as well write a general newspaper
advice column. As an Episcopalian priest, he could as easily be a Unitarian on
the liturgical side or for that matter a kindly secular humanist with ceremonial
leanings. What we know about him is more what he does not believe than what
he does believe.

Thus, in these novels he is shown to be unpopular with his fellow professionals, manipulated by (and, as best as he can, manipulating) his parishioners,
a cleric who would rather be anywhere solving a crime than home doing his
pastoral duties. He has been leaving sermons to late in the week, as late sometimes as Saturday night. Perhaps he has little theological to put into them.
Eventually, Buell is repaid in kind when, upon taking inventory of his posses-
sions after the move to the new rectory, "Martin said he'd found some of it, but
his trunkful of sermons was missing. Mrs. McCoy couldn't imagine anybody
wanting that. 'It's probably out at the dump,' she added consolingly" (*Back,*
105).

Buell sounds like a cleric who has essentially gone to seed in his parish.
He displays only one stellar talent, besides culinary aptitude and animal hus-
bandry, and that is catching nefarious Presbyterians with dazzling skill and great
aplomb. He seems a fine rector to have about, as long as someone in the choir
is being strangled, someone in the belfry is being lynched, or the vestry is being
methodically rubbed out.

The war Buell ultimately wages is close to home. It is one Buell fights
continually with himself and with his parishioners. Faith and courage, he recognizes, often thrive better in sudden desperate straits than in the grueling, wearing
disappointments of day-by-day life. Those who find faith rotting away within
them, oblivious as those around them are to that cancer, become the killers in
these books. The true battle for Buell is to resist becoming like these living
dead. His ministry exists to deliver others from them and unmask each new
wolf that his flock produces.

Simple, unaffected, common goodness is the safeguard. The lesson is
Ecclesiastes 5:18, simply eating and drinking and enjoying work in the days
God gives us. For Buell that is God's intention and the borders of goodness.
Anything more is the invitation to evil. Taken as a whole, the seven Buell tales
suggest that greed for an excess of anything—wealth, land, power—damages
others and ultimately turns back destruction on oneself. The self-sufficient yet
responsive rugged individualist of the classic West is the correct norm for

conduct. People should usurp no more than their share of money, power, or land from others. Each should live simply if cantankerously with others, settling for a simple, homely life in a small, roomy, communal setting. Any other approach spells destruction. Nor should anyone ever take others for granted. Quiet, predictable relations or neighbors may suddenly turn out to be pathological killers. And this is the point of all the painstaking barrage of sarcastic quips, deflating barbs, and leveling witticisms throughout the series. They are a safeguard against any character rising above his or her limited share of anything— talent, recognition, and affection included—because every excess, with the sole exception, apparently, of excessive sarcasm, leads to inevitable evil.

After 1965 Buell never again appeared in the fourteen years and six mysteries remaining until Scherf's death in 1979. As if to illustrate and summarize the necessity of wit, she ends Buell's adventures with a practical joke. Appropriately, in the final dirty trick of the series, author Scherf on their very last page left Buell and Bascomb stranded four hundred miles from Farrington.

19

Cop in a Cassock: Stephen Chance's Septimus

One of the most intriguing of the Anglican clerical sleuths is the creation of a writer who is himself a former parish priest and who, although trained originally as a mechanical engineer, branched out to serve in prisons and hospital administration, counsel youth, advise the BBC on religious affairs, teach English, eventually teach history at Malvern College, and, of course, write novels. Because of his many children's books, the Reverend Philip Turner's mysteries, written under the pseudonym "Stephen Chance," are often thoughtlessly filed in the juvenile sections of our public libraries. But the novels are hardly juvenile fare. Instead, these witty and delightful stories mark one of the hidden treasures of the Anglican ecclesiastical mysteries.

Like his creator, the Reverend Septimus Treloar, country parson, is a product of several career shifts. Turner has united the two strands of the sacred and secular mystery in one human by making a former police officer a cleric and enjoying the clash and resolution of the two roles in one character. Catalan and White approached this state by making their nuns daughters of police officers, yet apparently no one but Philip Turner thought of taking the final logical step. The only innovation left would be to make a clerical sleuth a tent-making parson, serving currently as a police officer. Until that time Septimus is unique and best approaches in one character the struggle for domination of law and grace, mercy and justice. Septimus' struggles provide a good culture in which to examine the interplay between the justice-oriented enforcer and the mercy-oriented reconciler. A seventh son of a Cornish soldier, Septimus progressed to the cloth beginning with his war service as a major, fighting in, among other places, the Holy Land. Then a career in police work, beginning as a constable in the east end of London and ending as chief inspector of the CID, left him with a broken nose and a rugged exterior: "His face really looked as if someone had tried to remodel it with a baseball bat . . . like a failed prize fighter" (*Ghost,* 10). To a parishioner he is like "'A big cat,' she thought, 'like a great grey panther'" (*Danedyke,* 12). To another he is like a "warhorse," a "gentle giant" (*Danedyke,* 41).

What is "not what it seems" in this clerical mystery is the mysterious cleric himself. Graying, unmarried, lonely, living "alone in his inconvenient rectory" (*Ghost*, 11), Septimus, if a "warhorse," is in one sense retired out to pasture. Yet his "shrewd eyes" (*Ghost*, 10) betoken a mind very much alert and active. Septimus is extremely observant, though he does not make a Nobel-prize performance out of it as Whitechurch's Westerham nearly does. Like Vicar Westerham, who is his inverse in age, Septimus likes to relax with a good half-pint of Guinness, and if his Latin has lapsed (*Ghost*, 34), his police skills certainly have not. He has a policeman's sixth-sense reliance on his feelings (e.g., *Stone*, 131), and he still bears so much of his prior profession about him that he is apt to be introduced as "an Anglican parson, though you wouldn't think it to look at him" (*Stone*, 44). Whatever may give other clerical sleuths pleasure, Septimus receives a "little glow of satisfaction at the double click of the complex deadlatch" (*Danedyke*, 14) on his church's door. He lifts fingerprints off suspected visitors by gratuitously pressing postcards of his church in their hands and then surreptitiously retrieving them. He memorizes their license plates, pats them apparently affectionately on the shoulders, gathering bits of fabric for clues. He dwarfs the otherwise tight relationships Sister Ursula, Brother Cadfael and Reverend Randollph have with the police by his ultimate claim as former coworker, the CID's own "beatified bobby" (*Danedyke*, 27), for whom his former colleagues will at times even breach security and risk their jobs.

Left over, too, is the salty vocabulary of the police. Despite his collar Septimus under stress seasons his speech with "curses" (*Ghost*, 27), those presumably above the standard ration of "damns" and "hells" grouped under the collective descriptive category. He labels his opponents "bastards" (*Danedyke*, 60), and in addition to employing that mild British swear word "bloody" (which alludes to Christ's blood), he drops the name of the deity vainly about. Being a former policeman, he "knew all the wrong phrases" and so "he cursed, fluently and comprehensively" (*Stone*, 19).

Unique to his character is his peculiar freedom with the truth. He lies blithely when he feels he needs to do so. He lies, we are told, with "immediate and engaging dishonesty" (*Ghost*, 36). He can claim he is the dean of a college and not a common clergyman (*Danedyke*, 56), reassume his old title to get past a skeptical innkeeper and a skeptical operator, and drop the portentous letters "MI5" with this completely fallacious hint of benefit to come: "We won't forget" (*Danedyke*, 47). To get information he tells "a clear-cut, totally convincing, and entirely fictitious story" (*Danedyke*, 84). Among his readily assumed personae is his favorite:

> Septimus slipped easily into his bumbling, vaguely benevolent, country parson act. . . . He looked the same. . . . But he had suddenly become a garrulous, well-intentioned backwoods

cleric without an idea in his head more complicated than choosing the hymns for the harvest festival service. (*Danedyke*, 84)

His church warden ironically reproves him:

"Bad example," said Tom. "That's what you are. Never thought I'd live to hear it. All those fibs. I shall jag in the churchwarden bit and join the Methodists."

"Parsons and coppers," said Septimus, his eyes on the road. "They're the best liars. Only way to keep up with the great British Public." (*Danedyke*, 86)

His creed seems to be clearly, "If the truth did not work, perhaps a lie might" (*Danedyke*, 111). He is also not above picking a lock, unlawfully entering, or helping himself to a piece of an uninvolved acquaintance's car in order to give chase (*Danedyke*, 58), a left-over police habit of commandeering what is needed to pursue criminals.

Yet his conscience is not entirely dead. When asked to give his word "as a reverend," "Septimus knew that once he gave his word he would have to keep it" (*Danedyke*, 117). Further, he may lie freely to criminals and to civilians from whom he wishes information, but he does have scruples about lying to the police. While keeping back "as much of the truth to himself as strict honesty would allow," he does feel "a little guilty about misleading Ted Harris, who was a good country copper" (*Danedyke*, 74). One gathers Septimus' loyalty is not to the truth *per se* but to those to whom he must choose to tell the truth or a lie. He judges the merit of doing so in regard to his opinion of the receiver. So his use of so-called objective truth seems totally subjected to his regard for the person to whom he is delivering information. This subjectivizing of morality extends to his service as a loyal church/state cleric discharging his civil duties by hastening to marry brides before "it'll start to show" (*Danedyke*, 72), or showing visitors around his church for the donation needed to keep it in repair and his parish budget solvent. He seems to be on comfortable terms with the total relativizing of Christianity to an ecclesiastical service he renders in the way that socialized medicine or public works are rendered. And glazed over all his activities is his policeman's endemic skepticism.

When a strange apparition occurs in the huge, stone Minster Saint Peter, the former CID investigator is asked:

"Do you think it's supernatural, Septimus?"

Septimus took out his pipe and clamped it between his teeth.

"Alisdair," he said, "I spent most of my life as a copper. I never investigated anything that hadn't got some sort of a villain at the back of it. Nearest I got to spirits was a fake medium who thieved a diamond brooch." (*Ghost*, 29)

To Septimus detection does not hold the charm it does to a Sister Mary Helen, and he does not take the delight in it that purely amateur sleuths like Dr. Mary Finney do. To him it is a commonplace, professional activity. When detecting, he reverts completely from cleric to cop, angrily cursing other drivers on the road (*Ghost,* 27) (what he needs is a flashing gumball), turning the professional's impatient contempt on inquisitive outsiders:

> "Have you formed any theories, Septimus?"
> He looked sourly at the Dean. Amateurs always talked about theories, whereas real detection was more like bricklaying. (*Ghost,* 30)

Like Soeur Angèle and her village priest, who, ironically, are the only ones in town to reject a vision of the Virgin Mary in *The Bell Ringer's Niece,* Septimus' commonplace workaday perspective rules out the supernatural with a policeman's skepticism (*Ghost,* 26). Therefore, we should not be surprised that his potential level of reversion is so situated that the discovery of the body of his beloved guard dog, Sir Handel, creates the catharsis that triggers his transformation from cleric back to cop. But his transition now carries with it a difference:

> In all his years with the police he had investigated murders, rapes, bank robberies, kidnappings. He had sent men to prison for more years than he cared to contemplate. He had sent four men to the gallows. In that time he had often been threatened with violence. But it had not meant much, because you could keep your job and your personal life separate. But now he was no longer a police officer he could not separate the one from the other. He was personally involved. And Sir Handel was dead. (*Danedyke,* 59)

Thus, the transition is not complete. His purely objectivized professionalism, if such a thing truly exists, is marred by the fact that he is unprofessionally motivated by revenge (*Danedyke,* 65–66), the role of avenging angel assumed by the clerical sleuth. His human frailty achieves in one parishioner's eyes the goal of clerical crime authors, particularly Charles Merrill Smith, to present the clergy's essential humanity: "Over the last few days she had seen a country parson in a new light. Not just as 'the Rector,' but as a man with a history and feelings and problems of his own" (*Danedyke,* 65).

Septimus' reversions, then, are never complete, since, despite his history, his detecting prowess, his proclivity to the policeman's lot and life, he is now a cleric. What might be an eccentricity in a retired policeman, such as a propensity to whistle hymn tunes (*Danedyke,* 42) or read Thomas Traherne's *Centuries of Meditation* for relaxation (*Danedyke,* 66), runs much deeper. Theology stirs at the core of Septimus' basic orienting perspective despite all the failings in his character to recreate himself as the perfect "Rector." The combination of theology and life in Septimus' character and outlook can be glimpsed in his ability to describe for the parish school children exactly the terrain of Jesus' parable:

> Rosemary Horton had made a fine model of the Holy Land in the sand tray, and Septimus spent a happy half-hour discussing with her seven-year-olds—half of whom had never seen a hill—the story of the Good Samaritan, and how the road really did "go down," as the Bible said it did, from Jerusalem to Jericho. Septimus knew the road from personal experience, so he talked about it rather well. He did not think it necessary to tell Class 2 about the dead bodies he had seen on it, nor the fact that he had last driven down it in an armoured car. (*Danedyke*, 90–91)

As a soldier and a policeman he has experienced the depths of sin, and the need for mercy has apparently made him a preacher. Theology for him is a matter of looking at reality in a way that makes it tolerable and as explicable as possible eternally within the sober plight of humanity. This unwillingness to let sin rest as the human condition has caused him to invest in mercy:

> Surprised, he found he was praying for the soul of old Lovebody, and the organist, and the sea captain who had murdered him. "Mercy. Mercy. Mercy," the wretched old man had written. In his years with the police Septimus had seen precious little mercy. He was now old enough to understand its importance. He could only hope that Lovebody had found it. Grinning wryly at the contradictions in his own character, he got up and continued his silent prowl. (*Ghost*, 41).

His theology, then, mixes a hard-core addressing of sin with an easy, almost childlike dependence on God's gracious intervention. This volatile mixture often explodes into comically farcical form, as when, setting a trap for a miscreant, he advises his cohort, "'If he decides to have another look at your ropes, hit him with that, and I'll be on his back quick as Christ'll let me'" (*Danedyke*, 121).

As God is his model, he does not let mercy set aside his passion for justice (or in Septimus' case, revenge). Yet with the relative sense of compromise with which he has adjusted to the less-than-ideal nature of reality, he will bargain with criminals when he must, and as easily break those bargains as he can.

One effect of such an attitude is his clear understanding of what motivates a criminal. The Danedyke cup, like Reverend Randollph's later unholy Gutenberg Bible or Sebastian's phantasmagorical original manuscript of the Pentateuch, is a religious icon that, like a juggernaut, threatens everyone in its path through history. An image of the grail, it is "supposed to have belonged to Mary, the mother of Jesus, and to have been brought to England by Joseph of Arimathea" (*Danedyke*, 8).

Why would anyone wish to steal and horde such a relic? The explanation is similar to that which Charles Merrill Smith will later use to explain the blood shed in the quest for the Gutenberg Bible: "'So you can look at it and think, I've got it and no one else has. Just me and it. I'm unique'" (*Danedyke*, 62). The transference of significance from the thing possessed to the one possessing, worth imparted by what one has rather than who one is, is the aberrant working out of an inner sense of inferiority, a material attempt to supply by nefarious means a lack of a sense of one's own worth. Crime is thus motivated by a low self image. That theme of a sense of inferiority in those who commit crimes will run throughout the series. In each book crime comes about when those who feel themselves inferior and powerless seek by theft, adultery, fraud, hoax, magic, and ritual murder—all means outside the rules of society—to secure satisfaction from society's powerful superior. In each case, though sympathy and the desire to bestow mercy might come from the cleric, Septimus the cop wants to exact justice. Each side triumphs in direct proportion to the gravity with which together they consider the crime.

Another direct effect is to make Septimus essentially an Anglo-Catholic in outlook. The provision of ceremonially imputed mercy allows Septimus to protect morality while receiving, if not sanction, at least forgiveness for the moral lapses his actions will necessarily entail. Therefore, Septimus in *Septimus and the Danedyke Mystery* feels an affinity for the outlawed medieval Catholicism that lays behind the tale. As Septimus imagines the faith that used to be, he looks around his church and

> he saw through the eyes of the men who had suffered . . . the stark human tragedy behind the legends . . . the shrine they had loved and tended desecrated by unbelievers, their home—the great abbey to which they had devoted their lives—smashed and stripped and falling into ruin; what would seem to them the blasphemies of the Protestant rite, and the arrogant servants of Henry VIII coming in their avarice and their ignorance. . . . "A house of prayer . . . a den of thieves." One way and another he had devoted his life to that struggle, and he also was a lonely man. (*Danedyke*, 35–36)

Celibate by choice, deeply empathetic with his monkish predecessors, Septimus by the third book, *Septimus and the Stone of Offering,* even finds himself praying to Mary (*Stone*, 165). He is an Anglo-Catholic, indeed, and that is how he can resolve the cop/cleric, supernatural debunking/supernatural affirming, truth devaluing/truth valuing, law enforcing/law breaking paradoxes of his character. Such security will stand him in good stead when he encounters espionage, where nothing is secure or as it appears, in *Septimus and the Spy Ring* (1979).

In the first book he spends an enormous amount of time and energy locating, recapturing, and preserving the symbol of that faded Catholicism, the Danedyke Cup. With the relic safely interred in the church's bank vault, he moves in the second book against another harbinger from the past when the supposed ghost of an organist killed for adultery appears to have returned to haunt a great church, setting Septimus against the sins of the Protestant past.

The third book presents the reemergence of sacrificial Welsh religion to supplant Christianity. Thus, in each of the first three books an agent of the past attempts to undermine and replace the values of the present.

One peculiar aspect of his reverence for the past, however, is Septimus' gentle deference to a white witch in the second and third books. Curiously for a Christian cleric, author Turner obviously approves of white witchcraft, even to the point of having Septimus in the third book accept treatment for his wrenched knee from a white witch (*Stone,* 112). In what way can true Christianity appeal for aid to witchcraft? Are not the systems mutually opposed?

The biblical case for the incompatibility of Christianity and witchcraft can be found thoroughly documented in the work of German State Church (Lutheran) pastoral counselor Dr. Kurt E. Koch. Koch, who has authored an authoritative, extensively documented study *Seelsorge and Okkultismus,* published by Kregel as *Christian Counseling and Occultism* (1965), has explored the effect of white witchcraft on the rural German shepherds who practice it. He distinguishes white magic from black magic as "enchantment for protection, for defense, for healing, for fruitfulness, etc.," as opposed to conjuration and "enchantment for persecution, for vengeance, for defense, for healing, etc." (Koch, 121). He mentions "natural magic, which without any relation to the two aforementioned factors [devil and Bible-texts] assumes mysterious relatedness of all things one to another," and he notes, "These relations are considered fully natural, though not fully known, and can transcend the purely material. And this so-called natural magic seeks by influencing these relationships to accomplish magic results" (Koch, 120–21). Yet in case after case Koch notices that people brought to white witches and shepherds for healing or counseling receive, along with the cure, a "spiritual residue" that haunts them. Children who are brought for healing are plagued into adulthood. This residue fills their dreams with night terrors and their lives with increasing spiritual oppression. Confirming conclusions drawn from case studies by the psychologist Schmeïng, Koch cites the hundreds of cases he has documented in his own research: "In all cases with which I made contact in my 25 years of pastoral care through interviews, the occult treatments by this shepherd produced grievous psychic disturbances" (Koch, 53). After discarding numerous case studies by himself and others for medical or other scientific reasons or for possible error in the collecting of the material, he concludes of the remainder and of the psychic phenomenon regularly produced as aftereffect, "White magic has the same character as the black magic except that it appears in a religious dress" (Koch, 124–25).

Septimus', and his creator's, lapse on this point is particularly puzzling since in the sequel, *The Stone of Offering,* we are told of Septimus, "He knew a fair amount about the powers of witch doctors and the like. He had once been sent to Trinidad to help with an investigation into a particularly revolting ritual murder" (*Stone,* 63). Why then this compromise with witchcraft of any shade? The point, though raised, is not resolved in Turner's work.

Further confusing the issue, the third Septimus mystery, *The Stone of Offering,* pits Septimus against a would-be wizard, with no comment concerning the theological dilemma left hanging in the second book or the acceptance of treatment in the present one. The stone of offering is the final in a series of replicas of an ancient Welsh sacrificial altar which the vacationing Septimus discovers is at the core of a resuscitated Druidic religion, revived to oppose a proposal to flood a valley for a new dam. The Wales of *The Stone of Offering* is certainly not the Wales of Ellis Peters' Cadfael books, where freedom, family ties and justice prevail. Instead this Wales is a wild terrain of ancient incantation, which "goes back to the dark times before Christianity came to Cymru" (*Stone,* 57), disturbed in fitful slumber, about to wake and attack the invasion of the Christian English. How such a land would ever have produced a Brother Cadfael eight centuries earlier is unfathomable. At any rate the threatened return of Druidism may shed some light on our previous question. Perhaps what has excused "white witchcraft" in Philip Turner's eyes is its obsequiousness before Christianity as opposed to the evident hostility of the atavistic Druidical religion. A dagger in the heart of one of the sacrifices symbolically duplicates "a slate cross, as if someone had made an obscene mockery of an Easter garden, using the bird's breast as the hill of Calvary" (*Stone,* 17). This is "barbaric. It smacked of nameless rites from the pre-Christian dark ages" (*Stone,* 31). Viewing the sites of sacrifice, Septimus has presentiments of "an evil magic about the place" (*Stone,* 36). "His conscious mind told him that it was nothing but a deep pool in a mountain torrent, his subconscious knew it to be a place of great evil" (*Stone,* 41), "a hell brew flecked with yellow scum" (*Stone,* 40). Eventually he will learn in a terrifying climax of personal danger that the crazed would-be wizard does indeed intend "to call upon the old gods" (*Stone,* 157), reduplicating what is recorded in the traditional "Red Book of Evan Ddhu." According to Turner's legend, Welsh hero Evan Ddhu determines to withstand the English "by Christ and by Mary":

> But the wizard said, "Not so. For this Christ and this Mary are weak. And I called on the old gods of stream and wood, of lake and mountain, you should see other manner of happening." And Evan Ddhu said, "Let it be so." Hugh-ap-Llwyd took the white bird to the defiled grove by the edge of the lake and offered it with the sword of the new faith. (*Stone,* 60)

In reaction against this resurgence of ancient ritual evil, Septimus finds "his deep faith coming to his aid" (*Stone,* 37) as it has not had to do in the two prior books. Great evil evokes great faith, and Septimus' Christian faith, faced with such a potent challenge, responds. In danger of death, he finds himself praying to the "Lord Jesus" (*Stone,* 37); offering up the Lord's Prayer twice to calm himself in a moment of great distress (*Stone*, 134); positing theological questions on the "afterlife" (*Stone*, 38); feeling a divinely sanctioned predestined sense of well-being, as if "he were about to go and do what he had been born to accomplish"; sensing a kinship with St. John the Divine and the words of God's pleasure and reward in Revelation for those who "overcometh" (*Stone*, 132); reading his office faithfully; and finally rendering the funeral service for the fallen when only himself, a bystander, and God can hear (*Stone*, 185–86). The result of this surge of faith is that, with a policeman's instinctive sense of self-sacrifice, he exchanges himself for a child hostage, imaging in his person the Christ-act of agape love, offering his life for another's (*Stone*, 138). Thus one ritual in deadly consequence is offered in place of another, the incantation of magic pitted against the offices of Christianity.

Just as the "Minster Ghost" hoax followed a set pattern in its attempt to redepict an ancient murder pattern, the Welsh religious revival also follows a pattern, but an even deadlier one since it presages a future ritual murder. When the first three components of a Druidic rite are found sacrificed—"a white bird and a silver fish, a black lamb and a white child"—Septimus must rush to find its celebrant before the final human sacrifice of the Red Book is reenacted:

And Hugh-ap-Llwyd took a christen child from among the prisoners and laid him on the very stone of offering in the last citadel and offered him with the stone knife from the Druid grove. And the god of the mountain stream woke and shouted in his waking to the god of the lake. And in joy and in power the god of the lake called to the lord of the storm, and they three turned and rent the invader so that in the morning no place was found for him. (*Stone*, 125)

Philip Turner's writing here, creating for us the old Welsh legend, is indicative of the adroit writing that infuses the series with a sense of excitement, atmosphere, and charm. The writing toward the end of *The Stone of Offering* is intensely poignant as Septimus first calms the five-year-old hostage in one of the tenderest passages in the entire genre and second, with appropriate symbolism, plunges with his crazed captor into the Stygian labyrinths of a deep abandoned mineshaft, now a sacrificial cave, "as the cold gods of the underworld took back their own" (*Stone*, 143). As the horror overwhelms him, he finds the two foundational factors of his nature coming to his aid: "his police training" and "his faith," centering in Psalm 139's praise for the care-taking presence of God even in the bowels of the earth (*Stone*, 144). After the dazed Septimus is knocked unconscious for the third straight book, he begins to duplicate the symptoms of a punch-drunk pugilist, finding himself unable to remember anything but the Old Testament's "eye for an eye." This, we are told, had once been quoted to Septimus by a chief constable "as a philosophical basis for police work. To Septimus it had always seemed inadequate" (*Stone*, 162). Now, however, that the bared skeletons of his and the ancient pre-Christian faith battle in grotesque contest, the stern Judaic justice of the Judeo-Christian tradition momentarily supplants the mercy of Christianity, only to be itself instantly replaced when immediate danger is passed (*Stone*, 159). Whether or not this assignment of primal attributes to the sequence of faith is satisfactory, aptly the justice of the policeman and the mercy of the minister jostle in uneasy alliance within Septimus, each vying for precedence, each momentarily dominating the other. Can justice and mercy truly coexist? Must one finally have precedence over the other? In the confessions we attribute both traits perfectly to God. In our own imperfect lives, as the figure of Septimus so cogently lectures us, such is not the case. What we see when we look in the mirror of Septimus' struggles is humbling indeed.

20

Holy Horror: Barbara Ninde Byfield's Father Bede

In one of her exciting and beautifully illustrated children's horror stories, *The Haunted Church Bell* (1971), Barbara Ninde Byfield constructs a fantasy of haunted horror in the minds of village parishioners that is found eventually by a clever aristocratic outsider to have a normal, human explanation. In her first adult mystery, *Solemn High Murder* (1975), written with Frank L. Tedeschi, Byfield presents another microcosmic horror, an anonymously written novel, *Black Mass*, through the discovery of whose author comes the explanation for the murder of an Episcopalian priest.

The new clever outsider Father Simon Bede may not be knighted like Sir Roger de Rudisill of the children's story, but as a traditional third son whose eldest brother inherits the family fortune and second brother pursues a military career, he has turned to the Church for his bid for success (with appropriate levels of ambition and piety). Although C. A. Alington's archbishops began at the top, they would be but charges of the Reverend Dr. Simon Bede, who begins as no less than aide to the archbishop of Canterbury, working out of Lambeth Palace.

Blue-eyed, square and solid (*Solemn*, 84), Bede is a widower whose rugged looks and hairy chest compensate sufficiently for his thinning hair (*Solemn*, 10) so that he seems to women a "divine Englishman," "deep," "private looking," the "dark, broody type with hidden motives" (*Solemn*, 160). He seems a strange mixture for a priest, and such an influential one at that. Anglo-Catholic, as is St. Jude's, he can respond puerilely to the sight of a vestige of Rome in a New York Episcopal church with a flippant, "'Sucks to you, Noll Cromwell'" (*Solemn*, 27), can call another priest a "fastidious bastard" (*Solemn*, 134), and use the name of his God idly (e.g., *Solemn*, 163). He reads his horoscope and that of others he cares about (*Solemn*, 163) and is "openly fascinated" with sex magazines, though he does not buy them, feeling a need for a "healthier" middle ground between the "Thou Shalt" and "Thou Shalt Not" (*Solemn*, 162). He shivers after a nap (*Solemn*, 110). Though "half American" (*Solemn*, 107), he is himself of the "English clergy," "vowed, as Americans were not, to say their daily offices unfailingly" (*Solemn,* 17). He thinks the sensible thing for people to do after a disaster is to get "quite healthily drunk" (*Solemn,* 115). As far as thinking is concerned, while the archbishop's expressed comments may be succinct, Bede's are amorphous (*Solemn,* 55), more multifarious than one would expect an obviously ambitious and presumably driving man in his position to be. A member of the theological jet set, Bede reads a letter from his son, who is making an independent film in Norway, when "he himself had been swimming this morning in the Caribbean and some of the salt from that clear sea was now floating off his body in a bathtub in New York," while he muses on a "Bastille Day reception, at the French Embassy" (*Solemn,* 8).

But Bede is not just glitter. He's sensitive to the needs of a Caribbean congregation (*Solemn,* 1–2), and can roll up his vestment sleeves and be "damn helpful" to a New York congregation (*Solemn,* 99). Like his rugged namesake Saint Simon Peter and another less pious "Saint" Simon Templar, he is fully masculine, while he retains the aura of genteel scholarliness suggested by the Venerable Bede. With his healthy libido he has certainly teamed with Reverend C. P. Randollph to return the credibility of virility to the clergy. Yet, despite Bede's claims to virility, and Byfield's obviously solid research about the Church, Dr. Simon Bede, right-hand man to the archbishop of Canterbury, ecclesiastical diplomat and Anglican statesman, seems one of the least theologically integrated and realistic of the clerical sleuths. Perhaps the problem is that the author knows an enormous amount of information about the Church but does not know Christianity. Perhaps the fault lies in Bede's background—a Ph.D. in pastoral theology (counseling) with too much emphasis on Carl Rogers—or in the statesmanlike reserve that keeps him from judging anything (except blatant killers and Pentecostals). In any case, Bede seems to be more the stuff of daydreams than real life.

Quietly handsome, strong but diplomatically deft, with nearly faultless tact, Bede plays a kind of ecclesiastical Basil St. John to heroine Helen Bullock's rough-and-ready version of Brenda Starr. Helen Bullock is what every working woman might want to be. Independent and rugged, she is a successful photographer whose forty-odd years have taken her around the world. Brown, clad in T-shirts, at the reading glasses stage (*Solemn,* 171), her house a jumble of suitcases, Helen has a worldwide reputation and a Pulitzer Prize (*Solemn,* 10), reinforced by her classic collections of topical photographs in book form and her relationship with the prestigious *Globe* magazine. A freewheeling sort, she has "cursed audibly" when things have gone wrong while photographing a church service (*Solemn,* 65). But lest we mistake this supercompetent professional for some sort of big-game hunter in a bra with the "extraordinary visual memory" (*Solemn,* 177) of a Picasso and the build of a longshoreman, Helen is "very attractive" (*Solemn,* 8). She has "known since she was fifteen that her face was merely pleasant but her legs were sensational," and she is not above dangling those legs before a man she likes (*Solemn,* 147). Her friends may assure her she is really "a Puritan at heart" (*Solemn,* 160), but she seems to live by no creed any Puritan would recognize, believing, "Whatever happens, it feels good right now, and that's all that matters" (*Solemn,* 147). Therefore, as far as her relationships are concerned, "Houseguests were a bore; anybody she liked well enough to have stay with her should henceforth be her guest at a hotel. Either that, or, if she liked them well enough, share her bed" (*Solemn,* 63).

Bede is attracted to her, feeling, like his contemporary, the dashing, urbane Reverend Dr. Caesare Paul Randollph:

> I've always thought it a pity that the really committed churchwoman the world over, from administration to altar guild, has tended to look like she should really be in a black silk uniform passing cream cheese sandwiches at a tea party. (*Solemn,* 82)

Bede must be ready for what Sister Mary Helen calls "senility sessions" to reach such a conclusion, but at any rate he, like Randollph, has to go outside piety to find someone exciting, and though Helen is a parishioner, she seems at times more jaded than the respectful, lapsed Presbyterian agnostic Samantha Stack. She can give a sort of desperation prayer—"God, if you love me, let me find replacements for those plates before then!" (*Solemn,* 154)—but she only genuflects when she feels like it, and is apt to dismiss others' faith, as in, "Me, I think Jake'll never get over his wife dying, and I'll bet a lot of that praise crap is based on hate" (*Solemn,* 73). What brings these two together is a joint assignment at Manhattan's massive St. Jude's Episcopal Church.

Rector Dunstan Owsley has roped Helen into providing him free of charge a pictorial promotion for the church, while Bede is there to offer him a prominent position in the worldwide Anglican communion. When Owsley is murdered, their growing attraction leads them to a joint search for his killer. The key lies in a sensational pulp novel, *Black Mass,* whose setting and details sound eerily like St. Jude's.

Barbara Byfield is a witty writer (who else, for example, would have her killer wear a hunter green hat?). She can ink in a scene with a few deft strokes, like chronicling the cold flowing off overcoats, or shoes scraping "grittily" on a "bare hall floor" (*Solemn,* 89). Descriptions like this one of St. Jude's abound:

> It sat back from the street a generous thirty or more feet. . . . Bede thought immediately of a handsome dowager, who as a slim young girl many years ago had rather cleverly married wealth but had since rather carelessly put on weight, and in family portraits would now seat herself at the rear center, allowing several dainty grandchildren to attach themselves to her sides and a handsome tea table, or decorative teen-ager sprawling with a dog, to intervene in front. (*Solemn,* 4)

And there is this pungent catalogue of sense perceptions that make Bede as well as many of us who have "never set foot in St. Jude's" feel immediately at home:

> The unmistakable smells of damp stone, votive candles, incense-cured wood, and what he always swore was pure prayer were as comfortable and familiar as the cracked wooden handle of the shaving brush he had used for twenty-five years. (*Solemn*, 17)

Her children's horror tales, like *The Haunted Ghost, The Haunted Spy,* and *The Book of Weird* (originally entitled *The Glass Harmonica*), have given her such practice in the whimsical macabre that she can posit a domineering cleric appropriately reduced to dust and ashes on Ash Wednesday. Or she can draw a poignant, four-page portrait of an upper-class woman driven desperate by an alcoholic, financially-draining husband (*Solemn*, 49–52). With an artist's eye she can draw on the pathetic fallacy to depict the eclipsing of faith at the church of St. Jude's, named, after all, for the saint of lost causes, as even the early morning light is "grudging of hope in its grayness as it entered the clerestory windows far above the sanctuary" (*Solemn*, 37).

That "grudging of hope" is not merely for the murdered rector, but primarily for most of the women Byfield depicts. For the core of this and all Byfield's succeeding mysteries is that, dominated by overbearing man, woman becomes victim and avenger. Thus, Helen serves as a foil to a depressing parade of oppressed and desperate women. Perhaps this very theme is the central factor that slowly drains away Bede's character as the series progresses. Perhaps what progressively robs Bede of much of his humanity and theology is the same impetus that motivates the movement of each of the books: an apparent intense dislike of domineering males. In each of the four books a larger-than-life successful career man becomes the predator and eventual prey of the people who must share his sphere with him.

Father Dunstan Thurgood Owsley of *Solemn High Murder* is a highly successful and officious manipulator of lives who frustrates the happiness of his late relative's oppressed wife one time too many. Chip, the aggressive realtor of *Forever Wilt Thou Die,* quietly eliminates those who would withhold their property from his grandiose developmental schemes. Tricked by vengeance into an accident that leaves him a helpless quadriplegic, he and we are subjected to four appalling sadistic pages of gloating over his final paralysis by the oppressed wife of one of his victims who has turned the tables on him. Channing Adaams of *A Harder Thing than Triumph* is a larger-than-life diplomat whose domineering personality and agonizingly golden good looks order, dominate, and destroy the lives of those around him. Careless of others' well-being, he sees only his own desires and, thus blinded, is slaughtered by his own oppressed wife as payment for a sexual crime against her he committed twenty-five years before. The overbearing Stanley Overton of *A Parcel of Their Fortunes* has gained his fortune by deluding a widow into thinking her only son, who has changed identity to escape a future in the priesthood, has really died in a prison camp. Marrying her niece to ensure he receives the fortune is not enough; he must hunt down the unfortunate incognito years later and kill both him and his crippled son in his mania to protect his security.

Against each of these Bede appears to be more a contrast than another character. He is so eminently capable of great things and yet so thoughtful and empathetic. While solving a crime, he may tend to pout a bit (but never enough to cause prolonged open hostility in Helen) until his good nature soon returns. Further, Bede shares Helen's bed without a qualm—a clear case of "all this and heaven, too." His theological contemplation seems to center mainly on the comparison of simple, ancient examples of church architecture. In fact, a preoccupation with church architecture seems to be the main qualification for the Anglican priesthood in the series. It is certainly not morals or theology. Barbara Byfield uses this characteristic well in her first book, when Owsley's rapaciousness toward others' lives is neatly imaged by his relentless quest to gather up fittings from other churches to enhance his own monolithic stone pile. In the same way he appropriates the lives of those around him as necessary for his own success, and depersonalizes others to the degree that he refers to his petulant organist as "it" (*Solemn*, 26). He appropriates, for example, a lectern from a small church being torn down, while glibly reassuring "the embittered rector" that it will find a "fitting home" at St. Jude's (*Solemn*, 26). So he blocks the advance of one of his "boys," his long suffering assistant rector, since his chosen replacement will not be free for another year.

What is distressing is that Bede does not particularly disapprove. In fact, Bede benignly helps him obtain the lectern. Indeed, Bede appears to understand both the assistant's fury and the rector's rapacity. Bede is generally understanding but, like a typical politician, he seems to have become amoral. His tolerance can be insightful:

> Bede saw the classic therapy of talking about money, of dealing with what could be dealt with, hard and healthily at work. So many times as a young priest he had been appalled at the seeming vulgarity of families, the bitter squabbles over tea services or sugar spoons, the hard and bitter feuds in divorce over a piano, the scrapbooks, the gramophone records, and despaired of his fellow humans. Then, gradually, they had become his fellow humans in actuality as he had begun to see that it was sometimes the human way of coping with death, and that death in one of its aspects was the disappearance of life or of love, and to protest that vacuum and to delay accepting it no object was too trivial as a diversion, and that a tensely labored decision about a box of yellowing old lace could have its place in the scheme of things. (*Solemn*, 103–4)

Yet sometimes his tolerance is foolish, as in his unclerical liaison with Helen Bullock. Perhaps he has continued upon the path of actualizing his solidarity with "his fellow humans" by taking into his own person their relativity, their loose sexual morality, and their shallow acceptance of less than fatal examples of human manipulation, but such a move cannot but be detrimental to his faith and ministry. Thus, after Bede begins his affair with Helen, he finds himself in church "utterly unable to pray," sitting back instead "to relish the few days he had ahead with Helen" (*Solemn*, 181), and can only utter the set liturgical Angelus, "Hail Mary, full of grace." His eclipse has begun. He does not appear as much more than a reference in the second book, and by the time he reappears in the third book, he is being slowly replaced by Helen as sleuth. In the first book he takes the detecting lead; in the second she benefits by being on her own; in the third they work cooperatively and in complementary independence; and by the fourth book Helen is doing the detecting, assisted mainly by Simon's son Fergus, and occasionally by Simon. Therefore, only the first can truly be called a Bede book. The tale is all told in the promotional blurbs. In the first Helen is relegated to an oblique reference in the last paragraph on the end flap while by the fourth she has top billing.

While this overshadowing only affects Simon as a sleuth, far more serious is what affects him as a cleric. Fully active in ministry when he meets Helen in the first book, he has by his reappearance in the third book apparently precipitously effected early retirement from Lambeth and his ministry at just "fifty and a bit" (*Triumph*, 30). Perhaps the explanation for this turnabout is that Barbara Ninde Byfield is more interested in fielding a female heroine than a male hero. But this would only account for the dimming of his perspicacity, not his ministry. Therefore, we need an additional way to read his demise as cleric and as detective. Apparently, rather than mix the Chlorox of his calling with the ammonia of his liaison, he has left the active ministry. His is a bleak church, indeed, for rather than being a caretaker, he is now under the caretaking of a bishop who is "so absorbed" "in his own divorce" he does not have "much interest" in Bede's current "plans" (*Triumph*, 30).

Faith and practice are certainly in the eclipse in the Bede books. Immorality is rampant in the clergy we encounter, affecting not only Bede and his bishop, but also the murdered cleric as well as various candidates Lambeth is considering for top honors. And all this has been presaged for the series in the theological prejudices depicted in the very first book. Back in the St. Jude's saga, the most theological of the series, we had posed for us in microcosm the conflict and plight of faith in contemporary mainline Christianity. The particularly uninviting Christianity of the church of St. Jude's and, really, of the entire series, is captured in the image of a stone Christ: "A clever sculptor had recessed the eyes of the Christ so deeply that one could not be sure, from so great a distance below, whether or not he was being regarded at all by the Crucified" (*Solemn*, 18). Apparently not, since the truly active believers in the church have turned to a particularly loathsome brand of cultic communal "Pentecostalism." The so-called "Jesus people," as described in the book, mainly resemble Jim Jones' People's Temple-ites approaching their final stages of paranoia, or the remnants of the Children of God after David "Moses" Berg's increasingly evident paranoia had alienated the truly pious seekers of the group with their group sex, Transcendental Meditation, vain usage of God's name, slovenly personal habits, and shouting power struggles (*Solemn*, 160, 31, 124, 159).

On the traditional church's side the priests, with their ambitions and their loose morality, view with "wonder" the continual, "genuine," anticipatory piety of the nuns (*Solemn*, 180). The nuns on their side are "clutching" their "beads" (*Solemn*, 22), having their novitiates and would-be enlistees "lighting a candle at a small votive shrine to the Virgin" (*Solemn*, 20). Sweet and pious as they are, the nuns cast suspicious eyes at the Pentecostals with their emotionalism (which means to the traditionalists they do not take piety seriously), explaining, "Well, if they just didn't *smile* all the time. . . . I don't trust it" (*Solemn*, 22).

Barbara Ninde Byfield has certainly fired off a scathing indictment of the worldwide Anglican communion. How theologically bankrupt is the Anglican clergy that Byfield envisions? Among her charismatics there are no Dennis Bennetts of *Nine O'Clock in the Morning: An Episcopal Priest Discovers the Holy Spirit*, and no Vicar Sandfords with wives like Agnes Sandford. There is no Order of St. Luke. Among traditional believers there are no Michael Greens or John Stotts. All the priests presented appear so worldly they are indistinguishable from nonbelievers. True, sacramental theology has always been the key to understanding Anglicanism, and one who searches for a uniform theology or a uniform praxis searches incorrectly, for the sacrament is that which cleanses and restores the faithful. And in this spirit the centrality of confession is marked at Saint Jude's. In one particularly well drawn scene, Byfield recounts the calming of a congregation in turmoil by a curate beginning the "Our Father" while here and there a working police officer pauses covertly to cross himself (*Solemn*, 72). The prayer inserts itself with an extremely effective quiet dignity into the nervous laughter of the chief protagonists gathered together to cope with catastrophe, just as the sacraments enter, order and cleanse the fallen human lives of the faithful. Similarly, Bede before his liaison with Helen is capable of praying a fine liturgical prayer (e.g., *Solemn*, 151). Otherwise, dead or fanatical religiosity has supplanted a true heart-warming, salvific, loving, and appealing Christianity in Byfield's bleakly constructed theological world. In reaction Bede seems to have substituted for faith and ministry a surrogate devotion to church architecture with an avocation in gardening (e.g., *Solemn*, 83). As a result of this draining away of theology, practice, and even of presence in the second book, not until the end of the third and best book *A Harder Thing than Triumph*, when Simon reads a funeral service, is the reader shocked back to the realization that this is indeed a retired Anglican priest.

As the female professional heroine grows in prominence, this series seems to project a prolonged demise of the initial clerical sleuth within an all-encompassing daydream that the strong, domineering, aggressive, oppressive males of the world will eventually get theirs. In the meantime oppressed female readers can imagine they are the rough-and-ready, cute-and-capable Helen, with a dark, handsome, and caring Simon Bede awaiting their call—and he comes complete with the blessings of Heaven.

21

Gothic Heroine with a Collar:
Isabelle Holland's The Reverend Claire Aldington

In *Grenelle* (1976), Isabelle Holland wrote a clerical crime novel with a clerical criminal. "A very Now priest" who, "along with others of the repressed, the sixties had liberated" (*Grenelle,* 3, 5) has become a drug-pushing devil worshipper. But this demonic wolf in priest's clothing, who has designs upon becoming the priest of New York's plush town/gown parish, St. Anselm's, is foiled by heroine Susan Grenelle, "the daughter of an Anglican priest of the Episcopal Church" (*Grenelle,* 205).

In *A Death at St. Anselm's* (1984), the very church that Susan Grenelle stalwartly saved in 1976 becomes the parish of the only ordained female Protestant clerical sleuth in the genre, and the only woman of any persuasion entitled to be called "Reverend." (Soeur Angèle is Reverend Mother.) And what was true of the fallen minister in *Grenelle* becomes the solution for this book as well, when the people of St. Anselm's persist in their attempts to hire a homicidal lunatic with vestigial late 1960s paranoiac social solutions. This new minister will kill the church's business manager. Pitted against the crazed cleric, protagonist and ultimate clerical detective, the Reverend Claire Aldington, is perhaps the most reluctant detective of the entire subgenre, detecting only to escape suspicion herself when the mass of evidence mounts against her.

We have seen clerical sleuths accused of murder on rather a regular basis. But of all their motivations for solving crimes, Claire's is the most clearly to exonerate herself. The Reverend Doctor Claire Aldington of the Episcopal Diocese of New York is a thirty-five-year-old niece of a bishop (*St.,* 7) and five-year widow of the late Reverend Patrick Aldington, an enlightened leftover 1960s civil rights and antiwar activist priest.

Claire herself is a frustrated pastoral counselor whose big plans to expand her pastoral ministry are continually thwarted by the tight conservative money managers of the church. Her "therapy-oriented viewpoint" (*St.,* 12) and profession as a psychologist (*St.,* 12, 13) do little to temper her detestation for the "conservative contingent" of the church (*St.,* 9). In fact, Claire, despite her doctorate earned before seminary and all her professional background in clinical psychology (*St.,* 48), is a rather catty, unpleasant person who has a strong conflict in her perspective. The tension in the novel plays off this tension within her. On one hand, she spouts liberal jargon and abhors the church's conservatives, declaring them the enemy. On the other hand, her husband Patrick was "far more a feminist" (*St.,* 6), far more the rhetorician, even more a "progressive" (*St.,* 10) than she.

Claire is from a middle-class, midwestern background (*St.,* 146). She grew up riding work horses (*St.,* 148), a "practical, pragmatic, and rather down-to-earth" (*St.,* 149) woman who has married wealth and now lives in a fancy Park Avenue apartment, sending her children to private school, able to stay home on a comfortable inheritance from her husband's estate, but working instead in an off-Park-Avenue Sixty-Second Street parish house which runs a soup kitchen twice a week and a temporary shelter for up to twenty transients while catering religious services to the wealthy. Claire and her children are not happy. She and her son Jamie, who is eight, have reddish-brown hair, slightly wavy, heavy and thick, lightly freckled skin, and large hazel green eyes. While the son is plump, the mother is slight and flat-chested with delicate feet, but both share large and "frequently indiscreet" mouths (*St.,* 9). Much of the hostility turned out toward the world is caused by anorectic fifteen-year-old stepdaughter Martha, a child who pays through her illness for a misery of five years past and for its modern reminder. Claire is further "haunted by a strong feeling" that the lay people who attend morning prayers are "a lot nearer to God" than she is (*St.,* 11). As a result she compensates by trying to be superhuman.

In her family Claire does all the work. She does not give her children meaningful tasks. Rather than starting dinner, her eight- and fifteen-year-old are forced to wait for mama to return home and cook from scratch. Her well-equipped kitchen does not appear to contain a crockpot. If there is a microwave, it does not speed the process. All the children apparently do is clean their rooms and sit around watching television (Jamie) or working up a stellar psychosis (Martha). On the job Claire takes a steady stream of clients. She is pragmatic and so is "inclined to help people where they are," rather than to reach for an ideal and be enraged if they fall short (*St.,* 94). She would like to lower drastically or drop her fees altogether, volunteer cleaning out the toilets to assuage her guilt, anything as a penance for—what? her husband's death? her own comfortable lifestyle? the existence of poor in the world? a belief in her own bleeding-heart *mea culpa* rhetoric? general middle-class free-floating anxiety? her stepdaughter's condition? the very existence of evil and her inability to stem it or cure its effects? perhaps all of these? This physician needs to heal herself, but nonetheless she courageously faces the interpersonal conflicts among all the strong authoritarian figures who are her colleagues, refusing to order people around as they do, willing to face her own weaknesses and take into account those of others. She is a truthful person among power-mongering manipulators. Her philosophy is "On the whole, it's better to act your way out, rather than try to think your way out of feeling" (*St.*, 179).

Part of her tension comes from the fact that she is the daughter of a former district attorney and was converted by marriage to "the anti-war, pro-peace, pro-environment, anti-government, anti-business (you can fill out the rest)" movement (*St.*, 23). Despite this pedigree she disagrees with her extremist senior pastor, who does not want punishment exacted if the killer should prove to be poor. Claire retorts:

> I don't think it's giving way to the eye-for-an-eye approach to want the killer picked up, Norbert. And punished. . . . But I do think that to find the murderer and put him behind bars would be an act of signal mercy to the next person he's going to kill. (*St.*, 29)

Amid feelings of "gratitude and guilt" she lives with her family in a "roomy," "well appointed," "two doormen" apartment on East Eighty-Second Street between Fifth and Madison Avenues (*St.*, 36). In fact, to a great degree this is a story about rooms and apartments. Claire's world is bounded by her office and her apartment (especially her own room and the kitchen). It is also bounded by her dead husband's dead first wife's mother's apartment. Between these Claire moves through a dangerous world where anything can and does happen. In other rooms, such as the business office, there is murder. Outside of rooms, on the streets, the reporters swoop down on her. In the lower reaches of the Church, the Stygian depths, the transients like so many lost shades hunger for her comforts, for her affection. The tale reaches true terror when the horrors of these others rooms, these halls, these streets begin to spill out of their confines, piercing the protection of her professional routine and her office and apartment walls, invading her refuges. In her bedroom she receives telephone calls. In her office appears damning evidence. In her home, the illness of Martha's room, symbolized by hoarded spoiling food, threatens to become uncontainable, scurrying out the cracks in the form of roaches. And finally Claire's own living room is nearly transformed into her dying room. In that sense it might be appropriate to give this psychological novel a classically psychological analysis.

Claire's mental instability with its unresolved tensions could be read as being mirrored by the various rooms and passages through which she moves. Her repressed secret is symbolized by Martha, whose emergence into Claire's world of work precipitates Claire by mistaken identity (altered identity) into suspicion and nearly arrest. The secret recesses of her home and office are violated by Martha's illness and the murderer's surreptitiously planted proof. As Claire must come to grips with the implications of husband Patrick's life and death, Martha's disease, her colleague's accusations, and finally and most importantly her own true identity as person and minister, so do the secrets of her private rooms pour into the open, laid bare before herself and others, a cathartic revelation. In that sense, taking our Freudian reading further, the setting would actually be Claire's head, the parish house, her consciousness, the office, and her own private expertise. Her home would be her subconscious. Martha's room would be her id, the grandmother's home her superego, the halls and streets her public interaction with others. On the other hand, reading by characters, Brett Cunningham might be cast as her superego, the conservative reminder of her law-and-order upbringing, linking in with the grandmother's symbolizing of responsibility. Norbert would be her id, the wild abdication to desire, the abandonment, linked in with Martha's physical expression of self destruction.

Like Poe's archetypical Roderick Usher with his headlike house, Claire nearly is destroyed, but on the far side lie self-integration, self-acceptance, and love. The diseases are named. The patient is diagnosed. The physician can begin to be healed. The terror of this process is profound. The truest terror of all is not a terror confined to midnight in some dark and distant haunted house. It is terror that strikes suddenly in the late afternoon, when the streets are filled with commuters, on our very street, in our very home. Horror is sudden isolation, a cry no one hears, a plea no one answers, an assault no one prevents. And it is an honest and frightening look into the monster's den of our own minds.

Claire's insecurity is augmented by the inferiority she feels when comparing her faith with her parishioners'. Groping toward her own devotional life, she prays, having tried and failed in seminary at a Christian adaption of Zen Buddhist meditation:

> For me it didn't work. All I got was a severe case of frustration, a low opinion of my spiritual capacity and, for one hideous fortnight, hives. My more disorganized Christian method of abbreviated prayer, occasional one-way conversations with the Deity, bursts of conviction about the Presence of Reality and a maundering contemplation most successfully practiced when washing the dishes or watering the plants—all these worked better for me. (*St.,* 203)

She does not like blasphemy, has a high view of Jesus, believes in the Ten Commandments (*St.,* 225), has a liberally relaxed view of the confines of sexual activity that does not apply to the question of her own late husband's infidelity. But the center of her insecurity, the focus of the tension in her perspective, lies in the conflict between her liberal social action stance and her conservative upbringing. When the "bleeding heart" idealists with whom she works begin their apportioning guilt between society and the individual depending on whether the culprit is a "street person" or a WASP, Aldington reacts: "Sorry to sound a note of law and order, but even with street people murder is a crime" (*St.,* 61).

A genre as conservative as the mystery must reject the differential applicability of the law to individuals. There has to be agreement about the nature of crime to make the secular mystery work. If one individual commits the ultimate act of violence, we have murder. If several do it, we have conspiracy as well. If, say, a dozen do it, we have a terrorist group. If a group does it, we have mob violence and need martial law. If a good portion of the population does it, we have a revolution. If the entire population does it, we have a war. If that particular population wins, we have a heroic struggle for freedom. Within that system there cannot be as much room for vigilante work—though the Saint and others have made a career out of it—as in a genre where laws are less secure and enforced, such as the western. After all, if the police are corrupt, a detective turned vigilante is actually working for society, for the higher societal laws the police are violating. But the secular mystery is anchored on agreement that societal and divine decrees that murder is wrong will be enforced by the police and ultimately by the courts, though fallible. When whole classes begin to be excused, the genre's presuppositions are thrown into turmoil. The clerical crime novel, which recognizes a higher law that at times conflicts with societal law, leaves a latitude for this possibility. But in the case of murder, except possibly in a tale like Kienzle's *Death Wears a Red Hat,* the clerical crime novel usually draws the line.

So Claire Aldington, despite her newly liberal consciousness, becomes the agent for society's claims. Her colleagues recognize this strain and react either defensively, in the case of her liberal senior minister, or romantically, in the case of her conservative interim business manager. Claire may be confused about many things but about one thing she is clear: "Murder *is* the ultimate crime" (*St.,* 31).

Working within this clash of the newly liberalized but demeaning with the old hide-bound conservative who may yet provide a truer way if sensitive to individual needs, Isabelle Holland makes the case for conservatism. Holland lets Claire's slow cracking of the veneer of her liberal rhetoric meet with her discoveries that there is indeed a spark of human kindness in even the most ferocious banker-cum-church manager and that poor people who rise do so through hard work. The American Dream, if tarnished, is intact in this book. In this framework she explores such issues as who really owns the church. And she has her heroine discover most potently why vengeance has to be the Lord's, because people make too much turmoil out of exacting it and hurt too many other innocent people on the way (*St.,* 216).

A Death at St. Anselm's is a fascinating and powerful study of an ordained working widow torn between the compelling needs to care for her children and to pursue a career, not for monetary need but for her own sake. Isabelle Holland takes the structure of the gothic and crosses it with the psychological novel and the mystery, transforming the tired framework of a struggling heroine and a strong, silent, gruff, eligible but forbidding male with a secret into a powerful tale of psychological disorders and their effect on families, on ministry, on all of life.

Perhaps the most significant aspect of Holland's work for the subgenre is that *A Death at St. Anselm's* provides one of the very few examples of a first-person narrative in the clerical crime novel. Andrew Greeley's *Happy Are the Meek* has a multi-point perspective, with first-person narration for the cleric as well as for other characters, but one is hard-pressed to find other examples. Despite the fact that the subgenre seems to have as one of its general goals a demonstration that clerics are indeed human, the vast majority of entries maintain the distance of third-person narration. But Isabelle Holland's first-person narration eliminates that distance and puts us finally in the cleric's head. And in her style of psychological narrative, that becomes a sort of cerebral Cooke's tour—Through Darkest Clerical Conscious/Subconscious with Pun and Grammar. She achieves what also appears to be a goal of most if not all clerical crime novels, to reveal that things are not what they seem. Perhaps these two goals work together in her writing. Both *Grenelle* and *St. Anselm's* demonstrate that things are not what they appear to be by showing us that the clergy indeed are human, and this in both works by revealing a sinister side to the clergy, thereby completely upsetting previously conceived pietistic notions. This she accomplishes with all the minutiae and infinitesimal attention to psychological details that Leonard (Holton) Wibberley has celebrated in his essay on Father Bredder (Penzler, 27).

Why, an impatient reader might ask, this painstaking if fascinating and poignant attention to interpersonal details? Is it just for verisimilitude, simply to draw a set of characters for us? Or is something more going on here? Many complaints about romance, interpersonal relationships, complex settings or occupations in the mystery suggest that all these exotic and essentially tangential details merely detract from the advancing of the plot. In essence, they argue, the mystery is a puzzle and all material that does not aid in assembling the parts of the puzzle ought to be omitted. For these readers the mystery is merely a sophisticated form of the crossword puzzle. Rather than simply setting out propositions, like an equation, analogically, the mystery is seen as a word problem which the detective must set into the proper equation and solve. Criticism then focuses on the strength of the probability of each factor having an analogical relationship to its counterpart in real life. Of course, this is a proper part of mystery criticism, but it is by no means the whole. Rather, like looking at schoolchild problems of Mr. Green's chickens and the price of eggs, it allows the possibility that any consistent ciphers can be plugged into the radicals to form the problem. The story and its motivations are subservient to the set formula—hence, not a story, not a novel at all, but an extended word problem.

But if the mystery is to be a work of literature, that is, if it *is* to deal analogically with real human concerns, it must move beyond being a verbal form of a mathematic equation. The puzzle itself must flow from the complex "primeval" mass of human character and conflict, what Isabelle Holland aptly calls the "human condition," "mild and less mild depression, fear, anxiety about job, boyfriend, husband, a sense of failure, loneliness, despair; an all-around worry about not being able to cope" (*St.*, 57), growing into something more deadly. Out of this seething critical mass of personal and interpersonal struggle explodes a deadly fall-out of malignant solutions to an oppressive problem. Murder is the great violation of individual sovereignty, the complete rejection of social agreement, the ultimate defiance of the law of God.

What James Johnson does is examine the seething mass in the pressure cooker of human relationship to God. What Isabelle Holland does is examine it in human relationship to the self. The chief focus of this book is each individual's struggle to come to grips with what and who each really is. Is Claire Aldington a radical, middle-class moderate, an ordained minister, or simply a proxy for her dead husband? Out of her struggle she reaches out to the self-inflicted destructive struggle of her anorectic stepdaughter, to the conservative attempt at reclamation by strong, obnoxious, yet beneath-the-surface-something-more, classic, gothic Brett Cunningham.

We have here the classic gothic setting: confused, struggling, middle-class single woman is thrown into high-powered wealthy world. Strong sinister obnoxious male lead repulses yet attracts her. Disaster strikes. What to do? But Isabelle Holland uses this structure to do something more. By filling it with a murder, she throws the plot structure into the hybrid category of mystery/romance, giving it a moral focus. Then she concentrates on the psychological struggles of her characters, letting these struggles both reflect authentic life problems and produce the forward movement of the plot. What James Johnson consistently does more than any other author on a spiritual level Isabelle Holland does on an earthly level. Her characters, ordained though most of them may be, are less concerned with God than with staying out of the mental ward. Unpleasant and obnoxious though she may be, collar notwithstanding, the Reverend Claire Aldington strikes a truer ministerial note than many other more integrated and at times nearly superhuman clerical sleuths. She is in a true sense the image of a suffering servant.

22

Matthew Head's Dr. Mary Finney: Antimissionary?

With an acidity born of years of evaluating modern artwork, John Canaday once tossed off this cavalier dismissal of contemporary detective fiction:

> I stopped wasting money on new mystery novels years ago. Those I tried, stank. Except I do look on the stands for any new Lew Archer paperback. Hence my mystery reading is limited to re-reading; Simenon, who helps keep my French in condition; Rex Stout, since Archie Goodwin is always delightful; Matthew Head, whom I read between the lines as a personal diary. Dashiell Hammett and Raymond Chandler have been re-read so often that I no longer go back to them. (Winn, 454)

His allowance for four survivors pales by one quarter with the discovery that "Not only scholars stoop to protect identity. John Canaday, former art critic for the *New York Times,* poses on crime shelves as Matthew Head" (Winn, 45–46).

Appropriately the same bombast Canaday has used here on others was fired back in return. Jacques Barzun and Wendell Hertig Taylor, for example, dismissed his *Another Man's Life* as "not a success in this difficult and overattempted genre" (Barzun, 230) and critiqued *The Smell of Money:*

> The slow buildup, given by the young painter and curator Bill Echlen, is not much more convincing than the murder and its unreasoned unraveling, while the steady drone of snappy talk about this large complex of neurotics makes it hard to finish the book or care about its outcome. (Barzun, 231)

But for Canaday's equally acid-tongued missionary Dr. Mary Finney there is grudging respect as she bulls her way through Africa and on to Paris in several tales, while badgering her sister missionary Emily Collins and exposing felons.

Miss Finney, as she is usually respectfully called, is unique to clerical sleuths, not simply for her lack of ordination—which is shared by such colleagues as Sister Ursula and Brother Cadfael and may be simply a restriction of her times—but for the question of the authenticity of her calling. She seems unconvinced about not only religion in general but also often missionary work specifically, actively sowing doubt and pushing her long-suffering partner to swear, shoot people, and eventually curb her pietism.

The Mary Finney books are definitely the peak of John Edwin Canaday's output as a mystery writer, and they draw on the techniques developed in the various solo novels he composed before and during the series. Canaday specializes in breezy young male first-person narrators with good educations (Harvard—*The Smell of Money*, Yale—*The Accomplice*) and artistic, if superficial, outlooks on life. Hooper Taliaferro (pronounced Tolliver) evolved as the prime mutation of that movement—sophisticated and not too perceptive: "There was hardly a person at the Congo-Ruzi who wasn't trying to fool me one way or another, and most of them got away with it" (*Devil*, 36). Therefore he is prepared to be bowled over on our behalf by the perceptive Dr. Mary Finney, who is seldom, if ever, deceived for long:

> "I try to be as honest as I can," she told me, "but when it comes to other people out here I always look twice. It seems to me that everybody in this part of the world is two people. . . . Anyhow I always look twice, once on top and a good long time underneath." (*Devil*, 46–47)

Hooper Taliaferro is a university man (naturally), an American botanist who finds himself in the Congo during World War II. In *The Devil in the Bush* he is sent on inspection to the remote Congo-Ruzi station where nothing is as it seems. Among the odd assortment of characters he encounters are Miss Mary Finney, M.D., a medical missionary born in 1892 in Fort Scott, Kansas, and her partner Emily Collins, a "mousey" missionary from Milford, Connecticut (*Devil*, 52). An unlikely minister, Mary swears more than any other clerical sleuth, possibly excepting Septimus, proclaims her loose morality—"I lost my virginity, for whatever that was worth" (*Devil*, 98–99)—and generally lacks interest in religion. Yet, she fills a position for which women are today regularly ordained. Still, her impatience with religious words passes far beyond James Johnson's ideal. Unlike Johnson's protagonists she seems at times uninterested in the content as well. She articulates her relationship with her sister missionary in this way:

> "Emily's the soul-snatcher in this outfit," she said, "and I'm the doctor. We represent the body and the spirit between us. God knows why we haven't killed each other during the last twenty-five years, but we haven't." (*Devil*, 54)

Together they represent Canaday's view of the mind/body issue. Mary is earthy, plump, and ruddy, with a rough and ready demeanor, a rugged impatience with piety, a disrespect for ceremony, and an earthy common sense. Emily is a thin, frail, wispy woman, big on soul and short on about everything else, though she does get up enough gumption to shoot a villain in *The Cabinda Affair,* fainting immediately afterwards, of course.

Mary's view of herself is appropriately jaded: "I feel pretty bad. I'm a woman fifty years old, Hoopie. I'm a little overweight and I've always been homely, and I didn't get to bed last night. That's enough to depress anybody" (*Bush,* 156–57). Yet the saving grace of her own commonsense humility helps her dispense with the narcissism of the ego-centered, allowing her to focus her powers on others. She is an observer of people, but not in the "participant observer" sense. She acts, wasting no time on social amenities, bursting out her words in rough, crude explosions that yet are given with such good humor that they do not usually offend. This self-freed, others-focused orientation lets her peer below the surface, ferret out the truth of the crimes she encounters, and identify the culprits responsible. In that sense she performs her task as a police-woman not a cleric. Yet at the inevitable unveiling she does not deliver the culprits to justice. In *The Devil in the Bush* she writes a letter to the guilty and allows justice to be self-exacted, a technique she will use again in *The Cabinda Affair,* when her timely note kicks out the restraints for a thundering end. In her effective "poison pen" routine she separates herself from the Apostle Paul. Not only are her letters strong and weighty, but she can also follow up with a weighty "one-two" personal appearance as well. A private approach to religion perhaps best articulates her theological outlook. As she writes to Hooper Taliaferro in the letter that closes *The Cabinda Affair:*

> Emily will always be the same and so, I fear, shall I. I keep pumping the natives full of medicine and Emily keeps them up to scratch on their hymns. I have stopped arguing with Emily over the relationship of the body and the soul, because I'm sick of the first, and the second is my business. (*Cabinda,* 184)

Drawing on the tradition of Mycroft Holmes, Mary is a cerebral detective, questioning Hooper at length until his ordering of events falls to pieces and a new sinister depth of order begins to appear. Mary is, of course, none too gentle about her interrogating process, investing Mycroft's superiority with exasperation:

> "Just give me what you *know,* Hoop," she said crossly. "I don't give a damn what you *think,* sometimes I think you've got one of the most confused thinkers I ever saw. Things happen right under your nose and you don't know anything's happened at all." (*Cabinda,* 73)

For such an earthy scientist her method is surprisingly intuitive:

> When you've got a series of circumstances that have several unexplained elements, then you start out just imagining things, and if you can imagine just one thing that would explain all the

things you have a question about, then you've probably imagined something that's really true, and the nearer anything comes to explaining all the questions, the nearer you're getting to what's true. That way it's so simple. (*Cabinda*, 78)

This is the same technique she uses to solve the crime in all four of her books, and the same one Bill Echlen used in *The Smell of Money*. It thus appears to be John Canaday's version of what detection is—imagining a series of events that explains the data.

As supplier of the data and Miss Finney's Watson, Hooper has the indispensable quality of maintaining "a good descriptive memory. And a good auditory one" (*Cabinda*, 139). In fact that skill is his business: "Part of my job was always to go along with Tommy Slattery and remember as exactly as I could exactly what people had said—not just the content, but word for word" (*Cabinda*, 139). Conveniently Hoop is a human tape recorder who practices on people on the street and at parties, writing down what is said afterwards (*Cabinda*, 140) as a sort of nondiscriminatory Vicar Westerham—a perfect Watson. Hooper's other great contribution to Mary Finney is his encouraging admiration, which spurs her incisive induction to new heights. He thinks her invulnerable (*Cabinda*, 140). Thus he provides the perfect foil for her, his young, male, prim and proper, sophisticated dullness setting off her earthy, rugged, mature, womanly scientific perspicacity. He also displays a skeptical agnosticism:

> I looked at Emily Collins sitting there in the Hotel Metropole drinking out of her grandmother's china, with the ratty garden beyond the window, and wondered if she was ever assailed by doubts as to the bargain she had made, giving up the white fireplace and the delphiniums that should have gone with the teacups, in exchange for the immortal souls of a few puzzled native converts. (*Cabinda*, 137)

This agnosticism sets off a sparkle of authentic commitment to faith in Mary, the embers of a smoldering campfire normally buried deep in her own sense of privacy: "Miss Finney snapped, 'I'm a perfectly honest missionary and I'm a damn good tropical doctor'" (*Cabinda*, 124). Yet this same quiescently private approach to religion makes Mary a kind of reactant, people-oriented, counseling antimissionary in Emily's presence:

> "You may not know it, but that was a landmark in Emily's life. She's been working up to it for thirty years." She pulled herself up suddenly and said, "I've got to go to her! Did you hear her? Not a single word about spiritual values! See you at supper, Hoop. I think she needs someone to hold her hand." (*Cabinda*, 152)

Mary Finney is an odd clerical sleuth on two counts. As for the clerical aspect, she downplays religion at almost every opportunity, and as for the sleuth part, in *The Cabinda Affair* she gropes toward a solution but only partially achieves it. She does not appear at the end to have arrived at the full solution and seems as disturbed as anyone at a confession that comes by letter, enough disturbed so that Hooper worries about her.

More than any of the previous books, *The Congo Venus,* a story about a blonde bombshell who has been detonated and Mary's search for whoever lit her fuse, seeks to locate and categorize Mary Finney's unique approach for us. Mary defines herself solely as a doctor, though the best one operating within two hundred miles of the equator (*Venus,* 4):

> Miss Finney often said that in their relationship as missionaries she represented the flesh and the devil while Emily ran the soul and hymn department, and certainly Emily's costume symbolized complete renunciation of the body. (*Venus,* 42)

This is a neat decapitation of the old principle that woman is earthly while man is celestial. Instead, the two complementary halves of this mission team symbolically divide up the normal wholeness of any human, becoming together one fully human expression. As for Mary's sense of calling, however, in her typically jaded earthy manner she observes:

> Look at me. Do you think I'd be an aging female medical missionary sitting here on Hippopotamus Point at the rear end of nowhere if I'd had soft curly hair and no freckles and hadn't outweighed half the boys in town? I'd probably be the leading dowager in Fort Scott, Kansas, right now. Or maybe I'd even have got as far afield as Kansas City. I might have developed a local reputation for my angel food cake. (*Venus,* 17)

Hooper, on his side, assures us:

> My good friend Dr. Mary Finney isn't much given to formal philosophical statement, and she would wither you with one good snort if you intimated to her that she was any kind of philosopher, formal or the kind they call homely. (*Venus,* 4)

Yet in a nicely phrased bit of "homely" philosophy the paradoxically nonphilosophical Mary Finney (who also paradoxically does not approve of swearing while swearing like a longshoreman) observes that death is a kind of frame for life. While we live we are seen at moments with the distortion of a child's photograph—all feet or body or half a head, as whatever action or concern we are engaged in becomes prominent—but death smooths out the distortion and we can see the completed whole in better proportion (*Venus,* 5–6).

If the information coming to us about Mary is conflicting, near the end of *The Congo Venus* Mary and Emily, whose roles have been so meticulously defined, suddenly reverse them inexplicably. Perhaps Mary's inconsistencies can be understood ironically: that she does not fully understand the extent of her philosophical gifts, though she calls herself a vain woman. Her reversal comes in an ethical analysis, which is pure philosophical New Testament theologizing:

> She wanted Liliane dead; she tried to kill Liliane; she thinks at this minute that she succeeded in killing Liliane. If that doesn't make her a murderess I don't know what does. . . . But morally she is and morally is what really counts, the law being only an effort to standardize in applicable form a group moral code. (*Venus*, 136–37)

Emily's reversal, however, is far less probable and satisfying. Emily has been constructed throughout the books to be the worst kind of cultural missionary. In this book she even admits to teaching the natives Western hymns while refusing to allow them even to apply their own rhythms (*Venus*, 107). Are we then to accept her final glib approval of a fallen character's decision to become a pimp, living off the proceeds of prostitution: "Well, why not, if it makes everybody happy?" (*Venus*, 207)? This is not a mere "pragmatism" that is "naughty. The devil's methods in the Lord's work" (*Venus*, 203), as Hooper whimsically calls her other efforts to spread rumors to ferret out the murderer. Nor is it the discovery of hidden depths of character within Emily, as in the case of Mary cited earlier. Rather, this is the revelation of antithetical hypocrisy, which weakens rather than strengthens Emily's character. Perhaps, of course, this is only a ruse on Emily's part to shock Mary and thereby declare her independence from others' expectations. But the result seems to suggest that Emily is a closet hedonist.

Canaday never has come to grips with what accountability in missionary work would mean for Mary or Emily as he has written in no supervisor, no activities for Emily, and plenty of free time to traipse off and solve murders. In the same way Canaday has also not come to grips with the particular character he has created in Emily, though he apparently has with Mary's and Hooper's. Probably he is ineffectual in her case because he has not yet come to grips with what is attractive about Emily's faith. Canaday does not evidence any understanding of Christianity here but merely caricatures it. Therefore he cannot give any true depth of life to the character he has assigned to represent it. Only in the final book does he evidence any genuine affection for Emily, and only then does she begin to come to life.

In the fourth novel, published five years later, the war work is over. Hooper Taliaferro has been in Paris running an art gallery, now defunct, and exchanging the authentic for a civilized watering hole, called the Flea Club. On the opening page we learn that the span of time of his African sojourn of the first three books has been three years. Now he is ready to assume a new life.

Murder at the Flea Club (1955) shows us a new consciousness rising in Canaday's work. Our heroine is no longer Miss Finney but now either Dr. Finney or Mary Finney. No longer a mountain under the sheets, as in *The*

Cabinda Affair, "Dr. Finney is not a fat woman, but without question she is outsize" (*Flea,* 18). Though they are oddly dressed, uncosmeticized, and out of style, Mary and Emily are to Hooper "the two most fascinating women in France" (*Flea,* 19). His values in this case are sound ones.

Mary has been invited to Paris to lecture on her findings about leprosy. When the Sûreté invites Mary to address them on the murders she has solved, Emily jokingly invites her to solve one for them. The jest grows grotesquely serious when the dying body of the Flea Club's manager/singer Nicole turns up in an excavation hole. Using the same techniques of imagining from the data as in the earlier books and the long narrative answer of *The Cabinda Affair* and *The Congo Venus* (though with more interrogative and action interludes), Dr. Finney hears and dissects the data, reaching a solution that agrees with that of the Sûreté. Again, she is one of the most modestly depicted of the clerical sleuths. Through her analysis she reaches agreement with the official verdict rather than an astonishing new solution, though she does astound the professional police with her exhaustive data gathering and her reasoning from that data. She is able to fill in the gaps of the official inquiry and in this manner she nods to the genre by outdoing the police, though not by the conventional means of providing a new solution.

Toward Emily, who has been so consistently caricatured throughout the earlier books as a wispy, otherworldly soul-snatcher, Canaday has obviously warmed. She is still a bit fluttery and, conversely, regimented, yet the promising bud of her courage in *The Cabinda Affair*'s shooting incident has been blossoming. For instance, the effete character Freddy apologizes after describing the vomiting that accompanied his last great binge which ended in his desire to change:

> "I'm sorry if I'm disgusting you, Miss Collins."
> Emmy said bravely, "There are all varieties of spiritual experience and I'm sure some of the saints have had it in even more oblique forms than you did. . . . After all, it's the depth of inner experience that counts, not the associated surface manifestations. So I don't think Mr. Gratzhaufer's story is disgusting at all. That's what I'm trying to say. . . . I'm a missionary, Mr. Gratzhaufer. A good missionary is a much more resilient person than most people suspect. We have to be." (*Flea,* 196–97)

In context Freddy is impressed and so are we.

As for Hooper, his parabolic depiction of the fate of middle-aged women who fall for rakes could be entitled, "Bertie Wooster Does Theology." One thinks of a cross between P. G. Wodehouse and the popular cartoon of the 1950s "(Jimmy) Hatlo's Inferno," that updated comic reduction of Dante:

> You know they have this special section down in hell reserved for women like Audrey. It's lined with special mirrors and everywhere they look they see their faces enlarged so every pore

and wrinkle looks like something on a relief map of the Grand Canyon. Their hair is always falling out and every time they reach for their lipsticks they find they've lost them somewhere. The imps in charge are beautiful young men but they don't use pitchforks or anything, they just stand around talking to other imps disguised as beautiful young girls, and now and then one of them glances over at all the Audreys and says, "Look at that hideous old hag over there." It's one of the worst spots in the whole place. (*Flea*, 122–23)

Granted this is hardly Karl Barth or Carl Henry, but it contains some shrewd insights into the doctrine of humanity. Further, not all of Hooper's observations are comic. His reflections on the fall of the innocent character Tony are really quite moving:

I realized that Tony had carried quite a burden for me, representing, all alone, man's innate capacity for goodness in spite of the general brutalisation, deception, and chicane of the world. Now I thought he had dropped the ball, and whether or not the curious guilt I felt meant that I had failed somewhere, I knew I'd never feel the same about Tony again. I wouldn't have put it all like this at the moment; all I knew was that things changed, and left an uncomfortable empty feeling behind them. (*Flea*, 225–26)

The thing about Tony and The Flea Club is that he wasn't attracted to it by temperament; he was there to make a living, and once there, he was debauched by it. (*Flea*, 231)

The influence of P. G. Wodehouse is evident throughout this book, which is perhaps why it is one of the cleverest and most entertaining of the series. The Flea Club is like a more sinister and more profligate version of the Drones Club. Freddy Fayerweather Gratzhaufer is a heightened and effete version of Freddy Widgeon. The clever verbal sallies, picturesque aphorisms, aptly comic descriptions, and wise disguised observations of Hooper Taliaferro put him increasingly into the Wooster style, with Mary Finney emerging as a less ethereal (she does not shimmer), certainly less reserved Jeeves. Had Canaday continued, he might have achieved Wodehouse's goal from *The Little Nugget* to *The Ice in the Bedroom, The Butler Did It,* and *The Plot That Thickened* to write a comic crime novel. Canaday, however, had that touch of dissolution, that sinister quality that the innocent Wodehouse lacked. Wodehouse's mastery, particularly in the short story, lies in the sheer pellucid effervescence of his prose. Canaday, had he continued to master the fluidly buoyant prose style, might have added that darkening ink that would have polluted Wodehouse's sparkling innocence sufficiently to depict the true mystery's mandatory evil and help produce the comic crime novel. Wodehouse's villains are always grown up bad school children; Canaday's could kill.

As it was, Canaday took his bombast into art criticism, producing such appropriate works as *Embattled Critic* (1962) and *Culture Gulch: Notes on Art and Its Public in the 1960s* (1969), as well as *The Mainstream of Modern Art* (1959), *The Metropolitan Seminars in Art* (1958) and studies of Ben Shahn,

Grandma Moses, and Sienese painting, culminating in 1975 with *The New York Times Guide to Dining Out* and the 1973 book whose title brought all three of his interests (comedy, art, and food) together, *The Art Avocado*. Sadly, he never returned to the mystery or his humanizing of the missionaries, but in effect stayed behind in Paris reviving Hooper's art business, while the magnificent Dr. Finney, sitting on natives to give injections, badgering and loving Emily Collins, and catching culprits through the process of imagination, vanished into the bush.

23

Reverend Randollph
and the Sacred and Sanguinary Satires

Novelist Terence Lore Smith, reflecting in print upon his father the Reverend Dr. Charles Merrill Smith, once mused:

> He has a fine mind and an eloquent command of language combined with the barbed wit and instinct of the satirist. If you want to hold your own with him in dialogue, you must marshal logic and wit. In fact, all the males in our family and most in our circle of friends and acquaintances have and appreciate the gifts of verbal sparring. (*Drums,* 12)

In 1965 Charles Merrill Smith took his gifts of verbal sparring and wrote a best-seller for Doubleday & Company entitled *How to Become a Bishop without Being Religious.* Based loosely on the 1952 secular best-seller *How to Succeed in Business without Really Trying,* it managed to step out of the dismal parade of derivative Christian books which theologize secular successes and carve out a significant place for itself in popular theological literature.

In this first book Smith laid down the basis upon which he built the next twenty years of his writing. In *Bishop* Smith introduced his method of satire by authorial intrusion. A paternalistic, omniscient author, not necessarily equated with Smith, acts as consultant, providing charts, tips, tales, mathematical formulas, and encouragement, with only an occasional elbow shoving through the pasteboard to expose the bitterness of satire. In a "benediction" to this first book Smith himself emerges from behind the scenes to defend his polemic as an attempt to convince the congregational public "to accept the clergy as part of the human race" (*Bishop,* 129–30) and defend his "astringency" as not "excessive" since "I only call it as I see it" (*Bishop,* 130–31). In that sense the book as satire, a strange hybrid of fiction and nonfiction, introduces fictional elements while yet purportedly drawing its subject matter from real life. The locus of suggestions on salary, clothing, housing, and transportation assumes a middle-class readership, a factor eventually to become a major characteristic of Smith's approach. Similarly, the topics satirized—respectability, prejudice, appearance, material items, overconcern for the opinions of others, false pietism, ambition—stake out the ground for Smith's future polemics. *Bishop* in all its aspects, and perhaps as well because of its resounding success, certainly emerged as a seminal book for Charles Merrill Smith. Four years later came his second in what became a series of satires attacking various strongholds of popular North American Christian faith: hagiology in *When the Saints Go Marching Out* (1969); respectability in *Instant Status: Or How to Become a Pillar of the Upper Middle Class* (1972), a secularly oriented book influenced by Lawrence J. Peter and Raymond Hull's *The Peter Principle* (1969); and modern modes of prayer in *How to Talk to God When You Aren't Feeling Religious* (1971). All bear similar titles; all attack similar targets: middle-class hypocrisies.

Obviously, Smith's attack on middle-class Christianity is a love/hate exercise in self-criticism, for by his own admission and the confirmation of his son in their joint effort *Different Drums,* he has solidly located himself within a middle-class definition of Christianity. In *Bishop* he borrows the term "lover's quarrel" to describe his struggle with the Church and suggests this quarrel "is what every Christian—be he minister or layman—ought to do" (*Bishop,* 128). In *Different Drums* he observes, "I structured my life on the framework of the Protestant ethic. Experience has forced me to edit some of its rubrics, but I still live by it insofar as I am able, and have no wish to abandon it" (*Drums,* 70). Smith's personal vision of his involvement in and self-styled representation of the great amorphic American middle class explains why he values what he values and why he satirizes what he satirizes. He seems automatically to set himself against whatever seems out of phase for the proper maintenance and edification of middle-class Christianity.

In *Bishop* he scathingly separates the qualities of the "genuinely religious" from what he calls the "pious," observing that the genuinely religious are inner-directed, deeply convinced of their faith in God and therefore usually "tactless, making enemies unnecessarily and thus becoming an embarrassment to the church" (*Bishop,* 3). His satirical advice is to let such a one rent a hall to make speeches and leave the care of souls to the less zealous, thereby saving the Church from the charge of socialism and the clerical profession from disrepute. He likens the difference to the acquired taste for frozen orange juice that makes the freshly squeezed taste artificial. His disdain for mere apparent pietism is obvious, and yet there is a double barb in his words, for Smith seems also to suggest that excessive piety leads to a life of upheaval that may prove eventually to be shallow and religiously bigoted. Therefore, he rains contempt on "Jesus people," conversion experiences and evangelists. In *Different Drums* he notes his attendance at "countless revival meetings and services" where people claimed to be "saved." He notes they are just the same after conversion as before, merely reoriented so that a drunk becomes a "fanatical temperance worker," a Jesus freak is "still freaked out" (*Drums,* 111).

Smith, as a result, prefers his son's present state of agnosticism/atheism to an "old-fashioned conversion" in which he would have remained "fixed" in his fragmentation" in a countercultural lifestyle *(Drums,* 111–12). For Smith the 1960s counterculture was an odious nightmare of slovenly appearance, fragmented lifestyle, and "execrable" music. As his son has summarized their differences:

> My father's drum had much in common with the similar drums of his generation of the American middle class; he believed that conformity to the basic standards and cultural values of the middle class were necessary to a successful and happy life; he envisioned for his children the life of standard Protestant professional middle Americans. But my drum told me that lifestyle was not for me. *(Drums,* 155–56)

By the 1970s, after more than thirty years of parish ministry, a multiyear struggle with his son over lifestyle, and a near coronary that forced him into reflective and scholarly retirement, Smith altered many of the articles of his North American mainline Christian conventionalism. Yet his concern for pastoring the middle class remained central to his vision and to his writing.

All of his satires are aimed at protecting the middle class from what he sees to be its enemies: hypocritical ambition *(Bishop, Instant Status, Pearly Gates)* and excessive piety *(Saints, Talk).* His nonsatirical nonfiction is aimed at instilling a nonseditious but genuine middle-class morality *(Drums, Middle Class)* with corresponding advice to the shepherds of the middle class concerning how to help inspire it *(Workbook).*

These goals seemed to have shaped the intent of Charles Merrill Smith's nonfictional career up until the early 1970s when he began struggling with a church in Montclair, New Jersey, whose problems, according to son Terence Smith, "were nearly insoluble because the people who control the purse strings did not yet, perhaps still do not, see that their church was dying around them as a pointless and tiresome old ritual" *(Drums,* 151). This battle caused Smith to begin suffering what he called "galloping hypertension" and eventually forced him to retire "at the age of fifty to write" *(Wages:* dust jacket back cover). In 1974 *Reverend Randollph and the Wages of Sin,* his first novel, introduced the clerical sleuth the Reverend Caesare (Che-sah-ray) *(Wages,* 119) Paul Randollph, minister extraordinaire. Smith's sudden shift from nonfiction to mystery fiction, the genre in which he has since that date continued almost exclusively to write, should come as little surprise. Smith's satires, as hybrids of fictionalized nonfiction, offer a precedent for the creation of a character like Randollph. Indeed, Smith created one major fictional character long before he concocted Reverend Randollph. By repeating and interpreting his own biography in such books as *Different Drums, Case of the Middle Class Christian,* and *How to Talk to God When You Aren't Feeling Religious,* he has managed to expand his own life experience to the point of fiction. He has become in his books a symbol, a sort of third-class American Adam.

For example, in 1971 he wrote, "You see, we American Christians, especially of the middle class (to which I belong), like to compartmentalize life" (*Talk,* 1). He thus locates himself as a representative part of the whole and follows with a series of typical (and entertaining) middle-class prayers. By 1973 he is more definitively declaring, "I AM A MIDDLE-CLASS CHRISTIAN. Maybe I am *the* Middle-Class Christian, meaning that I am as typical of the species as anyone can be. Anyway, I am typical enough" (*Middle,* 13). By 1975 the presentation and style of his synechdochal persona has passed into all-American art: "My early memories, framed and hung, would pass for Currier and Ives prints" (*Drums,* 57). As an increasingly archetypal representative of the "typical middle class," Smith has become so archetypal and so extremely typical in his autobiographical descriptions that he now seems larger than life. All of middle-class America empties into his image. Through the medium of autobiographical nonfiction Charles Merrill Smith has created a persona out of himself.

But one wonders, how true is this persona of Smith's? Is it authentic either in fact or even in his own, his family's, and his circle's perceptions of him? Is Smith really so typical, so ordinary and prosaic as to blend into society, becoming by his sheer commonness typically representative? Such seems hardly the case. Actually by all accounts Smith was a flashy and unique human being. He seems anything but typical:

> My father was a good athlete, a superior student, handsome, well groomed and dressed, a successful young minister who, everywhere we lived, strengthened the already potent public image ministers automatically have in small to medium-sized Midwestern towns and cities. He was not afraid to be different, to have his own ideas, to be his own man. People often disagreed with him, but most respected him. (*Drums,* 11)

Similarly, Smith seems hardly typical as a member of the middle-class clergy, for the opinions he holds seem strangely at variance with those typically supposed to be held by a retired parish minister. In addition to accepting his son's atheism/agnosticism, he does not appear to disapprove of premarital sex (*Drums,* 74–75). He thinks of working for the Church as a part of the visible kingdom of God as a "ratiocination" any business executive might use (*Drums,* 80). Not only would he not now use the term kingdom of God to support a sectarian organization or explain his commitment to the Church (*Drums,* 81), but he also sees the entire enterprise of church recruitment as based on a false assumption:

> Any kind of regimented living is based on the assumption that everyone is alike, and that certain experiences and disciplines are bound to be beneficial for everyone. In later years I came to see that the program and emphasis of the church—any church—is founded on this

same conviction. A church attempts to process its people so that they will choose a set of values that the church believes to be good for them, and adopt a lifestyle the church considers normative for adherents of its particular sect.

At the time, though, I was hard at it trying to persuade people to accept a Methodist Christian world view and lifestyle. I was engaged in processing people, trying to turn out a standard personality. I was certain that my prescription would be good for them.

I can now see that this is the closed-end approach to dealing with people. It seeks to set boundaries and impose values. If people were all alike it might be justifiable. But people are not all alike, and what is good for one person may be bad for another. I now believe that religion and education should encourage an open-ended approach to life, that they should be liberating rather than restricting. (*Drums,* 85–86)

He has come to believe the behavior adults impose on children is best for adults not children. Similarly, the well-groomed, conventional youth, while still pleasing to Smith's eye, is simply less troublesome for adults than one "doing his own thing." Conforming behavior does not necessarily benefit such a youth. Smith came to feel his son's rebellion was right for his son (*Drums,* 71).

As a result, in *Different Drums* he no longer believes ministers' children should be in church (*Drums,* 90), but does believe parents should relate to children as to equal adults (*Drums,* 103), and strongly disagrees with the need for a "generation gap," arguing, "Parents, I do not believe it is possible, today, to relate to your children in the patriarchal style" (*Drums,* 106). Instead he laments the male-dominated culture and his past participation in it—"I know I found it distasteful. I also know I did it, too" (*Drums,* 109). He cites Margaret Mead as support for equalizing communication between parents and children, adding, "I wouldn't for a minute give aid and comfort to the anti-women's liberation people who cherish the myth that mothers are better fitted by nature than men for wise and beneficial parenthood" (*Drums,* 109). Thus, for him, childrearing is a team enterprise (*Drums,* 110).

He seems rather than a fixed pillar of the middle class to be a shooting star, swiftly falling from the middle-class firmament to the dark marginalism below. As for his typical middle-class faith, he attributes his calling to the Methodist ministry not to God but to subtle manipulation by his parents (*Drums,* 64). He recalls early antagonism against the Lord's Day Alliance and its Sunday blue laws, remembering, "So I refrained. But I smoldered" (*Drums,* 61). He believes he ought to have drawn more on his faith in childrearing than on the pattern cut out by culture (*Drums,* 110), and he recalls arguing with his son for the right of high schools and their experienced administrators to enforce discipline and dress codes as "about as dubious a pair of propositions as I have ever been guilty of advancing" (*Drums,* 71). He maintains the middle class has confused faith with culture, thereby enervating both:

> Here, it seems to me, is our insight into why religious faith in this country is so superficial. Most people, like me, allow our culture to shape our faith rather than the other way around. We often call the result religion, but it isn't, really. (*Drums*, 110)

As a result, Smith rejects most culturally accepted forms of religion like the conversion experience. He believes no minister can entrust his true feelings or personal problems to his bishop or the Church and advance (*Drums*, 82), and he has adopted an unclerical self-image. He fills his speech with sports images, calling his advance to a prestigious pulpit "getting into the pastoral major leagues" (*Drums*, 87), and terming the future "a new ball game" (*Drums*, 117). He sports flashy clothes and has driven a flashy car for years, beginning with "a bright red Dodge convertible with a white top and black and gold interior" (*Drums*, 25). In short, he consciously violates all the mock but actual rules for success he exposes in his satires, commenting upon himself wryly in the third person, "No doubt he would have been a bishop by now had he not chosen to write a book on *How to Become a Bishop without Being Religious*" (*Instant Status*, 6).

No, the typical middle-class Christian of the nonfiction books is hardly the Reverend Doctor Charles Merrill Smith of self-revelation and of eyewitness accounts. He is obviously a fiction, but a very useful one in attracting, engaging, and edifying readers, and, it would seem by the proliferation of these books, a profitable one. As Smith's first fictional character, his autobiographical self is thus successful. Bland, typical, revoltingly middle-class, his persona is the exact opposite of Smith and the exact opposite of the Reverend Doctor Caesare Paul ("C. P.") Randollph, a flashy athlete, scholar, clotheshorse, gourmet, litterateur, and fictional child spawned by a lifetime of Smith's difficult parishes and responding therapeutic and diagnostic satires. Randollph, as we have noted, was born during the collapse of Smith's parish ministry career from hypertension, the collapse of his lifelong quarrel with his son over lifestyle, and the subsequent lessening of his nonfiction satirical writing in favor of fiction. Heeding his son's* and wife's importunities, Smith retired to write.

Out of Smith's response to retirement came *Reverend Randollph and the Wages of Sin,* a 1974 offering by G. P. Putnam's Sons. The novel is blatantly about money. Randollph, a published California church historian, is brought to Chicago by his former colleague, the bishop, not as a cure of souls but as a sort of clerical auditor, to ascertain where the funds of the richest church in the diocese are disappearing. The Church of the Good Shepherd in Chicago's loop certainly compounds the raw material of Smith's own "ten most trying and difficult years of my life" (*Drums*, 88) in prestigious Wesley United Methodist

---

*Terence Lore Smith had just authored his mystery *The Thief Who Came to Dinner*, which was made into a movie starring Ryan O'Neal.

Church of Bloomington, Illinois, into something rather stellar. A forty-story, vaguely gothic structure, it combines a church with a luxury hotel and commercial office space. The church has grown fat off rentals while still retaining its basic so-called Puritan tendencies to starve its personnel and horde its revenues.

The tale begins in the impersonal transience of O'Hare Airport where the bishop and a future assistant await Randollph. Focusing on externals, the narrative introduces Randollph simply: "A nifty blue houndstooth Norfolk jacket over a navy turtleneck was too casual and too young-looking, even though there were specks of gray in the dark hair that came well over the collar of his jacket" (*Wages*, 11–12). For several paragraphs Randollph is perceived as no more than an impersonal set of natty clothes, only slowly emerging into personality. If the bishop has sought a materialistic counterpart for slick impersonal Good Shepherd, Randollph is certainly fighting fire with fire. Sharing Smith's "pleasure in being neat and stylishly turned out"—"Indeed I was probably a bit too well dressed and affected a wardrobe more flamboyant than was compatible with the image of a Methodist pastor" (*Drums*, 91)—Randollph is mistaken for an amorphous Madison Avenue or Hollywood product, a TV actor or director, for as his clothes indicate, his taste is exclusive in all material realms. He travels first class, especially when someone else is paying, orders his martinis with Bombay gin, and adopts a pretension of language. Though he claims a distaste for pretentious titles like "Doctor" or "Reverend," he affects an extra "l" in his name, identifying himself continentally under his initials C. P., and adopting an artificial continental style of language—e.g., "this Smelser chap" (*Wages*, 19) or "He must be a grim sort of chap" (*Wages*, 94). As Randollph reflects on the crass, gaudy elegance of the interior of the Church of the Good Shepherd: "The whole effect was of spirituality gone to seed, an ecclesiasticism in which money was an acceptable substitute for prayer. Randollph liked it. He supposed that this was because he liked color and didn't mind vulgarity" (*Wages*, 132). Randollph is more than a materialistic match for Good Shepherd. He is a problem solver by nature (*Wages*, 16). Bigger than average, he is a former professional football star, and his approach to solving Good Shepherd's problems is an athletically sound one. He immediately affects a good offensive.

Once Randollph begins to act, he slowly gains definition. If he has begun as merely a set of clothes to his colleagues, or a vague pastoral presence to the transient parishioners or the entrenched white collar criminals on the board, his assumption of power begins to announce him. Soon we are seeing Randollph through a number of eyes, ranging from his own to the bishop's to those of Liz Casey, the police lieutenant's wife. In the same way, the other faceless characters in collision with him begin to emerge from the financial wasteland of life on the loop and become humans. Most dramatic of these, perhaps, is the murdered woman, Marianne Reedman. Most of the book, in point of fact, is a quest after the true identity of Marianne Reedman. Misunderstood by her parents, unappreciated by her husband, unknown by her peers, she begins as simply an annoyance to Randollph, a murdered woman who has not had the grace to die off church property. As Randollph pursues her memory in an effort to solve both her murder and his problems in one swoop, she begins to emerge. The financial wasteland has obscured Marianne her whole life long. The church of her upbringing is banked in the same vault as Good Shepherd. As Randollph speculates, membership in that church and in the Yale Club were about the same thing (*Wages,* 153). Her funeral oration at her home church is a dismal dust storm of William Cullen Bryant, Khalil Gibran, and a mere sprinkling of Scripture (*Wages,* 154). Marianne, like Randollph (and oddly like author Smith), is a victim of the past, particularly the parental past. Like Randollph and Smith, whose calls were the result of carefully directed youthful guidance, Marianne has been victimized by the good intentions of her parents and imprisoned in a loveless "respectable" marriage. Cut off from love, she maintains a life of appearances until her death exposes all.

In strange parallel, the past has also determined the life of her murderer. The Puritan past, coupled with personal adulterous tragedy, has set Clarabelle Creedy, the church's housekeeper, on a collision course with Marianne Reedman. In adultery one has found life, the other death. (Clarabelle's husband was slaughtered for philandering by the natives). When their trajectories collide, the death found by Clarabelle engulfs Marianne. Only through discovering who Marianne really was can Randollph solve her death and find its author. And the process of distinguishing truth from appearances exposes a number of other characters as well: Arnie Uhlinger, Professor Don Miller, Ward Reedman. In that sense this book might be considered an exercise in humanization—the recovery of authentic selves from the synthetic gold-plating of materialism. And yet the materialism is never ultimately rejected. In the end, Good Shepherd is merely restored to its former condition, and the charade of living is carried on. Why is there not a breaking off of the hypocrisy once it is exposed?

To understand this failure is to understand Smith's pastoral purpose in his writing. To end the materialistic hybridizing of Christianity that passes for religion at Good Shepherd would be to upset radically the way of life of both the church and the many it serves. This would be an act of radical religion, an act more suitable to one who should rent a hall, as *Bishop* has told us, than to one who should run a church (*Bishop,* 3). It would ultimately change the middle class (in this case the upper middle class) rather than merely improve it. The difference is fundamental to Smith's vision. Why, one might ask, has he even chosen to write in such a genre as the murder mystery? Because, I believe, the murder mystery more than any other genre of popular literature maintains middle-class mores. The assumption of the mystery is that the disruption of society by the crime of murder must be redressed. Guilt must be assigned, order must be restored, restitution must be made, society must be returned to its former state. The mystery is a literature of maintenance.

Smith focuses, then, more upon the maintenance and undergirding of conventional mores than on religion. When those mores alter in society, as the freer acceptance of sexuality outside the boundaries of heterosexual marriage has altered, then his religious attitudes alter with it. Philosopher William K. Frankena in his *Ethics* has noted, "As a social system of regulation, morality is like law on the one hand and convention or etiquette on the other" (Frankena, *Ethics*, 6). Having drawn this similarity, Frankena proceeds to distinguish morality from convention or etiquette, since it deals with matters of crucial importance while etiquette concerns itself with "considerations of appearance, taste, and convenience" (Frankena, *Ethics*, 6). Morality is similar to law since it shares law's concern for "crucial" matters. Yet it does not share law's dependence for creation and enforcement on acts of judicatories.

In Smith's and Randollph's vision, on the other hand, there seems to be a conjunction of morality with etiquette or convention. Both Smith and his creation put a high premium on appearance, on clothes, on "culture" and social grace. At the same time, in regard to religion, Randollph, like Smith, seems to prefer a refined, well-cultured atheist/agnostic like Terence Smith or Samantha Stack to a graceless, though fervent, believer like the little brown man who wants to convert Moslems (*Wages*, 182). Similarly, in practice, Randollph prefers an extramarital, though discreet, athletic tussle in the hay on the eve of entering seminary to a public campaign against pornography. The line, of course, is drawn at murder, but the rule seems to be consistent. What does not seriously undermine a comfortable middle-class existence and does not physically damage other people is an acceptable mode of Christian behavior. Thus, the atheist Samantha resembles the early Christians in Randollph's eyes (*Wages*, 30).

The result of this view is the truncating of serious religious values in favor of the maintenance of the status quo. For one salient illustration one can ask, how feminist is this book, despite its lip service to feminist lingo? Randollph sees no level of exploitation or dehumanization in pornography. Indeed, the book presents none. The only serious issue cited is censorship. Randollph champions the right of any "man" to read what he wants (*Wages*, 101). And only exploitative, graceless buffoons champion the opposing view. In regard to the women depicted, Marianne, a thirty-eight-year-old woman, is ceaselessly referred to as a "girl." Samantha Stack is a melange of conflicts. Her lip service to feminist rhetoric clashes discordantly with her continual references to herself as a sexual object. She calls other women "broads" or "girls" and maintains no self-respect or dignity in her personal references. She seems gauche and bold yet easily unnerved by the masterful Randollph, though her sheer forwardness in speculating upon seducing him can unnerve him as well. To Dan Gantry women are "skirt" or "a dish" (e.g., *Wages*, 71). He presupposes "hysterical females" will interrupt the police interrogation (*Wages*, 78). And these characters cited are all the heroes and heroines! When the female protagonist, Samantha, can dismiss a blatant sexual advance as "He always pats my fanny" (*Wages*, 94), call her thirty-year-old self a "girl," and be assisted by a pretty little chirpy "girl" on the job, we know we are not dealing with a feminist novel. We are dealing with the middle-class pasteurization of feminism into the cute rhetoric and sprightly conventionality of teenagers.

Similarly, the presence of the living God is more an appearance, a cameo shot, than a radical disturbing reality in the novel. For Samantha Stack God is a question mark (*Wages*, 30). For Dan Gantry God exists as a swear word: "Good Lord" (*Wages*, 12); "God, she's heavy" (*Wages*, 66); "Oh, jumping Jesus" (*Wages*, 68). For Randollph God is continually defined more by what Randollph rejects about God than by what he affirms. He separates himself from the "hard-nosed deity," the "God of wrath" of midwestern Christians, a God he supposes is credited to the climate (*Wages*, 92). He separates himself from the Bruce Barton-like God of Good Shepherd board member Bobbie Torgeson (*Wages*, 136), and from the God of his own conservative past, the "religion of the unexamined premise" (*Wages*, 182), which he preached as a conservative Christian athlete. Now he sees that kind of religion as an inaccurate view of reality (*Wages*, 98).

Instead, Randollph has traded a conservative religion for a malaise of the spirit (*Wages*, 171). He no longer spends long hours in prayer and devotion, and he does not hold "conventional pious attitudes" (*Wages*, 97). Among his rejected views are belief in "Satan's presence." He calls this "purple theological prose" (*Wages*, 123). He dismisses the Bible as outmoded (*Wages*, 249). He does not believe in converting members of other faiths to Christianity (*Wages*, 182). He considers the question of the trinity "so trivial an issue" (*Wages*, 127); he misinterprets Paul's powerful resurrection passage in 1 Corinthians 15 to suggest procreation rather than burial, thus dismissing it as "glorious sounding, sublimely phrased nonsense" (*Wages*, 136) and "lilting dualistic goop" (*Wages*, 137). In its place he offers no "cheap assurance of a better beyond where Marianne was now dwelling in a happiness unknowable to mortals" (*Wages*, 138). Instead, the stuff of his sermons resembles a mild sort of antinomianistic positive thinking. It contains no cross, no repentance, simply new attitudes to leave "repressive rules" behind. Jesus' role was to get people "to think in new ways, to open up to the possibilities in life" (*Wages*, 48).

This does not mean that Randollph has no faith remaining. He does believe in God (*Wages*, 138), and, of all things, in original sin (*Wages*, 139). And, echoing a bit of Clarabelle Creedy, he half seriously considers doing penance for his indulgences (*Wages*, 140). In that sense Randollph has mild overtones of a pre-Reformation Roman Catholic, without the benefit of confession and absolution. Certainly, the criminals and conventioneers he serves have no apparent sense of the presence of the living God. Only in the bishop do we see more than a glimmer of the memory of faith, though the bishop does label the resurrection pejoratively "a dubious piece of history" (*Wages*, 209), and he buries the radical demands of his faith in the day-by-day rubble of utilitarian compromise. In opposition to Randollph's relativized view that crime requires not punishment but merely apprehension to prevent further crimes (*Wages*, 137), however, the bishop does believe in both justice and mercy (*Wages*, 254), subject, of course, to the exigencies of administration. This relativized quasi-Christianity leaves the assurance of God's presence to fanatics like Clarabelle Creedy and charlatans like evangelist Jeff Davis Troutman, who himself is riddled with Good Shepherd's deadening materialistic outlook—"That's money in the bank for the Lord" (*Wages*, 101)—and who steps forth as the first of a parade of execrable fundamentalists throughout the series. As a result, for the heroes and heroines of the novel, God never seems to emerge as more than a bit of rhetoric.

The drama of faith, then, is played out by doubters who see their meaning in the nostalgic rituals of the church. Good Shepherd before and under Randollph serves

> the middle class, which owned every socially respectable American denomination, lock, font, and pulpit. . . . They were here to worship the God of Abraham, Isaac, and the American way of life. They were here to squeeze the last drop of experience from a festive venture, fully deductible, to the big city. They were here, some of them, shaky with hangovers and guilty thoughts of indulgences unthinkable in Grand Forks or Ottumwa, for some supposed process of atonement (which accounted for the astounding number of twenty-dollar bills in the offering plate). They were here because it was Sunday morning, and going to church was what they customarily did on Sunday morning. (*Wages*, 47)

Randollph does not find this lukewarm behavior "spewable" but instead "commendable" and not "entirely disreputable" (*Wages*, 47). Instead, like the acceptable atheist Samantha Stack, these worshippers are good status quo people, solid middle-class pillars who do not maintain a moral chip on their shoulders like the Calvinists (*Wages*, 169) and therefore do not upset the middle-class grace of living. In this point the work of the satires and that of this fictional piece come together. The novel is not simply an Arminian diatribe against Calvin and Calvinism, though it is that (*Wages*, 110), but like the satires, it is a polemic against the disruption of middle-class Christendom, a sort of comic answer, if you will, to the attack on Christendom by the disturbed and disturbing marginalized satirist Søren Kierkegaard.

Indeed, the book itself is certainly a good part satire, as mere examination of the names of the characters reveals. In its choice of names the book engages in a sort of comic allegory with serious overtones. Though Randollph emerges from being a mere set of clothes, the bishop never fully emerges from being the bishop. To the end of the book, indeed, to the end of the series we never know him by his full name. He is either Freddy informally or the bishop formally, a man either removed from or engulfed by his role. If anything, he seems the whimsical embodiment of all the Machiavellian advice in *How to Become a Bishop without Being Religious,* though his winsome personality prevents him from becoming vicious. The "smarmy O. B. Smelser" is obviously a play on smelling body odor, (B.O.), as Samantha Stack is colloquially and literally "stacked," and Mrs. Creedy is the embodiment of creeping creedaliam. Dan Gantry is the nemesis of Elmer Gantry (*Wages,* 71), though Randollph once really ran off the playing field, escaping to a new life. As a satire the book takes broad and exaggerated hyperbolic strokes at its targets. The real Athletes in Action, for example, is not merely a group of men playing a boy's game and preaching a simplistic religion. Since 1974, when it "began a ministry in five cities to meet the spiritual needs of professional athletes," it has focused on treating Christian athletes as "ordinary people" in "a society that makes sports heroes into demigods." It concentrates on "the drug problem" among athletes, helping "society see that superstars are people, vulnerable to sin, hardship, pain, and failure." It deals with the loneliness, "divorce and separation" and the familial fragmentation that has produced a higher divorce rate among male athletes than the national average since "with everyone enthralled with her husband, a wife feels like a nonperson, an accessory." It deals with the pressure to perform, the constant pressure of maintaining an image, the discordance of being labeled "hypocrites" if a television camera catches them swearing, throwing a clipboard or starting a fight. Finally, "A major part of the sports minister's role is preparing athletes, spiritually and practically, for life after football." And all those facets described are functions of the most conservative of the athletic Christian ministries, the one run by Campus Crusade, normally the model target for caricature by more liberal Christians (Frame, "Christianity," 37). Thus, like the satires, *Reverend Randollph and the Wages of Sin* slashes out with a meat cleaver at evangelists, Calvinists and Christian athletes.

Happily, the series did not end with this first novel. Instead *Wages* merely served as a springboard to the second book of the series, *Reverend Randollph and the Avenging Angel.* Henry Fielding reportedly began his tale *Joseph Andrews* as a scathing satire on Samuel Richardson's *Pamela* and came to feel an affection for his protagonist on the way, eventually shifting gears and making it a fine novel in its own right. In a similar way in *Reverend Randollph and the Avenging Angel,* Charles Merrill Smith leaves some of his preoccupation with satire behind and launches out into a fine, meaningful and eventually edifying novel. Coming three years after *Wages, Avenging Angel* found Smith back at active pastoring of the United Methodist Church of Troy, Kansas, teaching creative writing part-time at Highland College and spending "about half [his] time writing" (*Avenging Angel*, end flap, dust jacket). *Avenging Angel* is a stylistic *tour de force*, a witty delight brimming with dexterous writing.

Perhaps the power of the book originates in its source in the biblical account of Tamar, Amnon, and Absalom. In his opening encapsulation of the tale, Smith neatly foreshadows both the theme of the novel and the solution of the puzzle embedded in Randollph's antagonistic catalogue against a fundamentalist defender of the literature of the book of books: "History, short stories, love poetry, letters, murder, sex, incest, almost anything you can think of" (*Angel*, 14). Smith's technique is brilliantly subtle. He gives us the solution of the oncoming murder on page 14 (as he will do again on page 12 of *Reverend Randollph and the Holy Terror*), but the way he palms the ace misleads us. He has dazzled us with the old verbal shell game. It is a masterful stroke.

Equally masterful is the way he employs again the technique of anonymity with which he began *Wages,* yet here the style of its usage and the force of its effect are entirely different. In *Wages,* the anonymity of Randollph's introduction detached us from his character and made us judge him by the same external and superficial standards as his peers do, only eventually allowing us to peer below the surface and reconcile the person within with the image without. *Avenging Angel,* by contrast, immediately drowns us in the anonymous yet intensely intimate consciousness of a would-be murderer. From word one we are plunged into the whirlpool of the logic of evil. Dragged below the surface into the mind of the prospective killer, we think his thoughts and are inundated with foreboding. Thus, in startling contrast we are not drawn into the tale as we were in *Wages* by the use of anonymity. Rather, we are immediately engulfed by it. By the time we are dumped on Randollph's doorstep a page later, like a sacked corpse by Al Capone, our attention has been so commandeered by the anonymous evil that we see it lurking everywhere and so fail to catch its solution in Smith's brash sleight-of-hand juggling in Randollph's speech. Thus the felicity of style serves to mask truth in the tale as much as it serves to reveal it.

In one sense, *Avenging Angel* is a book about false appearances—from the surface cordiality that disguises an innocent competition between Sam and Lisa over Randollph's past attention to the deadly charades of Valorous Julian, whether respectable doctor, loving half-brother or avenging destroyer. While these deceptions are occurring among the characters, the style of the book reflects the theme of illusion, particularly in its use of the pathetic fallacy:

> Outside, a thin warm rain was lightly washing the city's streets and sidewalks, reflecting in the lights of passing traffic the illusion of cleanliness. (*Angel,* 42)

Ultimately the book develops its theme of illusion versus reality into a theological reflection about the puzzling nature of God. Put another way, the book poses a reflected puzzle about God in its speculation on the nature of God's agent, the avenging angel, for the concept of the avenging angel appears to include both murderer and retributor: "Avenging angels aren't too particular about who they punish. . . . If one of you is innocent, so what? If you're both innocent, well, that's tough" (*Angel,* 129). When a frightened character responds that that is "cold-blooded," the reply is, "Avenging angels usually are" (*Angel,* 129). The God reflected in this reading of the character and role of the angel of death is a monstrous God, one who inflicts punishment, then exacts revenge. This deity resembles the God of the so-called "hyper-Calvinism" who assigns guilt to people, does not choose to elect them, then punishes them eternally for the imputed sin. Against such an image of God Smith has Randollph react, as he did in *Wages,* where hyper-Calvinism was apparently lumped together with all Calvinism.

Against this divine sadism expressed in *Avenging Angel,* Randollph's theological hesitancy to ascribe any power or legislation to God is perhaps understandable. We have seen how hesitant both Smith and subsequently Randollph are to express God's disapproval of such standard Protestant peccadillos as profanity, premarital sex, heresy, atheism. Randollph's studied hesitancy even prompts him at times to hold conflicting opinions in his theology. His habitual reluctance to prefer conversion to Christianity to continuance in Islam, for example, flies in the face of his parallel assertion that he is a Christian. In this hesitancy he is not simply a Jeremiah Pembroke, who, innocent of theology, thinks all faiths are the same because he cares for none. Randollph has instead become a theological agnostic who seriously and consciously works on the presupposition that he cannot determine what is a preferable faith for the varied human race. Just as he did not consider the exploitation and oppression of women by pornography in *Wages,* similarly he takes no note that officially, at least for Moslems, women are considered chattel. A classic warrior heaven in Moslem thought is totally male oriented. Women serve tables and sexual requests. Jesus is a prophet who was saved from the cross by God's sleight of hand and thus provides no salvation from sin. Salvation, therefore, can only be assured by dying in battle for the faith—hence the jihad, the holy war, and the pugnacity of the Moslem faithful. Christianity, at least, pays lip service to love, and faithful sincere Christians can occasionally be badgered into exercising it. Moslems cannot in the same way. Are the faiths, then, really the same? Would a true feminist, or a Christian pacifist (though we cannot call Randollph the latter) affirm both? Randollph's hesitancy thus engenders internal conflicts in his theology, but they are inevitable since his overriding concern, his theological hermeneutic is to avoid the conclusion about God that the avenging angel holds. Thus Randollph at least half holds the conviction, or perhaps it is the desire, that God does not intervene in the affairs of mere mortals (*Angel,* 53). His concern dictates conclusions that at times drop him in a camp with the openly agnostic Samantha Stack—thus perhaps their affinity.

One pertinent place we see this tension of avoidance and conclusion is in Randollph's treatment of evil, what we might call his theodicy. Randollph's concern again is a good one. He does not want to agree that all the evil we experience can be reduced to punishment for our temporal sins, or a sort of heavenly tit for tat that makes our lives a controlled series of negative reinforcements, until we are either terminated by one shock too many or we end a quivering neurotic mass of inhibitions compelled into goodness. The point is well taken, but to do so, Randollph feels constrained to jettison the Christian understanding of a caring deity. Randollph's mistake leads ultimately not merely to flushing the proverbial baby with the bath, but to doubting whether there was ever a baby in the water in the first place, while affirming the efficacy and, indeed, the necessity of the ritual of the empty tub, i.e., the Church of the Good Shepherd in its solemn worship. Hence, his bizarre defense of the value of missions not to enlighten people about Christ but to keep the Church from going dead (*Angel,* 135). To some degree, good concerns lead to unsatisfactory conclusions.

This is not to imply, however, that Randollph's theology has not changed, grown, or deepened since *Wages.* Certainly in the realm of money and materialism Smith deepens Randollph's character. Money is raised as a motivation for the murder on page 138, making the book appear for a time a true sequel to *Wages,* but ultimately money is not what this book is about. Randollph also does a fine job counseling a parishioner against the excessive opulence of his "expensive living and consumer debt" (*Angel,* 97). Randollph's admonishment to live at a more modest level is a relief to the parishioner, for his tendency to live at such a high standard has obviously burdened him. Randollph's counseling is excellent and it has helped the troubled, yet when the cleansed parishioner leaves, Randollph berates himself inexplicably for relying on "fallacious theology" (*Angel,* 98). Fortunately, he followed his instincts, rather than his shaky sense of reason.

These clashes of Randollph's reason with pastoral experiences provide some of the finest moments in Smith's portrayal of the teacher becoming pastor. True, some of the tension can be traced to Smith's own views, for example that people's values, not their natures, change, a view expressed both in *Different Drums* and, by Randollph, in *Avenging Angel* (*Angel,* 62). Yet other views of Randollph's are altered as the bishop, again in his role as ironic giver of sage if satirical advice (e.g., *Angel,* 199), takes the fledgling pastor Randollph in tow. One such incident speaks in depth to the function of the mystery as the maintainer of social order as it articulates Smith's own pastoral conviction that the role of the clergy is to help maintain the equilibrium of the middle class.

The message of the restoration of order peaks in the bishop's and Randollph's counseling visit to the Julians. The bishop's strength in silence and his apt quiet prayer that encourages a return to normalcy are the strong medicine disruption needs. The scene works in itself and in its expression of the Christian faith. On his own Randollph continues his learning process, taking over the role of the elusive Henry Sloane, Good Shepherd's pastor of visitation (*Angel,* 168), who did not appear in *Wages* and is not listed on the church's roster of ministers in *Fall from Grace, Inc.*, but reappears in *Reverend Randollph and the Holy Terror* and may have been conjured up originally just for this scene. Randollph's resultant visitation at the Julian clinic fulfills the expressed goal of Smith's very first satire *How to Become a Bishop without Being Religious,* for it presents the clergy as fully human. Through the medium of his visit we peer into Randollph's fears, his uncertainties, his resentments, and his resignation. The deft touches of detail of the clergy room (*Angel,* 203–4) symbolize all the privileges, benefits and detriments of the occupation. The authenticity of experience in the writing in undeniable.

As Randollph continues the humanizing process begun in *Wages,* some of the fierce prejudices of the first book begin to soften and fall away. Thus, we are nearly prepared for the radical break in *Fall from Grace,* when Randollph advocates on behalf of a supposed fundamentalist, Prince Hartman (though there is no cross or repentance in this promiscuous minister's theology—only a doctrine of athletic fitness, a conservative variant of the short-lived "salvation and health" spinoff of early process thought).

Further, Randollph softens his hard line on the Association of Athletes for Christ which came in for such a drubbing in *Wages* (*Fall,* 14). We know he has looked at the group in a manner different from the way he did as a pious player; now perhaps he is looking again. He looks at Hartman differently, at other people differently, at the murders differently. With this deepening of perspective, Randollph achieves an ever higher level of humanity and ceases to be simply a vehicle by which to lampoon—by the contrast of speech, sophistication, and subtlety—the crass theological simplicity of the unwashed conservatives he encounters. Hartman, too, steps out of the monotonous goose-step parade of cardboard charlatans and buffoons who have represented not simply TV frauds but all religious conservatives, the shabby and glittering (e.g., Clarabelle Creedy, the little brown man, Jeff Davis Troutman, and the sputtering Pastor Wakefield). Randollph's growing tolerance seems to peak by the end of the book. He has certainly come quite a distance from being simply a stuffed suit of clothes. He has come to be a fuller, more mature individual, and with this blossoming into selfhood, Randollph is now ready to become interdependent with another full individual in marriage.

In *The Holy Terror,* Randollph's marital bliss cements the process of humanization and toleration that has progressed through his funeral counseling, his hospital visitations, his acceptance of Prince Hartman. The conjugal act defines for him God and humanity and thereby puts him in clearer, more loving communication with both:

> This, it went through his mind, is why they coined the word "ineffable." This ultimate melding with the one you loved. This unsortable mingling of tenderness and lust and affection and desire sharp as pain. This natural act so spiritual that it expressed the inexpressible. This blind, driven coupling which made sense out of God and creation. This animal experience through which the meaning of life could be glimpsed. This ecstasy which built to an explosion of sensation and revelation. (*Terror*, 18)

Tolerance, then, and more tolerance is the result, and, therefore, it is only to be expected that this is a book in defense of the need for tolerance. Randollph, as we have seen, tolerates pornography to ensure a free press. Sam and Randollph tolerate each other's views as Sam determines to tolerate the women of the Church of the Good Shepherd and they determine to tolerate her. At Randollph's installation all the clergy of different faiths tolerate each other. Only the Holy Terror does not. On a rampage of rebellion against the tight religious restrictions that he believes have ruined his life, the unknown killer called the Holy Terror lashes out against falsely pious religious appearances by systematically annihilating apparently pious preachers with nefarious pasts—a program somewhat similar to that in William Kienzle's *The Rosary Murders* and in Smith's last book, finished posthumously by his son Terence and published in 1986 as *Reverend Randollph and the Splendid Samaritan*. When Randollph is added incongruously to the hit list, his comfortable gothic penthouse becomes a citadel besieged and his life a nightmare of anxiety. In his descriptions of the clerical victims Smith's satirical rapier flashes once more with brilliant incisiveness, deftly carving masterful cameos of religious hypocrites, particularly media ones, in a manner all Christians of all persuasions can applaud. These hucksters who have given the faith such a seamy name are adroitly lampooned, then chillingly poleaxed by the Holy Terror. But the most chilling thing about the Terror's capital retribution is that the Terror can and does make mistakes. The glib and cold-hearted foreshadowing of the earlier avenging angel—"If one of you is innocent, so what? If you're both innocent, well, that's tough" (*Angel*, 129)—is catastrophically realized as the Terror slaughters the innocent Bishop O'Manny, mistaking him for Randollph, and butchers the blameless Rabbi Lehman on the basis of incorrect information. The book's apology for tolerance is brought effectively home by Randollph in his conclusive statement "'That's the trouble with playing God,' Randollph said. 'We never have all the information God has'" (*Terror*, 231). The genre of mystery, dealing with strong themes of life and death, can at its finest moments, as it does here, illustrate the need for human attitudes and conventions that ensure, prolong, and enhance life.

Hand in hand with the theme of tolerance, Smith's corresponding theme of distrusting appearances takes on a new benign dimension in *Terror*. Randollph has developed a suspicion of appearances to the extent he can see below the surface of human convention to divine what is beneath. Now as the Holy Terror stalks him and turns his life into a waking nightmare, his circle of family and friends draws tightly around him and strives to maintain the illusion of normalcy in Randollph's life. Randollph, of course, sees behind the facade, but he recognizes these are calming, not merely deceiving, appearances and is grateful for the love behind the acting. "Randollph appreciated this light talk acting out the concept that life was normal even though it wasn't" (*Terror*, 105).

If the nature of the use of appearances changes in *Holy Terror*, so, too, do some of the standard revelations of appearances alter. Despite a possibly prophetic quality to Randollph's opening observation to Sam that atheism may actually be Christianity in disguise back in *Wages of Sin* (*Wages*, 30), Sam's self-styled atheism/agnosticism has remained a constant in each of the books. Now in *Terror*, however, that secure foundation begins to slip perceptibly. Perhaps the first rather innocent instance occurs when, as the pastor's new wife, she is suddenly asked at her women's guild reception when she prays, and she answers automatically, "'I don't.'" Then she silently breathes what could either be a prayer or a blasphemy, "'Oh, Jesus, what's going to happen now?'" (*Terror*, 193). At the end of her ordeal, after she believes she has won Good Shepherd's women over, she whispers less ambiguously, "'Thank you, dear God'" (*Terror*, 195). Later when she believes she knows the identity of the Terror to be an intimate friend, she clearly entreats God through her tears, "'Pray God it isn't so,' she sobbed. 'Oh, God, don't let it be so!'" (*Terror*, 210). By the next book *The Unholy Bible* her refuge in prayer in time of trouble has become too regular to be ignored or to escape comment. "'O God,' she whispered, 'please make Randollph safe and bring him back to me.' It never occurred to her that she didn't believe in God or prayer" (*Bible*, 85). We have already noted the change in Randollph; what about the one in Samantha? As an unbeliever, she serves a regular convention in religious fiction. Like MacPhee in C. S. Lewis' *That Hideous Strength*, the nonbeliever functions as contrast or foil, not simply as potential convert. Sam, of course, sets off the belief that surrounds her: Clarence's, the bishop's, and presumably Dan's, as well as Randollph's. Now she is hobnobbing with all the women in Good Shepherd's guild and so is exposed not only to "smarmy" believers' faith but to the attractive Susan Fosterman's as well. Apparently, belief is not odious, repulsive, or impossible to Samantha. As her prayers show, it is remaking its mark. Samantha may learn what C. S. Lewis did when he wrote of himself, "A young man who wishes to remain a sound Atheist cannot be too careful. . . . There are traps everywhere" (Lewis, *Joy*, 191).

Another set of appearances challenged in the series and literally assaulted in *Holy Terror* is the stock literary figure of the anemic, otherworldly cleric.

Mysteries historically have intoned a dull litany of shabby, bumbling, naive clerics, a tedious roster of scrawny seminarians and starry-eyed rectors. Not since P. G. Wodehouse's marvelous beefy curates, however, has the male ministry had a shot of B-12 to match the tough new jocks of the Randollph series. The bishop may be dumpy physically, but he and Randollph can polish off a cop and a professional jock at poker (*Terror*, 226). Dan Gantry is identified as a "big guy," and repeats his decking of a hired killer in *Avenging Angel* by helping floor the Holy Terror (*Terror*, 227). Sticky Henderson, on the other hand, the supposed tough guy, the professional jock, is also a gourmet chef, reminiscent of Robert Parker's detective Spenser, so new dimensions are blossoming everywhere here. These instances, of course, salvage the males only. The figure of the Reverend Natalie Fisk and subsequent female clergy might have built an equally strong image of ministering women as the series continued.

With all the world altering, all the old images in turmoil, tolerance of the new is imperative, and a figure like the Holy Terror, who, as *Wages'* Clarabell Creedy, has been damaged by a strict Calvinist background, has no place. Indeed, all six novels unite in this overriding concern.

The theme of tolerance, then, is the impetus that moves *Reverend Randollph and the Holy Terror,* and inversely, the condemnation of fanaticism motivates its sequel *Reverend Randollph and the Unholy Bible.* If the *Holy Terror* has made the point by summoning up numerous positive examples of tolerant people of a variety of faiths (rabbis, priests, clerics, laity) to contrast with the Terror, *The Unholy Bible* ushers in a parade of contrasting fanatics, each more deadly than the last. The point is made in shocking inverse. In *The Unholy Bible* a true believer will go to any length to serve the object, the idol let us say, of that belief. A gangster will, on one hand, give millions of dollars and consider it a bargain or, on the other hand, will as readily remove by murder any human obstacles to his idolatrous quest for an object of ultimate beauty. A lawyer will kill to protect the cherished reputation of the firm he has built, and a priest will throw away his hope of glory and a lifetime of good works to reach his desire.

Given the response of fanaticism, any object of such an unholy quest becomes an idol. A holy Bible becomes an unholy Bible when a sacrilegious devotion is directed toward it. Thus, the novel becomes a parable of the misuse of the holy and functions as a depiction of the seven deadly sins alive in the fanaticism of pious people. By no accident does Randollph spend the book trying to sketch out a series on the seven sins, because the book becomes a cogent illustration of these sins—alive first in the obvious fanatics and soon discovered even in presumably normal characters like Randollph and his intimates (*Bible*, 34, 193).

In contrast the seven Christian virtues stand in judgment on him and everyone in the book. Thus, Randollph approaches a kind of paranoia of piety in this book despite his protests about the nonpious quality of his life. In past books he has turned his attention periodically to the presence of spiritual pride in himself or others, but in *The Unholy Bible,* like Holmes' Sister Ursula, he seems obsessed with it. We have seen already in previous books how he half jokes about penance, how he punishes himself, and how he quickly corrects or deflates others' egos when he thinks he perceives spiritual pride. In *The Unholy Bible* the instances are numerous and ultimately produce a pathetic sort of penance levied upon a killer. Perhaps Randollph is so continually obsessed because he has not come to grips satisfactorily with his own purgation. In *The Holy Terror* the narrative argued a "flaw" in the "soul" craves "the cleansing of personal suffering" and covets the salvation awarded to a martyr *(Terror,* 21). As the statement stands it is misleading, and possibly such a theology has misled Randollph. True, only a masochist will wish to suffer unduly, but there is a real and valid cathartic need for purgation in those who have sinned. A healthy spirit needs retribution exacted and absolution given.

What Randollph does not apply to himself or others is the full significance of the doctrine of justification. God's mercy never sets aside God's justice. This is a common mistake in popular theology. The result is that though sin is then removed in the sinner's eyes, guilt remains. But God's mercy does not set aside God's justice—it fulfills it. The bishop may cavalierly dismiss the doctrine of substitution: "I'm afraid there aren't any [good hymns about sin], C. P. At least none come to mind. Too many of them use blood atonement as their theme. I think blood atonement has no cogency for the 'modern mind'" *(Bible,* 161). But the point of this doctrine is that the concept of the blood atonement affirms that Christ has atoned. Christians do not escape punishment; they receive it in the person of Christ. Thus, they are justified and the guilt removed. Now that this restoration has been effected, Christians have no need for meticulous attention to lapse and penance. Repentance is still in order when sins are committed, but there need be no unhealthy obsession with ferreting out sin in the psyche. Now, if in the passage about coveting the salvation awarded a martyr, Christ is being identified with the envied martyr, then of course the passage is right. But since Christ is not the obvious referent, the reading appears askew and privative. Randollph's adoption of a similar view is probably traceable to the guilt he continually feels living in Good Shepherd's luxury. In addition to the permanent pastorate of Good Shepherd, marriage to the famed Samantha Stack, the bishop's continuing friendship and advocacy, ministrations by the incomparable Clarence, and constant celebration in the media, Randollph receives one million dollars and custody of the world's finest Gutenberg Bible. About all he is missing now is a pet duck. Though Randollph gives the Bible and money away, he has still had the right of ultimate choice as far as wealth and opportunity are concerned. In that sense he has actualized the goal of middle-class aspiration: independent and completely comfortable freedom of choice.

Thus from the vantage point of *The Unholy Bible,* the Reverend C. P. Randollph is certainly the stuff of which middle-class dreams are made. Of all the clerical detectives that have been imagined since Chesterton's Father Brown, none has been so much fun to follow as Randollph. He is certainly Horatio Alger in a white dickey. Randollph is what every male professional wants to be: a superb athlete, worshipped by the world at large, the desire of women, and the envy of less masculine men.

Still, Randollph can be fragile. His ego needs the affectation of an extra "l" in his name to set him apart. He needs clothes and cuisine. Before the superlative Sam, he needed a steady supply of starlets to keep his libido at nontoxic level and maintain the equilibrium of his physically-oriented, gymnastic self-image. But Randollph, despite occasional minor scratches, generally escapes Smith's razor-sharp rapier as few other characters besides the bishop do. A succession of bloated pretenders to theological respectability go down before Randollph's verbal sallies. Even Samantha can be bested by Randollph's wit, but it is a rare moment when the ego-bloated, pedantic Randollph ever gets a good thrust of the pin. How can the sardonic Charles Merrill Smith resist?

He can resist because Randollph, we we have seen, functions as more than just a character in a novel for Smith. As a sequel to the epitomized middle-class narrator of the earlier satires, Randollph is an ideal, a fleshed out repository of everybody's "What I should have saids" rolled up into a glorification of Smith's own athletic past, his premiums of good clothes, good food, good cars, the obverse of his largely middle-class parishes, the augmented extension of the prestige parishes he finally achieved, the instant celebratory arrival at status and economic comfort that Smith himself painstakingly paid for on the installment plan a book at a time, a parish at a time, over more than thirty years of struggling pastoral ministry. In only ten or so years off the playing field, Randollph has it all, while he is still only in his early forties and young enough to enjoy it—a doctorate, a reputation, a media-star spouse, a luxurious dream of a church setting.

For any minister reading, Randollph is certainly therapeutic, especially after a hard bout with the board of deacons. But is he ultimately, authentically edifying? Do Randollph's comedies actually reflect enough of the world we know to do more than deceive us? Or is this in any way the point of how they serve us? Do his cardboard misrepresentations of conservatives, seminarians, and missionaries really mislead us? Is the exhilaration one feels when Randollph burns a pass into a hostile bunch of seminarians, verbally outspars the antipornography religious pundits, shows up the cops with his insights, and dazzles the TV audience with his glittering wit and charm really good for us? In one sense, yes, and in another, no.

The Randollph series induces catharsis for liberal Christians, particularly clerics, oppressed by fundamentalists who assail them on television, charismatics who draw off their church membership, secularized parishioners who plague them with questions like "What do you *really* do with your time?" But the series also distorts good and evil, misrepresenting Randollph's adversaries by reducing them to unfeeling nonhumans. Essentially, these books dehumanize the image of their enemies. They also can simplify complex issues of race, biblical authority, and sexism until only an imbecile would hold a view opposite to Randollph's.

In their best moments, when they rise above polemic, the books can make some profoundly moving and truthful statements about life, the essential humanity of the clergy, and the caring interaction of people. As in the counseling scene I extolled in *Avenging Angel,* they can show by example the raw healing power of a potently comforting, living, sensitively human Christian faith. Even their polemical quality can be edifying when it serves the best function of satire, exposing the fraudulent, deflating the unjustly puffed up, uncovering the true motive beneath the pious subterfuge. Perhaps I am asking too much of satire, whose nature, after all, is to poke fun at our foibles and by that means present an even deeper challenge to middle-class complacency than would mere exhortation. However, given Reverend Smith's lifetime of painstaking pastoral care of the middle class, I think not. Such a veritable genius should have been able to differentiate between the paring knife and the meat cleaver, between satire and sarcasm.

With what conclusion then are we left? Is the Randollph series merely kitsch? Is it a retired minister's self indulgence, good for a few cathartic moments but ultimately misleading? I underscore there is nothing wrong with occasional euphoria, just as there is nothing wrong with an occasional strawberry sundae. Both of them salvage us from moribund asceticism. But a steady diet—especially one that reduces the opposition to dehumanized cardboard—ultimately lies to us about the true nature of the world.

Thus, where Smith's satirical novels merely scorch believers like the utterly harmless and well-meaning little brown man, they contribute to the disunity of the Church and are to be regretted. In spite of the sheer scope of his ingenious creations, his vast gifts of wit, language, construction, and humor, Smith can do us a keen disservice in his lapses. Where he turns the floodlight on manipulation, malignant self-deception or downright fraud, however, he goes beyond his prejudices and champions us all in an attack on our real enemies. When he cuts, then heals and restores, he produces an exhilarating pastiche of real value as well as real entertainment. But greater than all of these, perhaps, is Smith's one great achievement. Few Christian writers actively help us look above the pimps, the pushers, and the hustlers to see the pastor—a consciousness-raising that is the goal of every authentic city minister. In the virile, thoroughly attractive, and intelligent clerical hunk Randollph, Charles Merrill Smith at his best moments elevated our gaze to what God sees in everyone who serves heaven on earth—a potential champion.

24

God in the Fiction of Flagellation: James L. Johnson's
Code Name Sebastian Series

The presence of opulence and the distance of God in Charles Merrill Smith's
Reverend Randollph series stand in sharp contrast to the Sebastian spy sagas of
James Leonard Johnson. Starkly ascetic and charged with a nearly overwhelming preoccupation with God, Sebastian espouses a hybrid of the theologies of
St. John of the Cross and Dietrich Bonhoeffer, set in the hard-boiled religious
fiction tradition of Lon Woodrum. With such a sense of the immanence of deity,
one would expect to see the hand of God at work everywhere in these cross and
dagger novels, yet the elusiveness of authenticated glimpses of God's working
becomes the theme of the series. Actual documentation of God's work by the
characters becomes minuscule and ultimately equivocal.

Sebastian's creator, James Leonard Johnson, lived a robust life in the
adventure of religion. Returning from World War II, he traveled to Nigeria as
a missionary, eventually editing *African Challenge* and establishing it as the
premier Christian magazine in Africa at the time. From Africa he returned to the
United States to write sixteen books, direct *Evangelical Literature Overseas,*
establish the graduate communications department at Wheaton College in Illinois, and serve the World Relief organization as associate director of resource
development. A person who threw himself with passion into all he did, the
marvelous James Johnson died in 1987, the twentieth anniversary of Sebastian's
appearance and the publication year of his final adventure, *Trackless Seas.*

Sebastian may at first appear not to be as clearly a clerical detective as
Reverend Randollph, Father Brown, Rabbi Small, or Septimus, but instead is a
kind of clerical espionage agent. Yet Dorothy Sayers in her definitive *Omnibus
of Crime* collections has widened the definition of crime novels to include horror
and international crime. Crime novel historian Howard Haycraft has included
such espionage writers as Eric Ambler in his *Murder for Pleasure: The Life and
Times of the Detective Story,* noting, "Eric Ambler . . . has brought it [the
spy-and-intrigue story] close to a legitimate marriage with detection" (Haycraft,
Life, 205). And following the two world wars, such classic detective fiction

writers as Agatha Christie have blended tales of espionage into classical detective novels to the degree that Haycraft's wedding has in some instances taken place. Sebastian is one such instance, since every novel turns on a variation of the "whodunit" question. The first novel, *Code Name Sebastian*, asks in classic "whodunit" fashion, "Who is Agent Christopher who has caused the airplane to crash?" The rest turn on the query, "What is actually happening here?" From the first novel, things are never what they appear to be to Sebastian. And just as the movings of the human manipulators are mysterious, so are the corresponding movings of God. Sebastian tends to meet the dilemmas before him on an adapted model of Father Brown, investing his attention in the people involved.

This is not to say that Sebastian begins his series with an overwhelming sense of God's presence and a correspondingly deep conviction of his call. In point of fact, our opening glimpse of Sebastian, through a letter to his intimate friend and foil of normalcy, parishioner Les Bennington, reveals a disappointed widower, a burnt-out failure in ministry, a groper for a God whose presence has fled him. Despairing at his inability to recover from the death of his wife, who died taking a stance for social justice that Sebastian could not muster the courage to do, his long-suffering congregation has sent him to tour the Holy Land. When, failing to revive his faith, he leaves early, his plane crashes in the desert, where he meets Israeli agent Barbara Churchill, a plane load of espionage suspects, and, most disrupting of all, the ferocious God of Israel—encounters that will change him irrevocably.

Against these realities, Sebastian's initial solitariness belies his true unconscious theology, which is so intensely communal as to depend for motivation on the existence of women in his life. Just as in the first book his wife died, "taking with her the big meaning of his own life and the drive that had kept him alive in the ministry" (*Code*, 69), so in the fifth book, *Last Train from Canton*, with the loss of his wife's replacement Barbara Churchill, "Humanly he felt no drive for any of these things without her being alive somewhere" (*Train*, 31). Thus, Sebastian wanders in the desert of his own loneliness. In the opening book that internal desert is externalized for him in a few short pages, as the crash flings Sebastian into a survival trek across the Negev that is as spiritual as it is physical.

The use of environment to show internal state is a staple technique Johnson will employ again and again with extreme effectiveness as the series progresses. In *Code Name Sebastian* Sebastian's deprivation is mirrored in the desert. In *The Nine Lives of Alphonse* and *Trackless Seas* the mirror is the ocean. In *A Handful of Dominoes* it is bombed-out East Berlin. In *A Piece of the Moon Is Missing* it is the desolate Arctic. By thus employing the pathetic fallacy, Johnson echoes St. John of the Cross in his depiction of the two spiritual conditions, the dark night of the senses and the generally misunderstood dark night of the soul.

Rather than metaphors of despair, as these two spiritual states are normally construed in popular theology, the two concepts describe the purgative preparation of the soul as it approaches God. As the human draws near to the Divine Lover, the senses shut down since the spiritual cannot be sensorially perceived. Thus, the human passes into the condition of night when the five senses can no longer provide information. Then as the soul progresses past the failure of sense perception, it passes into the realm of the dark night of the soul. Ultimate night deepens until the soul passes into the agony of oblivion at its penultimate painful moment, being purged of all sin, unconscious, agonizing for the presence of God. At the depth of that deprivation, the ultimate moment of extreme night, the Divine Lover engulfs the purgated soul into the Eternal Oneness, the mystic's great All. For Sebastian the cutting of human ties has begun that process. And as he struggles, book after book, through spiritual and physical terrain that is stark, bleak, fierce, as his body thins ascetically, as his vision recurrently fails, he finally loses consciousness. In his physical and emotional deprivation at the end of nearly every tale he catches a misty sense of God, a vague glimpse of the Presence that others perceive around him—e.g., "You have a Presence about you" (*Moon,* 204).

Sebastian achieves Saint John's journey by following the prescription of Bonhoeffer:

> Bonhoeffer said, "The church must get out of the cloister and into the world . . . man is challenged to participate in the sufferings of God at the hands of a godless world. He must therefore plunge himself into the life of a godless world without attempting to gloss over its ungodliness with a veneer of religion or trying to transfigure it. He must live a worldly life and so participate in the suffering of God. To be a Christian does not mean to be religious in a particular way, to cultivate some form of asceticism . . . but to be a man." I've read Bonhoeffer before, but I never got the significance of that until yesterday when I reviewed all that happened to me in the desert. (*Code,* 268)

Sebastian's plunge does punish his body, humanize him, and at the same time draw him away from the false image of God his comfort has cultivated and toward the presence of God that Bonhoeffer has described: a God who suffers in the suffering of creation and who can only be approached through one's own experience of suffering. Hence comes my appellation for Johnson's fiction—the fiction of flagellation—for suffering must be sought in lieu of the easily available comforts of this dying world.

In his plunge into the desert Sebastian begins the Judeo-Christian experience again, like Elisha receiving the mantle cast upon him, like Moses finding himself the unwilling leader of a recalcitrant wandering people (*Code,* 95). He must find El Shaddai in the wilderness in order for him and his charges to survive, for the desert itself poses a problem for the God he has been preaching in his comfortable suburban parish in Nashville, Wisconsin. The Bedouins call the Negev "the bone that sticks in God's throat." It is the leftover of creation that taunts and defies even God the Creator "to conceive life out of this void" (*Code*, 22). This world is beyond "the neat pattern" of even science. As Sparks the navigator observes, "This kind of world doesn't follow the normal pattern of things" (*Code*, 90). In this chaos "reason and faith locked horns again" as the scientists who survived with Sebastian compete with him to deliver the wanderers (*Code*, 30).

Sebastian, true to the form of his life thus far, wants no part of the leadership being thrust upon him by an embittered Barbara Churchill, who wants to prove for personal reasons that the Church has failed. She adroitly argues that his maleness means he must lead, though succeeding books and particularly *A Piece of the Moon Is Missing* prove her argument is totally specious, since she refuses to follow any male's directions, defying the chief of Apollo Security and Sebastian with equal ease. The naive sexist Sebastian, however, agrees with the navigator Sparks that leadership is "a job for a man" (*Code*, 90); hence the onset of his longed-for yet involuntary passion. Barbara wishes to set Sebastian up for failure, because the macrocosmic example of the Church permitting the Holocaust and the microcosmic example of her own missionary father refusing to help freedom fighters have moved her to reject the Church. So, too, the scientist Brelsford battles Sebastian because of personal antagonism against a father whose simplistic faith caused family hardship. The squirming Sebastian is impaled on the hook of their accusations. He is equated with the Church in Germany for charging suffering "to God's account" and not seeking as a "man of God" to "relieve human suffering when and where you can" (*Code*, 61). And Sebastian is shamed. "For the first time in his ministerial life, the antiseptic-safe world of his Christian isolationism was caught in the balance, and it carried very little weight at all" (*Code*, 63). In contrast he is "thrilled" by the "magnificence" of her competency and involvement (*Code*, 63) and so he allows himself to be pushed. All his life he has looked like Abraham Lincoln and now the irony strikes him, for like Lincoln and Moses, he must lead a captive people out of duress.

As he becomes involved, he begins to loosen up. He now learns to light cigarettes for others, a previously loathsome business for a cultural fundamentalist (*Code*, 70–71). He hesitates to continue to employ his neat, pat, past answers. When the timid Ida Randolph queries, "I pray all the time . . . what have we now but prayer?" he replies simply, "It'll go a long way" (*Code*, 102), refusing to be drawn any longer into the simple conclusion that prayer is, indeed, all they have. Also changing is his preaching pattern: he begins to silence the claims he made about God back in Wisconsin. Now he is telling people less and relying more on his actions to speak (*Code*, 106). At the heart of this quieting of his words is the gnawing challenge of the desert that his "altars and organ music" faith is inappropriate here (*Code,* 107). The ex-Nazi Eaton articulates the desert's challenge:

> What does a simple clergyman whose life is cut along so plain a line know anything about complex things like deserts? You with your spiritual common denominator for everything in life—you who try to divide God into everything and expect it to come out all wrapped up in gay ribbon? You with your blind concept of the universe that says everything runs like a big watch and all you have to do is let it run by itself and life will be one big garden of roses, ha? (*Code,* 104)

And so the survivors push Sebastian to have his God produce a miracle. But the God Sebastian has worshipped for so long is nowhere to be found:

> He closed the Bible and tried prayer. His soul cried out, but no words came. Something would form way deep inside him, but would not rise to his lips. It was as if everything framed in his thoughts was not applicable, and he suddenly felt himself totally cut off from any sense of God, any presence, any contacts at all that might diffuse new hope within himself. All he felt now was incrimination of his past, his years of ministering in the non-critical areas of life, of pontificating on those safe and sure postulates that never demanded proof. And he knew then that his prayers couldn't form on his lips because they were words that were trite, meaningless, words addressed for the God of the comfortable, safe, and sure way of life he had in Nashville. He knew nothing of the God in crisis, the God of the Negev, the God of the impossible—he had reshaped God to his own form of Santa Claus and Easter bunny who could deliver gaily wrapped packages and chocolate eggs but who couldn't be counted on to alter the agony of the human condition. How then could he pray to God here, a different God in his own mind altogether, a God he had never tried, proved, or seen work anywhere? (*Code,* 172)

Thus, Sebastian in his increasing suffering with and for his companions must meet, as Moses met in the desert, a new God of adversity. Sebastian receives, as Moses did, a staff of authority by which he is jeeringly challenged to strike water from the rocks. But, unlike Moses, Sebastian finds no water, and even if he had, the scientist Brelsford is already prepared for a naturalistic explanation of the phenomenon (*Code,* 110). A cloud of dust does not lead Sebastian's people; it pursues them, and it represents communist agents coming to kill them. Like Christ, Sebastian is taunted to pray for his own deliverance and theirs, and, like Christ, he has made his descent into hell (*Code,* 167), but, unlike Christ, he is suffering as well for his own sins. The Christ he has always represented is a "Christ who died a neat, sophisticated death on a church steeple with the organ playing," "demanding nothing of God and expecting nothing in return" (*Code,* 181). But now by his acts of responsibility he is being purged of this Christ and being formed in the image of the Suffering Servant, cleansed at last of the haunting accusatory dreams that recreate his wife's death in his stead (*Code,* 222) until he finally concludes: "It's taken me awhile to realize that there won't be any quick seminary solutions to this one, and I know that I can't expect any miracle from God bigger than what I'm prepared to do to be a practical solution to this problem" (*Code*, 181). Thus, he must struggle, carrying his taunters, with no neat miracle to deliver them.

Yet as the disappointed jeer around him that no miracle is taking place, ironically a miracle is occurring, as Barbara finally perceives, in Sebastian's internal wasteland. Sebastian is changing. In his opening letter he had lamented the lack of "some kind of miracle in my life brought about by this trip" (*Code*, 8). Now he is developing a warm communal sense for the atheists, the taunters who share his adversity (*Code*, 211). And from their hate they turn to a grudging, growing respect for him. The clinging Ida Randolph delivers an unexpected expression of sympathy similar to that which another "Randollph," Reverend Randollph, invoked in *Holy Terror* when his life appeared forfeit: "You poor man. . . . I never thought of ministers who suffered with mankind as you have had to do here—what sins must you account for?" (*Code*, 225–26). Sebastian, like the goal of Smith's satires, has proved ministers are human. And as the book reaches climax, all the threads come together to weave a new tapestry of life and faith out of Sebastian's unused "unproven faith" (*Code*, 226).

Sebastian has contended, "Every man must sooner or later come to the impossible where reason has to yield to faith—when that time comes for you, only then can you determine if Deity is inconsistent with His being" (*Code*, 112). When that time comes for Sebastian, in his delirium—after the accomplishment of his John of the Cross-like deprivation, after he has suffered in the place of Christ, hearing the taunt "He saved others, himself he cannot save" (*Code*, 235), after he has called on the God of Moses (*Code*, 236), after he has sought God with the totality of his being—he babbles Psalm 139, God's presence is everywhere, with him in heaven or, if he should make his bed in hell, "behold, thou art there" (*Code*, 253). Sebastian has met the God of the desert and has delivered the people as he has promised. He has put the lie to Barbara, to Brelsford, and to his own doubts. Now others must affirm his miracle, for Sebastian no longer speaks his claims. Duncan Alexander calls it "a bloody miracle," ironically employing the mild British swear word whose referent is Christ's blood (*Code*, 241). Barbara concludes in tears for her own father and faith:

> You say you have seen no miracle in that desert to prove God? Well, understand me well now . . . the greatest miracle out there is what happened to you, Sebastian . . . you came into that desert weak, all mush, whining about the need to be detached from the bruised, confused people who had survived . . . remember? I hated you, I despised you that night for that weakness . . . well the end of the journey was different . . . you were in a sense invincible . . . not miraculous . . . but you were a man risen to the commission to lift the helpless, to daringly, in instances, effect deliverance when you even didn't know how . . . to me, that is my concept of God in the universe . . . and you brought Him to me in all His glory. (*Code*, 260)

The Christ of the steeples, the God of organ music is gone from Sebastian, just as weak, soft, sulking, indecisive Sebastian has died along with this unresurrected Jesus of comfort. Now that the Barak that Deborah has forced to do battle has triumphed, the miracle and presence and reality of God have become more visible to those around him than Sebastian's faltering words ever had conveyed. The "weakest element in society," the Church, has triumphed potently in the stumbling doggedness of the reduced and baffled Sebastian (*Code,* 257), and now he must adjust his life to this God of the unexpected. Like Jacob, he is in a sense renamed, given by Barbara the "Code Name Sebastian." He must now wander into a new way of life to continue to get to know the God he has found.

This he does in three more excellent adventures, including the superb story *A Handful of Dominoes,* which, like *Reverend Randollph and the Avenging Angel,* is built on a biblical theme. In each of these tales God is a force whose vague intentions Sebastian might guess—e.g., "[He was] not really sure what he was supposed to do or if God intended him to do much more than give counsel to an old friend" (*Alphonse,* 21). Immanent revelation only becomes clear as Sebastian acts: no action, no revelation. So Sebastian becomes a gambler of God: "Okay . . . let's put it all on the line" (*Alphonse,* 232). Because he really wants to know himself, he again lets people push him into seeking a miracle (*Alphonse,* 233). The ascerbic Joe pegs him correctly:

> "Straight from corn alley!" Joe chided. "The old 'rally round the flag, boys,' hey, preach? But I know what you want out of this trip—you want a pocket-sized miracle from God to crow about. You want as tough a job as you can find, so if you pull it off you can tell everybody that God did it—and maybe you think I'll wind up saluting God, too. Well, I'll tell you one thing, man of the cloth, if you are thinking of taking the same God out on Alphonse as you did last night on the PT boat, forget it!" (*Alphonse,* 85)

Sebastian hardly defends himself any longer. Growing more and more silent, he simply acts as God's hands. Rescuing victims inadvertently caught in the vice of international intrigue, suffering with them and sometimes in their stead, and eventually being beaten into insensibility, he relies on God's actions to rescue him and some of his charges. But Sebastian leaves increasingly to others the interpretation and affirmation that God has acted. Pressed to interpretation, he claims:

> Well, then, that's the eternal difference between politics and religion. You see things in terms of a hemisphere—we go a step further and try to see God's view, that every man has value. I'll put my aims straight for the record, Mr. Mathews: I want God to be out there, I want to demonstrate a living Christ, to show that He still loves mankind, that in all that bleeding mass of Cuba, where people are clawing their way out, God is there to help them up. . . . That may

> sound idealistic to you, sir, and to your partners here, but that's the way it is. And when you drop your depth charges on us out there, you can think about that. (*Alphonse*, 158)

Sebastian's last name, we might observe, is reminiscent of the Sebastinians immortalized for us by Jesus in his tale of the Good Samaritan—the central image of Sebastian's new ministry. Sebastian's first name, of course, is Raymond. In *The Nine Lives of Alphonse* the character El Dorado acknowledges that Sebastian has helped him find "the sun" (*Alphonse*, 273). And the "Rayman" spreads a little of God's light in the bleak darkness of the fallen world. The spiritually and modernly electrified Good Samaritan Sebastian realizes that "living in this world" is like "grabbing a high-voltage wire" (*Alphonse*, 73). Sebastian finds he needs all his power just to stay alive, not to mention to bring life to others.

Sebastian is learning the lesson Johnson has taught another character, the enigmatic Blake, jaded supervisor of a decimated missionary aviation outfit in *The Death of Kings:*

> In the meantime, you must let the deed articulate the word. The proof of words, definitions and terms in the lexicon of God is through their final verification in experience. God delights to prove Himself to you in this way. (*Kings*, 325)

or again:

> "God never gave *me* any blank checks, Willie," Sebastian returned. "I draw only on what I have. Sometimes it's pretty lean, the supply of miracles; sometimes they even come from people I least expect. Sometimes there aren't any. I sweat it out and keep trying the doors; some I even kick in when necessary. And since I'm no operator like you, when things happen, I figure it has to be God . . . understand?" (*Dominoes*, 149)

The God who forces an ascetic lifestyle on Sebastian seems to consume not only the flesh and the comforts and pleasures of the flesh, but also ultimately the life spirit as well. In *A Handful of Dominoes* investigator Margot Schell observes this when, pushed to the wall in her attempts to help Sebastian escape, she strikes out at the extreme demands of Sebastian's deity. In eerie anticipation of Joyce Carol Oates' later *Son of the Morning,* wherein God is depicted as a hungry maw that engulfs what it has created (Oates, 325), Margot assails Sebastian's rapacious God: " 'So it is my life you demand now too, is it?' she returned with a grating harshness in her voice. 'That hungry God of yours demands the full sacrifice; is that it?' " (*Dominoes*, 186). But Sebastian demurs, and his denial captures the difference between the God who demands all of Sebastian and the unconscious consuming maw of Oates: " 'No, Margot,' he said softly. . . . 'If you want forgiveness for what you did to your parents, then ask God for it. You can't win that by running a hundred miles for me or Dettmann' "

(*Dominoes,* 186–87). Mere sacrifice, mere giving is not enough, for the debt, the guilt that causes sacrifice, is not simply paid to God. The debt of self-sacrifice is owed to other people. To become Christ-like to the world, to stand in for God, is to be sacrificed for others as Christ was sacrificed. This is what Johnny Vandermeer's invitation to get involved in East Berlin has meant to Sebastian: "It was more as if he were spelling out the debt Sebastian owed him, whatever it was, or as if he owed Berlin the same things he gave out in the Negev and Cuba" (*Dominoes,* 33). And it is when one is willing to pay that price that one encounters the God of sacrifice, suffering along in one's sacrifice.

God for Sebastian is a rescuer who plucks people out of the death throes of this world. Once they are plucked, their task is to join the rescue squad, diving back into the struggle to pluck out others, whatever the cost. It is the same principle that has moved him to risk death for his reprehensible lookalike Udal. To Margot's disgusted derision, "Udal was hardly worth it—he stank of his own corruption. Didn't they tell you that?" Sebastian replies, "A little . . . but I don't believe God stops being concerned just by the smell or even the sight of a man." She counters, "That's a well-worn platitude. Can't you be original?" But Sebastian concludes, "I don't think I can improve on Deity" (*Dominoes,* 133–34). When Margot ultimately makes that sacrifice, at cost of her life, she too is cleansed of her sin of causing the arrest of her parents, as Sebastian in the Negev had been cleansed of his sin against his wife, and she too finds Sebastian's God of rescue and forgiveness. With such a code and such an attitude one would expect Sebastian to reek of "holier-than-thou" pride, but he is increasingly humbled by his experiences. The withdrawal and deprivation serve to humanize him as they deepen him spiritually.

Sebastian spends his energy making allowances for others' behavior. He defends Jews' worship of God in Hitler's Germany by asserting a domino theory of their faith being replaced securely in the creation of Israel. He importunes hesitant engineers to allow Christian Dettmann, a boy who has just tried to kill Sebastian à la Udal, to ride in the giant earth-moving cranes the boy admires. Though he takes the strictest interpretation of Christian faith upon himself, Sebastian is kind and forgiving to others. He will endure any amount of suffering and deprivation to help those who scorn him, and through this active willingness, his God is revealed as an attractive one. Sebastian has also stopped pressuring people into faith. Often now he does not interfere but lets people struggle for themselves. He even allows them to maintain their own artifices if he believes exposing them will cause undue suffering (e.g., *Dominoes,* 152). He can pursue a self-deceiver ruthlessly or he can let one alone if he believes the deceit covers personal pain. Sebastian's insistence on his God's concern for the individual now has made him a truly caring counselor, who does not value the insistence on *all* truth over the needs of people. He can expound a cauterizing truth when necessary, but he can also let people struggle themselves as he remains silent. Like his vision of God, he puts concern for people over politics, dogma, personal power, even his own safety; hence he is continually delivered, though not, of course, unscathed. Sebastian's God is hard on believers who serve him, though not on unbelievers or hostile critics. Toward them both Sebastian and his God are gentle, caring, and willing to rescue.

Sebastian's rejection of signs and wonders and his physical asceticism parallel his devaluation of mere religious trappings and relics. We have already seen how he has rejected the Christ of altars, organ music, steeples. When in *Dominoes* spies dangle before him the prospect of fetching out the original manuscript of the Pentateuch, Sebastian, unlike Randollph in *Reverend Randollph and the Unholy Bible,* is unimpressed. He replies there is no original manuscript of the Pentateuch, but even if there were, it would not usurp the place of true devotion to God. Sebastian, while affirming Scripture, has gone further than any mere attack on biblical inerrancy and instead rejects the appropriation of its words to replace action in the ministry. He would not subscribe, for example, to the Van Tillian view of the words of Scripture having power in themselves. For Sebastian the words have power because they are linked to lives in which God has acted. Therefore, merely to appropriate the words without that context of action is useless, for God's truth dwells not in the words alone but in the actions, the "Word incarnate," so to speak, just as Paul sees the rule of God coming not by words alone but by power (1 Cor. 4:20).

The bulk of words that do come Sebastian's way by the close of the fourth book are so hostile as to make a reader wonder whether they are really warranted. Johnson has reduced Sebastian to beaten unconsciousness in book after book, and character after character has showered such blistering vituperation on him that one wonders whether the author has lost his point in an ocean of caustic opposition. On the verge of World War II, Leonard Hodgson, canon residentiary of Winchester Cathedral, while working on a series of sermons later published under the title *The Lord's Prayer,* reflected about the responsibility of authors to their characters. As he watched Hitler destroying in macrocosm, he came in the microcosm of literature to find himself searching for "what I can only describe as a truly Christian spirit, the spirit of understanding love towards the characters they contain" (Hodgson, 66–67). In writing of novels that "claim to represent modern literature," he notes:

> It may be a poor kind of literary criticism, but I find myself more and more coming to ask of a novelist, Does he really care for the characters he is creating, or does he regard them as rather despicable specimens for his superior brain to dissect in its laboratory? The authors of the two books I have mentioned belong clearly to the former class, and their books are books which we cannot read without a truly Christian enlargement of our human sympathies. (Hodgson, 67)

Has Johnson's flagellation of Sebastian overdone it? Does he as a creator owe anything to his creation Sebastian, mirrored in the caring of the Great Creator he espouses? Has he lost his point by making the Bonhoefferian world outside the faith lack verisimilitude in the sheer overwhelming heinousness of its attacks? I think by the time of *A Piece of the Moon Is Missing* he has. And, perhaps, the perceptive Johnson thought so too. A month and a day before he died, Johnson wrote his funeral service, entitled "Jim's Last Word." In it he wrote:

> Take time to smell the roses. . . . I failed to do that as much as I should. Don't forget to walk a mile every day. I didn't. So now you know how important that is. Take time to look at the stars on those warm July nights. . . . And let God have His rightful place at your side in that. To amplify the images, the sounds, the whisper of the good earth quietly breathing around you . . . then you will be closer than ever to the reality of His Being. (Arnold, 4)

Similarly, near the close of *A Piece of the Moon Is Missing,* Johnson begins to relax the pressure on Sebastian when he isolates him and Barbara Churchill in an igloo. In a refreshing change, Sebastian finds himself stirred so deeply "that he was sure he was going to do that very thing he knew could only fulfill and heighten their love. And at this moment, he knew it was right; it was only the two of them before God in this lonely place" (*Moon,* 160). So much for Sebastian's no-drinking-smoking-movies cultural fundamentalism. His God has now proved to be the authentic Scriptural God on whose right hand are pleasures forevermore, as Lewis depicts in *The Screwtape Letters* and in the happy connubial intercourse that ends *That Hideous Strength.* When Sebastian, prior enemy of comfort, decides to relax, subzero arctic misery, a bleeding hand and a wounded lover are hardly sufficient detriments. Barbara, however, identifying positive "God-signs" hanging over him and not wanting to violate "that Presence," encourages him to complete his missions of mercy, plucking him from the jaws of sex, however right it might be before God. No wonder, with all the criticism, cold, adversity, and this final deprivation, he utters this exasperated prayer: "God, there's just so much any man can take in a day" (*Moon,* 192).

Along with his character's relaxation, author Johnson now throws in a couple of "damns" and "hells" in the text, along with the kind of role reversal he can allow among swinging singles: "A single man or woman can afford to play with these possibilities of role reversal; a married man or woman with children has far more at stake" (*Man,* 123). This is the reason why Barbara and Sebastian can only get married when Barbara is reduced to near destruction at the end of *Trackless Seas.* For the magnificent freewheeling Barbara would be stuck in the home, where a married woman's "primary fulfillment was centered" (*Man,* 129) for Johnson. So Barbara wisely side-steps Sebastian's proposals as long as she is able and continues to lead him.

But the easing of pressure on Sebastian is to continue, and by *The Last Train to Canton* a number of changes occur. There is considerably less vituperation, and Sebastian's environment no longer provides regular deprivation (though at the climax Sebastian does pass out from exhaustion as he did in *Code*). In fact, Johnson goes to excess in the other direction, completely rewriting Sebastian's history. If these books were canonical, *The Last Train from Canton* would surely be seen as spurious, as pseudepigraphical, for the internal disparities in style and content are so great that in some instances they are impossible to reconcile with the preceding four novels.

The Sebastian to whom we are introduced seems at the outset much the same Sebastian we have been viewing all along. Now at forty, his vision has been scaled down to the simple litany, "This is the day which the Lord hath made; I will rejoice and be glad in it" (*Train*, 41). He has come to live day by day. Yet, for him, as an encounter with an old associate in the intrigue business reveals, "The past would not die" (*Train*, 44). In continuity with *A Piece of the Moon Is Missing,* he is still a man under sentence of death, suffering in his internal winter with those on the death row of this world.

Yet, as we soon discover, the past that would not die is not the past that we have come to associate with Sebastian in the previous four books. We are given the new information that he was nicknamed "Tote" in his high school days, and are expected to accept that as a teenager

> He was always toting someone else's load, whether it was a poor skinny kid's schoolbooks or camp pack or whatever. He even carried half the senior class in math, right, Tote? That's why it was not a surprise to me when he went into the ministry . . . no sir. (*Train*, 48)

Sebastian? Our I-don't-want-to-get-involved Sebastian? And further, we are told:

> I remember once when Tote carried an injured farmer nine miles through a snowstorm in thirty-six below weather. I remember when we were going down the Colorado for our high school graduation outing . . . and one of the guys fell overboard and was dragged under. Tote jumped out and followed that kid for miles downriver until he finally pulled him out. (*Train*, 114)

What is the point of this new prequel in flashbacks? Why has Johnson suddenly changed the pitiful loser of the pre-*Code Name Sebastian* days into an heroic alter ego named Tote? This rewriting of history only serves to undercut the entire point of the earlier books, that any namby-pamby Christian who chooses to get involved can turn into a tiger for Christ.

Further, there has been a noticeable change in his sexual attitudes. Perhaps the extent to which his fundamentalist restraints flew out the igloo in *A Piece of the Moon Is Missing* accounts for some of the striking aberrations in this book. After all the restraint he showed in *A Handful of Dominoes* toward Margot Schell, his remarkable nonperformance when jumped by Maria in *The Nine Lives of Alphonse*, and the monastic fealty of his pent-up love for Barbara now in the forefront of his consciousness with the new hope she may yet live, what on earth is he doing casually kissing Linn Wu-Sung, whom he has just met? Is this not wholly out of character? It is one thing to jump his lover Barbara before the rightness in the eyes of God, and it is quite another to indulge in casual dalliance on a plush tour around Hong Kong.

Sebastian's self-understanding as well as his prehistory have undergone some strange alterations. In *A Piece of the Moon Is Missing*, the book just prior to this one, we learned that "for the first time since he had put his clergy cloth aside, along with his sermon notes, and taken on the mantle of a churchman's James Bond, Sebastian felt doubt" (*Moon*, 25). Now we are told, "He was not a spy, nor was he trained in espionage—no James Bond in any dimension. He was simply a man of God who found hurt and pain and tried to ease it" (*Train*, 31). Perhaps only his hairdresser knows for sure.

But the biggest contradiction lies in "the memory of Ann, his wife, who had died in the car accident while he was still a pastor in Wisconsin. . . . But she was a face faded out by time" (*Train*, 29). Actually more than her face has been faded out by time; in *Code Name Sebastian* his wife's name was Carol (*Code*, 66, 67, 69, 222). Did Johnson actually write this book? Or are we dealing with a deutero-James Johnson? We note near the copyright there is an unusual note: "Edited and designed by Judith E. Markham" (*Train*, 2). One wonders just how much editing and designing she did.

Without question the new history of Sebastian as the heroic Tote, the ever-present help in time of need, clashes with the code of noninvolvement that set up the tensions in the first book. The new overt sensuality in his character aimed at someone other than Barbara Churchill, especially while he carries the newfound hope that she lives, strikes another false chord.

To Linn's puzzled observation—"I have known clergymen who were starchy, really colossal boors. . . . Nothing about you is boring"—Sebastian replies, "I'm just a bit different . . . not odd, mind you . . . just different. God hates stereotypes, you know that? So maybe He made me a bit out of the mold?" The text tells us: "She seemed satisfied with that" (*Train*, 53), but we are not. The whole point of the Negev experience was that Sebastian was every soft Christian who needs to be incarnated in this world to meet God truly. If we assent that God made Sebastian out of the mold, the lesson that "Christianity in action is his theme" (*Code*, back jacket cover) is irretrievably lost.

And if Sebastian is now somehow different, perhaps Sebastian's God will turn out to be different as well. And indeed now God, or his creator Johnson, or Ur-Johnsonus, or the editor, is giving him a break at last. Perhaps his God has let up on him because Sebastian has finally learned his lesson. Gone are his ornate prayers; he simply converses with God as a respectful friend or child: "'God,' he said, 'thank You . . . thank You she's still alive'" (*Train*, 79). God is no longer antiquated and obscured behind his "thees" and "thous." Sebastian also has a social conscience now. He is enraged at the way refugees are made pawns in political games.He still resists the utilitarian claim that sensitivity is outmoded in the Orient (*Train*, 91–92) or that "this place has no morality: nobody plays fair game. Everybody cheats everybody else. If you learn to play by the rules, you live—if you don't you go down" (*Train*, 189). Sebastian has learned his lesson: "Anyway, giving someone else a break is the biggest thing you can do with your life" (*Train*, 198). And so he is no longer obsessed with God, obsessed with guilt, obsessed with his own flagellation. Now he can quote from the Old Covenant as well as the new one, and the words he finds are words of comfort, not simply words of accusation: "'In the Book of Proverbs,' he said to Clyde, 'it says "when a man's ways please the Lord, He makes even his enemies to be at peace with him"'" (*Train*, 165). Perhaps this is the point of the change in Sebastian's character and the rewriting of his history. James L. Johnson has altered the emphasis in his theology between *A Piece of the Moon Is Missing* and *The Last Train to Canton*. In the intervening years, actually one year before *Last Train*, Johnson wrote a nonfiction book for Harvest House entitled *How to Enjoy Life and Not Feel Guilty*. In it he wrote:

> However, the Bible is not a book of rules. It lists behavioral principles mostly. The Bible does not persistently define morality in every given situation. It does provide a broad plain of ethics, values, and morality that a man can interpret and apply to himself in cooperation with the Spirit of God within him. God stayed away from listing specific rules in every case, perhaps because He knew that some of those rules would alter later with culture change. . . .
>
> When the Bible is taken only as a book of *rules* and not a book of *life*, a person can't help but feel guilt and anxiety constantly. (*Enjoy Life*, 15)

The old straight-by-the-Book Sebastian certainly felt anxiety and guilt demanding he pay some indefinable debt in the Negev, Cuba, East Berlin, the Arctic. His God demanded of him that he play by the rules, and he hardly enjoyed life. But just as that passionate breakthrough in the Arctic seemed to suggest a morality, right in God's eyes, that did not fit Sebastian's conventional behavioral rules, so perhaps Sebastian can now posit a God who is not so excessively demanding and sadistic in the requirements that are levied on followers. God's rescue program would not seem to alter so radically with a person's commitment but would continue as God, still with care, brings the committed through sanctification. In parallel all those outside the faith could hardly hate with the uniform vehemence of the many of the first four books. More true to experience is the ironic skepticism of Bobby Boyington, who both admires Sebastian and considers him naive. Sebastian seems more a bumbler who has precipitated much of his own agony and is salvaged periodically by his patient God. Perhaps those earlier people hated not his God but the whining Sebastian, and they sublimated their hostility into striking him theologically in what he valued. The offense, then, was to the Christian, not solely to the cross. By the time Sebastian has matured into *Trackless Seas,* both he and his God are met with respect. *Last Train* summarizes his ministry well:

> Yet, the mark of God was on him. He had plowed through those four bizarre experiences, missing death only by inches in each of them. He had to believe God was in it, that somehow he had left something behind in people's lives that they would not have received otherwise. He had blundered in and out of those places, running scared most of the time, unsure always as to why he was there. (*Train,* 31)

This passage mirrors reality as it pictures a minister stumbling along in the ministry, aided and salvaged by a caring God who suffers not only with other people but also with the minister himself.

If what I have surmised herein is correct, there would still be no need for the dexterous James Johnson to have altered his story so radically. Why could he not simply have allowed Sebastian to grow naturally through his experiences to the point where God no longer has to prune and purgate him so extremely and can show him a loving side? Is the truth actually that the God depicted in his previous books could never have softened up enough to lay off Sebastian?

But James Johnson did break God, Sebastian, and God in Sebastian's perspective out of the old limited mold in one last adventure, *Trackless Seas.* In that finale a scarred and desperate Sebastian finds final resolution on one last great ocean, ending by saving both a few victims individually and the world entirely from disaster, salvaging and finally cementing his relationship with Barbara Churchill, and being vindicated one last time in his reliance on God's existence, on God's immanent nature, on God's caring for the value of individual humans. Ultimately Sebastian has learned that God's mission is for believers to suffer along with other humans' suffering. Resolutely acting upon his understanding of the nature of God as the Suffering Servant, he becomes in his own incarnational representation of God's great ministry a small but similarly present aid to those who suffer.

Post-Mortem

The Ministerial Mystery/Mysterium

> *And as she was being led away to be destroyed, behold! an angel of the Lord arrived. And the angel, just as ordered, gave a spirit of discernment to a youth, Daniel. And Daniel, shouldering aside the crowd, stationed himself in the middle of them and said, "Are you such fools, sons of Israel? Without questioning or finding out plainly, you sentence to death a daughter of Israel? Now separate them a distance from one another for me so that I may cross-examine them."*
>
> *Susannah,* according to the Septuagint, 44–51

An act of heaven, the great mysterium suddenly opens to someone in a crowd. A simple bystander instantly filled with God's perspicacity cries out against injustice. Inexorably, the young Daniel of *Susannah,* the Rabbi Daniel of *Bel and the Dragon,* small and insignificant, bumbling Father Brown, young and callow Vicar Westerham, elfish and amorphic Sister Ursula, and the other instruments of God's justice, move with the guidance of grace to truth, accusation, indictment, justice, mercy. When the revelation of heaven comes, the light of God's truth illumines all the dark and hidden secrets of humanity. But what was it like a moment before, when the youth Daniel stood helpless and sorrowful, when the people struggled to discern the murky truth in all the waning flicker of human honesty? When their appointed judges swore they testified truth and yet the wailing testimony of Susannah's children, her family, her friends and servants declared her blameless purity? How must the people have struggled and strained and longed for insight, for that glimpse of certain truth? The moment before, this time of uncertainty, confusion, and bafflement—this is the moment of the mystery. A crime is alleged. A suspect is apprehended. The people sit in judgment. But who lies? Which one is telling the truth? What does this fact mean? What does that one mean? Are these clues or irrelevant data? The responsibility for a future and often a life is in the hands of the people in every case of an accused Susannah. What really happened? Who is innocent? Who is guilty? What is the truth? Down which course of inquiry does truth and justice lie? These are the questions the mystery asks.

As any detective, whether a member of the professional police or an amateur sleuth, discovers, the quest to solve a mystery leads deeper and deeper into the identity and nature of truth, good, evil, justice, mercy. The responsibility to attain justice leads deeper and deeper to the root cause of justice, the great source of all definitions, the great well of discernment, the seat of the absolute, the great mysterium that flows in dark voluminous billows from the heart of God. Humans search through the murky confusion of the mystery. God reveals the deep mysterium. Herein lies the paradox. Humans must search, but God must reveal. The paradox of human action and God's sovereignty is central to theology. The human quest is through mystery to solution. God's solution is the revelation of the mysterium. The clerical sleuth is the human touched by the divine who stands in the breach between quest and revelation, the human detective/the divine emissary, questing through the mystery while enlightened by the mysterium. All other quests reflect this one. The search for any truth is ultimately a search for God's truth, since all true perspective points to God and comes from God, if God is indeed the repository and well-spring of truth (justice) and loving kindness (mercy), as God declares in Exodus 34:6.

The mystery and mysterium, then, are two ways of looking at the same profoundly central issue, the human dilemma as touched by the divine. In the mystery a crime is committed, evil has intruded in a world of innocence. Separating the innocent from the evil becomes the task of the good. "Why do you call me good?" Jesus asked in Mark 10:18. Only God is good. God is good and all goodness comes from God. The judiciary conduit of justice, then, when justice is truly sought, is the instrument of God. But, of course, true justice sears all, culprit and instrument as well. Increasingly in the contemporary mystery, evil is recognized as present in all, detective as well as culprit, even while those who have given themselves over to evil in action are apprehended for it and punished. For that reason, among others, the cleric is also the instrument of God's mercy, the hand of the Christ who came not as judgment but as bail, as settlement of fine, the biblical symbol of the ransom for many. "I am not a policeman," one of the newest born clerical sleuths at this time of writing, Blackie Ryan, affirms. No, the cleric is not a policeman, though Father Bredder is called a celestial one. Instead, the cleric stands as the servant of the savior, the bearer of good tidings, the bringer of reconciliation. The cleric is part of God's viaduct of mercy, flowing, as Shakespeare's Portia assured Shylock in *The Merchant of Venice* (4.1.185), like the gentle rain from heaven. But it is a rain of blood. Mercy is bought through murder: the slaughter of the sacrificial lamb, the murder of the messiah, the slaying of the savior.

What the clerical sleuth welds together is the instrument of justice with the instrument of mercy. In the theologically paradoxical situation of humans searching/God revealing comes an equally paradoxical figure, the instrument of justice and the instrument of mercy fused, the clerical sleuth. The mystery and the mysterium meet in that figure. As a human the clerical detective searches, sifting through evidence, hunting down the traces, sorting out the truth from the lies, unmasking the culprit, vindicating the innocent. As an emissary of God the detecting cleric brings God's message of mercy with God's message of justice, bearing the captive before God's bar and acting in the savior's image to bring repentance and reconciliation. The nature and intention of the human and divine meet actively in the ministerial sleuth as they met ontologically in the figure of Jesus the Christ. The clerical sleuth again is led to the discovery of God's mysterium while questing for the resolution of the human mystery.

So, then, the mystery is the human search through evil, murder, and theft for good, justice, redemption, restoration. The mysterium is God's revelation of secret good in this fallen world. The clerical sleuth, like the mediator Christ, stands in the gap between the questing mystery and the revealing mysterium, a detecting human filled with God's perspicacity. The clerical sleuth would appear at first view, then, to be the great Christ type in literature. As for mirroring the other attributes of the Christ, the various clerical sleuths do bring mercy and triumph over the powers of darkness. Some demonstrate to fellow characters proper conduct and attitudes toward God's laws governing humans. None of them, however, practices vicarious atonement, nor do they in themselves satisfy God's demand for justice. Rather, they point out the culprit and either turn the culprit over to the police, directly over to God, or over to both. Once in a while, as in McInerny's *Rest in Pieces,* they have to let the culprit go. They do not, however, suffer the culprit's just punishment in the culprit's place.

In fact, as instruments of God's mercy as well as justice, they often reveal a grim interpretation of what mercy is. Justice in the clerical crime novel is primarily retributive rather than distributive. The mercy often welded to it is equally fierce. Perhaps Father Brown and Brother Cadfael may let murderers go with penances of service, but the bulk of the clerical sleuths and particularly all seven of the nuns, Reverend Randollph, Vicar Westerham, and Fathers Buell and Septimus have no compunction about turning perpetrators over to the police. Sister Simon, in fact, has no compunction about shooting them herself. To a shocked listener, Sister Mary Teresa details the severe nature of her justice and mercy:

> "You and I—society—do not have the power to forgive a murder. God does that. And the death penalty does not interfere with God's mercy. It may be an instrument of it" (Quill, *Above,* 127)

If the clerical sleuth is to be seen as a Christ type, then the selection of style would have to be made between prophet, priest, and ruler. It would include suffering servant only in the sense that a sleuth will visit the culprit in jail after the apprehension and will minister to the victims. But no clerical sleuth sits permanently in jail in place of the culprit. That unique action is reserved for the true Christ. Still, just as Oscar James Campbell has pointed out that "in many of the cycles of mystery plays there is a kind of Last Judgment play in which Justice and Mercy . . . debate for the soul of mankind . . . as often in the miracle plays, mercy triumphs" (Campbell, 265), so in the modern mystery, and very often in the clerical crime novel, mercy, even if of a grim variety, triumphs.

Humans need justice and mercy, and they look to the clergy to help provide it. G. K. Chesterton reportedly took some children to see Andrew Lang's pasteurized version of a fairy tale in which the ending had been altered so that an evil cat was reprimanded and punished rather than slain. As they left the theater, the children were outraged at this miscarriage of justice. Chesterton noted that children are innocent and naturally want justice, while adults are not and therefore prefer mercy. The need for both justice and mercy, however, as Chesterton's own mysteries reveal, is a basic human need that Karl Menninger, in *Whatever Became of Sin?*, observes must be satisfied. The mystery genre vicariously serves that dual need.

The Questions in the Mystery

In what way does the mystery vicariously serve the human need for justice and mercy, for balance in the universe? The secular mystery asks what is the nature of good and evil? How can evil be exposed and eradicated? How successful can that enterprise be? Whether recognized or not, the existence of God is the lodestar of the mystery genre. C. S. Lewis has pointed out in his collection of broadcast talks, *Mere Christianity*, that whenever people ask questions such as those above, or even protest, "You can't do that to me," they are appealing to an absolute standard in the universe. The reply "why not?" is answered by the forging of local, state, national, and international laws. Thus, not only is the secular quest through mystery a reflection of the greater sacred quest for the mysterium, but the absolute to which those laws appeal is also the gold standard behind the currency of justice that is the medium of exchange among the sleuth, the police, the judge and jury, and usually the culprit as well. If the mystery, like the judicial system it depicts, deals with central, universal human questions of right and wrong, then, as in the case of many of the laws of various cultures and of agreed-upon international laws, there will be common denominators that can be found throughout the genre, reducing and unifying the various quests represented. There are at least three central ones in the clerical crime novel.

The first common denominator is that things are not what they seem. If the clerical crime novel—as well as the saintly sidekick, clerical criminal and general clerical participant novels—repeat one phrase endlessly and explicitly, it is that things are rarely what they appear on the surface to be.

Related to this is the nearly universal factor that the clerics themselves are regularly misjudged. Clerics are not what they appear to be. What are they? The ministerial mystery lectures over and over again that clerics are humans, tempted in every way that others are, and many times not without sin. That this very human cleric can begin to detect and with God-given perspicacity solve crimes astounds the unsuspecting citizen, who has viewed the cleric as off in a saintly cloud, a complete huckster and reprobate, a subhuman hypocrite in a sanctimonious bubble, or anything but a complete human. And when that cleric's full humanity is realized, the secular witness is never prepared for that flash of God's perspicacity that illumines the Daniel in the crowd.

Third, murder is a sin against God. The ecclesiastical mystery teaches that murder offends not only society but also the Giver of life and causes God's agent, the cleric, to take appropriate action.

Perhaps a fourth common denominator could be added. Virtually all clerical sleuths seem obsessed with combatting pride in themselves. Fathers Brown and Bredder, the Reverends Randollph and Sebastian, and Sister Ursula particularly suffer from this disease, being all but incapacitated at times by severe attacks of mental self-flagellation.

Further, none of the detectives seems ashamed of vocation or calling. Those who do, like Dorothy Salisbury Davis' Father Joseph McMahon of *Where the Dark Streets Go,* or Christopher Leach's Lucius Rumsey of *Blood Games,* have one foot well out of the vocation. Both of these saintly sidekicks, incidentally, leave their callings at the end of their novels. Ray Sebastian may have a foot out of his pastorate, or both feet out actually, but not out of his faith. He merely needs to discover what that faith authentically is. The clerical sleuths are as firm in their beliefs as the seculars they encounter are confused in theirs. When fiction reduces to life and death, the Rumseys and McMahons are sent packing and the Ursulas and Sister Johns and Dowlings rise to the occasion. The bulk of clerical sleuths take the exact opposite position of Herman Hesse's Gustav in *Steppenwolf:* "I'm a professor of theology if you want to know. But, the Lord be praised, there's no occasion for theology now, my boy. It's war. Come on!" (Hesse, 205). When it is war, for the clerical sleuth it is precisely the occasion for theology.

Theologizing, of course, frees the clerical sleuth from being bogged down in the police routine which, as Mary Teresa points out, dulls the official mind. The police, of course, notice this freedom, sometimes with mild resentment. As Lieutenant Minardi chides Father Bredder:

"Ah well, you amateur detectives," said the lieutenant. "You have an easy time of it. You don't have to keep tabs on anybody. Every case is nice and fresh and new. New crimes, new set of characters. Nothing to clutter your mind up with out of the past. Nothing unsolved. But we in the police department—we live with unfinished business all the time. . . ." (Holton, *Flowers*, 16)

In this light we might conclude that if the mystery genre is, indeed, a secularization of the great religious quest into the mysterium, the secrets of God, then an appropriate bridge between these two poles, the bloodline between parent and child, may well be found in the ordained investigator, the policing preacher, the "clergy cop." So far there have not been any police who are simultaneously preachers, but there have been near models of this end point. Both Sister Ursula and Soeur Angèle are daughters of police officers, as was Sister Simon. Ursula had intended a career in law enforcement. Septimus had had a career as a chief investigator before turning cleric. In his figure, perhaps, the fusion is most intensely reproduced, the welding of the police procedural and the clerical crime novel. But the form is not institutionalized. Septimus uses the machinery of Scotland Yard as a favor. Methodologically, the best of Marric's, Wambaugh's, and McBain's police studies focus on the machinelike scientific/forensic quest fleshed out in the humanity of the investigators in a way no ministerial mystery seems interested in doing. Against these models all the clerical sleuths seem to be hunting for Father Bredder's "spiritual fingerprints." The focus in the final analysis is essentially theological. This is what interests the writers and by inference the readers who wolf down these theological thrillers. Does this all suggest that people read mysteries to expose and deal with their own struggles with right and wrong? Is the reading of clerical crime novels, like church attendance and confession, a kind of purgative action? Do people put themselves in the place of the criminal who is caught and punished as well as in the place of the detective who takes the right actions, brings about the moral resolutions and achieves the resultant happy ending? Such could well be the appeal.

Common Themes in the Clerical Crime Novel

Within the literature there is both direct and indirect evidence of an obvious fraternity of clerical crime authors. The influence of Chesterton's Father Brown is pervasive throughout the genre. Verbal tributes are made in William Kienzle's books to Ralph McInerny's. Leonard Holton takes careful pains to contrast his cleric with Father Brown, revealing a knowledge of Father Brown's character and ministry, his modus operandi. Carol Anne O'Marie, of course, pays overt tribute to a plethora of crime writers, and nearly all clerical crime series of any length eventually join her in overt tribute to Father Brown. In addition, outside the genre, James Johnson's Sebastian regularly compares himself with James Bond.

Covertly, we discover that various threads of plots run through the sub-genre, whether they are the product of conscious design or not. For example, G. K. Chesterton, in "The Wrong Shape," establishes an Indian mystic whose sinister powers are suspected to be the cause of death. They are not. He is a fraud. H. H. Holmes adopts and reworks Chesterton's ideas for *Nine Times Nine* to show the incompatibility of eastern religion and Catholicism. His fake avatar claims to kill by astral projection but is also innocent of the crime. Dorothy Gilman picks up Holmes' "Sister Ursula" as a disguise for an escaped thug and redeems the image of the yellow-robed guru, revealing in contrast a compatibility of Catholicism with eastern religion, a new syncretism. But Andrew M. Greeley in *Happy Are the Meek* redivorces the robed fake mystic with his "Nine Times Nine" theology of hate from anything that smacks of healthy Catholicism or true religion. Again the guru claims a killing by astral projection. Again he lies.

Another thread that runs consistently through the Roman Catholic clerical crime novel is a persistent hostility directed at Reformed/Calvinist/Puritan faith. Chesterton's accusation that the Reformed, though good, are not Christian yields Calvinist villain after villain as recently as Gilman's 1975 outing. Relief comes only in the most contemporary additions to the Roman Catholic corpus.

Theologically, too, we have noted the peculiarity that amiability seems paralleled to theological denomination and content. And we noted that of all the denominational entries, the Anglican/Episcopalian clerical sleuths are the least overtly theological. While detecting vicars abound, there is precious little overt theology in their series. The extent of the drought may be seen in Septimus, who seems to be exactly what he is—a retired copper who has taken orders. His clerical investigations simply replace his secular ones, religious crimes replacing secular crimes. That he curbs his oaths when hitting his thumb seems his lone concession to his calling. What makes him a cleric? What makes Simon Bede a cleric with his absence of theology and his swinging lifestyle? Apparently, Bede himself is not certain, for after his first outing he seeks early retirement from his vocation. Perhaps the right hand of the archbishop of Canterbury has escaped defrocking by a thumbnail's breadth. But to recognize that Anglican/Episcopalian theology is not a consistent monolith of scholastic thought but a mode of praxis is to understand not only the theological silence of the Anglican sleuths but also the nature of the contemporary interpretation of Anglican piety. As Anglican priest/professor Father Dean Borgman explains, worldwide Anglicanism is filled with acceptable options that are not necessarily consistent with one another, and Anglicans resist systematizing in favor of a life of faith fleshed out in good works. The action of the cleric is the statement of theology. For all the theological words in his series, this is the position toward which Ray Sebastian gropes, albeit without the conscious lack of consistency.

Another major plot thread that runs through these series is the attempted use of a holy book or holy relic for purposes of manipulation, for example to short-circuit purgatory by giving a gift of great piety. The saintly sidekick novel *The Issue of the Bishop's Blood* attempts this ploy in regards to a living stigmata saint. The unholy Bible of Randollph's 1983 outing of the same name is the reason for murder—in a similar "holy cause," one dictated by personal pride. And in an attempt to lure Sebastian into a suicide mission to East Germany, a reputed original autograph of the Pentateuch is dangled before him.

In many of the longer, multivolume series there seems to be an overriding structural peculiarity, a kind of safety valve incorporated to drain off theological excesses. Thus, in these larger series one book seems to stand aside from the others and define itself against the remainder, qualifying the points the rest of the books make. In the Rabbi Small series, for example, *Wednesday the Rabbi Got Wet* serves this function. In Father Dowling's it is *Thicker than Water*. In Ray Sebastian's it would be *Last Train from Canton*. Somehow these prolonged arguments eventually require a safety valve, as if the author has suddenly become conscious of the contrived nature of the argument and feels the need to create a distance between inevitable conclusions and scholarly detachment. Perhaps the arguments have simply grown old and are ceasing to work as effectively as they did when the series first made its bold declarations. Perhaps this is a form of subtle self-destruction, a theological counterpart to Conan Doyle heaving Holmes off a cliff, but I think it is more likely to be a form of self-control, preventing the argument from becoming a didactic *cul de sac* when the world and the surprising nature of God keep revealing new evidence that bursts out of neat categories. Proof of this contention is the fact that these series in effect do not destruct but keep going on, sometimes returning to previous arguments, sometimes, as in the case of Holton's Father Bredder, staying with the modifications.

Such common threads and attributes should not delude critics into supposing that these clerical crime novels are simply clonic replicas of each other stamped out on indistinguishable word processors. Witness the care of Umberto Eco's crafting. His achievement, completed in only three years, absorbed an enormous amount of painstaking work. In the first year of his writing he explored long registers of books that would be found in a medieval library, wrote complete biographies for his fictional monks, some of whom do not appear in the book at all but would be in the monastery, conducted extensive architectural investigations, studied floorplans of abbeys. As he notes:

> The film director Marco Ferreri once said to me that my dialogue is like a movie's because it lasts exactly the right length of time. It had to. When two of my characters spoke while walking

from the refectory to the cloister, I wrote with the plan before my eyes; and when they reached their destination, they stopped talking. (Eco, *Postscript,* 25)

Duplicated in his style is the slow and measured pace of abbey life. The "long didactic passages" of the first one hundred pages serve for Eco as a kind of "penance" or "initiation" for the reader (Eco, *Postscript,* 41). This is superior crafting, indeed, and the unifying of form and content.

Qualities of the Clerical Sleuth

In sweeping down the aisles of the presbytery of clerical sleuths, we might wonder what if any similarities emerge when we attempt to form a composite picture of what authors have valued in their fictional clerics. In many other novels clerics are caricatured, pictured as thin, unworldly, ascetic anomalies, marooned on the bar of some half-sunken wreck of gothic architecture like a piece of ecclesiastical flotsam. Worse yet, the cleric can be huckster, a smooth-talking Elmer Gantry with a roving eye and a set of sticky fingers that draw banknotes like a paper magnet. Or often these days we find a zealous do-gooder, a bit out of phase with the lingo of the world, but fired up with an earnestness that doubtless sublimates a repressed libido. The clerical crime novel, however, refreshingly presents a healthy cleric as heroine/hero, the chief protagonist who determines the action. Thus, rather than presenting us a picture of someone's ill-researched hearsay of what ministers are like or, worse yet, someone's fleshed out antipathy to a strict upbringing, authors in this subgenre strive to create attractive, recognizably human clerics.

Further, the clerical crime novel, unlike many churches' pulpit committees, does not discriminate on the basis of age. While young clerics are represented by Whitechurch's Westerham, Sister Ursula, one of the archdeacons, Soeur Angèle, Sister Simon, Rabbi Small, and Sister Hyacinthe, older clerics include the other of Alington's archdeacons, Martin Buell, Septimus, Simon Bede, Roger Dowling, Brother Cadfael, Father Koesler, Sister Mary Teresa, and Sister Mary Helen. Marys Teresa and Helen, like Casey's Father Haggerty, are in their seventies. The rest are in middle age. Though Bredder begins at forty, he ages into his late fifties during the series, moving across the terrain of the middle years. Isabelle Holland's Claire Aldington, while in her thirties, has two children. Rabbi Small begins in his twenties but ages to his forties in his latest books. The fifties seem a popular age for clerical sleuths, and many of them spend their best detecting years in what for a scholar is normally considered the integrative height of the creating and synthesizing scholarly powers.

Whether the sleuths are chiefly urban or suburban is difficult to tell since many of them move around incessantly. Father Brown served, of course, every conceivable locale: urban, suburban, rural. Following in his model, Soeur

Angèle wandered from cities to small towns to missionary work abroad. Head's two missionaries ranged around Africa and ended in Paris, while Eco's Brother William roamed apparently from enigma to enigma. Even Alington's archdeacons relocate to be near one another. On the other hand, Westerham has a landed country vicarage, Buell, a small town, while Sister Simon is attached to a large hospital, and Bredder, Randollph, Sister Mary Teresa, Claire Aldington, and Blackie Ryan are all urban-based. Father Koesler may as well have saved the move to a nearby locale for his attraction is to the center city. Rabbi Small's home is a small, tight New England town, a sore trial for him, while Roger Dowling finds new life in backwash Fox River, his hermitage cum awakening new world. The monks are abbey-bound, so Cadfael, Brother Barnabas, and eventually Sister Ursula become tied to a church location (though Cadfael likes to roam abroad). Sisters John and Hyacinthe seem to recreate their convent wherever they go, while Septimus has such a responsibility in his large ancient stone monument of a church that sheer maintenance keeps his action located. Ray Sebastian's parish is the world at large, while Simon Bede now seems in and of the world.

As far as their vocations, however, we have already noted that, outside of Bede's retirement, they are secure in their callings, if in Sebastian's case the exact details are a little difficult to articulate to others. No wonder we see no bishop in the Father Brown series. Without a sense of humor like Randollph's Freddie and Ryan's Sean Cronin or a secret admiration for the powers of detection like Bredder's bishop, he would long since be sanitarium fodder trying to keep his mercurial charge in line. Those who do question their vocations, we have noted, are soon gone.

As far as shared beliefs, with the possible exception of Blackie Ryan, they are all agreed, even Randollph, upon the reality of original sin and the need for punishment—though off the record of his shamelessly forgiving God, Ryan's Irish temper often leads to a desire to slug some particularly loathsome human predator. All of the clerical sleuths believe in God (with the possible exception at times of Rabbi Small), though doubtless they would disagree upon who exactly God is. None of them is Calvinist, though Cadfael certainly comes close to this position, as do Bredder and a surprising number of the Roman Catholic sleuths. Randollph's opinions of others and their just desserts are enough to make even some hyper-Calvinists blanch, while Ray Sebastian in his earlier preenlightened days would toe a hard line against the chronically wicked. Father Brown, despite his protests, would understand. Secure in God's goodness and the sureness of God's justice, the clerical sleuths, though annoyed at times by ambiguity in their reasoning, can live with the confusion that makes some of their constabulary counterparts howl with frustration. As Father Bredder neatly explains in *Flowers by Request:*

"No," said the priest. "I am more confused than ever." He smiled. "That's good though," he added. "It means that we're getting somewhere. The more confusing things become, the closer we are to a solution. Confusion is only the state of getting rid of untruths so as to prepare oneself for the recognition and acceptance of the truth. It is always so. Even in finding God we are confused first."

Pacey gave him a nervous look. He was afraid he was in for a sermon, and the prospect made him uneasy, for he liked to avoid thinking of anything more than driving his hack and saving his feet. But Father Bredder said nothing further and they continued the journey back to town in silence. (Holton, *Flowers*, 99)

As we see by Father Bredder's example, clerical sleuths, unlike many of their authentic counterparts, know when to shut up. Silence, particularly in counseling the bereaved, is a regular part of the ministries of Father Buell, Randollph's Bishop Freddie, Blackie Ryan, the later Ray Sebastian, Bede, when he ministers, Fathers Dowling, Koesler, and of course, Father Brown. They have learned the lesson of Simon, the son of Rabban Gamaliel, that many words bring about sin. All these clerical sleuths also seem to pray, though some practice it and rely upon it to a greater degree than others. This practice is well suited for the mystery, for St. Francis of Sales in his monumental *The Love of God* has observed: "Prayer is called mystical, because of the hidden nature of the conversation" (Francis, *Love,* 219). Thus, prayer engages the mystical experience to explore and explain the mystery experience. St. Francis, too, has observed that the same qualities that produce holiness produce premeditated crime, another juxtaposition of the human dilemma with the divine call. As he has observed about meditation, "All it means is thinking intently and repeatedly about something in such a way as to give rise to good or bad emotions. . . . Meditation, therefore, has a good purpose or an evil purpose" (Francis, *Love,* 221). While the criminal plots the crime, the cleric mulls the solution, one in communion with evil, the other in communion with God. Is the mystery, then, Manichaen—a matching of two powerful forces against each other for the soul of the universe? No, because, as we have pointed out, good is the more powerful and the ultimate winner. According to the *Christianity Today* editor, evangelical theologian J. I. Packer, who is not afraid to be practical or clear while systematizing his theology, the mystery is Judeo-Christian:

Also, these are stories of a kind that would never have existed without the Christian gospel. Culturally, they are Christian fairy tales, with savior heroes and plots that end in what Tolkien called a *eucatastrophe*—whereby things come right after seeming to go irrevocably wrong. . . . The gospel of Christ is the archetype of all such stories. Paganism unleavened by Christianity, on the other hand, was and always will be pessimistic at heart. (Packer, "'Tecs," 12)

This is not to say that all other faiths could not or would not have detectives or counterparts of clerical detectives. One can find fictional detectives who are at least influenced by eastern religion from the Bombay police force to Japan and other points east, but, perhaps with their understandings of God, sin, and justice, they would not exactly resemble the Judeo-Christian clerical sleuths.

These, of course, as we have mentioned, are often obsessed with a characteristic sense of pride. As Father Bredder discovers, in *The Secret of the Doubting Saint,* "how false had been this little area of hidden pride within him" (Holton, *Saint,* 33), so do they all seem that to discover and weep over their hidden pride—the nearly immobilized Sister Ursula, Ray Sebastian, Father Brown, and, of course, Reverend Randollph, who also is acute at unearthing pride in others and knowing what to do about it. As for pugnaciousness in rooting out pride and often in rooting out criminals, we have seen that the Roman Catholic sisters are certainly a ferocious lot. Sister Mary Teresa packs her luger, Sister Simon can use it. Sisters John and Hyacinthe prefer the blunt instrument and long kitchen knife, while Randollph is not averse to breaking a few heads with his bare hands when the situation calls for action. Martin Buell could probably get physical. Septimus could definitely get physical, while Father Bredder and Ray Sebastian will use physical force as nonviolently as possible. Septimus, Cadfael, and Bredder have all seen combat action, and the experience has figured in all of their callings. Whether fighting the Saracens or the Japanese in another century, each has desired a better way to deal with people than through violence. Randollph has engaged in the war games of professional football, while Koesler, a fair amateur, has enjoyed watching them.

Still, most of the clerical sleuths would obviously prefer love, even if regularly sublimated, than war. Blackie Ryan and the later Father Koesler are perhaps the most pathetic in their frustrated libidos. Septimus nurtures his hopeless, sublimated love for the young Rosemary Horton, channeling his passion into fatherly affection. Sebastian is a widower who actively loves Barbara Churchill and, in *Last Train to Canton,* spreads his affection a bit loosely to others as well. Randollph has honorably married Samantha Stack, while Mary Finney, Brother Cadfael (before he was a brother), and Simon Bede (after) have all had affairs. Blackie Ryan seems to be one of the few Greeley clerics to escape sexual liberation, while Vicar Westerham, Alington's younger archdeacon and apparently Claire Aldington (?) get the spouse of their dreams. Rabbi Small, of course, has a normal home life—an anomaly in the genre—and the rest of the celibates apparently manage the best they can.

Innocence is, perhaps, the other side of that coin, and the balance between innocence and experience has characterized the genre ever since Father Brown appeared to display the one while actually possessing the other. Some clerics keep up this facade of innocence, while others authentically are innocent. Some arrive already ripe with experience, and still others achieve their experience as their series unfolds. So the young of our earlier list tend to be innocent and, depending on how many books they are afforded, they grow in wisdom and experience. Some of the young, like Westerham, however, arrive already equipped with powers that astound. But innocence is not merely the province of the young. The monastic—the Allisons' Brother Barnabas, Gilman's two sisters, or Sister Mary Helen (who is not, however, monastic)—are chiefly innocent as well. The rest tend to be experienced, some like Father Dowling nearly the victims of their experience. While some of these may be, like Father Brown, regularly misjudged, some, like Brother Cadfael, are obviously at first glance shrewd adversaries who need to be regarded carefully.

All of these sleuths are compassionate—though Randollph sometimes a bit thinly. All of them, if Buell gruffly, can be kind. All of them are forgiving. Most of them are nonjudgmental, though Randollph, again, has a severe eye, and no one puts anything over on Roger Dowling or Rabbi Small. Claire Aldington can get nasty, Buell can get gruff and cutting, Mary Teresa can get imperious, and Rabbi Small can get sharp, but they all can be called to accountability, and even Bede, whose morals seem the most slippery, has basically learned to tolerate others' foibles, in his case a bit too well. Many are robust, but all, including the frailest—Sister Mary Helen or the saintly sidekick Father Haggerty—have a massive inner strength. All have suffered—Randollph at least internally—and many suffer regularly in their series. Ray Sebastian looks like a hockey veteran after a brawl. And out of their own suffering comes understanding. They all have time for people.

They are in the last analysis struggling humans who possess one or more attractive virtues, along with a minor vice or two, as well. Paradoxically, they are more innocent and otherworldly than the rest of us humans while managing to be just as human in their failings and, as a result, endlessly forgiving. They are the straight, strong human conduit for a God who forgives. And these qualities are what is essentially attractive about the clerical sleuths.

These sleuths are also always conveniently available. Chesterton, as we noted in our study of Father Brown, chuckles in his *Autobiography* about what he calls the "flaw" of Father Brown, always seeming to be hanging around a house where a murder was about to be done (Chesterton, *Autobiography*, 339–40). This is pushing the old saw "where a priest is is death" a bit far. Although in reality most amateurs would not dream of interfering in police work and few clergy would even have the time to, a cleric makes a fine fictional detective because ministers are so often present when grieving people suffer from evil. Further, a pastor is used to taking charge. As Philip Turner, himself an Anglican priest, records of Septimus, "The habit of taking charge, of telling stricken people what to do, was so ingrained that it never occurred to him that he was acting in an authoritarian fashion" (Chance, *Stone*, 130). With all these attractive characteristics, God's sidekick looks pretty exciting and preaches a comforting gospel of justice and mercy that reveals a God anyone would like to know.

Qualities Missing in the Clerical Sleuths

Despite the rich diversity in clerical detectives, and in the face of the even richer diversity in the authentic Judeo-Christian tradition, there are wide gaps in the clerical sleuths' ranks. There are no minority ministerial sleuths. The closest entry we have is Ramon Toussaint, the syncretistic, deadly deacon of the Koesler series. Randollph stomped out the closest aspirant to being a black protestant cleric in *Fall from Grace*. There are no excons. The short-lived televised Father Noah "Hardstep" Rivers did not last long enough to solve mysteries. There are no tent-making cops who are clerics. In fact, all the clerics get by without tent-making jobs. Sebastian apparently lives on air or what is left of his previous bankroll.

Economically, nearly all the clerical sleuths come from white middle-class backgrounds and families. The exceptions are the youth Daniel, whose background is unclear in *Susannah*, Father Brown, whose background is solid Essex rustic farming stock, Brother Barnabas, whose family are commoners, and the saintly sidekick Father Joseph McMahon, who identifies his family as working class. Otherwise, we have the solid blue-collar professional children of police officers, Sister Ursula and Sister Simon, as well as the white-collar children of a small-town district attorney in Claire Aldington, or of a professor in Ray Sebastian. Father Bredder is solid American farming stock, which probably means a conservative middle-class upbringing. Cadfael might appear a serf, but his background romance with Richildas suggests his family was part of the infant middle class. Soeur Angèle's cousin is a noble, and her medical education suggests a background of wealth and influence. Alington's archdeacons wield power as if they were born to it, and Westerham is comfortable with his servants. Koesler's family background is conservative Catholic, perhaps rising from working class to middle class. No one appears to be the scarred survivor of a broken home. That is left to the more divergent sidekicks like the obviously poor Lucius Rumsey of *Blood Games*. Even Randollph's background appears middle class, his wealth coming from his football earnings. Thus, economically all the authentic clerical sleuths appear to be from the upper working class through the middle class to the upper middle class, with a possible borderline case in Soeur Angèle. Ethnically there are no Oriental, Indian, Native American, Black, Eskimo, or Latin clerical detectives. The Rabbi, of course, is Jewish.

In regard to prior occupations, we have ex-doctor Soeur Angèle, ex-soldier Cadfael, ex-football player Randollph, as well as ex-police officer Septimus and would-be police officer Ursula. These last, as we have noted, come closest to engaging professionally in both forms of law enforcement, celestial and earthly. A close model in real life is Father Martin Bell, author of such collections of creative writing as Seabury Press' *The Way of the Wolf*. The Reverend Bell is not only an Episcopal priest who has served parishes in Michigan and Indiana and a chaplaincy to the University of Michigan in Ann Arbor, but also a senior partner in the Wittlinger Agency, a firm of private detectives who specialize in criminal defense investigations and in locating missing persons.

Writers interested in developing the genre might give us, for example, a black cleric, a Latin cleric, a cleric tent-making as police officer or prison guard, or an ex-convict cleric, who would provide an obvious target for the formularistic initial suspicions of the police.

As the limitations of these protagonists reveal, the clerical crime novel is really a conservative exercise in reaffirming values. In that sense the genre is hardly stirring up the Church or the marketplace with a radical redefinition of the figure of the pastor. Instead, outside of Leach's quasimystery, it reasserts that no matter what evil rages, the traditionally strong cleric will step in and calm the storm. No wonder all the characters they meet are confused by Blackie Ryan's feminism and Sean Cronin's anti-punitiveness. The rest of their packaging—white, middle to upper class, powerful, authoritative, humble (except Randollph)—looks the same as that of their peers. So the restoration of order is a divine task entrusted to those society has come to trust. As in Iris Murdoch's *The Time of the Angels,* agnostic society wants to know that, even if ignored, neglected, normally shunted aside, the Church is still there like an almost outgrown parent to fix things if they get out of hand. The effect of the entire subgenre is to assure the fallen-away world that someone is there if needed, a security sufficient to let it sleep at night. In that sense what is missing tells us what is not wanted. What is included tells us what is wanted. Clerical candidates who fall outside the white middle class are not included. Further, truly ordained women are a scarce commodity. Reverend Natalie Fisk has just appeared as a seminary pastor-in-training at the end of the Randollph corpus while Claire Aldington struggles as a neurotic specialized minister, a pastoral counselor who is low down in the echelons of power in her parish's organization. While her colleagues are called "Father," she is always carefully addressed as "Reverend." There is apparently not even a familial counterpart for her title that would duplicate the kind of authority the term "Father" invokes. In this sense, the clerical crime novel, two-thirds of whose writers are lay people and one-third religious professionals, might be of interest to churches as one gauge of the current state of attitudes within and without the churches. It certainly reveals the need for consciousness-raising if people's image of the ideal cleric is ever truly to represent the wide variety of authentic leaders in international Christendom.

But Why a Murder?

The subgenre may be immensely valuable to the Church as an indicator of people's pictures of clerics, and to theologians as a secularization of the great

sacred mysterium in the mystery, as a theological literature which is not dull
and pedantic but alive, exciting, and marketable. But why does it have to be so
gruesome in subject matter? Why a murder for its mystery? As Father Bredder
has noted in *Flowers by Request,* "People gather around accidents. They flee
murder. . . . Murder is the oldest of man's crimes. It is horror, plain horror, that
makes men flee it" (Holton, *Flowers,* 21).

Mystery writers have argued that only wrongful death has the gravity to
carry a novel along, that a theft is not weighty enough to sustain reader interest
through some two or three hundred pages of a novel. While this may be true,
such an answer simply begs the question. Why is a theft normally not sufficient
to carry a novel through its many pages? Murder brings the topic to the final
basic level of life-and-death significance. The mysterium, the sacred secret of
God revealed, and the mystery, the quest of humans to understand, are, in the
final analysis, of life-and-death significance to us all. Murder serves in the same
way as do themes of terminal illnesses, war, grave accidents, or death-defying
struggle against the elements, in all of which few survive to tell the tale or make
sense of the experience. They all bring matters to a basic level. Murder adds to
this the dimension of morality. Whereas these other situations (with the exception of war) fit under the category of catastrophe, murder fits under tragedy.
Usually the tragedy is double-pronged. Investigations in the fictional morality
plays called the modern murder mystery inevitably reveal not only the moral
flaw in the murderer, but many compellingly "sound" motives for doing in the
victim, and not only the harm done to society resulting from this action, but
often also the benefit.

In addition, contemporary North American society, particularly in its literature, may have become so morally confused that many other actions formerly
considered crimes are seen as excusable. The proverbial moral "shades of gray"
have so obscured contemporary vision that writers stumble around in mainstream literature lost in a fog of moral ambiguity. At murder most of us, and
certainly our courts, draw the line. So murder becomes a milestone, a border,
a wall against which people can ricochet opinions in the handball match of
human moral casuistry. Murder is that bottom line against which all other human
action can be tested. The first great sin after the loss of paradise, it is the primal
human consequence of the loss of Eden, the ultimate rejection of the gift of the
Giver of life. Here, in more clear-cut perspective than in any other human
activity, one can measure right and wrong, observe where people have fallen
and where vengeance is exacted. Here God's province, the knowledge and
wielding of good and evil, becomes a human task. People take possession of the
tree of the knowledge of good and evil and batter one another with its limbs.
So we have murder by blunt instrument, Cain's primal means. People even use
its coldly balanced rule as the means of righting error: justice without mercy.
So Peter Wimsey leaves his captured doctor with a gun to do the "right thing,"

a normal British convention, so normal that it can be spoofed by Ian Fleming in the Bond short story "Octopussy."

Into this cruel abuse and vengeance comes the mercy of God. Into the mechanically cold and dehumanized human justice—which, as St. Augustine pointed out in *The City of God,* sometimes vindicates the innocent at cost of their lives—comes the emissary of the one to whom vengeance belongs, the healer of broken hearts. The great Judge is also the patcher of fragmented lives, the restorer of grace, and that Judge sends as emissary and conduit the clerical sleuth.

Murder recreates the primal sin of the fallen world just as pride and rebellion recreate the edenic one. So the emissary who walks now where God once walked in the cool of the human evening strides out to do in counterpart what God does, calling to Adam and Eve to know where they have gone, what they have done, and what can be done and must be done about it temporally and ultimately.

In a literary mystery, then, a writer and then a reader can summon these great themes, using them to mold a world that will lead people to reflect creatively on what is right and what is wrong. For clerical crime writers, two-thirds to three-quarters of whom are laypeople, the exercise gives a chance to construct a world built upon theological principles and see if it looks anything like the world they live in. The one-quarter to one-third ordained or ex-ordained writers can do the same. For these and for the clerical reader, the genre is as well a therapeutic booster shot in the arm, a paper steroid that can bolster up flagging commitment and enthusiasm and help the weary runner stumble on. Murder also is a suitable topic for those interested in theology. Perhaps people have killed as much for theological as for any other reasons, including love, gain, patriotism, self-defense, protection of home and family, and all the other human ideals, virtues, and qualities for which we regularly slaughter one another. The clerical crime novel is fantasy of the first order that incarnates in extended parable the eschatalogical truth that good will triumph over evil. When Father Brown wins, God's wisdom, that dancer at creation, wins. When Randollph scores off evil, God's might scores. When Sister Ursula triumphs, God's wit triumphs. Perhaps discouraged ministers should have the best examples of the genre prescribed to them in daily doses.

The ultimate truth that the mysterium, God's secret, reveals to the true human questor is that good can triumph over evil. The Christian hope is that heaven can begin here and now in people's lives together. The clerical crime novel is its heralding paean of praise. What the Psalmist affirms is that the last laugh will be God's, so people might as well enjoy themselves and their lives now in view of that destination. The smart traveler likes to view a few travelogues before the trip.

Appendix

Graph of the Clerical Crime Novel in English

Timeline markers: 1910, 1920, 1930, 1940, 1950, 1960, 1970, 1980

G. K. Chesteron (British) **Father Brown** (Roman Catholic)   5 Collections and 1 Short story
Setting: Great Britain

V. L. Whitechurch (British) **Vicar Westerham** (Anglican)
Setting: Great Britain   5 Novels

H. H. Holmes (American) **Sister Ursula** (Roman Catholic)
Setting: America   2 Novels/Short Stories

Matthew Head (American) **Dr. Finney/Miss Collins** (Protestant)
Setting: Africa/France   4 Novels

C. A. Alington (British) **Archdeacons** (Anglican)
Setting: Great Britain   4 Novels

Margaret Scherf (American) **Father Buell** (Episcopalian)
Setting: America   7 Novels

Henri Catalan (French) **Soeur Angèle** (Roman Catholic)
Setting: France   3 Novels in English

Margaret Ann Hubbard (American) **Sister Simon** (Roman Catholic)
Setting: America   1 Novel

Leonard Holton (American) **Father Bredder** (Roman Catholic)
Setting: America   11 Novels

Harry Kemelman (American) **Rabbi Small** (Jewish)
Setting: America   9 Novels and 1 Short Story

James Johnson (American) **Rev. Sebastian** (Protestant)
Setting: America   6 Novels

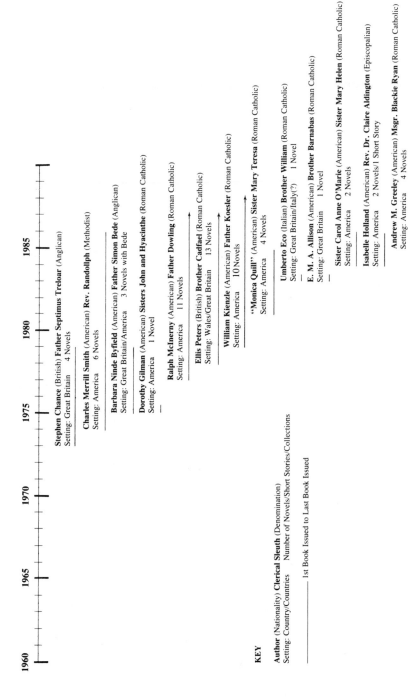

1960 1965 1970 1975 1980 1985

Stephen Chance (British) **Father Septimus Treloar** (Anglican)
Setting: Great Britain   4 Novels

Charles Merrill Smith (American) **Rev. Randollph** (Methodist)
Setting: America   6 Novels

Barbara Ninde Byfield (American) **Father Simon Bede** (Anglican)
Setting: Great Britain/America   3 Novels with Bede

Dorothy Gilman (American) **Sisters John and Hyacinthe** (Roman Catholic)
Setting: America   1 Novel

Ralph McInerny (American) **Father Dowling** (Roman Catholic)
Setting: America   11 Novels

Ellis Peters (British) **Brother Cadfael** (Roman Catholic)
Setting: Wales/Great Britain   13 Novels

William Kienzle (American) **Father Koesler** (Roman Catholic)
Setting: America   10 Novels

"Monica Quill" (American) **Sister Mary Teresa** (Roman Catholic)
Setting: America   4 Novels

Umberto Eco (Italian) **Brother William** (Roman Catholic)
Setting: Great Britain/Italy(?)   1 Novel

E. M. A. Allison (American) **Brother Barnabas** (Roman Catholic)
Setting: Great Britain   1 Novel

Sister Carol Anne O'Marie (American) **Sister Mary Helen** (Roman Catholic)
Setting: America   2 Novels

Isabelle Holland (American) **Rev. Dr. Claire Aldington** (Episcopalian)
Setting: America   2 Novels/1 Short Story

Andrew M. Greeley (American) **Msgr. Blackie Ryan** (Roman Catholic)
Setting: America   4 Novels

Joseph Telushkin (American) **Daniel Winter** (Jewish)
Setting: America   1 Novel

KEY

Author (Nationality) **Clerical Sleuth** (Denomination)
Setting: Country/Countries   Number of Novels/Short Stories/Collections

———— 1st Book Issued to Last Book Issued

Bibliography

The Clerical Crime Novel in English

Alington, C. A.
   1946   *Archdeacons Afloat*. London: Faber and Faber Limited.
   1947   *Archdeacons Ashore*. London: Faber and Faber Limited.
   1949   *Blackmail in Blankshire*. London: Faber and Faber Limited.
   1950   *Gold and Gaiters*. London: Faber and Faber Limited.
Allison, E. M. A.
   1983   *Through the Valley of Death*. Garden City, N.Y.: Doubleday & Co.
Byfield, Barbara Ninde
   1975   *Solemn High Murder* (with Frank L. Tedeschi). Garden City, N.Y.: Doubleday & Co.
   1976   *Forever Wilt Thou Die*. Garden City, N.Y.: Doubleday & Co.
   1977   *A Harder Thing than Triumph*. Garden City, N.Y.: Doubleday & Co.
   1979   *A Parcel of Their Fortunes*. Garden City, N.Y.: Doubleday & Co.
Catalan, Henri
   1955   *Soeur Angèle and the Embarrassed Ladies*. New York: Sheed and Ward.
   1956   *Soeur Angèle and the Ghosts of Chambord*. New York: Sheed and Ward.
   1957   *Soeur Angèle and the Bell Ringer's Niece*. New York: Sheed and Ward.
Chance, Stephen
   1973   *Septimus and the Danedyke Mystery*. New York: Thomas Nelson, Inc.
   1974   *Septimus and the Minster Ghost Mystery*. New York: Thomas Nelson, Inc.
   1977   *The Stone of Offering*. New York: Thomas Nelson, Inc.
   1979   *Septimus and the Spy Ring*. London: Bodley.
Charles, R. H., ed.
   1913   *The Apocrypha and Pseudepigrapha of the Old Testament in English*, vol. 1. Oxford: Oxford University Press (contains *Bel and the Dragon* and *Susannah*).
Chesterton, Gilbert Keith
   1951   *The Father Brown Omnibus*. New York: Dodd, Mead & Co. (contains *The Innocence of Father Brown, The Wisdom of Father Brown, The Incredulity of Father Brown, The Secret of Father Brown, The Scandal of Father Brown,* and "The Vampire of the Village").
Eco, Umberto
   1983   *The Name of the Rose*, trans. by William Weaver. New York: Harcourt Brace Jovanovich, Publishers.
Gilman, Dorothy
   1975   *A Nun in the Closet*. Garden City, N.Y.: Doubleday & Co.

Greeley, Andrew M.

   1985   *Virgin and Martyr*. New York: Warner Books.

   1985   *Happy Are the Meek*. New York: Warner Books.

   1986   *The Angels of September*. New York: Warner Books.

   1986   *Happy Are the Clean of Heart*. New York: Warner Books.

Head, Matthew

   1949   *The Cabinda Affair*. New York: Simon and Schuster.

   1950   *The Congo Venus*. New York: Simon and Schuster.

   1973   *The Devil in the Bush*. New York: W. W. Norton & Co. (originally published 1945).

   1981   *Murder at the Flea Club*. New York: Harper & Row Publishers (originally published 1955).

Holland, Isabelle

   1984   *A Death at St. Anselm's*. Garden City, N.Y.: Doubleday & Co.

   1986   *A Lover Scorned*. Garden City, N.Y.: Doubleday & Co.

Holmes, H. H.

   1942   *Rocket to the Morgue*. U.S.A.: A Phantom Mystery.

   1945   *Nine Times Nine*. New York: Penguin Books (originally published 1940).

Holton, Leonard

   1959   *The Saint Maker*. New York: Dodd, Mead & Company.

   1960   *A Pact with Satan*. New York: Dodd, Mead & Company.

   1961   *Secret of the Doubting Saint*. New York: Dodd, Mead & Company.

   1963   *Deliver Us from Wolves*. New York: Dodd, Mead & Company.

   1964   *Flowers by Request*. New York: Dodd, Mead & Company.

   1966   *Out of the Depths*. New York: Dodd, Mead & Company.

   1968   *A Touch of Jonah*. New York: Dodd, Mead & Company.

   1970   *A Problem in Angels*. New York: Dodd, Mead & Company.

   1972   *The Mirror of Hell*. New York: Dodd, Mead & Company.

   1974   *The Devil to Play*. New York: Dodd, Mead & Company.

   1977   *A Corner of Paradise*. New York: St. Martin's Press.

Hubbard, Margaret Ann

   1959   *Sister Simon's Murder Case*. Milwaukee: The Bruce Publishing Company.

Johnson, James L.

   1967   *Code Name Sebastian*. New York: J. B. Lippincott Company.

   1968   *The Nine Lives of Alphonse*. New York: J. B. Lippincott Company.

   1970   *A Handful of Dominoes*. New York: J. B. Lippincott Company.

   1974   *A Piece of the Moon Is Missing*. New York: A. J. Holman Company.

   1981   *The Last Train from Canton*. Grand Rapids: Zondervan Publishing House.

   1987   *Trackless Seas*. Westchester, Ill.: Crossway Books.

Kemelman, Harry

   1964   *Friday the Rabbi Slept Late*. New York: Crown Publishers, Inc.

   1966   *Saturday the Rabbi Went Hungry*. New York: Crown Publishers, Inc.

   1969   *Sunday the Rabbi Stayed Home*. New York: G. P. Putnam's Sons.

   1972   *Monday the Rabbi Took Off*. New York: G. P. Putnam's Sons.

   1973   *Tuesday the Rabbi Saw Red*. New York: Arthur Field's Books, Inc.

   1976   *Wednesday the Rabbi Got Wet*. New York: William Morrow and Company, Inc.

   1978   *Thursday the Rabbi Walked Out*. New York: William Morrow and Company, Inc.

   1981   *Conversations with Rabbi Small*. New York: William Morrow and Company, Inc.

   1985   *Someday the Rabbi Will Leave*. New York: William Morrow and Company, Inc.

   1987   *One Fine Day the Rabbi Bought a Cross*. New York: William Morrow and Company, Inc.

Kienzle, William X.
    1979   *The Rosary Murders*. Kansas City: Andrews and McMeel, Inc.
    1980   *Death Wears a Red Hat*. Kansas City: Andrews and McMeel, Inc.
    1981   *Mind over Murder*. Kansas City: Andrews and McMeel, Inc.
    1982   *Assault with Intent*. Kansas City: Andrews and McMeel, Inc.
    1983   *Shadow of Death*. Kansas City: Andrews and McMeel, Inc.
    1984   *Kill and Tell*. Kansas City: Andrews and McMeel, Inc.
    1985   *Sudden Death*. Kansas City: Andrews, McMeel, & Parker.
    1986   *Deathbed*. Kansas City: Andrews, McMeel, & Parker.
    1987   *Deadline for a Critic*. Kansas City: Andrews, McMeel, & Parker.
    1988   *Marked for Murder*. Kansas City: Andrews and McMeel.
McInerny, Ralph
    1977   *Her Death of Cold*. New York: The Vanguard Press.
    1977   *The Seventh Station*. New York: The Vanguard Press.
    1978   *Bishop as Pawn*. New York: The Vanguard Press.
    1979   *Lying Three*. New York: The Vanguard Press.
    1980   *Second Vespers*. New York: The Vanguard Press.
    1981   *Thicker than Water*. New York: The Vanguard Press.
    1982   *A Loss of Patients*. New York: The Vanguard Press.
    1983   *The Grass Widow*. New York: The Vanguard Press.
    1984   *Getting a Way with Murder*. New York: The Vanguard Press.
    1985   *Rest in Pieces*. New York: The Vanguard Press.
    1987   *The Basket Case*. New York: St. Martin's Press.
O'Marie, Sister Carol Anne
    1984   *A Novena for Murder*. New York: Charles Scribner's Sons.
    1986   *Advent of Dying*. New York: Delacorte Press.
Peters, Ellis
    1978   *A Morbid Taste for Bones*. New York: William Morrow and Co., Inc.
    1980   *One Corpse Too Many*. New York: William Morrow and Co., Inc.
    1981   *Monk's-Hood*. New York: William Morrow and Co., Inc.
    1981   *Saint Peter's Fair*. New York: William Morrow and Co., Inc.
    1982   *The Leper of St. Giles*. New York: William Morrow and Co., Inc.
    1983   *The Virgin in the Ice*. New York: William Morrow and Co., Inc.
    1983   *The Sanctuary Sparrow*. New York: William Morrow and Co., Inc.
    1984   *The Devil's Novice*. New York: William Morrow and Co., Inc.
    1984   *Dead Man's Ransom*. New York: William Morrow and Co., Inc.
    1985   *The Pilgrim of Hate*. New York: William Morrow and Co., Inc.
    1985   *An Excellent Mystery*. New York: William Morrow and Co., Inc.
    1986   *The Raven in the Foregate*. New York: William Morrow and Co., Inc.
    1987   *The Rose Rent*. New York: William Morrow and Co., Inc.
Quill, Monica
    1981   *Not a Blessed Thing*. New York: The Vanguard Press.
    1982   *Let Us Prey*. New York: The Vanguard Press.
    1984   *And Then There Was Nun*. New York: The Vanguard Press.
    1985   *Nun of the Above*. New York: The Vanguard Press.
Scherf, Margaret
    1948   *Always Murder a Friend*. Garden City, N. Y.: Doubleday & Co.
    1950   *For the Love of Murder*. New York: The American Mercury Inc. (Bestseller Mystery No. B126) (originally, 1949 *Gilbert's Last Toothache*, Garden City, N.Y.: Doubleday & Co., Inc.).

1950   *The Cautious Custard Pie.* Garden City, N.Y.: Doubleday & Co.

1952   *The Elk and the Evidence.* Garden City, N.Y.: Doubleday & Co.

1956   *The Cautious Overshoes.* Garden City, N.Y.: Doubleday & Co.

1959   *Never Turn Your Back.* Garden City, N.Y.: Doubleday & Co.

1965   *The Corpse in the Flannel Nightgown.* Garden City, N.Y.: Doubleday & Co.

Smith, Charles Merrill

1974   *Reverend Randollph and the Wages of Sin.* New York: G. P. Putnam's Sons.

1977   *Reverend Randollph and the Avenging Angel.* New York: G. P. Putnam's Sons.

1978   *Reverend Randollph and the Fall from Grace, Inc.* New York: G. P. Putnam's Sons.

1980   *Reverend Randollph and the Holy Terror.* New York: G. P. Putnam's Sons.

1983   *Reverend Randollph and the Unholy Bible.* New York: G. P. Putnam's Sons.

1986   *Reverend Randollph and the Splendid Samaritan* (with Terrence Lore Smith). New York: G. P. Putnam's Sons.

Whitechurch, Victor Lorenzo

1927   *The Crime at Diana's Pool.* New York: Duffield and Company.

Other Works Consulted

Aland, Kurt, et al.

1975   *The Greek New Testament,* 3rd ed. New York: United Bible Societies

Alington, C. A.

1927   *Elementary Christianity.* New York: Longmans, Green and Co.

1932   *Christian Outlines: An Introduction to Religion.* New York: The Macmillan Company.

1942   *Christianity in England.* New York: Oxford University Press.

1948   *The Life Everlasting.* London: The Religious Book Club.

Altizer, Thomas, et al.

1982   *Deconstruction and Theology.* New York: Crossroad.

Arnold, Margaret and Glenn

1987   "Jim Johnson's Tale: Pastor Founded Wheaton Media Program." *Spirited People.*

Angus, Samuel

1928   *The Mystery—Religions and Christianity: A Study in the Religious Background of Early Christianity.* London: John Murray.

Augustine, St.

1949   *The Confessions of Saint Augustine,* trans. by Edward P. Pusey. New York: The Modern Library.

1963   *The City of God,* trans. by J. W. C. Wand. London: Oxford University Press.

Bartel, Roland, James S. Ackerman, and Thayer S. Warshaw

1975   *Biblical Images in Literature.* Nashville: Abingdon Press.

Basney, Lionel

1974   "Corpses, Clues, and the Truth." *Christianity Today,* 8/30:16–17.

Barzun, Jacques and Wendell Hertig Taylor

1971   *A Catalogue of Crime.* New York: Harper & Row, Publishers.

Bemont, Charles and G. Monod

1902   *Medieval Europe from 395 to 1270,* trans. by Mary Sloan, ed. by George Burton Adams. New York: Henry Holt and Company.

Bianchi, Ugo

1976   *The Greek Mysteries.* Leiden: E. J. Brill.

Bloom, Harold, et al.

1979   *Deconstruction and Criticism.* New York: The Seabury Press.

Boyd, Ian
  1975 *The Novels of G. K. Chesterton: A Study in Art and Propaganda*. New York: Barnes & Noble Books.
Braun, Martin
  1938 *History and Romance in Graeco-Oriental Literature*. Oxford: Basil Blackwell.
Bray, Alison S.
  1981 "A Melodramatic Morsel Blending This World, the Nether and the Other." *The Review of Books and Religion*. Mid-October:8.
Brown, Francis, S. R. Driver, and Charles Briggs
  1953 *A Hebrew and English Lexicon of the Old Testament*. Oxford: Oxford University Press.
Bruce, F. F.
  1959 *Biblical Exegesis in the Qumran Texts*. Grand Rapids: William B. Eerdmans Publishing Company.
Budd, Elaine
  1983 "Women of Mystery," *Review*, November.
Burchfield, R. W., ed.
  1976 *A Supplement to the Oxford English Dictionary*, vol. 2. Oxford: Oxford University Press.
Butler, Diana
  1985 "Lord Peter Wimsey and the Theological Art of Detective Fiction." Unpublished paper, July 24, 1985:7.
Buxbaum, Laura
  1985 "Religion Is Growing in the Soviet Union." Hamilton-Wenham *Chronicle*. 4/3.
Campbell, Oscar James
  1949 *The Living Shakespeare: Twenty-Two Plays and the Sonnets*. New York: The Macmillan Company.
Certain Members of the Detection Club
  1979 *The Floating Admiral*. Boston: The Gregg Press.
Chatman, Seymour, Umberto Eco, and Jean-Marie Klinkenberg
  1979 *A Semiotic Landscape: Proceedings of the First Congress of the International Association for Semiotic Studies, Milan, June, 1974*. New York: Moulton Publishers.
Chesneaux, Jean, Umberto Eco, and Gino Nebiolo, joint comp.
  1973 *The People's Comic Book*. trans. by Endymion Wilkinson. Garden City, N.Y.: Doubleday & Co.
Chesterton, Gilbert Keith
  1905 *Heretics*. London: The Bodley Head.
  1912 *Manalive*. New York: John Lane Company.
  1919 *All Things Considered*. London: Methuen & Co., Ltd.
  1922 *Eugenics and Other Evils*. New York: Cassell and Co., Ltd.
  1936 *The Autobiography of G. K. Chesterton*. New York: Sheed & Ward.
  1939 *Alarms and Discursions*. London: Methuen & Co., Ltd.
  1946 "A Defence of Detective Stories," in Haycraft, Howard, ed. *The Art of the Mystery Story*. New York: Grosset & Dunlap.
  1984 "How to Write a Detective Story." *The Chesterton Review*, 10/2:111–18.
Christie, Agatha
  1927 *The Murder of Roger Ackroyd*. New York: Dodd, Mead and Company.
Clanton, Maryruth C.
  1985 "The Case of the Armchair Sleuth." *Mature Years*. 17/4 (Summer):50–55.
Coates, John
  1979 "Chesterton and the Meaning of Adventure." *The Chesterton Review*, 5/2 (Spring–Summer):278–99.

Dale, Alzina Stone
    1982   *The Outline of Sanity*. Grand Rapids: William B. Eerdmans Publishing Company.
Danby, Herbert
    1933   *The Mishnah*. Oxford: Oxford University Press.
Denison, D. C.
    1984   "P. D. James." *The Boston Globe Magazine,* 11/4:18, 20.
Dentan, Robert C.
    1954   *The Apocrypha, Bridge of the Testaments*. Greenwich, Conn.: The Seabury Press.
De Quincey, Thomas
    1912   *The English Mail-Coach and Other Essays*. New York: E. P. Dutton & Co., Inc.
Dillard, Annie
    1982   *Living by Fiction*. New York: Harper & Row Publishers.
Doyle, Sir Arthur Conan
    1892–1930   *The Complete Sherlock Holmes*. Garden City, N.Y.: Doubleday & Co.
Eco, Umberto
    1976   *A Theory of Semiotics*. Bloomington: Indiana University Press.
    1984   *Postscript to "The Name of the Rose."* New York: Harcourt Brace Jovanovich, Publishers.
Entrevernes Group, The
    1978   *Signs and Parables: Semiotics and Gospel Texts*. Pittsburgh: The Pickwick Press.
Erickson, Joyce Quiring
    1983   "What Difference? The Theory and Practice of Feminist Criticism." *Christianity & Literature,* 33/1 (Fall):65–74.
Ferguson, John
    1977   *An Illustrated Encyclopedia of Mysticism and the Mystery Religions*. New York: The Seabury Press.
Frame, Randy
    1984   "Christianity Comes of Age in the NFL." *Christianity Today,* 28/1:36–37.
Frankena, William K.
    1963   *Ethics*. Englewood Cliffs, N.J.: Prentice-Hall, Inc.
Francis of Sales, St.
    1962   *The Love of God: A Treatise,* trans. by Vincent Kerns. Westminster, Md.: The Newman Press.
Fritsch, C. T.
    1962   "Apocrypha." *The Interpreter's Dictionary of the Bible*. Nashville: Abingdon.
Gallico, Paul
    1961   "Introduction." Ian Fleming's *Gilt-Edged Bonds*. New York: The Macmillan Company.
Garcia, Guy D.
    1984   "People." *Time*. 2/6:63.
Gardner, Erle Stanley
    1969   *The Case of the Fabulous Fake*. Roslyn, N.Y.: Walter J. Black, Inc.
Greeley, Andrew M.
    1982   *Thy Brother's Wife*. New York: Warner Books.
    1983   *Ascent into Hell*. New York: Warner Books.
    1987   *Patience of a Saint*. New York: Warner Books.
Guthrie, Donald
    1970   *New Testament Introduction*. Downers Grove, Ill.: Inter-Varsity Press.
Hatch, Edwin and Henry A. Redpath
    1983   *A Concordance to the Septuagint and the Other Greek Versions of the Old Testament (Including the Apocryphal Books)*. Grand Rapids: Baker Book House.

Haycraft, Howard

1941   *Murder for Pleasure: The Life and Times of the Detective Story.* New York: D. Appleton-Century Company, Inc.

1946   *The Art of the Mystery Story.* New York: Grosset & Dunlap.

Helsa, David H.

1978   "Religion and Literature: The Second Stage." *Journal of the American Academy of Religion.* 46/2(6:78):181–92.

Herr, Dan and Joel Wells

1961   *Bodies and Souls.* Garden City, N.Y.: Doubleday & Co.

Hesse, Herman

1963   *Steppenwolf.* New York: The Modern Library.

Hodgson, Leonard

1934   *The Lord's Prayer.* London: Longmans, Green and Co.

Hoenig, S. B.

1962   "Bel and the Dragon." *The Interpreter's Dictionary of the Bible.* Nashville: Abingdon.

1962   "Susanna." *The Interpreter's Dictionary of the Bible.* Nashville: Abingdon.

Holland, Isabelle

1976   *Grenelle.* New York: Rawson Associates Publishers, Inc.

1985   *Flight of the Archangel.* New York: Doubleday & Co.

Hubbard, Margaret Ann

1950   *Murder Takes the Veil.* Milwaukee: The Bruce Publishing Company.

1952   *Murder at St. Dennis.* Milwaukee: The Bruce Publishing Company.

1966   *Step Softly on My Grave.* Milwaukee: The Bruce Publishing Company.

Hubin, Allen J.

1984   *Crime Fiction 1749–1980: A Comprehensive Bibliography.* New York: Garland Publishing, Inc.

1988   *1981–1985 Supplement to Crime Fiction 1749–1980.* New York: Garland Publishing, Inc.

Johnson, James L.

1974   *The Death of Kings.* Garden City, N.Y.: Doubleday & Co.

1977   *What Every Woman Should Know about a Man.* Grand Rapids: Zondervan Publishing House.

1980   *How To Enjoy Life and Not Feel Guilty.* Irvine, Calif.: Harvest House Publishers.

Josephus, Flavius

n.d.   "Against Apion." *The Works of Flavius Josephus, The Learned and Authentic Jewish Historian and Celebrated Warrior. With Three Dissertations, concerning Jesus Christ, John the Baptist, James the Just, God's Command to Abraham, and Explanatory Notes and Observations,* trans. by William Whiston, A.M. Baltimore: Armstrong and Berry.

Kakutani, Michiko

1984   "Mysteries Join the Mainstream." *The New York Times Book Review,* 89/3(1/15):36.

Kelley, Kathy

1984   "A Nun in the Closet." Unpublished book critique.

Kelly, J. N. D.

1960   *Early Christian Doctrines.* New York: Harper & Row, Publishers.

Kemelman, Harry

1967   *The Nine Mile Walk.* New York: G. P. Putnam's Sons.

Kittel, Gerhard

1967   *Theological Dictionary of the New Testament,* vol. 4. Grand Rapids: William B. Eerdmans Publishing Company.

Kittel, Rudolph, ed.

1961   *Biblia Hebraica.* Stuttgart: Württembergische Bibelanstalt.

Koch, Kurt E.
   1965   *Christian Counseling and Occultism*. Grand Rapids: Kregel Publications.
Kümmel, Werner Georg
   1975   *Introduction to the New Testament,* trans. by Howard Clark Kee. Nashville: Abingdon.
Lea, F. A.
   1945   *The Wild Knight of Battersea: G. K. Chesterton*. London: James Clarke & Co., Ltd.
Leach, Christopher
   1983   *Texas Station*. New York: Harcourt Brace Jovanovich, Publishers (original title: *Blood Games*).
Lewis, C. S.
   1955   *Surprised by Joy: The Shape of My Early Life*. New York: Harcourt, Brace & World, Inc.
   1961   *An Experiment in Criticism*. Cambridge: Cambridge University Press.
   1970   *The Lion, the Witch, and the Wardrobe*. New York: Collier Books.
Lewis, Matthew Gregory
   1952   *The Monk*. New York: Grove Press.
Liddell, Henry George and Robert Scott
   1968   *A Greek-English Lexicon*. Oxford: Oxford University Press.
Longenecker, Richard
   1975   *Biblical Exegesis in the Apostolic Period*. William B. Eerdmans Publishing Company.
McInerny, Ralph
   1966   *Thomism in an Age of Renewal*. Garden City, N.Y.: Doubleday & Co., Inc.
   1970   *A History of Western Philosophy,* vol. 2. Notre Dame: University of Notre Dame Press.
   1982   *St. Thomas Aquinas*. Notre Dame: University of Notre Dame Press.
   1982   *Ethica Thomistica: The Moral Philosophy of Thomas Aquinas*. Washington, D.C.: The Catholic University of America Press.
   1983   *Connolly's Life*. New York: Atheneum.
Malory, Sir Thomas
   1962   *Le Morte d'Arthur,* trans. by Keith Baines. New York: Bramhall House.
Mason, A. E. W.
   1935   *Dilemmas*. New York: Doubleday, Doran & Co., Inc.
Men against Patriarchy
   1983   *Off Their Backs . . . And on Our Own Two Feet*. Philadelphia: New Society Publishers.
Metzger, Bruce M.
   1957   *An Introduction to the Apocrypha*. New York: Oxford University Press.
Montgomery, James
   1927   *A Critical and Exegetical Commentary on the Book of Daniel*. Edinburgh: T. & T. Clark.
Murray, James H. H., Henry Bradley, W. A. Craigie, and C. T. Onions
   1933   *The Oxford English Dictionary,* vol. 6. Oxford: Oxford University Press.
Nash, Ogden
   1941   *The Face Is Familiar*. Garden City, N.Y.: Garden City Publishing Company, Inc.
Oates, Joyce Carol
   1978   *Son of the Morning*. New York: The Vanguard Press, Inc.
Oberman, Heiko A.
   1978   "Fourteenth-Century Religious Thought: A Premature Profile." *Speculum* 53/1(January):80–93.
Oesterley, W. O. E.
   1914   *The Books of the Apocrypha: Their Origin, Teaching and Contents*. London: Robert Scott.
Packer, J. I.
   1962   *"Fundamentalism" and the Word of God*. Grand Rapids: William B. Eerdmans Publishing Co.

1985 "'Tecs, Thrillers and Westerns." *Christianity Today,* 29/16(11:8):12.
Patte, Daniel
1976 *What Is Structural Exegesis?* Philadelphia: Fortress Press.
Penzler, Otto, ed.
1978 *The Great Detectives.* Boston: Little, Brown and Company.
Pollard, Alfred W.
1914 *English Miracle Plays, Moralities, and Interludes,* 6th ed. Oxford: Oxford University Press.
Prosser, Eleanor
1961 *Drama and Religion in the English Mystery Plays: A Re-evaluation.* Stanford University Press.
Queen, Ellery, ed.
1943 *The Great Women Detectives and Criminals: The Female of the Species.* Garden City, N.Y.: Blue Ribbon Books.
Reilly, John M., ed.
1985 *Twentieth Century Crime and Mystery Writers,* 2nd ed. New York: St. Martin's Press.
Sayers, Dorothy L., ed.
1929 *The Omnibus of Crime.* Garden City, N.Y.: Garden City Publishing Company.
1932 *The Second Omnibus of Crime.* New York: Coward-McCann, Inc.
Scheick, William J.
1977–78 "The Twilight Harlequinade of Chesterton's Father Brown Stories." *The Chesterton Review* 4/1:104–14.
Scherf, Margaret
1942 *They Came to Kill.* New York: G.P. Putnam's Sons.
1960 *Wedding Train.* Garden City, N.Y.: Doubleday & Co.
1971 *The Beautiful Birthday Cake.* Garden City, N.Y.: Doubleday & Co.
Schmoller, Alfred
1963 *Handkonkordanz zum griechischen Neuen Testament.* Stuttgart: Württembergische Bibelanstalt.
Schuerer, Emil
1973 *The History of the Jewish People in the Age of Jesus Christ,* vol. 1. Edinburgh: T. & T. Clark Ltd.
Slung, Michele B., ed.
1975 *Crime on Her Mind.* New York: Pantheon Books.
Smith, Charles Merrill
1965 *How to Become a Bishop without Being Religious.* Garden City, N.Y.: Doubleday & Company.
1969 *When the Saints Go Marching out.* Garden City: Doubleday & Co.
1971 *The Pearly Gates Syndicate, or How to Sell Real Estate in Heaven.* Garden City, N.Y.: Doubleday & Co.
1972 *Instant Status or How to Become a Pillar of the Upper Middle Class.* Garden City, N.Y.: Doubleday & Co.
1973 *How to Talk to God When You Aren't Feeling Religious.* New York: Bantam Books.
1973 *The Case of a Middle Class Christian.* Waco: Word Books.
1975 *Different Drums* (with Terrence Lore Smith). New York: Saturday Review Press/E.P. Dutton and Co., Inc.
Spencer, Aída Besançon
1984 *Paul's Literary Style: A Stylistic and Historical Comparison of II Corinthians 11:16–12:13, Romans 8:9–39, and Philippians 3:2–4:13.* Jackson, Miss.: Evangelical Theological Society.

1985 *Beyond the Curse: Women Called to Ministry*. Nashville: Thomas Nelson Publishers.
Spencer, William David
  1980 "Rastafari: Poverty and Apostasy in Paradise." *The Journal of Pastoral Practice* 4/4:63–
       71.
  1985 "Manchild by the Rivers of Babylon: An Analysis of Rastafari's Churchly versus Sectarian
       Aspects to Interpret the Present and Predict the Future of the Rastafarian Experience in the
       United States." Wheaton College, Wheaton, Ill.: The Billy Graham Center Archives.
  1988 "James Johnson's Sebastian: A Heroic Legacy." *Christianity Today*, 32/2 (2/5):58.
Spitzer, Leo
  1948 *Linguistics and Literary History: Essay in Stylistics*. Princeton: Princeton University Press.
  1949 *A Method of Interpreting Literature*. Northampton, Mass.: Smith College.
Sprug, Joseph W.
  1966 *An Index to G. K. Chesterton*. Washington, D.C.: The Catholic University of America
       Press.
Stevenson, W. B.
  1958 *Detective Fiction*. Cambridge: The National Book League.
  1963 "Detective Fiction." *Collier's Encyclopedia*, vol. 8. The Crowell-Collier Publishing Com-
       pany.
Tanenbaum, Marc H., Marvin R. Wilson, and A. James Rudin, eds.
  1978 *Evangelicals and Jews in Conversation on Scripture, Theology, and History*. Grand Rap-
       ids: Baker Book House.
Tani, Stefano
  1984 *The Doomed Detective: The Contribution of the Detective Novel to Postmodern American
       and Italian Fiction*. Carbondale and Edwardsville: Southern Illinois University Press.
Teresa of Avila
  1979 *The Interior Castle*, trans. by Kieran Kavanaugh O.C.D. and Otilio Rodriguez O.C.D.
       New York: The Paulist Press.
Thomas Aquinas, St.
  1975 *Summa Contra Gentiles*. Notre Dame: University of Notre Dame Press.
Thomas, R. George
  1966 *Ten Miracle Plays*. Evanston: Northwestern University Press.
Tucker, Ruth A. and Walter Liefeld
  1987 *Daughters of the Church*. Grand Rapids: Zondervan Publishing House.
Updike, John
  1975 *A Month of Sundays*. New York: Alfred A. Knopf.
USA Today
  1985 "Church: No Proof Statue Wept." 9/19:3A.
Van Nostrand, Albert
  1973 *The Denatured Novel*. Westport, Conn.: Greenwood Press.
Wells, H. G.
  1934 *Seven Famous Novels*. New York: Alfred A. Knopf.
Whitechurch, Victor Lorenzo
  1924 *A Bishop out of Residence*. New York: Duffield and Company.
  1925 *The Templeton Case*. London: John Long, Ltd.
  1926 *The Dean and Jecinora*. London: T. Fisher Unwin Ltd.
  1929 *The Robbery at Rudwick House*. New York: Duffield and Company.
  1930 *First and Last*. New York: Duffield and Company.
Winn, Dilys, ed.
  1977 *Murder Ink: The Mystery Reader's Companion*. New York: Workman Publishing Com-
       pany, Inc.

Winks, Robin
    1982   *Modus Operandi: An Excursion into Detective Fiction.* Boston: David R. Godine, Publisher.
Winks, Robin, ed.
    1980   *Detective Fiction.* Englewood Cliffs, New Jersey: Prentice-Hall, Inc.
Wodehouse, P. G.
    1972   *The World of Mr. Mulliner.* New York: Taplinger Publishing Company.
Woolfe, Rosemary
    1972   *The English Mystery Plays.* Berkeley: University of California Press.

General Index

Carpocrates, 187
Capote, Truman, 91
Carr, John Dickson, 99, 102
Case for Three Detectives, A, 99
Casey, Robert, 12
Casuistry, 143, 318
Catalan, Henri, 107–13, 114, 228
Catalogue of Crime, A, 102, 149, 195, 255
"Certain Members of the Detection Club," 193–94
Chance, Stephen, 228–38, 315
Chandler, Raymond, 24, 43, 177
Charles, R. H., 20, 21n., 25
Chesterton, G. K., 50, 52, 69, 76–100; rules for detective fiction, 76–77; longevity of his work, 88–89, 89n.; 163, 194, 211, 306, 308–9
Chesterton Review, The, 98
Chill, The, 24
Christian Science, 81
Cristian Counseling and Occultism, 235
Christianity Today, 50, 276, 313
Christie, Agatha, 83, 149, 167, 194, 211, 288
Christos Paschon, 7
Circular Staircase, The, 149n.
City of God, The, 318
Clanton, Maryruth C., 149n.
Clark, Linda, 88
Clerical crime novel: common themes, 306–7, 308–10, 319; definition, 12–13; extended parable, 319; gauge of Church's attitudes, 317; reaffirms conservative values, 316–17, 319; two-thirds of authors are laypeople, 317
Clerical detectives: accused of murder, 84, 166, 215; celestial police officer, 105, 127, 130, 304; characteristics: similar, 110, 165, 307, 311–15; and different, 315–17; Christ-type, 305; definition, 11; and human law, 11, 29, 82, 305; mete out God's justice, 82, 99, 106, 294, 303, 315; with mercy, 304, 319; reach back to mysterium, 9–11, 74, 304; reveal humanity of clergy, 125, 152, 160, 202, 232, 286, 292, 306–7, 311
Coles, The, 194
Color Purple, The, 174
Colossians 1:26–27, 5; 2:2–3, 6; 4:3–4, 6
Conan Doyle, Sir Arthur, 44, 72, 110, 141, 310
Common Sense in Education, 36
"Constancy of Susanna, The," 8
Cooper, James Fenimore, 10
1 Corinthians 1:18a, 79; 1:27, 79; 2:1, 5; 2:7, 5; 4:1, 5; 13, 109; 13:2, 5; 14:2, 5; 15, 274; 15:51, 5
Crime at Diana's Pool, The, 101
Crime on Her Mind, 101
Crofts, Freeman Wills, 194

"Cui bono?," 144
Curtain, 185
Cyril of Jerusalem, 17

Dale, Alzina Stone, 76, 88
Daniel 2:18–19, 4; 2:27–30, 4; 2:47, 4; 4:6, 4
Daniel, 3, 11, 31–33, 34, 92, 122, 213, 303
Dante Alighieri, 261
Dark of the Moon, 99
David, 124
Davidson, Benjamin, 3
Davis, Dorothy Salisbury, 12, 307
"De contemptu mundi," 57
"Dead, The," 87
Death of Kings, The, 294
Deborah, 293
Deep Purple Lament, The, 24
"Defense of Detective Stories, A," 50, 78
Denison, D. C., 165
Dentan, R. C., 21 note
De Quincey, Thomas, 69, 76, 81
Derush, 3
"Devout: Vicars, Curates and Relentlessly Inquisitive Clerics, The," 211
Didache, 8
Different Drums, 264–71
Din Torah, 31, 32, 35
Dionysius the Areopagite, 53
Doomed Detective, The, 43, 52
"Donkey, The," 85
"Don't Guess, Let Me Tell You," 149n.
Double Story, A, 101
Druidism, 236–38
Dupuy-Mazuel, Henri. *See* Catalan, Henri

Eastern mysticism, 147, 154, 155, 171, 308–9, 313
Eco, Umberto, 43–59, 310
Ecclesiastes, 104; 5:18, 226
Ecclesiasticus. *See* Sirach
Eden, 62–65, 83
Elderton, William, 8
Elisha, 289
"Ellery Queen's Mystery Magazine," 36
English Miracle Plays, Moralities, and Interludes, 7
Entrevernes Group, The, 49
Ephesians 1:9, 5; 3:3–4, 5; 3:9–10, 5; 5:32, 5
Erickson, Joyce, 150
2 Esdras 14:4–6, 18
Essenes, 19, 105
Ethica Thomistica, 134
Ethics, 273
Eugenics, 91
Evil and the God of Love, 189
Exodus 34:6, 304

Ulysses, 209
Unification, 105, 171
Unitarianism, 226
Universalism, 68
Updike, John, 186
Ursula, Saint, 151
U.S.A. Today, 112

Van Til, Cornelius, 296
Vanity Fair, 93
Vatican II, 133
Vaticanus (B), 21n.
Vidocq, Eugène François, 10, 97
Vincent De Paul, Saint, 107, 113
Vodun, 168
Vuillamy, C. E., 12
Vulgate, 21n.

Wales: as edenic sanctuary, 63–64; as pagan, 235, 236–38
Walker, Alice, 174
Wallace, Edgar, 91
Wambaugh, Joseph, 308
Wangerin, Walter, Jr., 123
Warriner, Thurmin, 12, 162
Way of the Wolf, The, 318
Webb, Jack, 12
Wedding Train, 223

Wellhausen, Julius, 18
Western genre (compared to mystery), 251
Westminster divines, 66
Whatever Became of Sin?, 306
Where the Dark Streets Go, 12, 307
White, William Anthony Parker. *See* Holmes, H. H.
Whitechurch, Canon Victor Lorenzo, 165, 193–205; definition of how to write a mystery, 195, 214
Whitehead, Alfred North, 184
Wibberley, Leonard Patrick O'Conner. *See* Holton, Leonard
Wilde, Oscar, 180
William of Occam, 44–49
Wind in the Willows, The, 209
Wisdom of Solomon 2:22, 2; 6:22, 2; 14:15,23, 2–3
Witchcraft, 155, 235–36
Wittenburg Door, The, 25
Wittgenstein, Ludwig, 47
Wodehouse, P. G., 102, 209, 211, 261–63, 282
"Women of Mystery," 148–49
Woodrum, Lon, 287
Woolf, Rosemary, 9
"Writer as Detective Hero, The," 165
Wyclif, John, 73

Index of Fictional Characters